Battleground for the Union
The Era of the Civil War and Reconstruction 1848–1877

William L. Barney

Department of History
University of North Carolina at Chapel Hill

PRENTICE HALL, Englewood Cliffs, N.J. 07632

Library of Congress Cataloging-in-Publication Data

Barney, William L.
   Battleground for the Union : the era of the Civil War and
reconstruction, 1848-1877 / William L. Barney.
      p.   cm.
   Bibliography: p.
   Includes index.
   ISBN 0-13-069386-3
   1. United States--History--Civil War, 1861-1865. 2. United
States--History--Civil War, 1861-1865--Causes. 3. Reconstruction.
4. United States--History--1849-1877. 5. Slave rights. 6. Slavery-
-United States--History--19th century.   I. Title.
E468.B318   1990
973.7--dc20   89-8552
                                                          CIP

Editorial/production supervision and
  interior design: Joe Scordato
Cover design: Lundgren Graphics, Ltd.
Manufacturing buyers: Carol Bystrom and Ed O'Dougherty
Photo research: Barbara Schultz

10

ISBN 0-13-069386-3

PRENTICE-HALL INTERNATIONAL (UK) LIMITED, *London*
PRENTICE-HALL OF AUSTRALIA PTY. LIMITED, *Sydney*
PRENTICE-HALL CANADA INC., *Toronto*
PRENTICE-HALL HISPANOAMERICANA, S.A., *Mexico*
PRENTICE-HALL OF INDIA PRIVATE LIMITED, *New Delhi*
PRENTICE-HALL OF JAPAN, INC., *Tokyo*
SIMON & SCHUSTER ASIA PTE. LTD., *Singapore*
EDITORA PRENTICE-HALL DO BRASIL, LTDA., *Rio de Janeiro*

For Elaine
In more ways than there are days

Contents

Preface

Battleground for the Union, which is a one-volume synthesis on the Civil War era, has been written to suggest how passionate struggles over the meaning of the Union comprised the unifying theme in the lives of those mid-nineteenth-century Americans who went to war against each other. The legacy of these struggles, gained at the terrible cost of the Civil War, was an American nation committed in principle to freedom and equality. In the years from 1848 to 1877, the central ambiguities of the original Union of 1787 were finally resolved. The United States was indeed an indivisible nation and not just a federated union of states that could reclaim sovereign powers of local self-determination and divide the Union. The dual commitment to freedom and slavery in the original Constitution could not persist. The rights of liberty enshrined in the Declaration of Independence did, after all, apply to all Americans, black and white.

In relating the story of the Civil War years, I have supplemented my own research with what I believe is the best and most significant recent research. The highlights of this research are summarized in the suggested readings at the end of each chapter. Although the text follows a traditional chronological framework, I have sought throughout to maintain a breadth of vision that places the coming of the Civil War, the war itself, and its aftermath in Reconstruction in the context of the broad changes that were transforming American society in the middle decades of the nineteenth century. My aim has been to balance the narrative with an analytical approach that suggests various lines of interpretation for the key events that are related. I hope that this conceptual context will encourage readers to approach history as a process of inquiry and discovery, both for the past and for the present as shaped by the past. Certainly, the issues of equality and justice so heatedly debated by Americans in the era of the Civil War are still very much alive and unresolved in the America of today.

Scholars whose findings and insights proved to be invaluable, colleagues and students who patiently listened to and improved my thinking on this project while it was in progress, Steve Dalphin, my editor at Prentice Hall, whose advice was always helpful, and, most emphatically, Rosalie Radcliffe, my typist in the Department of History in Chapel Hill, and quite simply the best typist who ever was, all played a major role in the completion of this text. I would like to thank those who reviewed the manuscript for this text: Bill Cecil-Fronsman, University of Wisconsin; Archie P. McDonald, Stephen F. Austin State University; Keith Ian Polakoff, California State University; Donald M. Jacobs, Northeastern University; and Gabor S. Boritt, Gettysburg College.

As with my past work, my family—Elaine, Kristina, and Jeremy—offered more support and encouragement than I ever deserved. By being herself, my wife Elaine offered the greatest encouragement of all.

William L. Barney
Chapel Hill

1

The Federal
Union
at Midcentury

"Spacious avenues that begin in nothing, and lead nowhere; streets, mile-long, that only want houses, roads and inhabitants; public buildings that need but a public to be complete; and ornaments of great thoroughfares, which only lack great thoroughfares to ornament—are its leading features."[1] Such was Charles Dickens' description of Washington, D.C., in 1842. Dickens, the famed British novelist, as well as many other foreign visitors, was struck by the gap between America's pretensions to greatness and the weakness of its centralized government. Nothing better symbolized that gap than the unfulfilled promise of the American capital itself.

Yet, as Americans, ever sensitive to outside criticism, were quick to point out, the United States of the 1840s was emerging as a great power. In the first half of the nineteenth century, both its population and land area had more than tripled. At the same time, strong economic growth had underwritten a level of per capita income that was second in the world only to that of Britain's. Prosperous, confident, and, above all, free, that was how Americans, or at least the adult white males who made up the political citizenry, viewed themselves and their country. Their republic had none of the hated trappings of legal privilege and coercive power deemed essential to social order and effective governance in the Old World. No officially government-sanctioned church, legal aristocracy, or large standing armies in peacetime had ever taken root in America. To be sure, the central government in

The unfinished dome on the U.S. Capitol was an ominous symbol of just how incomplete was the process of American nation-building in the 1850s.

Washington was weak, but, as a consequence, Americans were the most lightly taxed and least governed people of any major country, and they were all the freer for it. What Americans referred to as their experiment in liberty—the belief that the republic had a sacred mission to prove to a hostile world governed by force and the dictum of divine right that self-government could survive and flourish—was apparently a resounding success.

The United States by the midpoint of the nineteenth century was indeed a powerful country, but, as Dickens saw so clearly, it was not yet a "nation." The absence of a grand national capital was more than fitting for a country in which the citizenry profoundly feared centralized power and the potential authority of a national government with the legal and political means of directly exerting its will over them. There was no national currency issued by the federal government, no significant amount of national taxation (save for tariff duties on imports), and, most fundamentally, no definitive concept of citizenship to establish the primacy of national over state citizenship.

The weakness of the federal government flowed logically from the nature of the Union forged at Philadelphia in 1787. The Constitution of the Founding Fathers did not create a consolidated national state. It created a federated Union, which was defined by a division of sovereign powers between the federal government and the individual states. The newly devised federal government was given broad powers in the areas of commerce, coinage, foreign policy, and military affairs. Compared to the Articles of Confederation, which it replaced, the Constitution did create a more powerful centralized authority.

However, the national power conferred in the Constitution was limited in two fundamental ways. First, through an intricate system of checks and balances, each of the major elements in the federal government—Congress, the presidency, and the judiciary—had an effective veto over the actions of the other two branches of government. Second, all those powers not specifically delegated to the federal government were reserved for the states, which still retained their sovereign capacity to regulate and govern the daily lives of their citizens. Individual states, and the political subdivisions within those states, were the source of nearly all the legislation that directly affected the social and economic welfare of the citizenry. The result was federalism, a political system that divided and shared sovereign power between the overlapping and at times competing layers of government at the national, state, and local levels.

The source of ultimate sovereign power was left intentionally ambiguous, for any attempt to fix it either in the individual states or in the federal government would have prevented an agreement between the thirteen original states in favor of a new framework of government. There was no ambiguity, however, over the issue of the relationship between slavery and state sovereignty.

Of the exclusive powers retained by the states, none was as important as those that recognized the exclusive right of a state to regulate slavery within its jurisdiction. Without such an explicit recognition of their sovereign power over slavery, the slave states would never have joined the newly proposed Union. Thus, freedom for whites and slavery for blacks were constitutionally joined in the very creation of the antebellum Union.

In and of itself, this dual commitment to white liberty and black bondage was a standing barrier against the subsequent formation of a modern nation–state during the antebellum (pre-Civil War) period. Such a centralized government, with the power of acting on the citizenry regardless of locale or region, was simply too much of a threat to slavery in a Union composed of both free and slave states. However, as long as such a nation–state did not evolve, as long as political power remained diffused and fractured along the lines of federalism, the chances of a peaceful resolution of any bitter sectional division over slavery were correspondingly reduced. Without the means of exerting majority will through national institutions of government, or even the acceptance by a slave-holding minority of the constitutional right of an antislavery majority to exercise such power, any resolution of a division over slavery was, increasingly, likely to be settled by the sword and not by the ballot.

The outline of such a division first began to appear in the 1840s. Ironically, what triggered that division was the very process of economic and territorial growth that most Americans had always assumed was the surest evidence of the strength of the Union. This opening chapter will examine that process of growth and its social impact; it will then move on to the efforts of the major parties of the Jacksonian era, the Democrats and Whigs, to promote that growth and to channel reactions to it into a set of competing partisan loyalties that cut across sectional lines. The chapter will conclude with the election of 1848, the first presidential contest that confronted the issue that more than any other would split the Union, the expansion of slavery into the federal territories.

EXPANSION AND FEDERALISM

Whether measured by the people that it contained, the land area it encompassed, or the goods it produced, the United States grew at a prodigious rate during the first half of the nineteenth century. Continuing a pace that had set in by the early eighteenth century, the population was doubling every twenty-five years.

Increasing from 5.3 million in 1800 to 23.2 million in 1850, the American population was growing at a rate six times the world average. Yet, population density, measured by people per square mile of land area, remained far below the European average: In 1850, the average was 7.9, only marginally higher than the 6.1 average recorded at the beginning of the century. The reason for this was the continuous movement of Americans to new areas that came under the control of the federal government. The public domain, that is, land acquired and owned by the federal government, mushroomed from 233 million acres in 1800 to 1.4 billion acres by 1853.

Most remarkably, this exceptionally high demographic growth was accompanied by accelerating economic growth that resulted in a doubling of real average income. The American standard of living steadily improved while the population expanded, contrary to the gloomy predictions of the influential British economist, Thomas Malthus, whose *Essay on the Principle of Population* (1798) laid down the dictum that population increases invariably outstripped a given society's means of economic subsistence and, hence, produced poverty, distress, and war. But in America, the output of goods and services grew faster than the population.

What accounted for these extraordinary rates of growth in population, land, and output? The most important factor driving the population increase was the extremely high American birth rate, the highest recorded throughout the world in the nineteenth century. Thus, although some 2.5 million European immigrants entered the United States between 1800 and 1850, it was the natural increase of the native-born population, the excess of births over deaths, that explains seventy-five percent of the total population growth in that half century.

The reason why the American birth rate was so high is tied to the ready availability of cheap land. In the overwhelmingly agricultural America of the early nineteenth century—over eighty percent of the labor force was engaged in farming—land was the basis of independence and security, and children were an economic asset. The cost of farm labor was expensive and labor-saving machinery was virtually nonexistent, so children were needed to help out on the farm. The average American mother of 1800 gave birth to seven or more children. The sons, when settled on land that was subdivided from the original family holdings, would continue to be a source of economic assistance when their parents reached old age.

As a general rule, therefore, fertility rates in rural areas of antebellum America varied in accordance with the availability and price of the cultivable land needed to establish a family on its own farm. As population density rose and new farm land became increasingly scarce in older areas, fertility fell. Around the turn of the nineteenth century, the American birth rate began to decline. By midcentury, it had fallen nearly twenty-five percent, with the steepest declines occurring in the older rural districts of the Northeast. Nonetheless, the white birth rate in 1850 (an estimated forty-three births per 1,000 of population) was still extraordinarily high. The birth rate remained at historically very high levels because the land expansion promulgated by the federal government continually made cheap, fertile land, which was the basis of high population growth, available for settlement.

From the Louisiana Purchase of 1803 through the Gadsden Purchase of 1853, the federal government pursued expansionist policies that propelled the United States into the first ranks of the world's great landed powers. The purchase from Mexico in 1853 of a small strip of land that filled out the southern borders of the present states of Arizona and New Mexico completed an expansionist cycle that had quadrupled the country's size within the span of two generations. A combination of luck, diplomacy, and conquest accounted for this phenomenal pace of territorial acquisition. The most significant factor was the absence of strong enemies within North America. By European standards, the United States was a weak military power. More important, the Indians, Spaniards, and Mexicans, whom Americans pushed aside, were even weaker militarily.

The first great chunk of territory, some half a billion acres that doubled the size of the original United States, came with the Louisiana Purchase of 1803. Napoleon was willing to sell the middle third of the continent to President Thomas Jefferson because he needed money. England and France, the only foreign powers with military resources sufficient to block American expansion had they wished, were locked into a war that lasted from 1793 to 1815. Strapped for funds to finance the war, and frustrated by his inability to crush a slave rebellion on Haiti, a sugar island in the West Indies he had hoped to supply with foodstuffs from his holdings in North America, Napoleon unloaded the territory for $15 million. Jefferson and his secretary of state, James Madison, had helped force Napoleon's hand by covertly aiding the Haitian rebels with shipments of food.

Another 46 million acres came in the Florida acquisition of 1819 from Spain. The world's greatest imperial power in the sixteenth century, Spain had long since lapsed into military somnolence and economic decay. The determined American drive to secure the Spanish Floridas, the western province along the Alabama and Mississippi Gulf Coast, and the eastern province that is the present state of Florida, met with feeble resistance.

Under President James Madison, the United States seized West Florida, and Andrew Jackson's border campaign of 1818 exposed the hollowness of Spanish pretensions to sovereignty in East Florida. By 1819, Spain was reduced to the face-saving expedient of accepting an American assumption of up to $5 million in private claims against the Spanish government in return for a cession of all of Florida.

To acquire the bulk of the western third of the continent, the United States had to go to war. The Mexican War of 1846–1848 resulted in territorial gains that increased the size of the republic by nearly fifty percent. Although neither side made

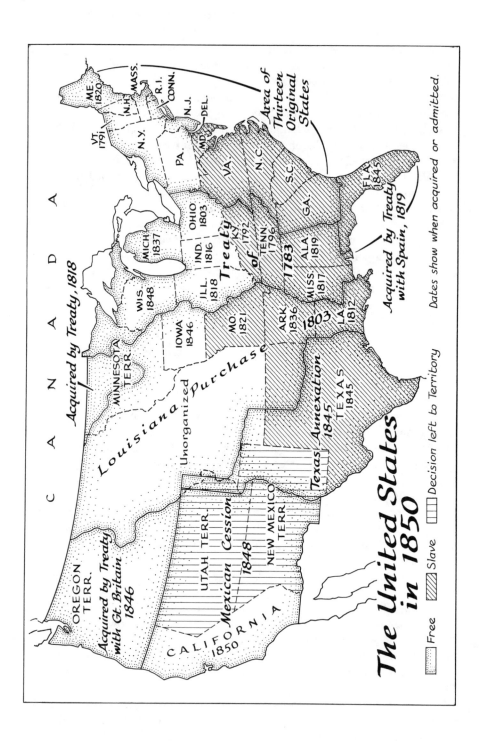

The United States in 1850

Area of Thirteen Original States

Acquired by Treaty with Spain, 1819

Dates show when acquired or admitted.

Acquired by Treaty, 1818

Acquired by Treaty with Gt. Britain 1846

OREGON TERR.

CANADA

MINNESOTA TERR.

Louisiana Purchase

Unorganized

UTAH TERR.

NEW MEXICO TERR.

Mexican Cession 1848

CALIFORNIA 1850

Texas Annexation 1845

TEXAS 1845

Treaty of 1783

1803

ME. 1820

VT. 1791

N.H.

MASS.

R.I.

CONN.

N.Y.

PA.

N.J.

DEL.

MD.

VA.

N.C.

S.C.

GA.

FLA. 1845

OHIO 1803

MICH. 1837

IND. 1816

ILL. 1818

WIS. 1848

IOWA 1846

MO. 1821

KY. 1792

TENN. 1796

ALA. 1819

MISS. 1817

ARK. 1836

LA. 1812

☐ Free   ▨ Slave   ▥ Decision left to Territory

6

much of an effort to avert the war, its most proximate cause was the aggressively expansionist policy of President James K. Polk.

Late in the administration of President John Tyler, Polk's predecessor, Congress extended an offer of annexation to the Republic of Texas, a former Mexican province, which had won its independence in 1836. The offer further embittered the already strained relations that existed between Mexico and the United States.

Mexico, which in the 1820s had encouraged American settlement in Texas in the mistaken hope that that would limit and control what was viewed as the inevitable Anglo push into its northern borderlands, had never accepted the loss of Texas. Mexico felt betrayed by the uprising of the Anglo-Texans in 1836 and was convinced that the United States was behind it. In particular, Mexico vehemently denied that the claim of Texas (and after Texas entered the Union in December 1845, the claim of the United States as well) to the Rio Grande River as its southern and western boundary had any legal foundation. By ordering American military forces into the disputed area and by provoking an armed response from Mexico in the spring of 1846, President Polk goaded Mexico into war.

Why had Polk incited the war? As he confided privately, he was determined to acquire California as an outlet to the Pacific. If Mexico was unwilling to sell California, then Polk was willing to fight to get it. The ensuing war was easily won by the United States. Strategically and tactically, Mexican forces were no match for the naval power and superior artillery of the American forces.

In retrospect, British intervention offered Mexico its only hope of emerging from a war with the United States with their northern borderlands intact. As the war crisis heated in the spring of 1846, such intervention did not seem improbable, at least to Mexico.

The United States and Britain were embroiled in a dispute over the Oregon country in the Pacific Northwest. The Polk Democrats had touched off the dispute. Contrary to a long-standing American offer to divide Oregon along the preexisting boundary to the east of the 49th parallel between the United States and Canada, which was a British colony, Polk pledged during the presidential campaign of 1844 to "reclaim" Oregon up to 54°40′. This was a boundary far north of any area which Americans had ever settled in Oregon. Although it appeared by the summer of 1845 that Polk was prepared to go to war over the issue, a compromise on the 49th parallel was reached in June 1846, a month after the outbreak of the Mexican–American war.

Political posturing aside, Polk had always favored such a compromise, and he was enough of a military strategist to realize the folly of plunging the country into a two-front war. As a result of the Oregon settlement, Polk was able to concentrate on Mexico, British–American trade continued to flourish, and Mexico lost a potential ally that could have served as a counterweight to American power.

Save for the Gadsden Purchase, the Mexican cession of territory in the 1848 treaty of Guadalupe Hidalgo rounded out the continental limits of the present United States. The Atlantic seaboard republic of 1800 now spanned a continent. To many white Americans, this extension of the flag had been divinely inspired. In a typical expression of this belief, Robert J. Walker, Polk's secretary of the treasury, spoke in 1847 of a "higher than any earthly power" that "directs our destiny, impels us onward, and has selected our great and happy country as a model and ultimate center of attraction for all the nations of the world."[2] Americans obviously believed that they were not engaged in empire-building in any materialistic, power-hungry European meaning of the term. Instead, their America, a republic born free in a world full of tyrants, was spreading its ideals of liberty and democracy across its natural territorial limits.

In laying claim to a providentially ordained exceptionalism among the countries of the world, Americans identified federalism as the moral and political basis for the genius of the American system. Acquired territories were not held as conquered provinces but were promised eventual co-equality when they entered the Union as states. Moreover, the range of interests and needs that new states brought into the Union would, it was argued, protect the liberties of Americans living in the older states.

The great threat to individual liberties in a republic ruled by the will of the majority was the creation of a tyrannical majority with the power to trample the rights of minorities. The likelihood of such a majority forming would be undercut by the infusion of new interest groups constantly limiting and offsetting the power of old political factions. Thus, the very expansion of the Union would maintain the balance between power and liberty. As Jefferson put it in his second Inaugural Address, "The larger our association, the less it will be shaken by local passions."[3]

The federal structure of 1787 consolidated diplomatic and military power in the hands of the federal government, especially the executive branch, and thereby gave the young republic the centralized authority and direction it needed to deal effectively with foreign powers and to embark on an expansionist program. In turn, much of this expansionist drive was shaped by demands that surfaced at the state and local levels of the federal system. These demands focused on expansionist issues of land and trade that were directly related to the economic self-interests and social aspirations of most of the citizenry.

When an English observer, Harriet Martineau, noted in the 1830s that "the possession of land is the aim of all action, generally speaking, and the cure for all social ills among men in the United States,"[4] she was but stating an American article of faith.

As celebrated in the Jeffersonian vision, land was the basis of independence and virtue. Its wide ownership and abundance in proportion to the population had enabled Americans to escape the tragedies of Europe, where the landless, whether as peasants on aristocratic estates or as wage laborers in the cities, were poor and dependent on others for their livelihood. Americans could remain free and prosperous as long as they had access to cheap, plentiful land and market outlets for the bounty of their farms. This was the vision that Jefferson acted on when he purchased the Louisiana Territory. Although initially hopeful only of acquiring the port of New Orleans, the outlet via the Mississippi River for the agricultural produce of the trans-Appalachian West, he seized the chance to double the size of the republic.

These same goals—land for the independent farmer and outlets to world markets for his crops—were the keys to the other expansionist surges of the antebellum republic. In both a strategic and an economic sense, the acquisition of Florida and the Gulf Coast opened up the Southeast for commercial agriculture. Polk plotted for and secured not only 500 million acres of land, but also the magnificent harbors of the Pacific, San Francisco, Monterey, and San Diego. All the while, merchants, farmers, and planters were pushing the frontiers of American settlement westward and demanding that federal military protection and political institutions catch up with them. Eastern Texas was Americanized before it entered the Union, and California was well on the way even before the Mexican War.

Western representatives, both north and south of the Ohio River, were the most incessant expansionists and the most ardent advocates of an aggressive Indian policy. In addition to negotiating the treaties that extinguished any legal title of the Indians to the land, the federal government provided the military force to expel the Native Americans from the path of white settlement. The first president to come out of the West, Andrew Jackson, pushed through the Indian Removal Act of 1830. Under its provisions, Indians were removed to reservations that were located west of the Mississippi River. By the time Polk became president in 1844, only about 30,000 Indians, out of a population of 125,000 in 1820, still lived east of the Mississippi. The frontier had spoken. The Jacksonian West from the Appalachians to the Mississippi was reserved for whites.

Apart from acquiring land and dispossessing Indians from it, the federal government quickly brought that land into the marketplace; that is, it encouraged the conversion of the public domain into private property. Revenue was the prime objective of the federal government in disposing of its land, and it soon became apparent that revenue would be maximized by a high volume of land sales based on a relatively inexpensive price. The first public land law of Congress in 1796 set down terms of a minimum price of $2 per acre and purchases in lots no smaller than 640 acres. From then on, the terms became increasingly liberal. After 1820, the minimum price was set at $1.25 per acre. The minimum purchase was reduced to 320, 160, and, after 1832, 80 acres. Settlers who "squatted" on the land before it had been surveyed and made available for sale in a public auction were assured in the Preemption Act of 1841 that they could purchase up to 160 acres at the minimum price when the auction was held. In a further concession to Western interests in Congress, the Graduation Act of 1854 reduced government land below the $1.25 minimum in proportion to the amount of time the land remained unsold on the market.

The ease with which individuals could acquire government land and the provisions for self-government and eventual statehood, first embodied in the Northwest Ordinance of 1787, were powerful inducements for the rapid settlement of the West. In 1800, only seven percent of Americans lived in the states and territories of the trans-Appalachian West. By 1860, one in two lived in these areas. Cheap, fertile soil was the magnet drawing Americans to the West, and revolutionary improvements in transportation after 1815 continuously widened markets for the crops grown on that soil. The result was a dramatic rise in population, agricultural output, and per capita income.

The development of steamboats, canals, and railroads unlocked the economic potential of the West. In the early nineteenth century, the prohibitively high cost of moving bulky agricultural commodities to market forced most farmers in the West to practice an economy of semi-subsistence. The first breakthrough in transportation came with the appearance of steamboats on Western rivers just after the War of 1812. Within a generation, downriver freight rates dropped by seventy percent and upriver ones by ninety percent. The completion of the Erie Canal in 1825 opened an all-water route from Buffalo, New York, on Lake Erie, to New York City. Merchants in New York now began to tap an immense interregional trade with farmers in the upper Midwest. Other East–West canals were built, though none was as profitable as the Erie. By 1840, some 3,000 miles of canals connected the Upper Mississippi and Ohio Valleys with the Great Lakes and the port cities on the Atlantic seaboard. Even by that year, however, railroads—a form of technology barely dreamed of a generation earlier—had overtaken canals in total mileage. Initially promoted by eastern merchants anxious to divert the western trade from rivals in port cities at the eastern terminus of interregional canals, the railroads linked the Great Lakes and the eastern seaboard by 1850. Western farmers could now choose between a series of transportation outlets to eastern markets, all of which were far cheaper and faster than anything that had existed in 1815.

Shown here under construction in the early 1820s, the Erie Canal was the most successful and famous of the antebellum canals.

The role of government at all levels of the federal system accounted for the speed with which Americans built a transport system that was the most advanced in the world by the middle of the nineteenth century. Public assistance was essential to meet the high construction costs of canals and railroads, about $25,000 per mile. Private sources of capital fell far short of the need, and most investors were leery in any event of risking their money in enterprises that would not earn a return for years, if at all. By antebellum standards, when the annual pre-1850 expenditures of the federal government barely averaged $25 million, the amounts of capital involved were enormous. Some $200 million were sunk into canals, seventy-three percent of which was provided by the states. The federal contribution consisted mainly of 4 million acres of land granted to the states as subsidies for canal construction. With the exception of the South, about three-quarters of the $1 billion invested in railroads through 1860 came from private sources. Still, before private investments at home and from abroad soared in the prosperous 1850s, state and municipal assistance had been critical in the formative railroad decades of the 1830s and 1840s. Apart from a lowering of tariff duties on iron used in railroad construction between 1830 and 1843, a reduction that saved the railroad companies $6 million, the assistance of the federal government once again took the form of land grants. About 20 million acres were granted to the states in the 1850s for the financing of railroads.

Constitutional scruples over the separation of powers limited the direct involvement of the federal government in the economy to stock subscriptions in three canal companies and the building of the National Road from Maryland to Illinois. Yet, the same scruples sanctioned a very activist role for the state governments in promoting, financing, and regulating economic development within their separate spheres of action. A host of federal court decisions set down a legal basis for this role, including the right of a state to charter corporations. A body of persons legally entrusted with certain rights and privileges for the purpose of carrying on the activities set forth in its charter, the corporation was a relatively new form of business organization that was used extensively by the states to develop their economies.

Prior to 1800, business corporations were very rare. Corporations that existed were public or quasi-public agencies used for town governments and religious, charitable, and educational institutions. After 1800, the states chartered thousands of corporations, and about two-thirds were in transportation. For most of the antebellum period, these corporations retained a quasi-public character. They were mixed enterprises in which state governments put up much of the capital, appointed many of the directors, and maintained an overall supervisory role. By combining public and private goals, these corporations ideally met the needs of the states. They promoted economic goals for local communities, without the reliance on stifling political bureaucracies that complete state ownership would have entailed. Most important, the ability of corporations to raise capital from a multitude of small investors freed the states from the need of having to impose heavy taxes to pay for internal improvements. Such taxes would have been suicidal for any officeholder to support in a political culture that equated taxes with governmental tyranny.

Federalism provided a stable but extremely competitive political environment in which demands for transportation improvements could rapidly be met. The result of these improvements was a tremendous release of economic energy as barriers of time and distance that had blocked the potential flow of goods to market drastically shrank. Within a forty-year period after the War of 1812, inland freight rates fell from fifty percent to ninety percent, and the time needed to travel from the East coast to commercial centers in the Midwest became measured in days instead of weeks. These gains in speed and efficiency enlarged the size of the home market, the area in which goods could profitably be distributed and sold, and continually drew more Americans into a market economy. Manufactured goods, which previously had been produced locally, at home, or not at all, were now purchased from distant markets with the income earned by selling cash crops for consumption elsewhere. Economic specialization and the division of labor, the two fundamental prerequisites for self-sustaining economic development, increasingly characterized the production of goods.

The Old Northwest, the contemporary name for the region north of the Ohio River and west of the Appalachian mountains, specialized in foodstuffs. South of the Ohio, the slave region of the Old Southwest specialized in cotton. Manufacturing became concentrated in the Northeast. The pace at which labor was becoming more specialized can be gauged by the increase in the non-agricultural labor force from seventeen percent of the total employed in 1800 to forty-five percent in 1850. As a consequence of these structural changes, per capita national product was growing three times faster than it had in the eighteenth century.

Transportation improvements triggered this economic growth, and the development of trade within and then between the regions drove it forward. The pivotal region was the West where gains in population, agricultural production, and per capita income were the greatest. By the early 1820s, regional terms of trade, the relationship of prices between eastern finished goods and western farm goods, shifted decisively in favor of the West. This shift encouraged more migration into the West and a greater commercialization of its agriculture. Every move to the West tended to lower the value of farm land in the East, and every eastward shipment of western foodstuffs added to the squeeze on eastern farmers unable to compete for markets against the low price and high volume of corn and wheat grown on the more fertile soils of the West. As a region, the Northeast responded by shifting its capital and labor into manufacturing. The sons and daughters of marginal eastern farmers comprised the bulk of this new manufacturing working class. They were consumers of western foodstuffs and producers of goods, which, especially after 1840, were purchased by western farmers with the income generated by market sales in the East. Measured by the value of the westward flow of goods along the Erie Canal, the home market in the West for manufactured goods grew almost ten-fold from the mid-1830s to the mid-1850s.

In marked contrast to the Old Northwest, the commercialized economy of the Old Southwest was always geared toward exports in the world market. As we have often been told, "Cotton was King" in the antebellum South, and it was so enthroned as the result of two concurrent developments at the end of the eighteenth century. Eli Whitney's cotton gin for removing the seeds from picked cotton opened up nearly all of the South below Virginia and Kentucky for the commercial cultivation of cotton. At the same time, technological innovations in the British textile industry were increasing enormously the demand for raw cotton. More so than any other area in the world, the South had the soil, climate, and labor system to meet this demand. The existence of slavery was critical. Cotton cultivation demanded hard, year-long labor that free whites were loathe to provide as wage workers for an employer. Slaves, of course, had no choice in the matter. They were held to the land, and their forced, unpaid labor permitted the South to take full advantage of its competitive advantages in the world market for cotton.

The center of cotton production moved steadily westward after 1800. The alluvial soils of the lower Mississippi Valley and the prairie lands of Alabama and Mississippi offered yields simply unattainable in the older regions of the South Atlantic states. As new cotton kingdoms were carved out in the Old Southwest, and as a labor supply of over 800,000 slaves was forced to migrate into the region, cotton production skyrocketed. After first reaching 100,000 bales in 1801, cotton production doubled by 1815. It doubled again by 1820, and finally leveled off at about 4 million bales by the late 1850s.

Throughout the antebellum period, more than three-quarters of the cotton crop was exported, most of it going to England. This export orientation of the Southern plantation economy speeded up the development of the entire U.S. economy. From the mid-1830s on, cotton alone accounted for sixty percent of the value of all American exports. Cotton-generated export earnings provided the cash to pay for European imports, and they enabled money centers in the Northeast to purchase foreign capital for investment in the diversifying economy of the North. Merchants, shippers, and bankers in the Northeast, and especially those in New York City, furnished the financial services needed to transport and market cotton. They thereby earned profits that could be plowed back into the industrialization of the Northeast. As for the plantation South, the very profitability of cotton production was a strong deterrent to diversification into manufacturing. The Southern demand for manufactured goods was met through imports from the Northeast. Additional amounts of cotton income were siphoned off through the purchases of grain and meat from the Old Northwest.

By mid-century, cotton no longer played as dynamic a role in spurring economic growth. Cotton earnings were still important, but the economy was increasingly fueled by the interregional links between the three specialized economies in the Northeast, Midwest, and South. The value of interregional trade grew half again as much as foreign trade between 1840 and 1860. In an economic parallel to the political logic of federalism, the regional separation of economic functions contributed to a greater economic whole.

GROWTH AND SECTIONALISM

Policy makers and common Americans alike had generally assumed that territorial expansion and economic growth would strengthen the Union. By the 1840s, this assumption was beginning to break down. Divisions rooted in the very process of growth were now generating sectional tensions that threatened the Union.

North–South tensions over slavery had existed since the founding of the republic, but they did not start to coalesce into rival ideologies based on notions of sectional separateness until the 1830s and 1840s. The key event in the formation of these ideologies was the founding in 1833 of the American Anti-Slavery Society, the organizational birth of Northern abolitionism and its unrelenting moral attack on slavery. Out of abolitionism and the Southern counter-response on behalf of slavery came sectional ideologies that posited a fundamental antagonism between the free North and the slave South. The emergence of these ideologies marked the point at which growing social and economic differences between the North and South were expressed in a moral conflict over the root meanings of freedom and equality in America. What was at stake was the meaning of America itself.

In the basic ways in which they organized their social and economic lives, Northern and Southern whites were much more similar in 1800 than half a century later. Nearly all Americans in 1800 earned their living directly from the land. Seven in ten Northerners and four in five Southerners worked in agriculture. Fewer than ten percent of the population in either section lived in cities or towns with a population of at least 2,500. Outside of the household system of production, manufacturing was negligible. The primary unit of social and economic organization was the farm family. Work, whether of children, women, or slaves, was governed by principles of dependency that rested on the traditional authority of the male household head. Wage labor, defined as a freely entered contractual obligation between economic equals, was emerging in the port cities of the Northeast, but most work still fell short of any ideal of free labor. Domestic servants, apprentices, and the widows and children who performed what little factory work was available were all viewed as social dependents in need of direct personal supervision.

By 1850 the patterns of social change in much of the North were increasingly different from those in the South. In New England and the Mid-Atlantic states, over one-quarter of the population now lived in cities, a proportion three times higher than in any region of the South. Less than half of all Northerners now worked in farm occupations. In the South the figure remained around eighty percent. Stimulated first by Jefferson's Embargo of 1807 and then by the cessation of British imports during the War of 1812, manufacturing became the most dynamic sector in the economy after 1809. The value of manufacturing output increased at a decennial rate of fifty-nine percent from 1809 to 1839 and then jumped by 153 percent in the 1840s. The vast bulk of this manufacturing activity occurred in the free states. The South in 1850 had less than one-eighth the per capita manufacturing output of the Northeast.

The presence or absence of slavery explained these divergent sectional paths.

The South's market economy was based on slave labor and export crops, and that economy could grow extensively without any major structural change. Indeed, the economic logic of slavery provided no incentives for urbanization, industrialization, and the population increases that cities and factories feed on. Local economic development did not increase the value of slaves, the major form of wealth in the South. Slaves constituted a movable form of capital, the value of which was set by the market demand for crops produced by slave labor. As long as that international demand was high, and as long as slaves could be moved to the areas of most profitable production, planters earned an annual return of eight to ten percent, which was at least equal to the profit margins of Northern manufacturers and commercial farmers.

In contrast to planters, Northern capitalists had to promote programs that could enhance the value of their immovable investments in land and factories. This was especially the case just after 1815, when the Northeast experienced heavy population losses to the West that simultaneously depressed land values and raised the wages of labor. Lacking the economic cushion enjoyed by planters in the Southeast of a lucrative cash crop in growing world demand, northeastern merchants and farmers stemmed and then reversed their population losses by pushing for intensive economic change. Capital was shifted out of international trade into domestic manufacturing. Transportation links were established between cities and their rural hinterlands and then between the eastern seaboard and the Midwest. Meanwhile, towns in the Old Northwest grew rapidly as local boosters competed to attract the population that would drive up local land values.

The North's promotional economic strategies were a success, and the payoff came in population numbers. The free and slave states were virtually even in population in 1800. By 1850, the Northern population was sixty percent larger, and this edge would grow to two to one by the eve of the Civil War. The North, but not the South, had an economy dynamic enough to absorb surplus rural populations that were migrating out of areas within both America and Europe. Despite a series of economic booms in the Old Southwest, the South as a region was losing its white population to the free states throughout the entire antebellum period.

More important, however, in accounting for the Northern population gains was the arrival of European immigrants. About 2.5 million immigrants entered the United States from 1800 to 1850, and decade after decade more than four in every five settled in the free states. Aside from a justifiable fear of contracting yellow fever or malaria in fever-ridden Southern ports with high mortality rates, the reason for the immigrants' sectional preference was obvious. They did not want to compete with slave labor, and they were well aware that manual labor was held in contempt by many Southern whites because of its association with a degraded race of slaves. The packet boats of the trans-Atlantic trade brought the immigrants to the port cities of the Northeast, and there most of them remained. Their numbers swelled the ranks of unskilled labor and accelerated the pace of both urbanization and industrialization. Half of all foreign-born Americans in 1850 lived in Massachusetts, New York, and Pennsylvania. Only one in ten were in the slave states.

The tide of Catholic immigrants became a flood during the Irish potato famine in the mid-1840s. Many native-born Protestants in the Northeast were convinced that the impoverished Irish peasants streaming into their cities needed to be educated in the virtues of American citizenship. It was no accident that Massachusetts, the state with the heaviest influx of Irish Catholics, passed the first compulsory school-attendance law in the early 1850s.

Since the 1830s, Massachusetts had taken the lead in committing the North to a state-supported system of public education. Unlike the South, where planters saw no need for an educated populace, and where nonslaveholders, locked into the folk mores of a traditional rural society, resisted the tax burden needed to support schools, the North made a sizeable investment in public education. The typical Northern county by 1850 had a population density two to three times greater than the median level in the South. Hence, the North had a concentrated tax base with which to fund local schools.

The absence of this fiscal commitment to public education in the South left the slave states with much higher rates of white illiteracy. About twenty percent of adult white males in the South of 1850 could not read or write, a level of illiteracy five to six times greater than in the North. This gap closed in the 1850s as some Southern states sought to improve their schools, but the Southern ratio of school children to white population remained under half of the Northern figure.

The North had more and better schools because public education served a vital need in its diversifying economy. As more and more Northern parents found themselves without land to pass on to their children, they compensated by providing their children with an education that could prepare them for nonfarm occupations. Schools, just as factories and railroads, were touted in the North as vehicles for economic advancement.

This different pace of material and cultural change in the free and slave states was crucial to the development of rival sectional ideologies. In particular, it was the meaning placed on those changes by individuals experiencing them that led to the growing belief that Americans were living in separate, different societies with conflicting interests and values. As the conditions of everyday life diverged above and below the Mason–Dixon line, an awareness of cultural and moral differences developed and sharpened.

By the middle decades of the antebellum period, many Northerners were proclaiming the moral and economic superiority of their free society over the South's slave society. In their view, the South had become a national embarrassment, a backward, stagnant region out of step with the progressive march of civilization in the nineteenth century. As Ralph Waldo Emerson, the Northern philosopher–reformer, argued in a public address in 1844:

> Slavery is no scholar, no improver; it does not love the whistle of the railroad; it does not love the newspaper, the mail-bag, a college, a book or a preacher who has the absurd whim of saying what he thinks; it does not increase the white population; it does not improve the soil, everything goes to decay.[5]

Emerson's audience in Concord, Massachusetts, would have found nothing remarkable in his indictment of slavery as a retrograde institution that stifled progress. What was remarkable was the extent to which this antislavery view had become a staple of thought in the trans-Atlantic community since 1800.

As late as the middle of the eighteenth century, slavery was widely viewed as a progressive institution responsible for economic expansion and development. Few whites on either side of the Atlantic would have denied that Europe reaped immense economic benefits from spearheading and exploiting the spread of plantation agriculture from the Mediterranean to the Americas between the fifteenth and eighteenth centuries. Slavery was at the core of huge and lucrative trading systems based on the sale of African slaves and the production, sale, and consumption of agricultural commodities extracted from their labor. The profits from this trade underwrote a rise in Europe's population, improved standards of living, and generated capital for intensive economic change. The first mass markets in European history were built around the slave crops of coffee, tobacco, cocoa, cotton, and sugar. Slavery contributed even more to European economic growth after 1790 when slave cotton from the American South fed England's industrial revolution in textiles. In short, the economic consequences of slavery seemingly left it invulnerable to the charge of being unprogressive. Yet, in a supreme irony, the very economic success of slavery led to its undoing.

The industrial revolution, which got underway in England in the last third of the eighteenth century and in the American North in the first third of the nineteenth, was based on wage labor. However exploited that labor was through low wages and long hours, it was legally free. For the first time in the history of the world, a system of mass production arose in which the labor force was not legally tied to the land or owned by a set of masters. This was a momentous change, and slave labor, when set against this historically new class of free labor, rather suddenly became vulnerable in a way in which it had not been before.

Despite the fact that the profits and products of slave labor were critical to the take-off stage of industrialization, it was now possible to conceive of economic growth without slaves. Indeed, slavery came to be viewed as a deterrent to such growth. As a matter of definition, the coerced labor of the slave did not produce wants that could be satisfied by spending wages on consumer goods. Historically, such wants had first been stimulated by slave crops, but future economic growth required the continuous creation of new wants and ever higher levels of consumption. Only the wages of free labor could provide the purchasing power needed for such consumption.

The frontal attack on slavery that made Emerson's indictment appear as a self-evident truth to his listeners in Concord originated with Quaker revivals in mid-eighteenth-century England. The Quakers, soon joined by Methodists and other evangelicals, were in the forefront of British abolitionism. Within a generation they built a mass movement that resulted in the British abolition of the African slave trade in 1807 and of slavery itself in the British West Indies by 1833. These were incredible accomplishments. What formerly had been the occasional religious voice denouncing slavery as a sin became an incessant moral chorus that no number of appeals to economic self-interest could shout down. England, the first nation to be affected by the industrial revolution, was also the one whose short-term economic interests would be most damaged by abolition. Nonetheless, the antislavery argument that free labor was inherently more productive than slave labor because of the incentives for material self-improvement held out by wages won more and more converts. Notwithstanding economic evidence to the contrary, it was now generally assumed that slavery was an inferior, outmoded means of production. Economically, as well as morally, slavery was damned as an anachronism that had to be swept away.

Trans-Atlantic ties between evangelical reformers nourished the early antislavery movement in America. Down to the 1820s, this movement could point to many successes. Slavery by then was a sectional, not a national, institution. Legal in all the thirteen colonies, slavery did not survive the Revolution intact. Citing the obvious contradiction between human bondage and the Revolutionary principles of liberty and equality grounded in universal natural rights, Northern reformers ended the institution outright in Massachusetts and by programs of gradual emancipation elsewhere.

Once New Jersey finally passed such a program in 1804, the division of the early Union into free and slave states was complete. Antislavery societies offered religious instruction to slaves, worked to protect Northern free blacks from being kidnapped and sold into slavery, and, above all, pressured Congress to abolish the African slave trade. Constitutionally enjoined from moving against the trade for a period of twenty years, Congress so moved in 1807. This, it was argued, would sound the death knoll for slavery. Falsely believing that slavery was dependent on the African trade for its survival, the antislavery forces assumed that cutting off the trade would wither the institution at its roots. Instead, it was antislavery optimism that withered.

After 1815 there could be no doubt that slavery was a thriving, expanding institution. In response to high prices for cotton, slavery spread to the Old Southwest and up the Mississippi Valley as far north as Missouri. As dramatized in the bitter debates over Missouri's admission as a slave state in 1821, slaveowners were increasingly aggressive and united in their defense of the institution. Their spokesmen in Congress blocked all proposals for gradual, compensated emancipation. They denounced the American Colonization Society for subverting their rights in slave property. Founded in 1816 by a bisectional group of antislavery reformers, the Society was based on the premise that planters would more readily manumit their slaves if they knew that ex-slaves would be encouraged to migrate to the Society's African colony in Liberia. The Colonization Society was a miserable failure. Planters feared the consequences for slave discipline of its espousal of piecemeal emancipation, and free blacks strongly protested its labeling of them as an inferior race unfit to live in America. They made it quite clear that they regarded America as their rightful home, and only a comparative handful, some 1,500, actually moved to Liberia in the 1820s.

Out of the antislavery setbacks of the 1820s emerged abolitionism, a more radicalized and militant antislavery movement. The involvement of women, especially educated, middle-class women from the Northeast, accounted for much of the energy and passion of abolitionism. Antebellum women were deprived of the right to vote, hold political office, or earn wages independent from the control of their husbands. Legally and culturally restricted to the home as their "proper" social sphere, women reformers found in abolitionism a means of extending their moral leadership from the home to the society at large. Abolitionism offered them both a cause of moral reform and an indictment of a male-dominated society that they could draw on to assert their rights as women. They applied notions of equality and individual rights used to condemn slavery to their own legal subordination within Northern society and built the ideological foundations for the women's rights movement of the 1840s. This movement culminated in the campaign for women's suffrage at the end of the Civil War.

The abolitionists declared war on slavery. The stakes could not be higher, and the war would be fought to the finish. In the words of William Lloyd Garrison, the fiery abolitionist editor of the *Liberator*,

> Enslave but a single human being, and the liberty of the world is put in peril....The war [against slavery] is a war of extermination; and I will perish before an inch shall be surrendered, seeing that the liberties of mankind, the happiness and harmony of the universe, and the authority and majesty of Almighty God, are involved in the issue.[6]

The abolitionists fought this war in the 1830s with the weapons of moral suasion. The movement drew its leadership and model of reform from evangelical Protestantism. A great wave of religious revivals in the 1820s and early 1830s had spread the message that the individual alone was accountable to God for his or her salvation. God had given everyone the moral freedom to accept or reject salvation, preached the revivalists. Through an admission of sin and the exercise of this free moral agency, the individual could will an infusion of God's forgiving grace in the conversion experience. The truly converted, those who had the moral self-discipline to commit themselves to Christian holiness, could aspire to lead lives of Christian perfectionism in which they cleansed themselves and society of sin. Here was the religious impulse which triggered a host of Northern reform movements aimed at social betterment in the antebellum period. The reformers established Sunday schools, Bible-tract societies, and missionary endeavors. They were instrumental in pushing through institutional changes that improved conditions for the caring of orphans, the confinement of the mentally ill, and the incarceration of criminals. They organized the temperance crusade, a mass-based reform movement that sought to banish the production and consumption of alcohol. The most radical of all these reform efforts was abolitionism.

Slavery, to the evangelical abolitionist, was the greatest sin because it denied its victims their God-given right to determine their own moral destiny. Worse than its brutalization of human beings, slavery made God's moral creatures into things, moral ciphers who were pieces of property.

The abolitionists tried to bring about a complete moral revolution. They sought to purge the North of the sin of indifference to the moral plight of the slave and the South of the sin of slavery itself. With an audacity that flew in the face of the overwhelming white prejudice against blacks, they even dared to proclaim that Christian benevolence demanded equality of political and economic rights for black Americans.

Employing techniques that foreshadowed much of mass advertising in the twentieth century, the abolitionists turned to the pulpit, schoolhouse, printing press, petition campaign, and lecturing circuit as vehicles to propagandize their message of the utter immorality of slavery. They were unshakable in their goal of immediate, uncompensated emancipation. However long the struggle might take, they insisted that individuals in an act of moral conscience immediately begin the work of dismantling slavery.

After a decade of intense agitation, the abolitionists seemingly had little to show for their efforts. They had built a permanent nucleus of local antislavery societies, but they had not freed a single slave. The South censored all incoming mail after 1835 and denied the abolitionists a hearing in the slave states. Congress, at the insistence of slave interests, refused to permit even a reading of abolitionist petitions after 1836. Mobs in the North broke up antislavery meetings and went on vicious rampages in which they attacked free blacks as well as known abolitionists. Wealthy Northern elites feared the economic consequences of emancipation and the possible loss of their own social leadership in the face of abolitionist appeals pitched directly at the mass of the citizenry. Unskilled workers feared for their jobs if the slaves were freed and moved to the North.

No more than one in twenty Northern whites was a committed abolitionist by 1840. This was a far cry from the millennially inspired vision of a society in which sin was blotted out by moral suasion. Garrison and his followers remained steadfast in their adherence to moral immediatism, but most abolitionists now turned to a new tactic to transmit immediatism into practical action. They organized an antislavery political party, the Liberty party.

Judged by its showing in the two presidential elections in which it ran candidates, 0.3 percent of the total popular vote in 1840 and 2.3 percent in 1844, the Liberty party was a resounding failure. Yet, in its decision to pursue voters through direct political action, the creation of the party signaled a critical turning point in the campaign against slavery. The public arena of voters now replaced the private sphere of conscience as the decisive terrain on which the abolitionists would battle slavery. Once this shift occurred, the way was open for building a broad reformist coalition that aligned Northerners critical of slavery for whatever reason with the much smaller number who had committed themselves on moral grounds to fight slavery.

The cement of the antislavery coalition that gradually started to emerge in the 1840s was a common vision of the good society. Relative to the late eighteenth century, Northern society by the 1840s had become much more open and fluid. Traditional social controls rooted in a localized and patriarchal world of small

As depicted by the abolitionists, slavery was a barbaric institution which turned even white women into savage brutes.

villages had eroded. In both secular and religious affairs, individuals had apparently broken free of traditional restraints. Just as evangelicalism had liberated individuals from the spiritual confines of an eighteenth-century Protestantism that had preached that individuals were powerless to achieve their own salvation from a wrathful God, so also did the widening economic opportunities free individuals from the social confines of the family farm and local village. If society were to be ordered, that order would have to come from the inner controls and self-reliance of the individual.

According to the value structure of the new middle class of manufacturers, entrepreneurs, and clerks, it was just such a self-ordered individual who was best equipped morally to take advantage of economic opportunities for advancement. Here was a secular world view that mirrored the abolitionists' religious vision of free moral agents achieving their own salvation and society's perfection through individual acts of conscience.

From either perspective, slavery stood out as a threatening anomaly. In depriving its victims of the right of moral self-government and the incentives for material self-improvement, slavery smothered individualism. It blocked both moral and material progress.

Only the outlines of a Northern antislavery coalition were in view before the Mexican War. Nonetheless, Southern political leaders had seen enough to convince them of the need to shore up the defense of slavery as a positive good. Critics of slavery within the South were forced to recant or leave the region. By 1845 the three major national denominations of Baptists, Methodists, and Presbyterians had all split over the slavery issue into distinctively sectional churches. Aware that they interpreted Biblical passages on slavery quite differently, and exhorted on by their ministers' sermons to view themselves as distinct peoples, Northern and Southern whites increasingly thought of themselves in sectional terms. Only the major political parties now remained as great unifying institutions.

THE PARTIES AND UNITY

In the absence of a powerful, centralized government, political parties were the great unifiers of the antebellum republic. The Democrats and Whigs, the major parties at midcentury, had formed in the 1830s as part of a political reorganization that replaced the former party competition of Federalists and Jeffersonian Republicans with a new alignment known as the Second Party System. By the presidential election of 1840, the Democrats and Whigs had reached a point of evenly balanced national competition based on two-party contests in all the states. Voters identified themselves in partisan, not sectional, terms. In the words of Martin Van Buren, one of the founders of the Democratic party, party loyalties acted as an "antidote for sectional prejudices by producing counteracting feelings."[7]

The Second Party System was the political expression of the same process of growth that so radically altered the society and economy of America after the War of 1812. On one hand, the very improvements in transportation and communication that allowed economic specialization in a market economy to take place also provided the technological means for reaching and organizing a mass electorate through a faster and cheaper diffusion of information. On the other hand, the transition from Jefferson's agrarian republic produced economic demands and grievances that provoked fierce political debates over the direction of economic change and the role of government in shaping that change. Voters were politicized at the same time as political leaders had acquired the means of mobilizing those voters into mass-based parties.

The emergence of the Second Party System during a period of accelerated economic development explains the dominance of economic issues in structuring the party appeals of the Whigs and Democrats. The parties differed sharply in their economic stands. The Whigs were the champions of the new capitalist economy. They favored the use of governmental power to promote and subsidize additional growth. They would pass high tariffs to protect American manufacturers and their laborers from cheap foreign competition. They would use governmental funds, at both the state and federal levels, as the basis for a circulatory currency of paper banknotes to provide a plentiful and stable supply of credit. They would encourage the chartering of corporations to pool investment capital for economic development, furnish public assistance for transportation projects designed to widen access to an expanding home market, and distribute the proceeds from the sale of public lands to the states as a fund for internal improvements.

In all these areas, the Democrats accused the Whigs of unwarranted, indeed unconstitutional, interference in the natural workings of a market economy. The Democrats insisted that they too favored prosperity, but they did not believe that prosperity depended on a system of privileges and inequalities, which they charged the Whigs with trying to create through the conferral of government favors. The Democrats denounced high tariffs as an unfair tax on the purchaser of manufactured goods. They attacked banks and other corporations as monopolistic combinations of aristocratic privileges that endangered individual liberties. For the Democrats, banknotes were not, as the Whigs claimed, the poor man's credit, but a devious form of manipulating the real value of goods and wages so as to enrich the few at the expense of the many. (These notes, technically interest-bearing loans redeemable on demand in specie, fluctuated in value according to the financial reputation and physical proximity of the bank of issue. Such fluctuations, charged the Democrats, encouraged reckless speculation and enabled the banks to reap unearned profits that added nothing to the real productive capacity of the economy.) As strict constructionists, the Democrats rejected any federal assistance to local economic projects as an unconstitutional infringement of states' rights. The Whigs' attempt to bypass constitutional objections through distribution of federal funds was assailed as a scheme to prop up the price of western land for the benefit of eastern speculators and as an excuse to keep the tariff high so as to maintain high levels of federal spending.

Party divisions over the economy represented much more than tactical sparrings over how best to achieve prosperity. It embodied a profound ambivalence over the social and ideological consequences of economic change. Many Americans viewed the new order of market relations that was evolving in the second quarter of the nineteenth century as a threat to the social foundations of their individual liberties.

Republicanism, an ideology that emerged during the 1780s as the political language and precepts of the Revolutionary generation, was founded on the principle that liberty could be secured only in a society of virtuous citizens. Civic virtue, the commitment to public good over private self-interest, was thought to be grounded in the economic independence of farmers and artisans. These small property holders and producers were free men who were hailed as defenders of individual liberties precisely because they were dependent on no one for their livelihoods. A spreading market economy, however, deprived them of their localized economic independence and progressively disrupted their social worlds rooted in the household production of the family farm and artisan shop.

After 1815 the relative stability of semi-subsistence rural economies gave way to the booms and busts of business cycles. Producers of all sorts were faced with the competition of outside goods that could now undersell them in local markets. Increasingly, status was measured not by one's place in the personalized networks of the local community but by one's wealth and membership in the new middle or working classes.

Most ominously, the advent of industrialization and the growth of cities seemingly confirmed the traditional fears of republicanism regarding the rise of an impoverished and corruptible class of social dependents. Factory laborers and the landless poor forced into crowded cities had always been singled out as potential threats to republican liberties. Without the economic independence necessary to nurture civic virtue, it was feared that they would be susceptible to the blandishments of any demagogue who sought power by trampling individual liberties.

The pace of change was an uneven one, and it affected different parts of the country at different times. Some regions, notably the Appalachian highlands and the Southern backcountry, remained relatively isolated from any direct contact with the market economy and thus maintained traditional social relationships based on kin and community. Nonetheless, the economic transition was rapid enough and pervasive enough to generate deeply held hopes and fears, which politicians were able to channel into effective party appeals. Voters responded to these appeals because the parties offered them clear-cut alternatives for pursuing issues and values that directly touched their daily lives.

The parties, like government itself, simultaneously operated on federal, state, and local levels. They were not built outward from a central power base in a national government but upward as a coalition of state-centered organizations. This structure, one that replicated the logic of federalism, was the key to the strength of the parties because it enabled the parties to link local concerns with broad national issues. As personified by the grassroots cadres of party workers who organized rallies, distributed partisan literature, and got out the vote from among their neighbors, the parties had deep roots in local communities. Values shared at the local level were the bedrock of party allegiance. By fashioning party appeals around these values and pledging to protect individuals from outside attacks on their values, the party managers succeeded in fusing loyalties to party, locality, and the republic.

Thus, the economic issues that served as focal points for party contests in the 1830s spoke not only to local battles over commercial development but also to divergent cultural outlooks and moral viewpoints. For example, the struggle over banks and corporations was part of a wider debate over competing notions of equity and public morality. For a Whig, a bank exercised prudent business judgment when it decided during a commercial panic to suspend the specie redemption of its banknotes because of a lack of reserves to pay off the notes at par. For a Democrat, such a suspension was a violation of a moral commitment to pay off one's debts. Why, asked the Democrats, should a private investor in a corporation have the legal privilege of limited liability, that is, the protection of being liable for any losses incurred by the corporation only to the extent of one's individual investment? Such privileges were not granted to the average hard-working citizen who, through no fault of his or her own, ran up debts that creditors could liquidate by forcing a sale of all the debtor's property.

Much more so than the Whigs, the Democrats feared that the benefits of prosperity would not be distributed equally and that the price of economic progress would be a loss of individual autonomy. The bulk of their constituency was drawn from small farmers in the backcountry who harbored suspicions of bankers as "paper aristocrats" and who rejected paying taxes for internal improvements that would disrupt the accustomed rhythms of their daily lives and enrich outsiders.

In urban areas, the Democrats could count on the support of unskilled laborers and artisans who had fallen into the ranks of wage labor after their skills and status had been eroded by the competition of factory-produced goods. These workers deeply resented their dependence on wage labor and the enormous gaps in wealth that accompanied early industrialization in the cities. By midcentury, two-thirds of the urban population had no measurable accumulation of property. The upper ten percent of the urban population owned about ninety percent of the total wealth. No wonder these workers voted for Democratic politicians who castigated banks and corporations as centers of aristocratic tyranny that hypocritically exalted labor as citizens while exploiting them as workers.

The mass constituency of the Democrats tended to come from the ranks of the "have-nots," and they were politically mobilized by an ideology of militant egalitarianism. The converse was generally true of the Whigs. Not surprisingly, the Whigs' promotion of economic change was popular with those Americans who had benefited from such change or expected to do so in the future. Prospering farmers, manufacturers, artisans-turned-businessmen, and the upwardly mobile middle class comprised the rank and file of Whig voters. In the South, the party drew heavily from the wealthier slaveholders, the town merchants and professionals economically tied to the planters, and the small farmers desirous of state-sponsored internal improvements.

Partly out of a need to explain and justify their own economic success, and partly out of the need to fend off Democratic charges that they were betraying the republican values of liberty and equality, the Whigs redefined the key concepts in the vocabulary of republicanism. The Whigs divorced freedom from its former material base in the direct ownership of productive property and redefined it as the unfettered right of the individual to enter into contractual arrangements for self-improvement in a market economy. For the Whigs, equality lost its former connotation of a comparatively broad distribution of property among the citizenry and instead became associated with a broad range of opportunities that permitted individuals to rise or fall according to their own merits and talent. These were the ideological grounds on which the Whigs touted their support for economic development as a program that would enhance equality for all Americans.

The Whigs' commitment to economic opportunity was closely related to their cultural and religious assumptions concerning the prerequisites for material success. Their rather formalistic definition of freedom—an individual was free as long as he could enter a contract of his own choosing—presupposed that any adult white male could shape his own destiny as long as he exercised sufficient self-restraint. The curbing of passions, the denial of immediate gratification, and the exercising of strict economy were the moral precepts of self-restraint preached by Whig ideology.

These precepts were part of a world view that blended ethnic, religious, and class outlooks into a coherent whole. This was the world view of the evangelical Yankee Protestants who dominated the Whig party in the North. These Protestants also tended to be the most economically successful Northerners. They were the entrepreneurs, manufacturers, and business leaders who were driving the economy forward. As they did so, they attributed their own material success to the moral values they had internalized as evangelicals. They had learned not to be slaves to their sinful passions but to be truly free by governing themselves through rigorous self-discipline. They worked hard, saved their capital, planned for the future, and, in improving themselves, glorified God through the fruits of their labor. Surely others could do the same if only they were taught the virtue of self-control, they felt. The Whigs themselves did the teaching through a network of reform organizations staffed by their wives and daughters.

In cultural, as well as economic, matters, the Whigs favored governmental activism to promote their vision of equality. Evangelical reform societies set up Sunday schools, distributed Bibles, sent missionaries to the new settlements in the West, and proselytized against the evils of alcohol and commercial activities on Sundays. When moral suasion failed, the evangelicals and their Whig allies turned to governmental coercion. Although a drive in the late 1820s to stop the Sunday delivery of mail was blocked by Democrats in Congress, the Whigs did succeed in having fifteen states pass prohibition laws by the 1850s. Temperance, or prohibition as it came to be known, was a mass crusade pledged to produce more efficient and dedicated workers and more disciplined, and therefore freer, Christian citizens. The Whigs also led the political campaigns to create public school systems in the North. Public education, promised the Whigs, would diffuse knowledge and equalize access to it. Schools would raise the skills of the labor force, teach the values of orderliness and regularity, and instruct youth in the basic tenets of Christianity.

The Whigs were not consciously trying to manipulate and control the masses, though it certainly seemed that way to their Democratic opponents. What the Whigs experienced as a moral imperative to help others to improve themselves was seen by the Democrats as a heavy-handed attempt to dictate to others in matters of individual conscience. Projecting themselves to the voters as the party of personal liberty and moral pluralism, the Democrats insisted that government had no right to regulate morality on behalf of any group.

The poor, wage laborers, immigrants, and Catholics were the prime targets of evangelical reform. By the 1840s these groups were becoming synonymous with each other as a foreign-born working class formed in Northern cities. Irish Catholic workers (and to a lesser extent, German workers) comprised a virtually solid bloc of Democratic voters. For ethnic, religious, and class reasons, these immigrants rejected the attempts of Whiggish evangelical employers to tell them how to order their lives and how to spend their leisure time. If nothing else, the Democrats promised to leave them alone to run their own lives. By the same token, Democratic farmers outside the market economy saw little need for the Whigs' expensive system of schools that interfered with their right to educate their children as they saw fit.

For the Democrats, the Whigs' meddling in the personal affairs of others was most dangerous when it touched on the rights of slaveholders. The Whigs were decidedly not abolitionists, but many of them in the North had strong moral feelings against slavery, and others agreed with the abolitionists that planters were a privileged aristocracy who wielded too much political power within the Union. In the state legislatures of the North, Whigs were much more likely than Democrats to vote for antislavery measures. It was Northern Whigs in the mid-1830s who introduced abolitionist petitions in Congress. Ninety percent of congressional Northern Whigs, but only twenty percent of Northern Democrats, voted against pro-Southern resolutions that denied Congress any authority over slavery in the District of Columbia and prohibited the House of Representatives from even discussing the content of antislavery petitions. These resolutions passed because Northern Democrats rallied behind their party leader, President Andrew Jackson.

A wealthy planter from Tennessee, Jackson had bitterly attacked the abolitionists in his annual message of 1835. He labeled them "incendiaries" and came close to sanctioning lynch law when he called upon Southern postmasters to publish the names of local subscribers to abolitionist publications. In one of the many ideological reverses that the defense of slavery forced on the Democrats, the party was now on record as denying Northerners their constitutional right to petition Congress. The party's stand on moral tolerance clearly did not encompass the opponents of slavery.

While Northern Whigs were attacking slavery, Southern Whigs were doing just the opposite. Politicians could not survive in the South if they were not trustworthy on the slavery issue. Both as slaveholders themselves and as shrewd politicians, Southern Whigs in Congress rallied to the defense of the institution. Moreover, they told the voters back home that they, not the Democrats, were the most ardent defenders of slavery. This tactic, one that exploited the slavery issue for partisan purposes, worked.

Largely because of Jackson's overwhelming popularity among Southern voters, the Whigs were a distant second party in the South as long as Jackson was president. However, in 1836, Jackson chose not to run, and his vice president, a New Yorker, Martin Van Buren, became the Democratic candidate for president. By claiming that Van Buren, by virtue of his being a Northerner, was unsafe on slavery, and by touting their candidate, Hugh White of Tennessee, as the slaveholding champion of Southern interests, the Whigs established the Second Party System in the South. In 1836, they carried four slave states and prepared the ground for their victorious campaign of 1840. Despite running a Northerner, William Henry Harrison of Indiana, the Whigs won eight of the thirteen slave states in 1840 in their first successful campaign for the presidency.

The fact that the Whigs could be a proslavery party in the South and an antislavery party in the North illustrated one of the great strengths of federalism. The system was so loose, and communications were so slow in the pre-telegraphic age, that politicians in the same party could say radically different things about the same issue in different parts of the Union.

Thus, for all the sound and fury of the political struggles over slavery, the country remained united. That unity emphatically did not rest on consensus over slavery, or on any other number of issues for that matter. Rather, it rested on conflicts that the parties exploited and channeled into partisan organizations that offered Americans competing choices for the defense and maintenance of their republican liberties. All the evidence indicates that voters believed their choice did make a difference, and they went to the polls in record numbers. Nearly eighty percent of the eligible electorate, virtually all adult white males, turned out in the presidential election of 1840, a three-fold increase since 1824.

Mass politics arrived in 1840, and on ethno-religious issues, as well as slavery, federalism prevented local divisions from polarizing into conflicts that could rip the republic apart. Divisions over such cultural issues as prohibition were quite deep at the local and state level, but politicians generally agreed that Congress had no say in such matters because these matters belonged within the constitutional purview of the states. Matters that Congress did take up were largely economic in nature, and here the parties could safely take a consistent stand throughout the country. Much of the divisiveness of local clashes over economic development was blunted by linking the issue to national party stands, while local, partisan disputes over religion and ethnicity could safely run their course without badly damaging the parties in Congress. In effect, the various layers of federalism simultaneously expressed and contained conflict. The parties were the popular institutions that served as an outlet for these conflicts. Most important, the parties did so in such a way as to convince their respective followers that party loyalty was the surest guarantee of republican liberties.

WAR AND PARTY STRAINS

Parties were the primary institutional antidote to sectionalism, and, as we noted earlier, space was the physical antidote. Beginning with Jefferson, a succession of presidents celebrated American expansion as an extension of the area of freedom. Abundant land represented not just an economic asset for agricultural growth but the social foundation for the self-reliant farmer whose economic independence was indispensable for the preservation of republican liberties. Denied room for its surplus population, America would soon suffer from the same overcrowded conditions that beset the Old World. Republican virtue would be destroyed as Americans, in Jefferson's vivid phraseology, got "piled upon one another in large cities, as in Europe, and go to eating one another as they do there."[8]

In addition to serving as a social and economic safety valve, expansion was hailed as a major counterweight to the potential threat of disunion. New states voluntarily entered the Union, supported the Union strongly, and strengthened it by counterbalancing the power of preexisting political factions. Thus, as President Polk stated in his inaugural address in 1845, "As our boundaries have been enlarged and our agricultural population has been spread over a large surface, our federative system has acquired additional strength and security."[9]

The benefits of past expansion and the need for future acquisitions were staples of Democratic ideology. In contrast, the Whigs were more reluctant to endorse expansion. The Whigs spoke for manufacturing and landed interests in the Northeast who stood to loose economically as the opening up of new lands in the West drained off population, drove up the wages of those workers who remained, and depressed land prices in the East. Many established Whig planters reasoned that an increased supply of cotton from the Southwest hurt them by lowering the price of their own cash crop. The Whigs also cited Roman history to argue that overly rapid expansion might well destroy the republic by forcing its conversion into an empire that relied on despotic controls to govern its far-flung possessions.

The most immediate danger posed by expansion in the 1830s was the rekindling of sectional antagonisms over the slavery issue. It was the expansion of slavery, not the existence of slavery per se, that had provoked the Missouri Compromise debates of 1820–1821, and it was the fear of reviving those divisive debates that had kept the slave republic of Texas outside the Union once it had won its independence from Mexico in 1836. Even such a staunch Democratic expansionist as President Jackson did not push for the admission of Texas. Jackson's successor, Martin Van Buren, followed suit, and in the Whigs' defeat of Van Buren in 1840, the annexation of Texas was a nonissue. What concerned voters most in that election was the nationwide depression that set in after the commercial panic of 1837. The Whigs won in 1840 by pledging to restore prosperity through governmental stimulation of the preexisting marketplace. Because the Whigs could neither enact their program nor restore prosperity, the Democrats regained the presidency in 1844.

The Whig program—a new national bank to replace the one destroyed by

Jackson during the Bank War of 1832–1833, a higher protective tariff, and the distribution of government funds to the states—was stymied through an accident of fate. "His Accidency," John Tyler of Virginia, assumed the presidency when William Henry Harrison died suddenly just a month after his inauguration. Tyler was a strict advocate of states' rights and a former Democrat who had broken with his old party over the threatened use of force by President Jackson to crush the attempt of South Carolina to nullify the tariffs of 1828 and 1832. Tyler had been on the Whig ticket to balance the ticket both geographically and ideologically. What was considered good politics in 1840 suddenly led to a party disaster in 1841.

As president, Tyler soon clashed with Henry Clay, the leader of the congressional Whigs, and vetoed key parts of the Whigs' economic legislation. The Whigs exacted a measure of revenge by reading Tyler out of the party; but they never fully recovered from his vetoes. Never again would they be handed what could be interpreted as a popular mandate to enact into legislation the congressional program of positive government that unified them as a party and that set them apart from the Democrats.

Meanwhile, Tyler, a president without a party, seized on the issue that he hoped would salvage his presidency. The issue was the immediate annexation of Texas, and here Tyler had the support of southern and western Democrats who used the Texas issue to wrest control of their party from Van Buren. These Democrats had wanted to dump Van Buren ever since his defeat in 1840. He had none of Jackson's dynamism, aroused little enthusiasm in the South, and was too tied to the economic policies of the 1830s at a time when ambitious, younger Democrats wanted to stake the party's future on territorial expansion.

Van Buren was vulnerable on Texas because he felt that a Democratic endorsement of the addition of a huge slave state to the Union would cost his party votes among antislavery Northerners. By equivocating on Texas, Van Buren lost his party's nomination for the presidency. Clay, the Whig nominee, also opposed immediate annexation.

The Democrats turned to James K. Polk of Tennessee, a close political friend of Jackson, and Polk headed a Democratic ticket that unabashedly demanded both Texas and the "reoccupation" of the Oregon Territory up to 54°40′. In a very close election in which the Liberty party siphoned off enough antislavery votes in New York to cost Clay the state, and possibly the election, Polk won an electoral majority with but a plurality (49.6 percent) of the popular vote, the first president to have done so. Nonetheless, the Democrats believed they had a mandate for expansion.

Polk acted on this belief when he pursued an aggressive foreign policy toward Mexico that touched off a war in which the United States reaped a territorial bonanza. In truth, Polk was probably not far off the mark in gauging the popularity of expansion. He had run strongest in the Lower South, the Mississippi Valley, and the Midwest, areas in which farmers and planters were anxious for a fresh start on new land after the lean years of the depression from 1837 to 1843. He also had significant support in eastern cities, where many read, and presumably agreed with, the expansionist philosophy of the penny press.

Mechanization during the previous decade had drastically increased press runs and lowered the cost of newspapers, and the penny press became an important medium for influencing public opinion. The political message of the urban dailies was a vulgarized version of Jeffersonian republicanism updated to shape and reflect the culture of the new urban class of wage laborers. The penny press dramaticized the lot of the laborers by publicizing their self-description as a class of degraded wage slaves, pilloried the Whigs for importing to America the hated factory system of the British, and promoted territorial expansion as the remedy for the miseries of the workers. It was a penny press editor, John O'Sullivan of New York, who coined the phrase "Manifest Destiny" in 1845, a phrase that, ever since, has served as a shorthand rationale of America's outward thrust in the 1840s. Polk had ample reason to believe that there was a national constituency behind Democratic expansionism.

As long as the issue was expansion per se, Polk was on safe ground in assuming that the Democrats could build and maintain a popular majority. After all, the basis behind the Democratic program of integrated expansion was that there would be something in it for virtually everybody. The open acres of Texas, California, and Oregon beckoned agrarians and speculators from both the West and the South. Ports and harbors on the Pacific coast were very attractive to northeastern merchants and shippers as jumping-off points for a growing trade with the Orient. Evangelicals were eager to claim the Far West for Protestantism.

If war came, as it did, then it easily could be celebrated as a triumph of republican virtue. Liberty-loving Americans, or so they convinced themselves, were spreading the blessings of freedom to impoverished Mexicans groaning under the weight of Catholic and aristocratic tyranny. Mexico and its dark-skinned peoples, so they believed, would be morally regenerated by the racially superior white Anglo-Saxon Protestants.

The flip side of the racially based egalitarianism used by American white males to level the pretensions of any would-be white aristocrat to superiority over them was itself a disdainful assumption of racial superiority over all nonwhite groups. American notions of democracy were racially exclusive and, once fused with the idea of a providentially guided Manifest Destiny, became both a rationale for and a rationalization of white expansion.

Within three months of the outbreak of the war in 1846, a Democratic representative from Pennsylvania, David Wilmot, introduced a rider to an appropriations bill that glaringly exposed Polk's one major miscalculation of the public's response to the war. Polk had assumed that the war would be popular because, in addition to its economic benefits, it could be portrayed as a crusade to extend the republic's free institutions. Polk might have been right, but he overlooked the fact that many Northerners now viewed slavery as incompatible with free institutions and as a distinct threat to their own liberty and property rights. Northern public opinion was willing to support the war, but only if it precluded the spread of slavery. That was the purpose of Wilmot's rider, the famous Wilmot Proviso, which called for the prohibition of slavery in any territory acquired from Mexico as a result of the war.

The Wilmot Proviso united Southern congressmen across party lines in a

American victories in the Mexican War, such as this one at Vera Cruz in March, 1847, were hailed by Americans as proof of the superiority of their democratic institutions.

heated defense of the right of slavery to expand. If such expansion were blocked, Southerners believed that slavery would soon become unprofitable as slaveholders exhausted the supply of fresh, arable land needed for plantation agriculture. Once slavery was confined to a fixed space, Southerners were convinced that a rising black population in the older slave states would reach socially dangerous levels that would trigger a race war in which whites would slaughter blacks out of self-defense.

The geographical diffusion of slavery had provided successive generations of farmers and planters with the means of both expanding slavery and its profits and of providing entry points for newcomers to the slaveholding class. The acquisition of land and slaves was the formula for economic success and social mobility in the South, and any national legislation that proposed to keep slavery out of newly acquired territory was viewed by Southern whites as a denial of their right to social and economic advancement.

In terms of sectional power, the prohibition of slavery from future territories, especially an area as large as the expected cession from Mexico, would reduce the South to political impotence. As free states were carved out of the territories and added to the Union, the South's ability to defend slavery from a hostile antislavery majority would steadily deteriorate.

In addition to the interlocking economic, racial, and political fears that it aroused in the minds of Southern whites, the Wilmot Proviso was also an intolerable affront to Southern notions of honor and equality. For Southern whites, acquiescence in the Wilmot Proviso would have been tantamount to the servile behavior demanded from a black slave. As free men, and as coequals in the Union, Southerners denounced the Wilmot Proviso as an unconstitutional and degrading violation of their rights. Wilmot had indeed struck at a raw nerve.

Wilmot's Proviso and a similar version of it in early 1847 twice passed the House by sectional votes but were blocked in the Senate. On both occasions, northern Democrats had led the congressional revolt against Polk's leadership, and about three-fourths of their party colleagues in the North went on record as opposing the expansion of slavery. Polk was genuinely surprised, and southern Democrats were stunned. They could expect such antislavery behavior from northern Whigs and even welcome it, for it gave the party an opportunity to close ranks around the defense of white liberties. But this was far more ominous. Slavery was safe only so long as northern Democrats joined their Southern brethren in a solid phalanx against any outside interference with the institution.

Despite the fact that it never became national legislation (and, given the certainty of a presidential veto, never had a chance of becoming a law), the Wilmot Proviso significantly strengthened the Northern antislavery movement. One of the main reasons for this was the fact that Wilmot was not an abolitionist. Indeed, he made it as clear as possible that he was not. "I have no squeamish sensitiveness on the subject of slavery—no morbid sympathy for the slave," he told the House in February 1847. Moreover, he favored territorial expansion and had fully backed the annexation of Texas, where slavery already existed. But Mexico had prohibited slavery in its provinces of California and New Mexico, and Wilmot would not sanction Americans' bringing their slaves into these territories if they were acquired from Mexico. These territories, Wilmot insisted, had to be reserved for free white labor as a land of opportunity "where the sons of toil, of my own race and own color, can live without the disgrace which association with negro slavery brings upon free labor."[10]

Wilmot's oblique attack on slavery was far more dangerous to Southern interests than the frontal moral assault of the abolitionists. The political genius of the attack was that it avoided moral condemnations of Southern whites and instead appealed directly to the economic, racial, and political self-interests of Northern whites. Many in the North, including members of Wilmot's Democratic party, deeply resented and feared what they viewed as the overweening Southern dominance of the federal government. Nearly all the presidents had been slaveholders, Southerners dominated the Supreme Court and key congressional committees, and federal armies had been used to rid the South of Indians on behalf of slave interests and were now apparently fighting to gain more territory for slavery. More than any other factor, it was this Northern anger at the Slave Power, a term first popularized in the early 1840s by antislavery Whigs in Congress, that explained the willingness of Northern congressmen to vote as a bloc during the Mexican War against the extension of slavery. This was how slavery entered the political center of the sectional storm that would destroy the Union within fifteen years.

Sectional antagonisms within the Democratic party prepared the ground for the revolt of northern Democrats led by Wilmot. Van Buren Democrats harbored grudges over the scuttling of Van Buren's renomination by southern Democrats. Polk made matters worse by apparently favoring Van Buren's political enemies in the distribution of federal patronage in New York. Democrats from Pennsylvania, a major manufacturing state, felt that Polk had broken a vague campaign promise to maintain tariff protection when he supported sharply lower duties in the Walker Tariff of 1846. Western Democrats felt betrayed on two counts. They had backed southern Democrats on the annexation of Texas, only to see those same Democrats back away from Polk's campaign pledge to acquire Oregon up to 54° 40' and vote instead for Polk's compromise with the British along the 49th parallel. Second, and in the same weeks leading up to the introduction of the Wilmot Proviso, Polk had angered western Democrats by vetoing a popular Rivers and Harbors Bill. Westerners wanted federal assistance for internal improvements around the Great Lakes. When Polk prevented their getting it, they accused the administration of unfairly discriminating against them. Quite inadvertently, Polk's very success in economic matters as a party ideologue of limited government had focused attention on slavery as the one area where party dissidents could vent their frustrations over the Southern dominance of the party.

As a party, the Whigs opposed the war and any territorial indemnity from Mexico. When Philip Hone, a retired New York merchant, grumbled in his diary that the country already had more than enough territory, and that the war was "unjust, unnecessary, and expensive,"[11] his fellow Whigs in the North, and significantly, most in the South as well, would have nodded in agreement. For a distinct minority of Whigs, found mostly in Massachusetts, the war was also blatantly immoral. These Conscience Whigs, as they were dubbed, bolted the party over its apparent hypocrisy in denouncing the war while simultaneously voting funds to wage it. Hypocritical or not, the party was not about to repeat the blunder of the Federalists during the War of 1812 and be politically crucified for failing to support American troops in the field.

Despite the defection of the Conscience Whigs, the party had every reason to believe that it would profit politically from the war. The congressional elections in the fall of 1846 returned a Whig majority to the House for the second (and last) time. Northern Whigs were unified as never before over their support for the Wilmot Proviso, while southern Whigs could blame the Democrats for introducing an issue so threatening to the South.

As for the obvious Whig problem of neutralizing their antislavery stand in the North among voters in the South, the war provided a solution. General Zachary Taylor, one of the war's great heroes, made it known that he was available for courting by the Whigs. Surely, no one could question the loyalty to slavery of this Louisiana planter who owned more than a hundred slaves.

Taylor, a newcomer to the Whigs, had no difficulty in accepting the presidential nomination from a party that pursued a no-platform strategy in 1848. Economic issues could not be stressed by the Whigs because prosperity had returned under a Democratic administration that pointedly reversed Whig priorities by lowering the

tariff and removing government deposits from private banks through the Independent Treasury System. Huge British demands for American grain pumped foreign
specie into the economy, and the financing of the Mexican War through short-term
treasury notes further primed the pump for economic recovery. Once the Senate
ratified the Treaty of Guadalupe-Hidalgo in March 1848, the war was over. No
longer could the Whigs whip up antiwar sentiment, and they could hardly call for
a return of the ceded Mexican territory. As for the great unresolved issue of the war,
the status of slavery in the new territories, the Whigs took no national stand. Such
evasion, by enabling the Whigs to run two distinctly sectional campaigns, was
superb politics. In the North the Whigs favored the Wilmot Proviso, and in the South
the Whigs pointed to Taylor as a defender of Southern rights.

The Democrats were just as evasive on slavery in 1848, though less obviously
so. To mend its political fences in the North and West, the party ran Lewis Cass of
Michigan for the presidency. Cass had a proven record of party regularity and was
acceptable to the South on the slavery issue. He rejected the Wilmot Proviso and
instead favored popular sovereignty as an equitable solution for the problem of
slavery in the territories. Disarmingly simple in its appeal, popular sovereignty
called for the actual settlers in the territories to decide the question of slavery for
themselves. This approach seemed to be inherently democratic. Moreover, it spoke
to the traditional Democratic stress on local rights and promised to remove a
potentially explosive problem from the national arena of congressional politics.

Popular sovereignty was far removed from the preferred solution of Southern
diehards who had rallied behind John Calhoun of South Carolina. They held that
the states were the equal co-owners of the territories and that the right of citizens
in all the states to carry their property (including slaves) into the territories could
not constitutionally be denied by Congress or by a territorial legislature, the legal
creature of Congress. Still, the Calhounites could live with popular sovereignty, at
least temporarily, because its ambiguity over just when the settlers could definitely
settle the slavery issue left a loophole through which a proslavery interpretation
could be pushed. Southern Democrats insisted that a territory could make a legally
binding decision on slavery only at its point of admission to statehood, that is, in a
state constitutional convention. In the interim period of territorial status (usually
several years), slavery, like any other form of property, had to be protected.

Northern Democrats rejected the proslavery interpretation of popular sovereignty. They believed that a legal decision on slavery could be made as soon as the
first territorial legislature met. Because of the expected dominance in the new
territories of Northern farmers, settlers who could more easily pull up stakes than
Southern planters, this early decision would presumably be an antislavery one.
Thus, much like the Whigs, the Democrats in 1848 could be antislavery in the North
and proslavery in the South.

The only party in 1848 that took an unequivocal stand on slavery in the
territories was a new one, the Free Soil party. Organized at a convention in Buffalo,
New York, in August 1848, the Free Soilers demanded that the federal government
separate itself from any support of slavery. In practice this meant a congressional

prohibition on slavery in the territories and federal initiatives against slavery in the District of Columbia and other areas where it had the constitutional right to act. As shown by their ticket of Van Buren for the presidency and Charles Francis Adams, John Quincy Adams' son and a Massachusetts Conscience Whig, for the vice presidency, the Free Soilers institutionalized many of the party strains generated by the war. Van Buren, and the New York Democrats who followed him out of the national party, had old political scores to settle. The Conscience Whigs were morally repulsed by their party's selection of the slaveholder Taylor. The third element in the Free Soil coalition consisted of former members of the Liberty party, who saw a chance to broaden the appeal of political antislavery. They were responsible for the antislavery bite of the Free Soil platform and for the tentative steps taken by the party on behalf of black equality in Northern society.

The Free Soilers made an impressive showing in 1848 for a new third party. They won ten percent of the overall vote and elected about a dozen congressmen. Although they garnered only a handful of votes below the Mason–Dixon line, their ringing slogan of "Free Soil, Free Labor, Free Men" was instrumental in swelling the Northern political antislavery vote to a level five times above that reached by the Liberty party in 1844. Still, they could not shake the traditional party attachments of eighty-five percent of the Northern electorate.

Despite the intrusion of the Free Soilers, the Second Party System held firm in 1848. As in the past, party competition between Democrats and Whigs solidified the loyalties of the voters not by stifling sectionalism but by reveling in it. In their intrasectional battles, each party accused the other of betraying sectional interests for or against slavery. Such politicking ran the obvious risk of dividing the country along a sectional axis, but it could be engaged in without destroying the Union as long as each of the parties was based on an intersectional alliance. Each of the parties thereby had a built-in incentive to cooperate eventually with its respective sectional wing and to compromise issues at the federal level that it recklessly exploited at the local level.

It was this task of compromise that faced the Second Party System once the returns were in from the election of 1848. The election was very close, and the Democrats and Whigs maintained their even competitive balance in both the free and the slave states. Taylor won, and Congress now turned to a resolution of the slavery crisis in the territories.

NOTES

1. Charles Dickens, *American Notes for General Circulation* (New York: Penguin, 1985), p. 164.
2. *Niles National Register,* vol. 73, Dec. 18, 1847, p. 255.
3. James D. Richardson, *A Compilation of the Messages and Papers of the Presidents, 1789–1897,* vol. 1 (Washington: Government Printing Office, 1896–1899), p. 379.
4. Harriet Martineau, *Society in America,* vol. 1 (London: Saunders and Otley, 1837), p. 91.

5. Quoted in David Brion Davis, *Slavery and Human Progress* (New York: Oxford University Press, 1984), p. 110.
6. *Selections from the Writings and Speeches of William Lloyd Garrison* (New York: New American, 1964), p. 142.
7. Quoted in Michael F. Holt, *The Political Crisis of the 1850s* (New York: John Wiley, 1978), p. 7.
8. Julian B. Boyd, ed., *The Papers of Thomas Jefferson,* vol. 12 (Princeton, N.J.: Princeton University Press, 1955), p. 442.
9. Richardson, vol. 4, p. 380.
10. *Congressional Globe,* 29 Congress, 2 Session, p. 354, and Appendix, p. 317.
11. Allan Nevins, ed., *The Diary of Philip Hone, 1828–1851* (New York: Kraus Reprint Co., 1969), p. 769.

SUGGESTED READINGS

ASHWORTH, JOHN, *"Agrarians" and "Aristocrats": Party Political Ideology in the United States, 1837–1846.* Atlantic Highlands, N.J.: Humanities Press, 1983.

BROCK, WILLIAM R., *Parties and Political Conscience: American Dilemmas, 1840–1850.* Millwood, N.Y.: KTO Press, 1979.

BRUCHEY, STUART, *The Roots of American Economic Growth, 1607–1861.* New York: Harper and Row, 1965.

DAVIS, DAVID BRION, *Slavery and Human Progress.* New York: Oxford University Press, 1984.

GERTEIS, LOUIS S., *Morality and Utility in American Antislavery Reform.* Chapel Hill, NC: University of North Carolina Press, 1987.

HIETALA, THOMAS R., *Manifest Design: Anxious Aggrandizement in Late Jacksonian America.* Ithaca, NY: Cornell University Press, 1985.

HOWE, DANIEL WALKER, *The Political Culture of American Whigs.* Chicago, Ill.: University of Chicago Press, 1979.

MCCORMICK, RICHARD P., *The Second American Party System: Party Formation in the Jacksonian Era.* Chapel Hill, N.C.: University of North Carolina Press, 1966.

NORTH, DOUGLAS C., *The Economic Growth of the United States, 1790–1860.* Englewood Cliffs, N.J.: Prentice Hall, 1961.

NUGENT, WALTER, *Structures of American Social History.* Bloomington, Ind.: Indiana University Press, 1981.

SELLERS, CHARLES G., *James K. Polk, Continentalist, 1843–1846.* Princeton, N.J.: Princeton University Press, 1966.

SILBEY, JOEL H., *The Shrine of Party: Congressional Voting Behavior, 1841–1852.* Pittsburgh, Pa: University of Pittsburgh Press, 1967.

SINGLETARY, OTIS, *The Mexican War.* Chicago, Ill.: University of Chicago Press, 1960.

STEWART, JAMES B., *Holy Warriors: The Abolitionists and American Slavery.* New York: Hill and Wang, 1976.

TAYLOR, GEORGE R., *The Transportation Revolution, 1815–1860.* New York: Harper and Row, 1951.

TURNER, FREDERICK JACKSON, *The United States, 1830–1850*. New York: Holt, Rinehart and Winston, 1935.

WALTERS, RONALD C., *The Antislavery Appeal: American Abolitionism after 1830*. Baltimore, Md.: Johns Hopkins University Press, 1976.

WRIGHT, GAVIN, *The Political Economy of the Cotton South*. New York: W.W. Norton, 1978.

2

Compromise
and Party
Strains

"Faction, Disunion & the love of mischief are put under, at least, for the present, & I hope for a long time."[1] With these words Daniel Webster, a Massachusetts Whig, echoed the sentiments of most Americans whose fears for the Union were relieved with the passage in the summer of 1850 of a series of measures known collectively as the Compromise of 1850. The republic had just survived its most serious sectional crisis.

Throughout 1849 and the early months of 1850, sectional tensions had spiraled to a point where a Texas congressman proclaimed that "we are absolutely engaged in a war against our own Government, the only free Government on earth!"[2] In this context, the Compromise of 1850 was indeed a peace treaty among Americans, one necessitated by the need to resolve the territorial issues raised by the Treaty of Guadalupe-Hidalgo, which had ended the Mexican War. The uproar created by the passage of the Kansas–Nebraska Act just 4 years later revealed, however, that the sections had arrived at only an armistice in 1850, not a final settlement of differences.

This chapter will explore why the sectional peace hoped for by Webster in the wake of the Compromise of 1850 proved to be so short-lived. A significant number of voters, represented in Congress by northern Whigs and southern Democrats, rejected key parts of the Compromise as a sellout to the other section. More important, and as was understood by perceptive politicians, the Compromise in fact had not settled the issue of slavery in the territories. At best, it had temporarily depoliticized the issue in one specific set of territories, those acquired from Mexico, and it had done so by artfully avoiding a decision over just what power a territorial legislature could exercise over slavery. Thus, the Compromise rested upon a studied ambiguity. In turn, the ambiguity permitted politicians in both sections to support the Compromise and indeed to declare its finality. Yet, the sheer dynamism of America's economic and geographic growth ensured that no territorial agreement of 1850 could be final for very long. The issue had to be fought again as soon as 1854 over the Kansas and Nebraska territories.

The Democrats and Whigs entered this battle in 1854 considerably weaker than they had been in 1850. They had moved closer together on first slavery and then the economy. As the ideological lines between the parties blurred, voters began to turn to a spate of single-issue new parties at the local and state level. The Whigs in particular were hurt by defections to a new anti-Catholic party, the Know-Nothings. Faced with an erosion of party strength, politicians now had an incentive to latch onto an issue that could revitalize partisan loyalties. They saw such an issue in the very one they had tried to bury in 1850: slavery in the territories. In pursuing this territorial issue, they unwittingly signed the death warrant of the Second Party System.

THE COMPROMISE OF 1850

For a political novice, Zachary Taylor faced a bevy of problems upon assuming the presidency in March 1849 that would have taxed the skills of the most experienced politician. The discovery of gold in California in early 1848 had touched off a predictable rush of population into the territory and heightened the importance of a rapid political organization of the territory through an enabling act of Congress. The same gold raised the stakes over the issue of free soil versus slavery. Neither faction backed down during the lame-duck session of Congress from December 1848 to March 1849, and California remained unorganized.

Another piece of the Mexican cession, what is now the eastern half of the state of New Mexico, was claimed by Texas on the grounds that it fell within the western boundary of the upper Rio Grande. Entangled with this boundary claim was the Texas debt, some $11 million in bonds that Texas had issued as an independent republic and pledged to redeem through its customs duties. Unable to pay off these bonds after Texas entered the Union and hence having ceded its customs collections to federal authorities, Texans now insisted that they had every right to seek compensation for their lost revenue by pressing their demand to eastern New Mexico, even to the point of a military invasion. Meanwhile, Mormon settlers in Utah and a free-soil group in New Mexico were in the early stages of organizing governments that claimed wildly overlapping boundaries. The whole question of who governed what on behalf of whom was one vast muddle in the Mexican cession.

The chances of Congress' resolving this muddle were further complicated by the eruption of long simmering tensions over slavery in the nation's capital. In December 1848, Northern votes in the House pushed through a resolution calling for the abolition of the slave trade in the District of Columbia. A resolution to abolish slavery itself in Washington failed to pass, though four out of five Northern congressmen voted for it. On top of this antislavery offensive, Northern bloc voting reaffirmed the commitment of the House to the Wilmot Proviso in California and New Mexico. The power of numbers, in this case the greater voting weight of the free states in the House of Representatives, was threatening vital Southern interests. In his Southern Address of January 1849, John Calhoun called on Southern politicians to unite across party lines before it was too late to resist what he decried as Northern aggressions.

Calhoun's call for Southern unity fell on deaf ears, especially those of Whigs. Only 48 out of 121 Southern congressmen signed the Address; of these, only two were Whigs. Nevertheless, outside of Congress, Calhoun's Address tapped into the resentments of many Southerners who agreed with him that the South was a beleaguered section whose constitutional rights in slave property were being violated by the North. Southern Democrats now had a rallying cry that they used effectively against the Whigs in the state and congressional elections of 1849. State legislatures in the South passed resolutions looking toward actions for redress if the North did not back down on the Wilmot Proviso. In the fall of 1849, a bipartisan convention in Mississippi issued a call for a Southern convention to meet at Nashville, Tennessee in June 1850, to discuss whatever collective steps were needed to be taken in order to protect Southern rights.

Much of the anger that fed into the popular momentum for Southern resistance to alleged Northern aggressions in 1849 stemmed from the shocked realization in the South that Zachary Taylor had turned out to be a Southern president with Northern principles. In an August 1849 speech in Pennsylvania, Taylor told his Northern audience that they need not worry over the spread of slavery. More important, his earlier actions as president revealed why Northerners could rest easy on the territorial issue. In the spring of 1849, Taylor sent Thomas King of Georgia to the West coast on a mission to encourage Californians to draft a state constitution and speedily apply to Congress for admission as a state. Taylor's strategy in New Mexico was the same. The assumption in both cases was that the new states would be free because of the precedent set by prior Mexican laws that barred slavery. Besides, Taylor and his advisers were convinced that the parched lands of the Mexican cession were economically unsuited for slavery and that most planters had no desire to take their slaves there. Instead of endless agitation on an issue that had become a point of honor for Southerners, Taylor proposed to take the whole issue out of the hands of Congress. The new states would decide the issue of slavery for themselves, as every one agreed they constitutionally could do. The North would have its free soil, and the South would escape the stigma of being denied its equal rights in the territories through the imposition of the Wilmot Proviso.

Taylor's plan had a blunt simplicity that befit his military nickname of "Old Rough and Ready." To outraged Southerners, that simplicity amounted to a deceitful scheme to shut slavery out of all the territories. No one expected Oregon to sanction slavery, and Taylor was about to keep slavery out of the Mexican cession, including the lucrative gold fields of California where slavery undoubtedly would have been quite profitable. To make matters worse, a free New Mexico, as envisioned by Taylor, would include the area claimed by the slave state of Texas. The result of denying the claim of Texas would be a net loss of land otherwise open to slavery.

To cover their party's Southern flank, congressional Whigs offered their own plan in opposition to Taylor's. It was introduced by Henry Clay of Kentucky in late January 1850. In place of simplicity, Clay's plan had the virtue of comprehensiveness. California would be admitted as a state under the free-soil constitution it had adopted in December 1849. The rest of the Mexican cession would be divided into the territories of New Mexico and Deseret (Utah) with no conditions being placed on the status of slavery. Texas would yield most of its claims on New Mexico in return for a partial federal assumption of the Texas public debt. The slave trade would be abolished in the District of Columbia, but the continuance of slavery there would specifically be reaffirmed. The South would receive a stronger fugitive slave act with federal provisions for its enforcement and a congressional pledge of noninterference in the interstate slave trade.

Clay's proposals set the stage for some of the best political theatre in the history of Congress. The grand triumvirate of the 1830s—Clay, Webster, and Calhoun—was aged and infirm, but before they exited (Calhoun died in March 1850 and Clay and Webster in 1852), they engaged in one final, moving debate. Clay recreated his role as the great compromiser of 1820 and 1833. A gaunt, dying Calhoun, all his remaining energy seemingly expressed in the blazing intensity of his eyes, sat impassively, huddled in a blanket, while his prepared speech was read on March 4 by Senator James Mason of Virginia. The tone of the exquisitely reasoned speech was calm, but its implications were chilling. Calhoun asserted that the North was inexorably destroying the equilibrium of sectional interests upon which rested true equality in the Union. Unless permanent guarantees were put in place to restore that equilibrium, he warned that any compromises would simply postpone the final day of reckoning for the Union.

Three days later, it was Webster's turn, and he lived up to his advanced billing. His renowned Seventh of March Speech soon became a lesson in patriotism and an exercise in memorization for Northern schoolchildren for the rest of the century. In eloquent and conciliatory phrases, Webster called on both sections to renounce the extremists in their midst, that is, abolitionists in the North and fire-eating disunionists in the South. The Wilmot Proviso was not necessary, he assured the North. God and the laws of nature had decreed that the arid Southwest was unfit for slavery, he continued, and in a concession to slavery that he never lived down among many of his erstwhile Northern supporters, Webster assured the South that it could count on a strengthened fugitive slave law. Running throughout the entire three-hour speech was a nearly mystical plea for the preservation of the Union.

However much political oratory stirred the large audiences in the congressional galleries, it failed to move the congressmen toward a sectional settlement. Congressional Whigs and President Taylor remained at loggerheads. Clay, rather than allowing Congress to vote on the individual parts of his compromise package, had wrapped up all of his territorial provisions into a single, or omnibus, bill. Unfortunately for Clay and the supporters of sectional compromise, the tactic only gave sectional opponents of one particular point a reason to vote against the entire package. For example, Northern congressmen did not want to face their constituents after having voted for a stronger fugitive slave law. Southern congressmen were equally reluctant to be accused of selling out Southern interests in California.

Then, in late June, the Texas–New Mexico controversy careened toward a possible civil war. News reached Washington that New Mexico, at Taylor's urging, had drawn up a free state constitution that incorporated the disputed area with Texas into its boundaries. Texans vowed to fight, and they could count on bipartisan Southern support. In a public letter published on July 4, Alexander Stephens, a leading Georgia Whig, warned Taylor that the cause of Texas was the cause of the South and "that the first Federal gun that shall be fired against the people of Texas, without the authority of law, will be the signal for the freemen from the Delaware to the Rio Grande to rally to the rescue."[3] Still, Taylor was adamant. He would use federal force to repel any invasion of New Mexico by Texas troops.

Taylor's sudden and unexpected death on July 9 defused this very dangerous crisis, the most serious one facing the Union in 1850. His successor, Millard Fillmore, was quite a different politician, one whose skills were now most needed.

Experienced in the infighting of New York state politics, where he had battled for control of the Whig party against William H. Seward, an early supporter of Taylor and the leader of the free-soil faction of the New York Whigs, Fillmore had the cautiously balanced touch of a seasoned politician. Thus, while he strengthened the federal garrison in New Mexico against a possible Texas invasion, he also deftly minimized the chances for such an invasion by mollifying the wounded pride of the Texans. He promised them that any final settlement of the boundary dispute would have to rest on the voluntary consent of Texas authorities. Without any fanfare he quietly shelved the New Mexico constitution when it arrived in Washington.

In a turnabout from Taylor's approach, Fillmore announced his support for Clay's compromise and packed his totally reconstituted cabinet with pro-compromise Whigs. Nonetheless, it took the parliamentary skills of a Democrat, Stephen A. Douglas of Illinois, to salvage a sectional settlement. The key to Douglas' strategy was breaking up Clay's combined bill into separate pieces of legislation. Douglas knew that only about one-quarter of the congressmen, mostly northern Democrats and Whigs from the Upper South, were pro compromise in the sense of favoring both the Northern and Southern positions in Clay's package. Starting with this group as a base, Douglas then built ad hoc coalitions behind each piece of legislation.

It was a clever strategy, and it worked because Douglas was enough of a political realist to know that cash and conferral of political favors would likely provide the necessary incentives to win over the uncommitted. Congressmen were encouraged to invest in Texas bonds, securities that then could be purchased for 45 cents on the dollar. Their value was sure to rise if Congress (i.e., many of the bondholders themselves) voted the money to redeem them. The payoff came in early September when Congress set aside $5 million for the Texas bondholders, many of whom by now were Northern speculators. Other doubtful congressmen, particularly from the Middle Atlantic states, were courted by offers of special investment deals in the Illinois Central Railroad, a pet project of Douglas' that Congress was about to subsidize with a huge grant of public land.

The last of the five measures that made up the Compromise of 1850 passed Congress on September 17. California would enter the Union as a free state; the slave trade would end in the District of Columbia; the South would receive a more stringent fugitive slave act; and Texas, with federal monies for its bondholders and an adjusted boundary that included 33,333 square miles more than offered in the original Clay bill, would no longer threaten war against the Union over New Mexico. Yet, in regard to slavery in the territories, the issue that had precipitated the whole crisis, it was not at all clear what had been settled. Congress had placed no restrictions on slavery in the territories of Utah and New Mexico. It was anyone's guess as to whether this meant an endorsement of the Northern position of popular sovereignty or the Southern position. Congress itself seemed to be covering all bets by explicitly providing that the issue of title to slaves in the territories could be appealed to the Supreme Court.

COMPROMISE AND CONSENSUS

If a valid test of a political compromise consists of the howls of protest registered by extremists on both sides of the political spectrum, then the Compromise of 1850 should have been quite durable. Southern radicals, those who believed that secession offered the only security for slavery in a Union increasingly dominated by a hostile Northern majority, attacked the Compromise as a sellout of Southern rights that confirmed the worst fears of the dying Calhoun. In their indictment, Southern honor and interests had been betrayed by the corrupt politicians of the major parties. As was summarized by Robert W. Barnwell of South Carolina,

> We went into the battle for the territory won by blood [and] we came out of the fight with all the territory given up to free soil & yet we are told that we have a great victory. We have paid ten millions, not to Texas but to stock jobbers to make a free soil state for a harbour for runaways & a boundary to keep us from growing. In fact this is certain no new slave holding state can ever be formed.[4]

On one major point the Southern radicals were certainly correct. The Compromise, or, more precisely, the possibility of one once Clay had presented an alternative to Taylor's free-state plan, derailed the secession movement spawned by the Southern reaction to the Wilmot Proviso. Secessionists controlled South Carolina in 1850 and, under the leadership of Governor John A. Quitman, were also quite strong in Mississippi. Significantly, these were the only two Southern states in 1850 where slaves outnumbered whites. White fears of losing control of the slaves were most intense in these states, and the radicals exploited those fears to good effect. In the rest of the South, however, whites continued to believe that their rights, including slavery, could best be maintained within the Union. However objectionable the Compromise of 1850 was to these whites, it emphatically did not endorse the Wilmot Proviso. As southern Whigs immediately pointed out, Southern honor had not been violated by a congressional prohibition of slavery in the territories. Once it could be plausibly argued that the South had turned back the threat to slave property posed by that prohibition, the secessionists quickly lost most of the popular ground they had gained in 1849.

The Nashville Convention, by the time it met in June 1850, had largely been reduced to a gathering of Democrats from the Lower South. Calhoun's call for a South united in defense of its rights had come to naught. Though there were plenty of fiery speeches in Nashville, the Convention's most radical act was a resolution calling for an extension to the Pacific of the Missouri Compromise line of 36°30'. When the Convention reassembled in November after the passage of the Compromise, attendance was down by half, and all that was left of the radical impulse were resolutions condemning the Compromise and asserting the right of secession. Meanwhile, state elections in late 1850 and early 1851 further weakened whatever momentum the secessionists had developed. Unionist tickets won handily in Mississippi, Alabama, and Georgia, and, in South Carolina, the secessionists were paralyzed by infighting between those who favored immediate secession by separate state action and those who supported cooperative secession in which a prearranged bloc of states would leave the Union together.

Secession had been defeated, but it was by no means dead. For all their failures, the radicals achieved two objectives that would be of inestimable importance for a later, and more successful, secession movement: They popularized secession as a constitutional right and placed Southern Unionism on a conditional basis. These conditions were spelled out in the Georgia Platform of December 1850. Drafted by a coalition of Georgia Unionists, the Platform reserved for Georgia the right to secede if Congress made any hostile move against slavery anywhere within the Union. In particular, the Platform stressed "that upon a faithful execution of the *Fugitive Slave Law*...depends the preservation of our much beloved Union."[5]

This emphasis on Northern adherence to the Fugitive Slave Act was consistent with Southern strategy during the debates over the Compromise of 1850. Once Clay had laid out his proposals in February, Southern moderates were painfully aware that any territorial settlement was likely to result in a substantive defeat for slaveholding interests. On top of that, the drive to abolish the slave trade in the District of Columbia would hand Northern opponents of slavery a great moral victory. Southern moderates needed an equivalent victory if they were to check the inroads of the radicals in the South and gain Southern acceptance for an overall sectional settlement. The moderates pinned their hopes for such a victory on a strengthened federal statute for the return of fugitive slaves.

The Fugitive Slave Act of 1850 gave Southern moderates the political victory they so desperately needed. The Constitution contained a fugitive slave clause that stipulated that interstate fugitives "held in Service or Labour" were to be returned to their masters. The Fugitive Slave Act of 1793 enacted that clause into national legislation but failed to set up any federal machinery for its enforcement. Slaveowners were thus forced to rely primarily upon state authorities for the assistance needed to capture their runaways. Such assistance was generally given until the 1820s. Subsequently, and at the behest of abolitionists and their political allies, several Northern states passed so-called Personal Liberty Laws. Initially designed to protect Northern free blacks from being kidnapped and sold into bondage, the laws were being used by the 1840s to prevent any state involvement in the arrest and rendition of fugitive slaves. Slaveholders were furious, and they accused Northerners of violating both the letter and the spirit of the Constitution. Slaveowners demanded new and tougher federal legislation, especially after the Supreme Court ruled in the 1842 case of *Prigg* v. *Pennsylvania* that the federal government had exclusive jurisdiction over fugitive slaves. They got it in 1850.

Northern congressmen gave their Southern colleagues a free hand in writing the new fugitive slave law. The result was an act that revealed how quickly Southern politicians would jettison states' rights when an enlargement of federal power would be in the best interests of slavery.

The Fugitive Slave Act of 1850 radically extended the police powers of the federal government. The Act empowered U.S. circuit courts to appoint federal commissioners with full authority to issue warrants for the arrest and rendition of suspected fugitives. These commissioners could also hold summary hearings in cases involving alleged runaways who had been seized by a claimant without a legal warrant. In such cases, all the slaveowners or their agents had to do to claim the alleged runaway was to present an affidavit of ownership (oral or written). The slave commissioner received a fee of $10 in cases where he ruled in favor of the claimant, but only $5 if he released the alleged fugitive. The Act allowed no jury trial, no writ of *habeas corpus,* and no testimony by the alleged fugitive on his or her own behalf. In their enforcement of this legislation, federal marshals could compel the assistance of bystanders and deputize them into a local posse. Failure to comply or to interfere with the Act in any way carried stiff penalties of up to 6 months in prison and $1000 in fines.

For Southern whites, this draconian new law was simply their just due as constitutional equals in a Union based on the mutual forbearance of diverse sectional values. Many sincerely believed that the Act would quell agitation over slavery by forcing Northerners to recognize that they had a legal and constitutional duty to uphold the institution. In fact, quite the opposite happened. For many Northerners, the Fugitive Slave Act was a moral abomination and a disgrace to any people professing to love liberty. Much more so than the abandonment of the

By depicting the slave catchers as invaders of Northern communities, the abolitionists were able to rally public opinion in the North against the Fugitive Slave Act. The servile figure on all fours in this 1851 lithograph is Daniel Webster, who was now caricatured as the lackey of the Slave Power.

Wilmot Proviso, the Act made the Compromise of 1850 contemptible to antislavery Northerners.

Handed their greatest propaganda vehicle since the Gag Rule of 1836, the abolitionists responded with a call for the open defiance of the Fugitive Slave Act. They seized on the frightening imagery of the Slave Power to explain the passage of the Act. First popularized as a political symbol by the Liberty party in the early 1840s, the Slave Power was an alleged conspiracy of slaveholders and their Northern lackeys who were said to be masterminding a vast plot to subvert the liberties of Northern whites by capturing control of the federal government for the purpose of expanding slavery and crushing all opposition to it. Who could now deny, abolitionists rhetorically asked, that the Slave Power was attempting to nationalize slavery by using the power of the federal government to deny fugitives the sanctuary of free soil in the Northern states? What could be more evil than to force Northerners to sin by complying with an inequitous law? There was a moral law, preached the abolitionists, higher than public duty or even private conscience. Adherence to that law obligated all good Christians to disobey a law as monstrous as one that endangered the liberties of all free blacks in the North and converted the free states into holding pens for the slave catchers. "It is not for you to choose whether you will or not obey such a law as this," argued the abolitionist minister, Samuel J. May. "You are as much under obligation not to obey it, as you are not to lie, steal, or commit murder."[6]

Spurred on by abolitionist invective, many Northern whites did openly defy the Fugitive Slave Act just after its passage. In the fall of 1850, menacing mobs contested the claims of slaveowners in several Northern cities, and two fugitives were smuggled out of the abolitionist stronghold of Boston before they could be claimed by their Georgian owner. Aside from holding protest meetings, Northern free blacks forcibly intervened on behalf of fugitives. A group of blacks rescued the fugitive Shadrach from a Boston courtroom in February 1851. That fall, a racially mixed crowd spirited away a fugitive, Jerry McHenry, from a courthouse in Syracuse, New York. In October 1851, defiant blacks killed a Maryland slaveowner who was attempting to reclaim a runaway slave in Christiana, Pennsylvania.

The uproar in the North over the Fugitive Slave Act died down after 1851. Within a year of its passage, most fugitives had already fled to Canada, and slaveowners were becoming more selective as to when they chose to invoke the federal law. Just as important, a conservative reaction had set in on behalf of the Union and law and order. For the rest of the decade, the Act generally was quietly, though sporadically, enforced. Some 300 blacks were returned to slavery under its provision, and federal tribunals ruled in favor of the alleged slaveowner in four out of every five cases.

The Fugitive Slave Act was a qualified success. It worked when the slaveowner chose to use it, but, of the estimated several hundred slaves who escaped to the North every year, only a small fraction were ever recaptured. Northern whites, but decidedly not blacks, grudgingly became reconciled to the Act as a necessary price for sectional harmony. Nonetheless, the enforcement of the act brought home to many Northern whites for the first time the ugly truths of slavery. In cities close to the slave border, such as Harrisburg, Pennsylvania, whites were shocked by the kidnapping of free blacks as alleged fugitives and the carrying off to slavery of fugitives who had lived peacefully in their midst for many years as hard working citizens. A Harrisburg lawyer, Charles Rawn, on being sent to Richmond, Virginia, in 1852 to purchase back the freedom of a black teamster who had been returned to slavery after living in Harrisburg for thirteen years, was morally sickened when he came face-to-face with a slave market:

> The more I see however the More I detest & abhor the *accursed* business. That it is *accursed* of Heaven I as firmly believe as that I believe in the Justice and goodness of God. And this Nation will yet weep over this National sin of slavery & a slave trade in sackcloth & ashes and the severer Judgment of a righteous God who will surely visit us as a Nation with our National sins.[7]

This moral revulsion, one that empathized with the slave but stopped short of openly defying federal law, was a powerful cultural force in the Northern middle class by the early 1850s, and it explains the incredible popularity of Harriet Beecher

The illustrations in *Uncle Tom's Cabin* included such heart-rending scenes as this hunting down of a runaway slave.

Stowe's *Uncle Tom's Cabin*. After appearing serially in the *National Era,* an abolitionist paper in Washington, D.C., *Uncle Tom's Cabin* was published as a novel in 1852. It was an immediate best seller. However much this fictionalized account of slavery can be criticized as a sentimentalized set piece of stereotyped morality, it brilliantly succeeded in making Northern whites feel for slaves as human beings and fellow Christians. An abolitionist tract without the invective, and an evangelical sermon without the hellfire and brimstone, the novel indicted slavery and all those implicated in it, Northern as well as Southern, for betraying America's Christian mission of mercy and love.

The popularity of *Uncle Tom's Cabin* dispelled any lingering Southern hope that the Northern acceptance of the Compromise of 1850 amounted to an endorsement of slavery. If the Compromise had failed as a symbolic reaffirmation of slavery and Southern values, it nonetheless remained rock solid as a political reality. Both of the major parties took their cue from President Fillmore when he pronounced the Compromise in his annual message of December 1850 as a "final and irrevocable" settlement. The House soon went on record as endorsing the finality of the settlement. Party orthodoxy now denounced any politician who threatened to upset the Compromise. Thus, although the state organizations of Whigs in the North were in general strongly opposed to the Fugitive Slave Act, the Whigs as a national party in Congress refused to take a stand against it or vote for its repeal. Abolitionists and antislavery Northerners, much like the Southern radicals, were left out in the political cold. Consensus on the Compromise was the byword of the major parties, and dissenters from that consensus would have to look beyond the Democrats and Whigs if they wanted to continue agitating the slavery issue.

PROSPERITY, CONSENSUS, AND THE ELECTION OF 1852

As Democrats and Whigs were agreeing not to disagree on the slavery issue, they were also reaching a consensus on the economic issues that previously had sharply differentiated them in the eyes of the voters. The economy entered a boom in 1849 that lasted until a short recession in late 1854. The prosperity of the early 1850s undercut the logic behind the traditional Whig stand in favor of government subsidies to stimulate the economy while it simultaneously pushed Democrats toward a more activist pro-business stance. The popular demand for more banks and railroad charters was so great that politicians in both parties outdid themselves in trying to meet it. In the process, party lines on the economy became hopelessly blurred.

The potato famine in Ireland and the Mexican War were the two events that triggered the economic boom. In 1845, an outbreak of potato rot destroyed the food supplies of the peasants in Ireland. Half of Ireland's population of 8 million was so poor that they could not afford bread, and the potato was virtually their only source of food. Before the epidemic of potato rot ran its course by the late 1840s, about 1 million Irish died of hunger. Another 1 million migrated to the United States between 1845 and 1854. Destitute and desperate for work at any wage, these Irish immigrants were a boon to industrialization in the Northeast. Given the decided preference of native-born American workers for economic independence over wage labor, the arrival of the Irish turned a relative shortage of factory labor into a surplus that American manufacturers eagerly drew on to expand production.

In addition to exporting cheap labor to the United States, the potato famine also resulted in a massive infusion of hard cash. The British government paid out close to half a billion dollars on emergency relief for American grain during the famine, and economic free traders used the famine as the pretext they had been looking for to repeal the high tariffs in the British Corn Laws that previously had kept out American grain. The value of American wheat exports quadrupled in 1847 over the level in 1846, and gold and silver flowed into the country as payment. In turn, rising cereal prices and increased supplies of specie had a multiplier effect throughout the economy. Higher farm prices touched off a new surge of settlement on western lands, and soon demands were heard for better transportation links between the West and the eastern seaboard. After barely budging from 1837 through 1847, new railroad mileage suddenly quadrupled in 1848.

The economic boom kicked off by the potato famine was carried forward by the fiscal impact of the Mexican War. As was noted earlier, deficit spending during the war stimulated the economy. In 1847, the federal government ran a budget deficit of $31 million, the highest ever recorded before the Civil War, and that deficit was financed by short-term treasury notes that circulated as currency. Just as the economic stimulant of federal expenditures was beginning to wear off in 1848, the discovery of gold in California rapidly increased the stock of specie. More gold, the metal (along with silver) held by banks as a reserve for currency and demand deposits, meant more circulating currency. After reaching a low of $158 million in 1842 during the post-1837 depression, the money supply swelled to $611 million by 1856. During the same period, wholesale commodity prices rose by 40 percent.

After 1849 the economy was, to put it simply, awash in money. Much of that money was funneled into railroads. Over $800 million in new construction was pumped into the railroads in the 1850s, and track mileage more than tripled to 31,000 miles. Most of the new track was laid down in the boom from 1849 to 1854. Four major trunklines were completed in the early 1850s—the Erie, Baltimore and Ohio, Pennsylvania, and New York Central—which, for the first time, offered direct rail service to the Atlantic seaboard for midwestern farmers. These same five years saw dramatic rises in the growth rates of all the major sectors of the economy. The value of agricultural production increased by thirty-three percent, mining by fifty-three percent, and manufacturing by thirty-seven percent.

This prosperity hopelessly muddled the traditional positions of Democrats and Whigs on the economy. Ever since Jackson's resounding Bank veto of 1832, the Democrats had spoken for agrarians who feared the commercialization of the economy. In the ringing rhetoric of the party, the power and privileges of banks were anathema to the egalitarian values of true republicanism. By the 1850s, however, more and more of these agrarians were finding the material rewards of the spreading market economy to be irresistible. So many voters now wanted to jump on the economic bandwagon that Democratic party unity on the bank issue completely broke down. In the Midwest, formerly a bastion of Democratic antibank sentiment, four states passed free banking laws in the early 1850s. Democrats joined Whigs in supporting legislation that opened banking to anyone who could back their issues of bank notes with specie reserves deposited with the state treasury. The party that had denounced banks in the 1830s as antirepublican monsters and bank notes as a swindle on the public now conceded that banking should be promoted to continue prosperity. To be sure, the party retained its antibank ideology, but its voting record on banks had become indistinguishable from that of Whigs.

The same was true of the former Democratic opposition to corporations. As many businesses were incorporated in the 1850s as in the entire first half of the century, and Democrats were now as likely to vote for new charters as were Whigs. State party battles over corporations persisted, but they no longer revolved around the issue of whether corporations should be chartered in the first place. Instead, the parties lined up in complex geographical groupings that pitted older corporate interests, such as the state-supported canals, against the newer ones, represented by the largely privately financed railroad companies.

The post-1848 prosperity was far more politically damaging to the Whigs than to the Democrats. While pro-business and anti-corporate Democrats were squabbling among themselves, with the former gaining the upper hand, the Whigs found themselves deprived of the issue that, more than any other, had defined them as a party. The Whigs matured as a party during the depression of the late 1830s, and the party was built around the appeal of a return to prosperity through governmental intervention in the economy. In the interlocking logic of Henry Clay's American System, high tariffs would be used to promote industrial capitalism; land prices would be kept high enough to prevent eastern workers from abandoning low wages for cheap western farms; and the revenues from tariffs and land sales would be recycled through the economy as subsidies for internal improvements to promote more industrial expansion. This Whig promise to get the economy moving again was what won the presidency for them in 1840. It also won the party a solid base of support in the South. Commercially minded Southerners were converted to Clay's economic nationalism in the 1830s, and they remained committed to it in the 1840s when cotton prices reached an antebellum low in 1845. Government subsidies for manufacturing and economic diversification held out the hope of reviving the South's depressed cotton economy.

As long as the economy suffered from a lack of private capital and remained mired in a slump, the Whigs' economic nationalism won votes and set them apart from the Democrats. Conversely, when prosperity returned and money became plentiful under the laissez-faire Polk Democrats, the Whigs' program became unnecessary and irrelevant. Nor could the Whigs point to past achievements to buttress appeals to voters on economic issues. Tyler's vetoes had checkmated the Clay Whigs in the early 1840s, and the Whigs thereafter could hardly point to what had never been in order to attract voters. Having never actually delivered on their economic promises, and unable to claim credit for prosperity when it did return, the Whigs ideologically floundered after 1848. Without the old issues of banks, tariffs, and credit, issues that the Democrats had coopted or discredited, the party was reduced to vague appeals on behalf of reform and respectability.

Prosperity under the Democrats removed the major ideological prop from underneath the Whigs, while Whigs themselves sawed away at the organizational prop of party unity through their savage infighting over the Compromise of 1850. To survive as a national party, the Whigs had to maintain a facade of unity behind the Compromise of 1850. President Fillmore, supported by the prestige of his new secretary of state, Daniel Webster, made support for the Compromise a test of party loyalty. This in turn infuriated Northern Whigs, most of whom were bitterly opposed to the Compromise. Its most detested feature, the Fugitive Slave Act, passed Congress only because enough Northern Whigs could be induced to absent themselves from the final vote. In an irony that bedeviled the Whigs, national Whig leaders from the North were irrevocably committed to measures that most Northern Whigs felt were proslavery. Once Fillmore and Webster began using federal patronage against anti-Compromise Whigs, the Northern wing of the party split into hostile camps. The contest was most heated in Fillmore's home state of New York, where his backers, the Silver Grays, fought a rearguard action against the free-soil supporters of William Seward for leadership of the party.

In the Lower South, the Whigs were even more badly damaged by the Compromise. Because President Taylor had been widely perceived as a Southern turncoat, a lackey of Seward's, and because northern Democrats under Douglas were chiefly responsible for the passage of the sectional settlement, Southern Whigs were deprived of the political advantage of claiming the Compromise as a party measure that protected the rights of the South. This was all the more galling because Southern Whigs had been more pro-Compromise than Southern Democrats. Thus, when Southern radicals threatened to bolt the Union and formed Southern Rights parties on the issue of secession, Southern Whigs dropped their old party label and joined new Union parties in opposition.

In Georgia, Alabama, and Mississippi, old party divisions were obliterated in the battles between secessionists and Unionists. The Union party coalitions were ostensibly bipartisan but in fact were dominated by the Democrats. Southern Whiggery was weakest in these three states (the Whigs never had a party organization in South Carolina, a Democratic state where the Second Party System never took hold) because they were the least economically diversified of any in the South. Georgia, Alabama, and Mississippi were the heart of the Cotton Kingdom, and Clay's economic nationalism attracted many followers only during the depression of the 1840s when planters were considering more balanced economic growth. When cotton prices turned upward in 1849, the economic ideas of Whiggery had even less of a hold on these planters. As a result, Whig strength in these states was ebbing quickly when the radicals precipitated the secession crisis of 1850.

Aware that they needed non-Whig votes to remain competitive in future state politics, Whigs in the Lower South eagerly joined the new Union parties, and they hoped that those parties would become permanent. They were always the junior partners in the parties, and they readily conceded most of the offices to pro-Compromise Democrats who could appeal to hill-country whites on behalf of the Union. By late 1851, the radicals admitted defeat and returned to the Democratic fold. Having lost their reason for being, the Southern Rights and Union parties disbanded. The Whigs were left weaker than ever. Their party organizations in the Lower South had been irreparably weakened, and the Whigs were now in a permanent minority.

The loss of party unity in the North and of morale in the Lower South spelled disaster for the Whigs in the election of 1852. For the last time, the Whigs dipped into the well of military heroes, and this time they came up dry. The candidate they selected, General Winfield Scott, the conqueror of Vera Cruz and Mexico City during the Mexican War, certainly had the name recognition the Whigs needed to attract new voters, but he faced an impossible political task. The very fact of his selection meant that the Whigs had rejected their incumbent president, Fillmore, and indicated how deeply the Fillmore–Seward feud had disrupted the party. Seward and other Northerners who had backed Taylor were fighting for their political lives. Denied party patronage by Fillmore and handicapped among anti-slavery voters in the North by his commitment to the Compromise of 1850, they insisted that Fillmore be dropped. In return for their reluctant acceptance of Scott, who refused to openly endorse the Compromise, the Southern Whigs demanded and received a national platform that unequivocally pledged the party to the finality of the Compromise, specifically including the Fugitive Slave Act. Saddled with a candidate who was disliked by Southern Whigs and a platform disliked by Northern Whigs, the party limped into the campaign of 1852.

The Democrats also promised to enforce the Compromise, but, unlike the Whigs, the Democrats had actually built a strong bisectional alliance in favor of the Compromise. Although northern Democrats might have personally disliked slavery, they were willing to vote for Southern rights for the sake of party unity. Whereas only three out of the fifty-three northern Whigs who voted on the Fugitive Slave bill favored it, twenty-six out of forty-two Northern Democrats did so. This support of their Northern wing was critical in enabling the pro-Compromise Democrats in the South to crush the secessionists, and, once the radicals were defeated, they too agreed that they could live with the Compromise so long as the North abided by it. Meanwhile, the party defectors of 1848, the Van Buren Democrats, abandoned their flirtation with the Free Soilers and returned to the Democratic party. The Compromise had eliminated the issue of the Wilmot Proviso, and Van Buren and his New York lieutenants were party professionals who were well aware that they needed the patronage jobs of a national party to retain their power base on the state level.

Big winners in the congressional elections of 1850, and united behind their own Mexican War general, Franklin Pierce of New Hampshire, the Democrats entered the presidential race fully expecting victory. They were not disappointed. Pierce carried all but the four traditionally Whig states of Tennessee, Kentucky, Vermont, and Massachusetts. The Free Soilers were even less of an irritant to the major parties than they had been in 1848. Stripped of Van Buren's followers, their share of the popular vote fell to five percent, half of their total in 1848. Scott picked up some of the former Free Soil vote, but even so his percentage of the Northern vote was slightly below Taylor's. In the Lower South the Whigs were routed. In the six states where Taylor had captured fifty percent of the vote, Scott's share plummeted to thirty-five percent. To all intents and purposes, the Lower South had seceded from the Second Party System between 1848 and 1852.

CORRUPTION, IMMIGRANTS, AND KNOW-NOTHINGS

The Second Party System was showing signs of age by 1852. It had collapsed in the Lower South, and elsewhere voters were starting to abandon the major parties. The total popular vote was up in 1852, but that was only because of the growth in population and the increase in the number of eligible voters. By one statistical estimate, ten percent of the Whigs who voted in 1848 sat out the election of 1852, seventeen percent of the Democrats did so, and about half of the Free Soilers abstained from voting. The drop off was particularly sharp in the slave states. Even in absolute numbers, fewer Southerners voted in 1852 than in 1848.

The root of the problem was the popular perception that the Democrats and Whigs no longer stood for anything distinctive. Both parties declared slavery off limits in the campaign of 1852. The flexibility in the federal system that had enabled the parties to pose as the opponents of slavery in one section and its proponents in the other was lost. It was the Whigs' national platform in support of the Compromise of 1850 that crippled Scott's campaign in the North. Unlike the past, when the

Whigs had no platform at all, northern Whigs were constrained from openly attacking slavery and hence could not fully exploit the antislavery vote. The cautious Fillmore administration had dampened the issue of expansionism, the parties had come together on the economy, and old party battles in the states over constitutional reform were largely settled when nine states wrote new constitutions between 1848 and 1854. The last remaining major difference between the parties, attitudes on immigrants and Catholics, was blurred when the Whigs courted the Irish Catholic vote in 1852. Desperate for votes in the North to make up for those they expected to lose in the South, the Whigs reversed their traditional stand of whipping up the cultural prejudices of Yankee Protestants against the Irish. They made much of the fact that Scott, though not a Catholic himself, had educated his daughters in Catholic convents. This new departure failed. The Whigs lost more votes among the nativist or anti-immigrant Protestants than they gained from the Irish Catholics.

If the parties were indistinguishable and refused to take stands on issues that really mattered to the voters, then the popular culture of republicanism taught Americans that the politicians must be corrupt. In a decade rent by sectionalism, this outcry of corruption was the one political sentiment widely shared by Northerners and Southerners. Speaking at an antislavery rally in April 1852, George W. Julian, an Indiana Whig, Free Soiler, and later a Republican, lamented what had happened to the parties.

> There was once a time when the Whig and Democratic parties were arrayed against each other upon certain tolerably well defined political issues. That time is past. These issues are obsolete....[The parties] are at this time pitted against each other in a mere scramble for place and power, however anxious their leaders may be to hide the fact from the eyes of the masses.[8]

Robert Toombs, a Georgia Whig, voiced the similar conclusion drawn by proslavery Southerners. For Toombs, the Democrats and Whigs had "degenerated into mere factions, adhering together by the common hope of public plunder. Their success would benefit nobody but themselves, and would be infinitely mischievous to the public weal."[9]

Factions had replaced parties, and plunder had taken the place of principles in public life. Most Northerners and Southerners were convinced of this by the early 1850s. In large measure they were so concerned because the culture of republicanism held that corruption was intrinsic to the process of government itself, and that power was always seeking to expand by subverting individual liberties, and that the spoils of public funds were the means by which the ambitious bought off men of good conscience and robbed the people of their freedoms. Formerly, the Democratic and Whig parties were hailed as the champions of self-government. By identifying different centers of tyrannical power for the voters, and by offering different programs to combat that tyranny, they seemingly gave the voters an opportunity to change their government in a meaningful way. Now that the parties apparently stood for nothing, that opportunity for change was gone. It was hard to escape the conclusion that the politicians, bought off by the surplus of cash, were putting their self-interests above the public good.

The traditional American grumbling about the corruptibility of their politicians turned into outright anger in the early 1850s, when evidence mounted that more and more politicians were in fact selling their votes and influence to the highest bidder. "We have reached a period when almost any act of legislation may be obtained for a price,"[10] moaned the Philadelphia *North American* in 1854. What was said of the Pennsylvania legislature was repeated for legislatures throughout the country. As for Congress, Toombs described the politicians who passed the Compromise of 1850 as "the worst specimens of legislators I have ever seen here."[11] For the rest of the decade, the reputation of congressmen grew steadily worse.

Although the proliferation of an urban press anxious to pounce on any exposé to boost sales made corruption more visible in the 1850s and exaggerated its extent, there is little doubt that corruption was increasing. The backdrop for most of this corruption was the economic boom after 1848. The boom produced easy money and unprecedented opportunities that could quickly be realized through state and federal aid.

The situation in Pennsylvania was illustrative of how quickly the business demand for political assistance picked up. In the depressed years of the 1840s, the legislature chartered an average of 28 corporations a year. In the first half of the 1850s the average jumped to 111. Despite the availability of general incorporation, most businesses in Pennsylvania and elsewhere wanted charters with special privileges. To get heard over their competitors clamoring for their own benefits, merchants increasingly turned to professional agents (known by the 1870s as lobbyists) to plead their case before the legislators. Overworked, deluged with a backlog of private bills, and generally with less than two years of experience because of the high turnover of offices in state elections, legislators were often happy with any assistance the hired agents could provide. That assistance commonly took the form of cash for a vote, cheap stock or investment opportunities in a company whose charter was coming up for a vote, or help in passing a bill that the constituents back home dearly wanted. Many legislators were sorely tempted to accept anything that made their jobs easier and more profitable.

The same scenario played itself out on the federal level, only here, the payoffs and corresponding rewards were much greater. Under tremendous pressure to provide transportation and communications facilities for the transcontinental dimensions of the country after the Mexican War, congressmen voted for lucrative subsidies for steamship, stage coach, and railroad companies. The disappointed rivals of those companies that received subsidies redoubled their efforts at the next session of Congress. Further magnifying the image of congressional corruption was the highly publicized issue of patronage. The parties largely financed themselves by rewarding loyal party editors and workers with federal contracts and jobs. With about 30,000 civilian jobs at its disposal in the 1850s, the federal government, or, more accurately, the particular party faction in power at a particular time, was the country's largest single employer. The wails of each disgruntled office seeker raised the pitch of the cries of corruption leveled against all the politicians.

As voters began to lose faith in the Second Party System as corrupt and meaningless, new, single-issue parties popped up at the local and state levels. Reform groups organized for honest government in a host of Northern cities and offered independent slates of candidates. Protestant foes of demon rum, emboldened by the passage of the Maine Law in 1851 that prohibited the sale of liquor, bolted the major parties and made temperance the leading issue in many of the Northern states by 1853. In both instances, the major group of voters who opposed change were the Catholic immigrants, the most rapidly growing element in the electorate. This, in turn, confirmed the belief of many native-born Protestants that foreign-born Catholics were the major source of the corruption that was polluting the republic. The stage was set for the emergence of a new party that could exploit the issue of anti-Catholicism.

The mass arrival of Catholic immigrants coincided with, and in part explained, wrenching economic changes in American life. The potato famine in Ireland, coupled with political and economic unrest in Europe that exploded in the suppressed revolutions of 1848, drove millions of peasants out of Europe. Most went to America. After first reaching 100,000 in 1842, immigration to the United States averaged nearly 300,000 a year between 1845 and 1854. Never before or since has the proportionate increase of the foreign born in the overall population been so great in a single ten-year period.

Not just the numbers were unprecedented. For the first time most of the immigrants were unskilled and Catholic. This was almost universally true of the Irish, and it was increasingly characteristic of the Germans, the second largest ethnic group in the new immigration. Such a sudden flood of impoverished strangers who spoke and worshipped differently than most Americans inevitably was going to produce tensions. When those same strangers readily could be targeted as the religious and economic enemies of American workers, tensions turned into hatred.

The economic boom after 1848 was immensely disruptive. As in any boom, there were economic losers as well as winners. For every town whose prosperity was assured by the coming of the railroads, there were many others who lost out and were consigned to straggling along as economic backwaters. Railroads spread, while turnpikes and canals deteriorated for lack of funds. Railroads brought in cheap goods and broke down localized monopolies of trade and production that had arisen precisely because localized economies had previously been insulated from outside competition. In particular, the completion in the early 1850s of four major trunk-line railroads out of the Midwest to the East threw thousands out of work whose jobs had been dependent on servicing the river trade.

California gold helped finance the new railroad construction, and that same gold was instrumental in driving up wholesale prices by thirty-three percent between 1849 and 1854. As the cost of living rose, wages for unskilled labor stayed flat at about 8 cents per hour. Wages for skilled labor kept pace with the boom, but only about one in five urban workers by the 1850s had a craft skill that could command the higher wage. The first wave of industrialization in cities had deci-mated many of the old crafts. As late as the 1820s, half of the urban working class was still involved in craft work with its traditional, self-regulated arrangement of masters, journeymen, and apprentices. Journeymen worked under master craftsmen and had a reasonable expectation of someday becoming masters themselves. Also included within the workshop of the master craftsmen were apprentices, young boys under a contractual arrangement to work without pay in return for room and board and training in the master's craft. This arrangement, and the security and eventual economic independence that it often provided, broke down when merchant capital-ists and ambitious master craftsmen reorganized production to increase output for the mass consumer markets in ready-made goods that were emerging. They by-passed the craft hierarchy, divided labor, and cheapened skills. In the industrialized crafts, such as the clothing trade, the productive process was broken up into its simplest parts, and wage laborers working at home or in outside shops run by wholesale manufacturers were constantly displacing skilled artisans. In New York City, the largest center of manufacturing, four-fifths of the working people by midcentury were wage laborers in what had become a glutted labor market. Although precise data are missing, most working-class families probably saw their real income decline during the boom from 1849 to 1854. In New York City a family of four in the mid-1850s needed an annual income of $400 to $600 to maintain a minimum budget, yet the average worker earned only about half of that in a year. This was an economic environment guaranteed to breed frustration and a search for scapegoats.

Immigrants, and the Irish Catholics in particular, became the scapegoats for native-born workers. Concentrated in the port cities of the Northeast, the Irish were a highly visible group set apart by their poverty and their tenacious loyalties to their own Church and religious rituals. In a host culture that was profoundly and militantly Protestant, it was the Catholicism of the Irish that made them appear so threatening to American liberties. Nativists pointed to the huge increase in Ameri-can Catholics from 600,000 in 1830 to 3,500,000 in 1850 and interpreted it as nothing less than a papal plot to enslave Protestant Americans.

The virulent anti-Catholicism of American Protestantism was cradled in the long struggle of English Calvinists against the imperial power of Catholic Spain in the sixteenth and seventeenth centuries. Out of the struggle came a belief in Protestantism as the embodiment of a universal quest for progress and civil liberties. By definition, Catholics were seen as the enemies of individual freedom, and thereby the American republic, because they had surrendered their free will to the absolutist claims of the pope in all matters of conscience. The slavish subservience of Catholics was the antithesis of an American individualism rooted in the respect of Protestantism for self-governance.

Even before the Irish arrived in record numbers, anti-Catholic hostility had sparked the burnings of convents and churches, and several election-day riots between Catholics and Protestants had embittered urban politics in the 1840s. Native-born craft workers threatened by rapid industrialization comprised the bulk

The Know-Nothings charged that the Irish and German immigrants, plied with whiskey and beer from the liquor interests, were corrupting American politics in the 1850s.

of these anti-Catholic mobs. When the Irish flooded labor markets after 1845, these Protestant workers had even more reason to blame the Catholic invasion for their deteriorating economic situation.

American-born workers in the eastern cities of the early 1850s felt besieged on all sides. Real incomes were down, the cost of food and rents was up, and job tenure was increasingly precarious. The quality of urban life was deteriorating. Housing was scarce and expensive. All the great cities on the eastern seaboard— Baltimore, Boston, New York, and Philadelphia—were overcrowded as their populations exploded anywhere from five to ten times over in the first half of the nineteenth century. Municipal governments struggled to cope with higher crime rates and soaring costs for poor relief. And the politicians were seemingly ever more corrupt and unresponsive to the real needs of the people.

Catholic immigrants could easily be blamed for these unsettling and frightening changes. The nativists charged that it was the pauperized labor of the Catholic foreigner that was driving down wages and bastardizing the crafts. The immigrants were also accused of driving up the cost of living through the abnormal demand generated by their sheer numbers. Immigrants, in the minds of the nativists, were accustomed to living in filth and squalor in Europe and thus were responsible for the slums and debasement of city life in America. Ignorant and depraved Catholics, the nativists believed, corrupted politics and sold their vote to the unholy alliance of the liquor interests and politicians, and, besotted with liquor, they squandered their wages and terrorized honest workers with their thievery.

Although the Irish themselves were the worst victims of the overcrowding, low wages, and poverty for which they were blamed, these charges of the nativists were immensely persuasive. After all, the Irish did resist temperance legislation, and they did vote as a bloc for the Democrats, the party of cultural toleration and the one that was much more open to newcomers than the Whigs. The Irish did make up a disproportionate number of the criminals and paupers. And their arrival in such large numbers did place tremendous burdens on overtaxed city services and worsen the competitive position of most native-born workers. Above all, however, the Irish were used as scapegoats because their presence could be portrayed as part of a popish conspiracy to destroy the republic.

For nativists, this plot first assumed a definite shape in 1853. In that year, Catholic bishops and their Democratic allies mounted a drive to block the reading of the Protestant Bible in the public schools and to secure tax monies for Catholic parochial schools. To Catholics, these proposals seemed eminently reasonable: Why should their children be indoctrinated in the Protestant version of the Bible? Why should Catholic taxpayers not have the right to divert their school taxes for the support of their own educational system?

To many Protestants, especially those in the working and lower-middle classes, the proposals signaled a papal assault on public education. Superstition and ignorance, not the free exchange of ideas, many Protestants alleged, were the hallmarks of a Catholic education. Clearly, the papal monarchists in Rome wanted to subvert the financial health of American schools as the first step in a plot to enslave the minds of American children, Americans were warned. Protestant workers, already alarmed over Catholic competition for jobs, now feared that the Catholics would destroy the public schools as an avenue of upward mobility for their children.

This new Catholic "menace" coincided with a sharp increase in Catholic voting. Many states prescribed a five-year naturalization period for citizenship, and thus the full voting impact of the surge in Catholic immigration of the late 1840s was delayed until the early 1850s. In response, and to protect their endangered republic and their place within it, nativist Protestants turned to the American party, a new anti-Catholic and anti-immigrant party. An outgrowth of local nativist associations in Northern cities, the most powerful of which was the Order of the Star Spangled Banner, founded in Philadelphia in 1849, the new party was popularly known as the Know-Nothings. Its members were pledged to secrecy and were told to reply "I know nothing" if asked about the party and its rituals.

The Know-Nothings offered strident nationalism and a sense of solidarity to Americans buffeted by rapid economic change and alienated from the major parties. They had a powerful appeal both because they had an explanation for what troubled Americans and because they had a solution for saving the republic. A papal plot was insidiously undermining the freedoms of Americans, the Know-Nothings decried; it was this plot that had inundated America with Europe's degraded poor, perverted its political institutions, and now threatened its schools. It was time for all true Americans to stand up and free the republic "from that monster which has long since made his appearance in our midst and is only waiting for the hour to approach to plant its flag of tyranny, persecution, and oppression among us."[12]

Translated into a political program, the crusade to save America consisted of extending the naturalization period for immigrants to twenty-one years, prohibiting the foreign born and Catholics from holding political office, upholding the use of the Protestant Bible in the public schools, deporting alien criminals and paupers, and imposing a head tax on immigrants to protect American workers from pauperized foreign labor. At the local level, the Know-Nothings supported temperance and a return to honest government in the hands of the people's candidates uncorrupted by the patronage and bribery of the major parties. A Know-Nothing leader in New York City captured perfectly the party's self-image of sober honesty:

> our party is the only one that pays its debts, don't drink bad liquor, don't vote but once a time, don't carry ballots to crowd into the ballot's box while two of the inspectors are off to get a drink; but are quiet, honorable and peaceful.[13]

The Know-Nothings experienced meteoric growth from late 1853 through 1855. The party burst into prominence when it swept the fall elections of 1854 in Massachusetts and ran strong congressional races in New York and Pennsylvania. By 1855, just a year after they had formed a national organization, the Know-Nothings were the major party in most of New England and a strong second to the Democrats in the Mid-Atlantic states, the Upper South, and California. The party had pockets of strength in the river towns of the Ohio Valley and was making major inroads in the Lower South. Driven into a minority status by the Democrats' unrelenting use of the issues of Southern rights, cotton state Whigs countered with the anti-foreign, anti-Catholic issues of the Know-Nothing movement.

Although the Know-Nothings drew converts from both of the major parties, the explosive rise of political nativism especially hurt the Whigs. In New England and the Mid-Atlantic states, where nativism was strongest, the typical Know-Nothing was a young artisan, clerk, or shopkeeper. Such middle-class and skilled working-class voters had been the backbone of the Whig party in Northern towns and cities. Because the Whigs apparently could not protect them from the disturbing changes that were disrupting their lives—changes symbolized by the Catholic immigrants—these voters bolted to the Know-Nothings.

Almost overnight, the Know-Nothings emerged as a political wildcard that upset the calculations of the politicians in the Second Party System. Democratic and Whig leaders expected the Kansas–Nebraska Act of 1854 to rejuvenate the faltering Second Party System by sharply redrawing the lines of party conflict. What caught them by surprise was the disruptive impact of the Know-Nothings on former party loyalties. By re-igniting the volatile issue of slavery's expansion, the Kansas–Nebraska Act triggered even more party defections and shattered what was left of the Second Party System.

MEXICO, CUBA, AND KANSAS–NEBRASKA

Although expansion was not a major issue in the presidential campaign of 1852, the incoming Democratic administration fully intended to revive the spread-eagle diplomacy of the Polk years. Like Polk, Pierce hoped that expansion would unite Americans by balancing the commercial interests of the North against the agrarian interests of the South. Nonetheless, and despite projected plans for the annexation of Alaska and the Hawaiian islands and persistent efforts to promote the commercial interests of Northern businessmen in Central America and the Pacific, the domination of Southerners in the Pierce administration steered its foreign policy toward the interests of the slave South.

In a coincidence that did not go unnoticed by Northerners, Pierce followed Polk in making the acquisition of Mexican territory his first major diplomatic objective. James Gadsden of South Carolina was appointed minister to Mexico with instructions to purchase up to 250,000 square miles of land in northern Mexico, including all of Lower California (an extension of California that separates the Gulf of California from the Pacific ocean). Understandably enough, after its losses in the recent war, Mexico balked at selling anywhere near that much territory. Gadsden was denied even so much as a port on the Gulf of California and had to settle for 54,000 square miles running through the valley of the Gila River in what is now the southern extremity of Arizona and New Mexico.

This land was a desert that seemed to hold no promise at all for plantation agriculture, but, even so, Northern senators suspected a Southern plot to acquire more slave territory. Why else, they asked, was Gadsden instructed to demand so much territory in the first place? Furthermore, many southern Democrats were on record as claiming that the South needed northern Mexico as an outlet for slavery. Their fears aroused, Northern senators threatened to block the ratification of the Gadsden Purchase. It passed only because its Southern supporters agreed to lop 9,000 square miles off of the original purchase.

At least the Pierce administration had gained a strip of land in the Gadsden Purchase that made feasible from an engineering viewpoint the construction of a possible Southern Pacific railroad from New Orleans to Los Angeles. Its efforts to acquire Cuba, the second major expansionist goal of the Southern Democrats, wound up in a fiasco that discredited the administration.

The United States had long wanted to acquire Cuba, a slave colony of Spain's, and in the early 1850s southern Democrats openly declared that they meant to have Cuba as a slave state to counterbalance the growing political power of the North. Cuba seemed ripe for the taking. A revolt against Spain had been crushed in 1848, but unrest continued to simmer. A Cuban junta in New York was actively working with Southern filibusterers (private military adventurers) led by ex-Governor John A. Quitman of Mississippi to launch a military attack to gain Cuba's independence from Spain. It was an open secret that Cuban sugar planters, infuriated by tentative steps that Spain was taking toward emancipation, would welcome annexation by the United States.

Had the Pierce administration made a concerted, unified effort to acquire Cuba, it probably could have done so. To be sure, such an acquisition would have aroused ferocious opposition. Antislavery Northerners would certainly have fought annexation. Nativists would have been horrified by the thought of what Cuban Catholics would mean for the Protestant values of America. Moreover, Southern unity on Cuba was more apparent than real. Sugar planters in Florida, Louisiana, and Texas opposed annexation because they would be ruined economically by the importation of duty-free Cuban sugar. The Whigs spoke for these planters and other Southern whites when they decried the folly of worsening race relations in the United States by incorporating the 200,000 free blacks of Cuba into the Union.

Still, variants of all these arguments against annexation had been used to no avail a decade earlier when southern Democrats and a renegade Whig president maneuvered the slave republic of Texas into the Union. If the Pierce administration had presented the country with the *fait accompli* of an American purchase or conquest of Cuba, it most likely had enough of a Democratic majority in Congress to make the acquisition of Cuba stick.

The Cuban issue had the potential to produce a terrible crisis for the Union. That crisis was stillborn, however, because of the inconsistencies of Democratic diplomacy and its failure to pry Cuba loose from Spain. Pierce and his secretary of state, William Marcy of New York, wavered between three strategies in their Cuban policy. At one time or another they favored buying the island, supporting its pro-American rebels, or simply looking the other way while American filibusterers seized Cuba. Each of these approaches worked at cross purposes with the others.

Finally, in the spring of 1854, Pierce decided to push for the purchase option and abandon the other two approaches. By then, however, the damage had already been done. Pierre Soulé of Louisiana, the flamboyant American minister to Spain and a favorite of the Cuban junta, had completely alienated the government in Madrid, and American filibusterers were left high and dry when Pierce abruptly announced that American neutrality laws against filibustering would be strictly enforced.

The upshot of this wildly inconsistent diplomacy was the Ostend Manifesto in October 1854. This policy memorandum on Cuba was prepared by the American ministers to Britain, France, and Spain. Named after the Belgian city of Ostend, where they met, it declared that Cuba "naturally" belonged to the American republic and that Americans would be justified in using any means at their disposal to acquire the island if continued Spanish possession threatened the internal security of the United States. Quickly leaked to the press, this private memorandum became a public badge of dishonor for the Pierce Democrats. Europeans and Americans alike scorned the administration for resorting to the tactics of a highway robber and for threatening an American invasion if Spain went ahead with its emancipation program in Cuba.

The Pierce Democrats badly botched the Cuban issue. Not only had they mishandled the South's last real chance of acquiring more slave territory, they had also held American diplomacy up to ridicule. Above all, they had intensified

Northern fears that the Slave Power controlled the Democratic party and would stop at nothing to expand slavery. Southern designs on Mexico and then Cuba predisposed many Northerners to expect the worst from the Pierce Democrats on the slavery issue. These Northerners then saw their worst fears realized when a political storm erupted over the Kansas–Nebraska Act in the spring of 1854.

For all the sectional uproar over the Kansas–Nebraska Act, railroads, not slavery, best explain its genesis. Proposals for a transcontinental railroad dated back to the mid-1840s, and the republic's leap to the Pacific during the Mexican War made the need for such a railroad imperative for both economic and strategic reasons. Building a Pacific railroad would be a prodigious undertaking that would require federal subsidies in the form of land grants. The potential rewards, of course, were enormous. Cities in the Mississippi Valley vied with each other to be designated as the eastern terminus of the railroad. Speculators and their political friends in these cities bought up raw land in the hopes of making a killing when the railroad came through. Indeed, so many groups wanted the railroad for so many reasons that they canceled each other out. Congress debated a slew of Pacific railroad bills in the early 1850s, and rejected them all.

No one had pushed longer or harder for a Pacific railroad bill than Stephen Douglas, chairman of the Senate Committee on Territories. Such a railroad was the key to his program for solidifying the Union and strengthening his Democratic party. Long identified as the chief spokesman for the Old Northwest and himself an avid speculator in Chicago real estate, Douglas wanted that railroad to have an eastern terminus in Chicago. He was certain that the railroad, once built under the sponsorship of the Democratic party, would spark an unprecedented economic boom in the Mississippi Valley and the entire trans-Mississippi West. The Democrats could then take credit for the economic good times and for having had the foresight to bury old sectional issues in a national commitment to develop the West.

Everything in this ambitious plan hinged upon congressional approval of a bill to organize the territory west of Iowa and Missouri and stretching to the Mormon country in Utah. This was the politically unorganized section of the Louisiana Purchase through which any northern or central route of a Pacific railroad would have to run. Public land could not be surveyed and made available as grants to a railroad until this expanse was politically organized into a territory by Congress.

When the 33rd Congress met in December 1853, Douglas knew that he had to move quickly on a territorial bill. Southern interests, with the backing of the secretary of war, Jefferson Davis of Mississippi, were about to secure the land in the Gadsden Purchase, which would put them at the top of the list for a federally supported transcontinental railroad. Projected from New Orleans to Los Angeles via El Paso, Texas, and the Gila River Valley, a southern Pacific railroad would pass entirely through states and the organized territory of New Mexico. It had administration support and did not have to overcome the organizational hurdles that faced a northern or central route. The South had taken the lead in the railroad sweepstakes. On top of that, and as it had repeatedly done in the past, the South had the votes to defeat any territorial bill for Nebraska, the Indian name for the area west of the Missouri River that Douglas wanted to organize.

Clearly, Douglas had to offer Southern congressmen inducements for supporting a Nebraska bill. Quite apart from the railroad issue, Southerners had opposed Douglas' Nebraska bills in the past because the territory he proposed to organize was part of the Louisiana Purchase north of 36°30′ and hence was prohibited to slavery under the Missouri Compromise of 1820. In the sectionally tense political environment after the Mexican War, Southerners had no intentions of voting in favor of any more free territory. Thus, Douglas used the only leverage that he had. The Nebraska bill that he introduced in January 1854 bypassed the Missouri Compromise prohibition by employing the exasperatingly vague language of popular sovereignty written into the territorial settlement of the Compromise of 1850. It was a crafty subterfuge, but it was not enough for the South. Just because Douglas had sidestepped the Missouri Compromise did not necessarily mean that its prohibition of slavery was no longer legally binding. If Douglas wanted to substitute popular sovereignty for the Missouri Compromise restriction, he would have to do it explicitly.

Douglas unwittingly had opened a Pandora's box of sectional animosities and political intrigue. The South backed his bill only after it was amended to declare the Missouri Compromise "inoperative and void." This fell short of an open repeal, but it came close enough to meet the demand of Southerners to be treated as equals in the territories. Significantly, the Senate amendment calling for repeal came from a southern Whig, Archibald Dixon of Kentucky. Here, finally, was an opportunity for southern Whigs to pose as more fervid champions of slavery than southern Democrats. Dixon was a Whig, but the Nebraska bill was a Democratic measure. Thus, free-soil Whigs in the North welcomed, and may even have encouraged, Dixon's initiative. Led by William Seward of New York, these Whigs had always felt stifled by Fillmore's insistence that they treat slavery as a closed issue; they wanted to pursue an aggressive antislavery position, and now they could do so. They expected to win big in the congressional elections of 1854 by blaming an extreme proslavery measure on the northern Democrats.

The nearly defunct Free Soil party pursued a radical version of this northern Whig strategy. Like the abolitionists, the Free Soilers were skilled agitators, and they well understood the value of Congress as a national platform from which to propagandize the cause of antislavery. They readily entered into anti-Whig coalitions with Democrats in Ohio and Massachusetts where, in return for Free Soil support in gaining control of the state legislatures, the Democrats sent Free Soilers to the U.S. Senate. These two Free Soil senators, Salmon P. Chase of Ohio and Charles Sumner of Massachusetts, were quick to see the possibilities offered by Douglas' revised Nebraska bill for reviving political antislavery in the North. Chase and Sumner, joined by four antislavery members from the House, drafted and published in late January 1854 one of the most remarkable and effective pieces of political propaganda in the history of American politics.

Their "Appeal of the Independent Democrats in Congress to the People of the

LIBERTY. THE FAIR MAID OF KANSAS_IN THE HANDS OF THE "BORDER RUFFIANS".

Antislavery opponents of the Kansas-Nebraska Act used political cartoons to portray President Pierce and other leading Democrats as vicious enemies of social order who were directly responsible for the violence in Kansas. The figure on the right, shown lifting a bloody scalp, is Stephen A. Douglas.

United States" hit the country like a bombshell. What was soon to become the Kansas–Nebraska Act was indelibly branded in the minds of many Northerners as "part and parcel of an atrocious plot" of the Slave Power "to exclude from the vast unoccupied region immigrants from the Old World and free laborers from our own States, and convert it into a dreary region of despotism inhabited by masters and slaves."[14] By seeking to overthrow the Missouri Compromise and win back for slavery territory forever consecrated to free labor, the Slave Power was breaking "a sacred pledge," they said, and defiling America's mission from God to serve as the world's beacon of freedom.

The Appeal of the Independent Democrats touched off a barrage of Northern protest against alleged Southern treachery. It immediately put northern Democrats on the defensive and converted what Douglas had expected to be a unifying measure of economic development into a divisive wedge of sectional rancor over slavery. Initially, Southern congressmen had shown no great interest in Douglas' bill. Now, stung by the ferocity of the Northern response, they rallied to its defense. Southerners could support the revised bill because it seemingly recognized the equal right of slaveholders to take their property into the territories. Probably few of them, however, envisioned that they would actually want to move to the Nebraska territory with their slaves. Those who did, such as Missouri slaveholders under the leadership of Senator David Atchinson, welcomed the division of the originally defined Nebraska Territory into the territories of Kansas, to the west of Missouri, and Nebraska, to the west of Iowa and Minnesota. This split was a tactical move on the part of Douglas to attract more railroad support to the bill, but it was widely interpreted in the North as a stratagem to deliver Kansas to the slave interests. Here was further evidence to many Northerners that Douglas was the tool of the Slave Power.

In a virtuoso display of parliamentary maneuvers and timely concessions, Douglas secured the passage of his bill. President Pierce, who earlier had thrown the full weight of his administration behind it, signed the Kansas–Nebraska Act on May 30, 1854. The act created two new territories out of all the remaining unorganized section of the Louisiana Purchase and legally opened both to slavery. Douglas had won, but at a terrible political cost to himself, his party, and the future of the Union.

Most Northerners never fully trusted Douglas again on the slavery issue after the Kansas–Nebraska Act. He felt their wrath almost at once. As he told the story, he could have found his way home to Illinois after the Kansas–Nebraska session of Congress by the light cast by the Douglas effigies being burned in bonfires along the railroad tracks. Upon learning that he would have to tamper with the Missouri Compromise, Douglas expected a tremendous political brawl. What he did not anticipate was the storm of moral indignation unleashed in the North.

Douglas personally had no strong moral feelings on slavery. As he publicly stated more than once, he did not care whether the people in a territory voted slavery up or down. The issue was one of economics, not morality. If climate and physical conditions favored the institution, the settlers would find it in their economic self-interest to support slavery. As for the territory that he wanted to organize, Douglas insisted that slavery could never be established on the cold, dry plains of Kansas and Nebraska. Thus, the repeal of the Missouri Compromise restriction raised no real issue of any practical importance. For Douglas, those who said otherwise were self-serving politicians and agitators who endangered the Union in their lust for power. True friends of the Union recognized that popular sovereignty would keep slavery out of the territories while simultaneously respecting Southern rights, he thought, and, moreover, by leaving the decision up to the actual settlers, it would do so in the most democratic manner possible.

Douglas' position made a good deal of sense to those who shared his amoral attitude toward slavery. However, he underestimated the number of Northerners for whom slavery had become a burning moral issue, especially after the Appeal of the Independent Democrats popularized the antislavery interpretation of the Kansas–Nebraska Act as a proslavery offensive and a shameful overthrow of a national pledge to the cause of freedom north of 36°30'. Even many Northerners who had no particular moral scruples against slavery, those who had accepted popular sovereignty as a fair solution to the issue of slavery in the territories of New Mexico and Utah, were swayed by the Appeal's argument. The frightening imagery of an aggressive Slave Power was more persuasive when slavery suddenly had a chance to move into the fertile region that lay just to the west of settled agricultural communities in the free states of the Midwest.

Douglas was accused, fairly or not, of betraying the interests of Northern free labor. The doctrine of popular sovereignty reopened sectional divisions over slavery

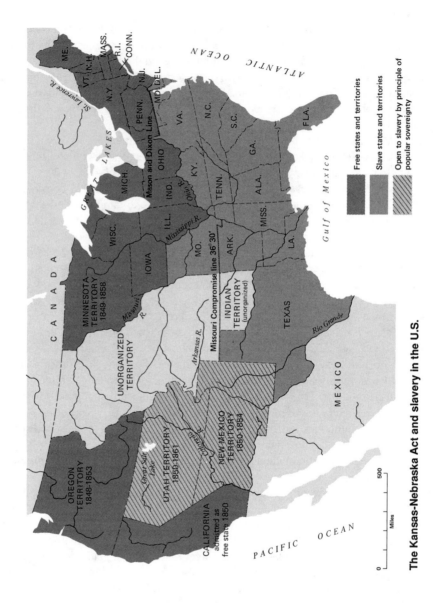

The Kansas-Nebraska Act and slavery in the U.S.

Free states and territories

Slave states and territories

Open to slavery by principle of popular sovereignty

that Douglas had hoped it would permanently close. By staking so much on a doctrine that many Northerners now perceived as an unfair, if not immoral, concession to the slave South, Douglas lost support in the North that he could not recoup in the South. The Pacific railroad bill that Douglas foresaw as the end objective of organizing the Kansas and Nebraska territories remained bottled up in Congress for the remainder of the decade, a victim of the sectional rivalries intensified by the Kansas–Nebraska Act.

The losses for Douglas' Democratic party were just as high. The instincts of northern Democrats told them that Douglas was playing with political dynamite in the Kansas–Nebraska Act, and they wanted nothing to do with it. Left to their own, most northern Democrats would have voted against the bill, and it never would have passed. To save the legislation, President Pierce used all the influence and patronage powers of his administration to wheel northern Democrats into line. After Senate approval of 37 to 14 in March, the crucial vote came up in the House in May. The bill passed 113 to 100, and in what otherwise was a nearly solid sectional pattern of voting, 44 northern Democrats provided the margin of victory. While one half of the northern Democrats succumbed to the administration's pressure and voted for the bill, every northern Whig voted against it. Northern Democrats paid the expected price in the fall elections of 1854. The party lost sixty-six of its ninety-one congressional seats in the free states.

As the northern Whigs had predicted, voters rejected the northern Democracy once it was blamed for the repeal of the Missouri Compromise restriction on slavery. Nonetheless, these Whigs had miscalculated the impact of the Kansas–Nebraska Act just as badly as had Douglas. Northern voters turned away from the Democrats, but they did not turn toward the Whig party. The reaction against the "Nebraska infamy" was so powerful and fears of the anti-Northern Slave Power so intense that the Whigs did not appear to be anti-Southern enough for many of the disgruntled voters. After all, southern Whigs had voted two to one for the Kansas–Nebraska Act, and any party such as the Whigs that still hoped to wage a national campaign for the presidency would have to make concessions to its Southern wing. Second, the Whigs had overlooked the fact that the partisan feelings of former Democrats were so strong that they simply would not join the Whig party. Consequently, opposition in the North to the Slave Power and the Democrats took the form of a new party. By the summer of 1854, anti-Nebraska coalitions were organizing in the North under the name of the Republican party.

Within a matter of months the Republicans emerged as the major opposition party to the Democrats in the Midwest, a region where the Whigs had usually been weak. The Republicans got off to a much slower start in New England and the Mid-Atlantic states. Here the Whigs had strong party organizations, and the Democrats desperately tried to disassociate themselves from the Kansas–Nebraska Act. Although voters in the Northeast were just as angry with the Democrats as those in the Midwest, the target of their wrath was more likely to be the Catholic immigrant than the Southern planter. Eastern Whigs had underestimated the appeal of nativism, and once again their strategy of capitalizing on the popular backlash against the

Kansas–Nebraska Act backfired. In 1854 the Know-Nothings decimated the ranks of the Whigs, as well as the Democrats, in the Northeast. They did so by picking up both the nativist and the antislavery vote.

The combined impact of the Kansas–Nebraska Act and political nativism destroyed the Second Party System in 1854. The Whigs were dead as a national organization. Its Northern wing was the backbone of a new and thoroughly section-alized party, the Republicans. Its Southern wing joined the Know-Nothings after Southerners identified Whiggery with Northern condemnation of the Kansas–Ne-braska Act. The Democrats still existed as a national organization, but the Southern domination of the party was now so strong that Northerners questioned whether it could serve their interests.

A new party system was emerging, and it was not at all clear in 1854 whether the Republicans or the Know-Nothings would replace the Whigs as the major opposition party to the Democrats. The outcome of the competition between these two new parties would be critical in determining whether the new party system assumed a highly sectionalized form that would threaten the preservation of the Union. Why and how that party sectionalization occurred will be examined in the next chapter.

NOTES

1. Charles M. Wiltse and Michael J. Bukner (eds.), *The Papers of Daniel Webster, Corre-spondence,* vol. 7 (Hanover, N.H.: The University Press of New England, 1986), p. 155.
2. D. H. Kaufman, in the *Congressional Globe,* 31 Congress. 1 Session, Appendix, Part II, p. 936.
3. *Washington Daily National Intelligence,* July 4, 1850, quoted in Mark J. Stegnaier, "Zachary Taylor versus the South," *Civil War History,* vol. 33, p. 229, 1987.
4. R. W. Barnwell to James H. Hammond, Sept. 9, 1850, in John Barnwell (ed.), " 'In the Hands of the Compromisers': Letters of Robert W. Barnwell to James H. Hammond," *Civil War History,* vol. 29, p. 166, 1983.
5. Quoted in David M. Polter, *The Impending Crisis, 1848–1861* (New York: Harper and Row, 1976), p. 128.
6. *Anti-Slavery Bugle,* April 5, 1851, cited in Jane H. Pease and William H. Pease, "Con-frontation and Abolition in the 1850s," *Journal of American History,* vol. 58, p. 926, 1972.
7. Quoted in Gerald C. Eggert, "Notes and Documents: A Pennsylvanian Visits the Rich-mond Slave Market," *Pennsylvania Magazine of History and Biography,* vol. 59, p. 575, 1985.
8. George W. Julian, *Speeches on Political Questions* (New York: Hurd and Houghton, 1872), pp. 74–75.
9. Ulrich B. Phillips (ed.), "Correspondence of Robert Toombs, A. H. Stephens, and Howell Cobb," *American Historical Association Annual Report,* vol. 2, p. 229, 1911.
10. Philadelphia *North American,* May 11, 1854, quoted in Douglas E. Bowers, "From Logrolling to Corruption: The Development of Lobbying in Pennsylvania, 1815–1861," *Journal of the Early Republic,* vol. 3, p. 460, 1983.
11. Quoted in Mark W. Summers, *The Plundering Generation: Corruption and the Crisis of the Union, 1849–1861* (New York: Oxford University Press, 1987), p. 186.

12. Nativist quote in Michael F. Holt, *The Political Crisis of the 1850s* (New York: John Wiley, 1978), p. 163.
13. Quoted in Edward K. Spann, *The New Metropolis: New York City, 1840–1857* (New York: Columbia University Press, 1981), p. 338.
14. For the Appeal of the Independent Democrats, see *Congressional Globe*, 33 Congress, 1 Session, Part I, pp. 281–282.

SUGGESTED READINGS

BAKER, JEAN, *Affairs of Party: The Political Culture of Northern Democrats in the Mid-Nineteenth Century.* Ithaca, N.Y.: Cornell University Press, 1983.

BILLINGTON, RAY ALLEN, *The Protestant Crusade, 1800–1860: A Study of the Origins of American Nativism.* New York: Macmillan, 1938.

BLUE, FREDERICK, J., *The Free Soilers: Third Party Politics, 1848–54.* Urbana, Ill.: University of Illinois Press, 1973.

CAMPBELL, STANLEY W., *The Slave Catchers: Enforcement of the Fugitive Slave Law, 1850–1860.* Chapel Hill, N.C.: University of North Carolina Press, 1968.

COOPER, WILLIAM J., JR., *The South and the Politics of Slavery, 1828–1856.* Baton Rouge, La.: Louisiana State University Press, 1978.

HAMILTON, HOLMAN, *Prologue to Conflict: The Crisis and Compromise of 1850.* Lexington, Ky.: University of Kentucky Press, 1964.

HANDLIN, OSCAR, *Boston's Immigrants, 1790–1880: A Study in Acculturation.* Cambridge, Mass.: Harvard University Press, 1941.

HOLT, MICHAEL F., *The Political Crisis of the 1850s.* New York: John Wiley, 1973.

JOHANNSEN, ROBERT E., *Stephen A. Douglas.* New York: Oxford University Press, 1973.

MAIZLISH, STEPHEN E., *The Triumph of Sectionalism: The Transformation of Ohio Politics, 1844–1856.* Kent, Ohio: Kent State University Press, 1983.

MORRISON, CHAPLAIN W., *Democratic Politics and Sectionalism: The Wilmot Proviso Controversy.* Chapel Hill, N.C.: University of North Carolina Press, 1967.

NIVEN, JOHN, *John C. Calhoun and the Price of Union.* Baton Rouge, La.: Louisiana State University Press, 1988.

POTTER, DAVID M., *The Impending Crisis, 1848–1861.* Completed by Don E. Fehrenbacker. New York: Harper and Row, 1976.

SMITH, ELBERT B., *The Presidencies of Zachary Taylor and Millard Fillmore.* Lawrence, Kansas: University Press of Kansas, 1988.

WILENTZ, SEAN, *Chants Democratic: New York City and the Rise of the American Working Class, 1788–1850.* New York: Oxford University Press, 1984.

3

Sectionalism and a New Party System

On the eve of the election of 1856, Martin Van Buren noted that "for the first time in our history" a major party was seeking to win the presidency which "has placed itself in a position which…cuts itself loose from all hope, if not desire, of assistance in the slave States." It "wishes to accomplish its mastery by its own unaided arm." Van Buren added that if this party, the Republicans, captured control of the federal government, "it would be against reason and experience to expect a Union, in which political mastery is so plainly exhibited and organized, to continue."[1]

Van Buren was hardly alone in 1856 when he warned that a Republican triumph would result in the collapse of the Union. The opponents of the Republicans in the North and many Southerners were sounding the same alarm. Because the Republicans were in fact a thoroughly sectionalized party organized only in the free states, they were vulnerable to the charge that their bid for federal power threatened the Union. Yet, this sectionalized nature of the Republicans was the essence of their appeal in the North.

The Republicans proudly and defiantly declared that they were an anti-Southern party that would protect the North from the encroachments of the Slave Power. "We must not stop till we have laid the Slave Power on its back," urged Charles Sumner to the cheers of Republicans holding their first state convention in Massachusetts.

To the overthrow of the Slave Power we are summoned by a double call, one political and the other philanthropic—first, to remove an oppressive tyranny from the National Government, and, secondly, to open the gates of Emancipation in the Slave States.[2]

To the charge that they were a sectional party, the Republicans replied that the older parties were the truly sectionalized ones for they had handed over the federal government to the sectional interests of slavery. Freedom was national and slavery was sectional, proclaimed the Republicans, and this belief was the bedrock of their new party. They charged that this great principle of the Founding Fathers had been abandoned by the Whigs and Democrats in their submission to the Slave Power.

The Northern belief in the Slave Power and its gigantic plot in the Kansas–Nebraska Act to repeal the Missouri Compromise gave birth to the Republican party. As long as that belief was continually reinforced by specific events and by the actions of the federal government, the Republicans could expect to grow in power. The Southern and Democratic opponents of the party were acutely aware of this basic dynamic that structured the appeal of the Republicans. They tried desperately to put an end to the agitation over slavery in the territories that was so fundamental to the origins and growth of the Republicans. Their efforts on the plains of Kansas and in the chambers of the Supreme Court, however, were so blatantly self-serving that they strengthened the Republican charge of a Slave Power in control of the federal government. In trying to deprive the Republicans of their single most effective issue, the Democrats succeeded only in hastening the sectionalization of American politics between 1854 and 1860. As a result of that sectionalization, the Republicans were the most powerful political party in the country by 1860.

REPUBLICANS VERSUS KNOW-NOTHINGS

The competition between the Republicans and Know-Nothings determined the major successor party to the Whigs in the North. In retrospect it is clear that antislavery had a wider and more lasting popular appeal than nativism, but many politicians were drawing just the opposite conclusion in 1854 and 1855. In such key eastern states as Massachusetts, New York, and Pennsylvania, the Know-Nothings handily defeated the first separate slate of Republican candidates. Far from being a foregone conclusion, the Republicans' triumph over the Know-Nothings by 1856 required political cunning and a bit of luck.

A majority of Northern congressmen elected in 1854 were both Know-Nothings and Republicans. This confusing result, one made possible by the secrecy of the Know-Nothing lodges, indicated that the two parties were competing for the same kind of anti-Democratic voter in the North. That voter was Protestant, nativist, likely to support temperance, and was antislavery, or at least anti-Nebraska. Since the Know-Nothings attacked the Kansas–Nebraska Act and were against the extension of slavery, they could attract antislavery Northerners, such as Baptists and

Methodists, who also feared popery and blamed popery for the alliance of the Irish Catholics and the Democratic liquor dealers.

Moreover, the Know-Nothings could appeal to workers with their own version of the Republican free-labor critique of the slave South. For the Republicans, slavery sapped the initiative and ambition of free labor by subjecting it to the degrading competition of slave labor. For the Know-Nothings, Catholicism was a form of spiritual and secular bondage that stifled progress and destroyed any hope of free labor for social advancement. The goal of the Know-Nothings in Indiana, the one midwestern state where they engulfed the anti-Nebraska movement, was an American republic that would "exhibit the glorious spectacle of a government without a king, religion without a Pope; a continent without a slave."[3] That was a goal with which few Republicans would quarrel.

The Know-Nothings more than held their own against the Republicans at the state and local levels. Yet, if the Know-Nothings were to be more than a passing protest movement, they would also have to operate at the national level, and it was here that the party's Achilles' heel was exposed. Initially, the Know-Nothings appeared to have a decided advantage over the Republicans in that they had a Southern wing. Thus, the Know-Nothings could make a plausible case to anti-Democrats in the North that they, not the Republicans, stood the best chance of defeating the Democrats in the presidential election of 1856. When delegates from the Northern and Southern wings of the party met to draft national resolutions in June 1855, this apparent strength immediately became a great liability. Nativism took a back seat to the slavery issue, and the Northern delegates walked out in protest of a resolution supporting the Kansas–Nebraska Act. A subsequent national convention in February 1856 confirmed the split, and the American party (Know-Nothings) was now permanently divided by slavery into two separate sectional parties.

The national rupture of the American party coincided with growing evidence at the local level that they had inherent limitations in building an anti-Democratic coalition in the North. Many antislavery Northerners were repelled by the open bigotry that tainted so much of Know-Nothingism. "I am not a Know-Nothing," wrote Abraham Lincoln of Illinois to a close friend in 1855. "How could I be? How can any one who abhors the oppression of negroes, be in favor of degrading classes of white people?"[4] The blanket condemnation of foreigners alienated German Protestants and Irish Protestants who otherwise would have been happy to join an anti-Catholic crusade. The secrecy and rituals of the Know-Nothing lodges offended Whigs who had entered politics as part of the popular movement in the 1820s and 1830s against the power and privileges of the Masonic Order. These Whigs hated the Know-Nothings and accused them of proscribing individual conscience and free choice in the same way as had the Masons. Indeed, to many of their opponents, the Know-Nothings were guilty of fostering the same slavish obedience for which the party had castigated the Catholic Church.

Unable to attract many new converts after the initial flush of enthusiasm wore off, the Know-Nothings also had trouble holding onto their original followers. Disenchantment set in quickly, because the party was unable to deliver on its promises. Congress did nothing to restrict immigration, lengthen the naturalization period, or ban Catholics and the foreign born from holding political office. Actual accomplishments at the state level consisted of little more than investigations into the alleged sexual perversions of priests in Catholic nunneries, some tightening up of voter registration laws, and temperance legislation.

Know-Nothingism also failed as a people's campaign against fraudulent elections and corrupt politicians. Violent election-day riots were commonplace in the Know-Nothing strongholds of Cincinnati, Louisville, and Baltimore, where immigrants battled nativists for access to the ballot box. These bloody brawls, and the open attempts to steal elections that accompanied them, made it appear as if the Know-Nothings were polluting the very electoral process they had promised to purify. Equally damaging in the eyes of erstwhile Know-Nothings was the manipulation of their party by experienced politicians. Antislavery Free Soilers in Massachusetts, conservative Fillmore Whigs in New York, and pro-business Democrats in Pennsylvania all used the Know-Nothings to further their own party ambitions as the Second Party System was breaking down. In most areas by 1856, the Know-Nothings were indistinguishable from the corrupt old parties they had pledged to replace.

As the weaknesses of political nativism surfaced, the Republicans skillfully exploited them to win over former Know-Nothings. While carefully distancing themselves from the secrecy and violence that had discredited Know-Nothingism, the Republicans developed an artful strategy to capitalize on the undeniable appeal of nativism. The key to that strategy was the drawing of a distinction between being anti-Catholic and anti-immigrant.

The Republicans played upon fears of popery but they stopped well short of condemning all immigrants as unAmerican. In this way, Republicans picked up the vote of both native-born and immigrant Protestants. By linking Catholicism to corruption and ignorance, and pledging to combat its evil influences, the Republicans reinforced their image as a party of reform and attracted voters disappointed with the failure of Know-Nothings to cleanse American politics. Meanwhile, most Republicans refrained from publicly criticizing the Know-Nothings. This made it easier for the party to win the endorsements of leading Know-Nothings and, where necessary, to share slates of state offices with them.

While Republicans at the state level were learning how to neutralize the appeal of nativism and use it to their own advantage, Republicans at the national level scored two significant victories over the Know-Nothings in early 1856. The first involved a protracted struggle over the selection of the Speaker of the House of Representatives. The Congress elected in the fall of 1854 after the Kansas–Nebraska battle first met in December 1855. The Democrats had lost their majority, and nativist and antislavery congressmen were vying with each other to fashion a controlling Northern majority. More adept at political infighting than the Know-Nothings, the Republicans won the struggle when Nathaniel P. Banks, a Know-Nothing recently turned Republican, was chosen Speaker on the 133rd ballot in early February. The Republicans had put together a coalition that combined out-

and-out antislavery congressmen with those who now placed antislavery above their commitment to nativism. This victory in the House contest marked the organizational birth of the Republicans at the national level. Three weeks later, the Republicans held their first national meeting in Pittsburgh.

In June 1856 the Republicans pulled off an even more stunning triumph. The North Americans (the now separate Northern wing of the Know-Nothings) intentionally scheduled their nominating convention for the presidency to take place a few days before the Republicans were to meet to select their candidate. Once the North American party chose their candidate, the Republicans would be in a tight bind. If the Republicans supported the North American party nominee, they would diminish their stature as an independent party, perhaps permanently. If the Republicans went ahead with their own candidate, they would be accused of placing selfish party interests above the need to maintain the unity of the antislavery, anti-Democratic coalition in the North. With a stroke of political genius the Republicans wiggled out of the bind by striking a secret deal with Nathaniel Banks, who once again doublecrossed the Know-Nothings.

First, the Republicans assisted Banks in winning the North American party nomination. Then, after delaying his acceptance until after the Republicans had made their choice, Banks turned around and rejected the nomination. The Know-Nothings were now in the same bind they had tried to fasten on the Republicans. Beaten at their own game, the North American party wound up seconding the Republicans' nominee, John C. Frémont.

The Republicans were clearly better politicians than the Know-Nothings. Yet, for all their successful political maneuverings, the Republicans were able to eclipse the Know-Nothings primarily because of the resurgence in 1856 of Northern fears over the Slave Power. This was the year in which the sectional conflict started to turn violent.

"BLEEDING KANSAS" AND THE ELECTION OF 1856

At the end of 1855, the Republicans were still running a poor second to the Know-Nothings in most of the North. The Republicans did not yet exist as a separate party organization in eight of the free states, and the Know-Nothings were the most powerful new party in the large electoral states of New York, Massachusetts, and Pennsylvania. To make matters worse, the Know-Nothings routed the Republicans in the Connecticut state election in the early spring of 1856. Then, beginning in May 1856, the political tide suddenly turned in favor of the Republicans. Two shocking events in May—the "sack of Lawrence," an attack by proslavery Missourians on the most important free-soil settlement in Kansas, and the savage beating of an antislavery senator, Charles Sumner, by a Southern congressman—dramatically personalized the Slave Power for Northerners as a barbaric force that threatened all decent values of civilized behavior.

The settlement of Kansas became politically and symbolically enmeshed in the struggle over slavery a month before the Kansas–Nebraska bill had even passed Congress. In April 1854, Eli Thayer, an antislavery Northerner, secured a charter from the Massachusetts legislature to incorporate the New England Emigrant Aid Society for the purpose of assisting free-state settlers to emigrate to the West. In the next two years the Emigrant Aid Society helped about 1,500 Northerners move to Kansas. They were only a small fraction of all those who had settled in Kansas by 1856, but the organized way in which they were recruited immediately aroused Southern fears of a Yankee plot to steal Kansas from the slave South. Egged on by the loud and tactless urgings of Senator David Atchison, Missourians vowed to repel this abolitionist invasion on their western border.

From the beginning, then, the question of who would control Kansas was cast in nearly mythic proportions for many Northerners and Southerners. Congressional leaders, the party press, and ideologues for or against slavery simply assumed that Kansas was now to be the battleground of freedom versus slavery. Their assumption became a self-fulfilling prophecy, and, in the process, disputes in Kansas that had little, if anything, to do with slavery were distorted to fit political preconceptions in both sections.

Most of the settlers in Kansas were nonslaveholding farmers from Missouri and other midwestern states, and they seemed not to have cared deeply about slavery one way or the other. What they did care about, and what brought them to Kansas in the first place, was land.

When they started to trickle into Kansas during the summer of 1854, no land was legally available. Indian titles had not yet been extinguished, and no public land had been surveyed and put on the market. This remained the case until the end of 1854, and for the next few years federal surveyors could hardly work fast enough to meet the demand for legal titles to land. As a result, disputes over land were endemic. Adding to the uncertainties was the scarcity of the type of land with which the settlers were familiar.

The open grasslands of Kansas were a new and psychologically threatening environment to farmers accustomed to the farming ecology of the more humid, wooded Midwest east of the Mississippi. The Kansas prairies lacked the wood, water, and easily broken soils that these farmers had taken for granted farther east. The very limited forested and well-watered areas were therefore in highest demand, and, quite independent of the slavery issue, settlers fought over who had clear title to them. Territorial officials, nearly all of whom were involved in real-estate speculations of their own, raised the stakes in these land disputes by promoting rival town sites for county seats and railroad depots.

Kansans fought among themselves primarily over land, not slavery. Nonetheless, to outsiders, the slavery issue provided the easiest and politically most useful way of explaining the outbreaks of violence in the territory. This projection onto Kansas of the sectional division over slavery became all the more persuasive when Kansas split into two hostile camps after the Missouri "border ruffians" had made a mockery of popular sovereignty.

Although Southerners believed that a territory could not make a final decision on slavery until it was ready to enter the Union as a state, they knew from experience that unless slavery arrived with the first settlers it would never be established. The early sanctioning of slavery in turn required a territorial slave code that would protect the institution and silence its critics. According to the Northern interpretation of popular sovereignty, a territorial legislature was empowered to prohibit slavery. Thus, control of the first territorial legislature in Kansas was of critical importance to the minority of proslavery and antislavery ideologues in the territory and to the politicians who had staked their reputations on the outcome of the slavery issue.

The election for the territorial legislature was scheduled for late March 1855. Owing to the geographical proximity of Missouri, Southerners had been a clear majority of the early settlers, but at this point it was uncertain whether they were outnumbered by the increasing flow of Northerners from the Midwest. Senator Atchison of Missouri did not want to risk the result of a fair and open election. He personally led a large band of Missourians who crossed the border and stuffed the ballot boxes in favor of proslavery delegates to the legislature. If slavery had not initially polarized Kansas, it did so now when it became inseparable from the issue of an honest expression of the will of the majority.

Antislavery Northerners had barely finished proclaiming that the Slave Power had stolen an election when the fraudulently elected legislature acted in just the manner that the Slave-Power theory would have predicted. The legislature passed a series of harsh laws that deprived antislavery Kansans of their basic constitutional rights. An oath of allegiance to slavery was now made a prerequisite for holding an office. Aiding a fugitive slave to escape was a capital offense, as was the distribution of abolitionist literature. The mere questioning of the right to hold slaves in the territory was a felony. Logically enough, the proslavery majority then ousted its few remaining antislavery members.

Passed over the vetoes of Pennsylvania Democrat Andrew Reeder, who was territorial governor and who was powerless to intervene without support from the Pierce administration in Washington, these drastic measures drove the free-state settlers into open opposition. By now, the free-state forces were undeniably a majority of the bona fide settlers in Kansas. They denied the legitimacy of the "bogus" legislature sitting in Lecompton, held their own extralegal elections, and organized a free-state government in Topeka in the fall of 1855.

Two rival governments were now in existence. Kansans divided over whether they viewed the Lecompton government as immoral or the Topeka government as illegal. It was impossible to remain neutral because basic duties of citizenship, such as paying taxes or serving on juries, performed for one of the governments were treasonable acts in the eyes of the other. The worst episodes of violence now erupted, and scattered guerrilla warfare was hyperbolized in the eastern press as the opening salvos of a civil war.

The stronghold of the free-state forces was Lawrence, the town that was also the center of the subsidizing activities of the Emigrant Aid Society. On May 21, 1856, a posse composed primarily of Missourians anxious for a shot at the "aboli-

The above sketch of Lawrence, Kansas, after Missourians burned and plundered the town in May 1856 shows the ruins of the Free Soil Hotel.

tionists" entered Lawrence to arrest free-state leaders who had defied the Lecompton government in the matter of the killing of a free-soil settler by a proslavery man. The free-state leaders had already fled, and the Missourians vented their frustrations by destroying any property they could get their hands on. Contrary to the impression in the eastern press, no one was killed, though property losses were high.

For a Republican party still struggling to establish itself as the major alternative to the Democrats in the North, Lawrence came as a godsend. After all, it was a northern Democrat, President Pierce, who had officially proclaimed the proslavery Lecompton government as the only legal one in Kansas and promised to back it to the hilt. The result, according to the Republicans, was the "sacking of Lawrence," the wanton killing of freedom-loving Kansans by Missouri savages doing the bidding of the Slave Power. This highly partisan and sectionalized portrayal of the Kansas tragedy rang true to many Northerners, for, on the very next day, May 22, Preston Brooks of South Carolina bashed Charles Sumner of Massachusetts senseless in the Senate chambers.

What happened was this: On May 19 and 20, Sumner had delivered perhaps his most famous speech in a long career noted for its oratory. The speech was called "The Crime Against Kansas,"[5] and it was a florid masterpiece that wove together classical allusions, lofty principles, and gutter invective in a stunning two-day performance. The speech itself deserves some attention not only because it was reproduced in the hundreds of thousands as a campaign document for the Republicans, but, even more so, because it set off a train of events that marked a critical turning point in the rise of the Republican party.

Sumner constructed the speech around the elaborate metaphor of "the rape of a virgin Territory," a very powerful symbol in a sexually prudish society, with which to express the North's sense of betrayal over the alleged invasion of Kansas by the proslavery forces. The purpose of the crime, the "hideous offspring" of the rape, was to be a slave state in Kansas. The crime itself was the Kansas–Nebraska Act, which exposed the territory of Kansas to the foul embrace of slavery. The crime was perpetrated "*first, by whipping in*" congressmen through executive patronage; "*secondly, by thrusting out of place*" the normal business of Congress; "*thirdly, by trampling under foot,*" House rules; and "*fourthly, by driving it to a close*" before the public had a chance to react.

Although several senators objected to this explicit sexual imagery as morally offensive and "unpatriotic," it was a representative from South Carolina, Preston Brooks, who was offended to the point of deciding to retaliate. Along with Douglas of Illinois, Senator Andrew Butler of South Carolina, a kinsman of Brooks', was singled out for personal attack by Sumner. After ridiculing Butler for the sham chivalry of vowing honor and courage only to his chosen "mistress..., the harlot, Slavery," Sumner stooped to the level of mocking Butler's minor speech impediment by scorning "the loose expectoration of his speech."

In Brooks' view, Sumner was a contemptuous dog who had villified his kinsman and his state. Unworthy by the Southern code of being challenged to a duel—only gentlemen fought duels—Sumner had to be thrashed like the dog that he was, Brooks reasoned.

It happened on May 22 after the Senate had adjourned for the day. Sumner was seated at his desk, writing letters, when, from behind, Brooks approached, carrying a gold-headed walking stick. He accused Sumner of libel, of castigating untruths about South Carolina and about Butler. When Sumner started to rise, Brooks beat him down with his walking stick. Sumner, unable to protect himself because his legs were pinned beneath his desk, was beaten into bloody unconsciousness. Three years it took before Sumner was physically able to resume his duties in the Senate.

This brutal, shocking attack gave the Republican party a martyr and ignited a veritable blaze of protest meetings in the North. No matter how the South reacted, the Republicans stood to gain politically.

As it was, the public reactions of Southerners gave Republicans their most effective weapon yet in their propaganda war against the South. In newspaper editorials and public rallies, Southerners did not stop with just hailing Brooks as a sectional hero who had upheld a civilized code of personal honor. They also went out of their way to insult and abuse antislavery Northerners. Sumner and his friends were denounced as traitors who long since should have been chastised or silenced.

"The truth is," exclaimed the Richmond *Enquirer,* "they have been suffered to run too long without collars. They must be lashed into submission."[6]

This Southern support for Brooks and the tauntings that accompanied it gave Republican recruitment a tremendous boost. By rallying behind Brooks, Southerners confirmed for many Northerners the Republican position that the attack on Sumner was not an isolated act of one brutal individual but the inevitable savagery spawned by a barbarous society of slaveholders. Southern actions and threats were showing that the Republicans were correct in their charging that the Slave Power endangered the liberties of Northern whites. "Has it come to this, that we must speak with baited breath in the presence of our Southern masters...?," asked the New York *Evening Post.* "Are we, too, slaves, slaves for life, a target for their brutal blows, when we do not comport ourselves to please them?"[7] Whether as middle-class evangelicals who had renounced the use of violence in their lives, or as good republican citizens who prized the Constitution and its protection of free speech, more and more Northerners had reason to join the Republicans. The imagery of the Slave Power was becoming more persuasive, they saw, and only the Republicans promised to protect Northerners from that enslaving menace to their own liberties and values.

The Republicans entered the campaign of 1856 with "Bleeding Kansas" and "Bleeding Sumner" emblazoned on their banners. The eventual status of slavery in Kansas was still very much up in the air, but the Republicans already had decisively won the propaganda battle over the territory.

To be sure, Southerners were burdened by the now politically impossible task of trying to defend an institution that most of the Western world denounced as a barbaric relic from the past. But Southerners compounded this weakness by failing to see how the recent communications revolution had made it possible to manufacture news as a politically marketable commodity.

It was Northern correspondents, especially those from Horace Greeley's New York *Tribune,* who reported to the nation what was going on in Kansas, and these reports invariably placed the pro-Southern side in the worst possible light. It was a Republican-dominated investigating committee appointed by the House, the Howard Committee, that gathered information on the Kansas disturbances and publicized its findings to the nation. For partisan reasons these findings downplayed the worst episode of bloodletting in Kansas, the murder of five ostensibly proslavery men at Pottawatomie Creek on the evening of May 24.

The murders were ghastly. The victims were dragged out of bed in the middle of the night, and their heads were split open by broadswords. It was no secret in Kansas that John Brown, a fanatical abolitionist, was responsible for the massacre. Yet, owing to the Northern press and the Howard Committee, public opinion in the North was not aroused by the slogan of "Abolitionist Butchery" or the "Pottawatomie Massacre."

The walking stick of Preston Brooks, not the broadsword of John Brown, was the most potent symbol of sectional violence in the election of 1856. Shocked by the violence that Republican publicists succeeded in blaming entirely upon the South and its slavish followers in the northern Democracy, antislavery Know-Nothings and conservative Northerners rushed into the Republican party. When Republicans met for their national convention in the middle of June, they correctly sensed that the party had turned the corner in its bid for Northern support.

The election of 1856 was a three-cornered contest. The Republicans ran John C. Frémont, a colorful military adventurer and a political newcomer. On both counts he was a shrewd choice. As an army officer and explorer in the Far West, he had earned a reputation as the "Pathfinder," a swashbuckling hero who played a prominent role in the glorious conquest of California during the Mexican War. Although he had done little fighting, his military aura strengthened the Republicans' claim that they would stand up to Southern aggressions. Frémont's youth (at age 43 he was the youngest candidate yet for the presidency) and lack of any prior identification with a party or faction were positive assets in the eyes of an electorate grown weary with politics as usual. Party professionals did not expect Frémont (or any Republican) to win in 1856, but they planned on using him as a stalking horse to help land the presidency by 1860.

The Republicans' platform was noteworthy for marking the first time in antebellum presidential politics that a major party took an unequivocal stand against slavery. The Republicans condemned the repeal of the Missouri Compromise, favored the immediate admission of Kansas as a free state, and called on the federal government to withhold all its support from slavery and to prohibit the institution in the territories. Much of this antislavery platform came straight from the creed of the Liberty and Free Soil parties. Former Whigs were responsible for a plank that was in favor of federally funded internal improvements, and the Republicans followed at least part of Douglas' strategy in 1854 by supporting a Pacific railroad.

The Democrats chose their candidate by a process of elimination. Pierce, their presidential incumbent, and Douglas, their party leader in the North, were ruled out because of their close association with the politically disastrous Kansas situation. Knowing that their Southern base was secure, the party settled on an uninspiring Northerner, James Buchanan, who had made a long career for himself by substituting party regularity for originality of political thought. Buchanan had faithfully served his party in a variety of posts since the 1820s and was the undisputed leader of a strong state machine in Pennsylvania, a critical state for the Democrats to carry in 1856. Having been the minister to Britain during the Pierce administration, he had the additional advantage of being untarnished by the Kansas issue. As expected, the Democrats ran squarely upon popular sovereignty and the absolute noninterference by Congress with slavery in the territories, states, or District of Columbia.

The third candidate was Millard Fillmore, the nominee of an American (Know-Nothing) party now noted more for its conservative Unionism than its rabid nativism. Fillmore was widely identified with the Compromise of 1850 and the enforcement of the Fugitive Slave Act. This, plus a platform that vaguely endorsed popular sovereignty, made him unacceptable to antislavery North American party adherents, who bolted to the Republicans. By the same token, these were the very

In the election of 1856 the American party charged that both the Republicans and Democrats were hopelessly corrupt. Millard Fillmore, the American presidential candidate, is depicted here as an honest farmer guarding the crib of government favors and offices from the thieving politicians. John C. Frémont is the rat closest to the door on the crib.

factors that made him attractive to the South American party, former Whigs searching for a new political home after 1854. Die-hard northern Whigs, still frightened by the radicalism of the Republicans on the slavery issue, also endorsed Fillmore.

For a sectionalized new party barely in existence for two years, the Republicans came astonishingly close to winning the election of 1856. Frémont carried eleven of the sixteen free states. Had he added Pennsylvania and either Indiana or Illinois, he would have won. Buchanan ran even stronger in the South than Frémont had in the North. With the exception of Maryland, the lone state carried by Fillmore, Buchanan swept the slave states, the source of two-thirds of his electoral vote.

Fillmore won only thirteen percent of the popular vote in the North, as opposed to forty-four percent in the South, but his candidacy definitely hurt the Republicans. The American party vote cost the Republicans three of the five free states they lost, New Jersey, Illinois, and California, and American party appeals to anti-Catholicism and pro-Unionism cut into the potential Republican vote throughout most of the lower North, the belt of states stretching westward from New Jersey. Seizing upon Frémont's French background and his marriage by a Catholic priest, the American party spread the false charge that Frémont was a Catholic and effectively attacked the Republicans for being harder on Southern whites than on foreign-born Catholics.

There was no mistaking the chief lesson of the election of 1856. American politics were polarizing around the sectional axis of the free and slave states. In 1856, New England joined the Lower South as a virtual one-party region. Republicans in New England now controlled 60 percent of the popular vote, the same dominant support that states' rights Democrats could count on in the Lower South. Voter turnout surged in 1856, but it increased particularly sharply in these two regions, an indication that sectional antagonisms were a more fundamental factor in galvanizing voter interest than two-party competition.

Between these two sectional extremes the Democrats as a national organization still held onto about half of the electorate. That hold was weakest in the North, and it was slipping fast outside of New England. The Democratic share of the popular vote in the North fell from fifty-one percent to forty-five percent between the presidential elections of 1852 and 1856. Even so, it was here that Buchanan gained his margin of victory. Southerners were threatening secession if the Republicans won in 1856, and those threats heightened the appeal of the Democrats in the North as the saviour of the Union. More than any other factor, that appeal put Buchanan into the White House.

His stay was a short one, however, because he failed to understand how quickly that appeal would turn hollow once Northerners became convinced that his pro-Southern administration was a captive of the Slave Power.

THE ILL-FATED BUCHANAN PRESIDENCY

Buchanan's presidency got off to the worst possible start. Two days after his inauguration, the Supreme Court handed down perhaps its most notorious decision ever. The case was *Dred Scott* versus *Sandford,* and it indelibly stamped the Buchanan Democrats for many Northerners as the willing accomplices of a Southern plot to spread slavery and strip Northern whites of their liberties.

Dred Scott was a Missouri slave who claimed his freedom on the grounds of prior residence in a free state and a free territory. Scott's owner in 1834, Dr. John Emerson, an army surgeon, had first taken him to Illinois, where slavery was banned by the Northwest Ordinance of 1787 and subsequently by the state's constitution, and then he took Scott to the Wisconsin Territory (later, part of Minnesota), where slavery was banned by the Missouri Compromise restriction. In 1838, Scott returned to Missouri with his master. After Emerson's death, Scott began his suit for freedom in 1846. Missouri courts first ruled for and then against him. By the time Scott's case was appealed to the Supreme Court, Mrs. Emerson, his owner by inheritance after the death of Dr. Emerson, had remarried to an antislavery politician and was living in Massachusetts. Under Missouri law she now had to relinquish control of her ex-husband's estate, including the slave, Dred Scott. Her brother, John Sanford (mistakenly misspelled Sandford in the official record of the case), assumed control of Scott. The important point in all this maneuvering was that Scott's case had come to the attention of antislavery Northerners who were determined to make it a *cause célèbre*.

For all its legal complexities, the Dred Scott case boiled down to two main points. Was Scott, as a black and as a slave, an American citizen entitled to bring suit in a federal court? Second, did Congress have the constitutional power in the Missouri Compromise or any other legislation to prohibit slavery in the federal territories?

Initially, it appeared that the Court would sidestep both issues by the simple expedient of affirming that the state law of Missouri was binding in the case. That was the decision reached by the Court in mid-February 1857. However, two antislavery justices, John McLean of Ohio and Benjamin R. Curtis of Massachusetts, refused to let the matter drop. They intended to write dissenting opinions upholding the constitutionality of the Missouri Compromise and declaring Scott a free man. Perhaps because they felt goaded and wanted to deprive the abolitionists of a propaganda victory, the five Southerners on the Court reversed course and came out in favor of a broad decision. Undoubtedly swaying them as well was the fact that Congress had been looking to the Court since the introduction of the Wilmot Proviso to settle the question of slavery in the territories once and for all.

One final piece had to fall into place before the Court would issue a sweeping decision. The five Southern justices, headed by Chief Justice Roger Taney of Maryland, all believed that the Missouri Compromise was unconstitutional. In an effort to avoid the charge of sectional bias if they alone comprised the anti-Scott majority on the Court, they wanted assurances that at least one Northern justice would go along with them. To that end they communicated with Buchanan, the president-elect, urging him to persuade Justice Robert Grier of Pennsylvania, his close friend and political ally, to join them in laying to rest the vexed issue of slavery in the territories. Buchanan, in an egregious violation of presidential ethics and the constitutional separation of the executive and judiciary, followed the suggestions of the Southern justices. He intervened, and Greer became the sixth justice in the majority against Scott and the Missouri Compromise.

Each of the nine justices wrote separate opinions. To the extent that a unified majority existed, Chief Justice Taney was its spokesman. Taney first ruled that Scott, either as a slave or as a black, was not a citizen of the United States and hence had no legal right to bring his suit in the first place. He based this argument on a distorted, even falsified, summary of the actual historical status of free blacks at the time of the ratification of the Constitution. According to Taney, the Founding Fathers never intended blacks to be granted national citizenship, that any rights of citizenship blacks *might* be granted had to come from the individual states and were legally binding only in those states. This latter argument ignored the fact that several states in 1787 and subsequently did confer citizenship on blacks. Nonexistent in Taney's view, these blacks, as citizens of states, were fully entitled under the Constitution to the rights of national citizenship.

Taney's ruling on the second major issue in the case, the constitutionality of the Missouri Compromise, could have been written by John Calhoun. It followed closely the reasoning developed by Calhoun in his opposition to the Wilmot Proviso: As a constitutionally recognized form of property, slavery could not be singled out for exclusion from the territories, the common property of all the states. It would have been just as illegal to deprive a New England farmer of his right to bring a horse into the territories. In either instance, the Fifth Amendment prohibited Congress from denying a citizen the use of his or her property without due process of law. As for the power conferred by the Constitution on Congress to make all necessary rules and regulations for the territories, Taney held that, in respect to slavery, this power was strictly limited to protecting the rights of the slaveholder. Property took precedence over liberty, and the Missouri Compromise restriction on slavery was declared void.

In retrospect, it is hard to imagine how anyone could have ever felt that this decision would quell, let alone settle, the volatile issue of slavery in the territories. Far from banking the fires of sectional discord, Buchanan and the Southern justices fanned them into a hotter blaze. In theoretical terms, the ruling that Congress was powerless to prohibit slavery in the territories eliminated the Republican party's main reason for existing. In practical terms, however, *Dred Scott* simply convinced even more Northerners of the reality of the Slave Power.

Buchanan had foolishly called attention to the Supreme Court's upcoming decision (which he knew in advance) in his Inaugural Address. This left him wide open to the subsequent Republican charge, voiced by Senator William Seward of New York, that his inauguration had been "desecrated by a coalition between the executive and judicial departments to undermine the national legislature and the liberties of the people."[8] Out on the Illinois prairies, Abraham Lincoln detected in the *Dred Scott* decision "another nice little niche, which we may, ere long, see filled with another Supreme Court decision, declaring that the Constitution of the United States does not permit a *state* to exclude slavery from its limits."[9] In short, the Republicans could now argue that the Slave Power had become even bolder, because, they believed, it had spread from Congress into the executive and judicial branches of the federal government and was about to launch its most heinous plot, the nationalization of slavery in all the states.

As a lawyer, Buchanan apparently believed that slavery in the territories could be treated solely as a judicial question, the resolution of which by the Supreme Court would put the matter to rest. By ignoring the immense moral and economic importance that most Northerners placed on free soil, he wound up discrediting the very legal process that he expected to restore sectional harmony. Naive as a lawyer, Buchanan was obtuse as a politician. In supporting *Dred Scott* he unwittingly set a trap for his own Democratic party.

Ever since its introduction by Lewis Cass in 1848, popular sovereignty had the great political advantage of ambiguity. As long as northern and southern Democrats could interpret it differently to meet their sectional needs, popular sovereignty unified the party. The *Dred Scott* decision removed that ambiguity. The Southern position denying the right of a territorial legislature to ban slavery before statehood was now apparently the law of the land. If Congress could not banish slavery, then surely it could not delegate a power that it did not have to a territorial legislature, its constitutional inferior that was created through an enabling act of Congress. By mandating the legality of slavery in the territories, *Dred Scott* set up a collision between the sectional wings of the Democratic party. Stephen Douglas had promised his Northern supporters that popular sovereignty would be a sure means of keeping the territories free.

The spotlight now shifted back to Kansas. To avoid a confrontation over popular sovereignty that would split his party in two, Buchanan had to bring Kansas into the Union as a state as quickly as possible. Such a move was also expected to silence the incessant Republican agitation over the outrage of the Slave Power in Kansas. Even though this meant forcing a slave-state constitution upon Kansas, Buchanan accepted the challenge. The logic behind eliminating the territorial status of Kansas was as compelling to him as the logic behind the *Dred Scott* ruling. The results were equally as disastrous.

By the fall of 1856 a measure of calm had returned to Kansas after the Pottawatomie massacre in the spring had nearly incited a full-blown civil war. Much of the credit for this rested with the tough but fair policies of John Geary, the territory's third governor. On the day of Buchanan's inauguration, Geary resigned. He was tired of threats on his life and furious over the actions of the Lecompton legislature, still the only officially recognized government in Kansas. Over Geary's veto, this proslavery legislature had passed a bill calling for a state constitutional convention that did not include a provision for a popular referendum on the constitution. Buchanan replaced Geary with Robert J. Walker, a Pennsylvanian by birth who had risen to political prominence as a Mississippi senator and member of Polk's cabinet. Walker was an excellent choice. He had administrative experience, influential friends in the South, and a genuine desire to oversee a fair resolution of the Kansas difficulties. Before he accepted the appointment, he secured Buchanan's commitment in writing that the administration was pledged to a peaceful and honest expression of the will of the majority in Kansas. Apparently, Kansans would have a chance after all to decide for themselves on any proposed constitution.

Although the free-state men comprised by now at least two-thirds of the voters, they refused to vote in the convention election called by the Lecompton legislature for June 1857. They denied the right of the "bogus" legislature to issue any such call and insisted, correctly as it turned out, that the election would be rigged. Only about 2,000 out of 24,000 eligible voters turned out in June, and, to no one's surprise, proslavery delegates were elected. When this convention met in September, it quickly adjourned to await the outcome of yet another election in Kansas. This one was for a new territorial legislature. Exhorted by Walker to vote, the free-state men participated, and, for the first time, they gained control of the official legislature when Walker tossed out some flagrantly fraudulent ballots cast for the proslavery men. Walker's actions in assuring an honest election were technically illegal (only the courts could review the election returns), and the proslavery forces accused him of throwing the election to the free soilers. Walker returned to the East in disgust, and those who wanted slavery in Kansas now played their trump card at the Lecompton constitutional convention.

The proslavery delegates at Lecompton seemingly went out of their way to flaunt the will of the free-state majority in Kansas. Not only did they draft a constitution that would make Kansas a slave state, but they also refused to submit the entire constitution to a popular vote. The only choice made available to the voters was whether to approve a version of the constitution that permitted more slaves to be brought into Kansas or one that prohibited such entry. In either case, the property rights in the roughly 200 slaves already in Kansas would be fully protected. In an election again boycotted by the free soilers, the constitution permitting additional slaves was approved in December. A month later, in an election called by the newly elected territorial legislature, the entire constitution was overwhelmingly voted down.

At the end of 1857 the Buchanan administration was at a crossroads, and Buchanan followed the southern fork in the road. Often mistakenly criticized for indecisiveness, Buchanan now made the most fateful decision of his presidency, and he stuck to it. He proclaimed the December referendum in favor of the Lecompton constitution a legitimate expression of the popular will in Kansas and totally committed his administration to the immediate admission of a slave-state Kansas under that constitution. Why did he break his pledge that Kansas would have a fair opportunity to vote slavery up or down? Part of the reason was surely the fact that Southerners now so completely dominated his Democratic party. Two-thirds of Buchanan's electoral vote had come from the slave states, and three in five Democratic congressmen came from the South. Moreover, Buchanan's closest political and social friends were Southerners, and this lonely old bachelor was quite dependent on their fellowship. Still, Buchanan could easily rationalize that he was pursuing the national will by supporting Lecompton. The agitation over slavery in the territories was a dire threat to the Union, and it simply had to stop, he felt. Once Kansas was out of the territorial stage, that agitation, logically enough, had to cease, and voters in Kansas were still perfectly free to write a new, free-state constitution if they so desired. Indeed, that is just what Buchanan expected to happen.

No more than 400 slaves had ever been in the Kansas territory at any given time, and their numbers were dropping. Even most Southerners agreed that slavery would never thrive there. What was critical to slaveholders, ever fearful of the growing antislavery majority in the North, was the principal that additional slave states could still be admitted to the Union. If Kansas eventually turned out not to be one of those slave states, at least the way was still open for Cuba and perhaps parts of northern Mexico. Why not, reasoned Buchanan, grant Southerners their point of honor, give Northerners the reality of what soon would be a new free state, and get on with the business of strengthening the Union?

Buchanan's legalistic reasoning made sense, but it immediately backed him into a political corner narrower than the one he was trying to escape. The Republicans, of course, were handed an issue that strengthened their case against the Slave Power. Far more damaging to the Democrats, however, was the open revolt of their

Northern wing against Buchanan's decision to ram the Lecompton constitution through Congress.

Douglas, the unquestioned leader of the northern Democrats, was up for reelection in 1858 and, politically, he could not afford to be identified with another surrender to the slave interests. Condemned in the North for championing the Kansas–Nebraska Act, discredited by the *Dred Scott* decision that ruled out an antislavery role for popular sovereignty, and now saddled with the Lecompton perversion of popular sovereignty, Douglas had to oppose Buchanan in order to shore up his political base in the North.

In a meeting in early December, Douglas informed Buchanan that he, Douglas, would be in opposition if the administration went ahead with its plans to force Lecompton on Congress. After the president then invoked the hallowed Andrew Jackson as an example of a party leader who crushed all Democrats who dared to oppose him, Douglas acidly retorted that Buchanan was forgetting that Jackson was now dead.

This angry confrontation set the tone for the invective that characterized the congressional debates over Lecompton. Insults were freely exchanged, revolvers were openly displayed, and several fights nearly broke out. The administration exerted tremendous pressure on northern Democrats to follow the party line. Contracts, bribes, and patronage jobs were the rewards that were dangled, and job dismissals and withholdings of party funds for reelection were the punishments that were promised.

As expected, Buchanan won outright in the Senate, but enough northern Democrats broke party ranks in the House to force a compromise that sent the Lecompton constitution back to Kansas for another popular vote. In August 1858, Kansas spurned the constitution and immediate statehood by more than a six-to-one margin. Elections in Kansas finally stopped being national news, and, in what almost amounted to a postscript, Kansas entered the Union as a free state in 1861.

The antebellum Democratic party never recovered from its self-inflicted wounds in the Lecompton battle. Douglas and Buchanan, now the most bitter of enemies, fought each other for control of the party's Northern wing. Meanwhile, southern Democrats assailed Douglas and his Northern supporters for betraying their interests. Douglas still aspired to head a united Democratic party in 1860, but, first, he had to gain his reelection as an Illinois senator against the combined opposition of the Republicans and Buchanan Democrats. His opponent was Abraham Lincoln, and American political lore was about to be enriched by the Lincoln–Douglas debates.

Although hardly as obscure as later legend would have it, Lincoln was little known in the East in 1858. Within his adopted state of Illinois, though, he was widely respected as a shrewd politician. Through hard work, a marriage into a prominent, slaveholding Kentucky family, and a very successful practice as a corporate lawyer, Lincoln had risen far above the poverty of a youth spend in crude frontier settlements in Kentucky, Indiana, and Illinois. As a lawyer riding the Illinois court circuit, Lincoln established the personal contacts and political friendships that would be invaluable in his rapid rise to the leadership of the Illinois Republican party in the late 1850s. It was also as a lawyer that he learned the art of persuasion, the ability to strip an issue down to its essentials and present it in a homespun idiom that country jurors or rural voters could easily understand. Perhaps the most valuable lesson that this self-taught politician learned on the Illinois prairies was how to relate to, and empathize with, a broad range of folk that made up in microcosm the America of the mid-nineteenth century: upland Southerners such as himself, Southern aristocrats represented by his wife's family, New England Yankees, and Germans and Irish. And, through the river trade on the Mississippi, Lincoln had enough of an acquaintance with black slaves to know that he despised the institution of slavery. As Lincoln put it in 1858, "I have always hated slavery, I think, as much as any Abolitionist..., but I have always been quiet about it until this new era of the introduction of the Nebraska Bill began."[10]

Not active in politics after a one-term stint as a Whig congressman during the Mexican War, Lincoln resumed his political career in the mid-1850s when the Kansas–Nebraska Act both deeply angered him and offered a new range of political opportunities. In the Republican party Lincoln saw a perfect vehicle for his political ambitions and his moral indignation. His acceptance speech for the Republican nomination for the Senate illustrated how skillfully Lincoln could combine partisan need with high moral purpose. This was the famous "House Divided" speech of June 1858.

> I believe this government cannot endure, permanently half *slave* and half *free*....Either the *opponents* of slavery will arrest the further spread of it, and place it where the public mind shall rest in the belief that it is in course of ultimate extinction, or its *advocates* will push it forward, till it shall become lawful in *all* the States, *old* as well as *new*—*North* as well as *South*. Have we no tendency to the latter condition?[11]

This theme of a fundamental conflict between slavery and freedom for dominance in America, a conflict now seemingly being won by slavery, was one that Lincoln repeatedly highlighted in his summer debates with Douglas. On the one hand, this revealed the courage of a politician who dared to force an open, public debate over the meaning and ultimate impact of slavery in American society. On the other hand, this emphasis on slavery as a moral and divisive issue was an incredibly sharp political tactic. Douglas had become something of a darling with eastern Republicans because of his open defiance of Buchanan over Lecompton. Some Republicans in the East even favored a party endorsement of Douglas's reelection bid. Thus, it was imperative for Lincoln to establish that deep moral differences still made Douglas unacceptable to the great bulk of Republicans, differences that completely overshadowed the temporary convergence of Douglas Democrats and Republicans in opposition to forcing slavery upon Kansas. By so doing, Lincoln was also staking out the main ideological position of the Republicans once Kansas could no longer be used as a rallying point for all Northerners opposed to slavery in the territories.

The key to Lincoln's attack on Douglas, and by extension the northern

Abraham Lincoln, shown here delivering a speech in his debate of 1858 with Stephen A. Douglas, emerged as a major leader of the Republican party in the late 1850s.

Democrats as a whole, was Douglas's "no care" attitude on slavery. During the Jonesboro debate Lincoln charged,

> When he invites any people willing to have slavery to establish it, he is blowing out the moral lights around us. When he says he "cares not whether slavery is voted down or voted up,"—that it is a sacred right of self government—he is in my judgment penetrating the human soul and eradicating the light of reason and the love of liberty in this American people.[12]

American democracy, Lincoln insisted, embodied a moral sense of purpose enshrined in the commitment of the Declaration of Independence to freedom as a national goal. By his moral insensitivity to slavery, Douglas denied that commitment, sapped the will of Northerners to resist the spread of slavery, and encouraged the slave interests to threaten Northern liberties in the Kansas–Nebraska Act and the *Dred Scott* decision. In other words, Lincoln named Douglas an accomplice of the Slave Power. Douglas was to blame for that "tendency" darkly hinted at in his "House Divided" speech, the drift of the nation toward the legalization of slavery everywhere at the behest of the Slave Power. All that was now needed, said Lincoln, was a second *Dred Scott* decision legalizing slavery in the Northern states.

Douglas counterattacked with his oft-repeated argument that popular sovereignty, if given a fair chance, still was the most democratic way of handling slavery in the territories. Aside from race-baiting Lincoln with the claim that the Republicans favored an amalgamation of the races out of their love for blacks, Douglas focused his attacks on the charge that the Republicans were disunionists. Yet, as Lincoln cleverly retorted, the Republicans had counseled legal compliance with the *Dred Scott* ruling, while it was Douglas himself who publicly proclaimed that the law of the land could be effectively nullified. In response to a direct question from Lincoln during the Freeport debate, Douglas admitted that, regardless of any

Supreme Court decision on the constitutional rights of slavery in the territories, the settlers could shut slavery out by failing to pass the slave codes necessary to protect the institution. Douglas had made the same argument before, but the publicity surrounding his so-called Freeport Doctrine eliminated his already slim chances of ever winning back the trust of the Southerners in the party.

Lincoln's political stock soared owing to the national exposure of his debates with Douglas. Still, he lost the election. More precisely, he came out on the short end of the balloting in the legislature where, as was the case throughout the nineteenth century, states chose their senators. Lincoln slightly outpolled Douglas in the popular vote for the legislators, who would actually elect a senator, but that edge was not large enough to overcome the holdover strength the Democrats had in the legislature.

Elsewhere in the fall elections of 1858 in the North, the Democrats suffered heavy losses. In the House, the Democrats lost twenty-one of their fifty-three seats from the free states. Anti-Lecompton sentiment clearly hurt the northern Democrats, but the party was also staggering under the burden of being in office when a financial panic paralyzed the Northern economy in the fall of 1857. A year later, much of the Northern economy was still in the doldrums.

A FINANCIAL PANIC AND A SLAVEHOLDERS' PANIC

The financial panic of 1857, on top of the *Dred Scott* decision and continuing troubles in Kansas, was the third major setback that ruined the Buchanan presidency before it barely had a chance to get underway. With a frightening suddenness, this financial crisis ended the long economic boom that had begun in the late 1840s.

The collapse of the New York branch of an Ohio bank in August 1857 touched off a financial crisis made virtually inevitable by the speculative excesses in an economy that had become overly dependent on European capital. By the mid-1850s, a time of unusually heavy foreign borrowings, the economy was clearly overheating. All the major indices of growth in the cyclical recovery from the depression of the early 1840s—land sales, domestic trade, money supply, real output, and new railroad mileage—peaked between 1854 and 1856. The climax of this business cycle was closely associated with the Crimean War of 1854–1856 between Russia and Turkey. The war closed off Russia as a source of wheat for Europe, and, consequently, demand for American wheat soared. In 1855, the price of American wheat reached its antebellum high, and there was a predictable surge in the sale of public lands in the Midwest. The end of the Crimean War reversed this sequence and popped the speculative bubble that was by now driving the economy.

Once the extraordinary European demand for American wheat ceased, the income of farmers and exporters quickly fell. The export earnings of huge grain sales no longer covered the interest charges on the imported European capital that had been invested in American securities, and gold exports increased in order to meet those costs. At the same time, the British began liquidating their holdings of

American bonds and securities, especially the railroad securities they had snapped up in the early 1850s. Interest rates in Britain had skyrocketed during the Crimean War, and British investors could now earn a much higher yield on their capital at home. These British sales drove down the price of American securities, now commonly used by banks as collateral for their loans. Faced with declining assets and a heavy demand on their specie reserves, the major Eastern banks frantically called in their loans, drove their debtors into bankruptcy, and suspended the specie redemption of their banknotes. By mid-October, when the panic was at its height, business in the Northeast was paralyzed.

The financial panic itself was relatively brief. The money-center banks in New York City, their reserves replenished by eastward shipments of California gold (the September shipment of $2 million was lost in a storm at sea), resumed specie payments in December. By the spring of 1858 most other banks had followed suit. Factories and mills reopened, and the worst of the business crisis had passed within a few months. Nonetheless, the economy did not regain its buoyancy of the early 1850s, and it lingered in a business recession for the remainder of the Buchanan presidency.

The overall price index fell by 16 percent in 1858 and remained flat until the Civil War. Hardest hit was the farm economy of the Midwest. Wheat prices collapsed by 40 percent between 1855 and 1859, and the arrival of settlers and capital from the East slowed to a trickle. New railroad construction, which had been centered in the Midwest, was off by one half at the end of the decade from its peak year of 1854. The manufacturing economy of the Northeast weathered the financial storm somewhat better. The value of manufactured goods continued to grow in the second half of the decade, although at a pace only half that achieved from 1848 to 1854. In contrast, the value of farm output stagnated after 1857.

Only one major regional economy emerged from the panic unscathed. Export demand for Southern staples remained high, cotton prices were firm, and planters gloated that King Cotton had saved the national economy from utter collapse.

Initially, the Democrats felt that the panic could work in their favor. Here was a splendid opportunity to shift the political spotlight away from Kansas and win back northern Democrats lost to the Republicans by reviving traditional Democratic rhetoric against the greed of bankers and the evils of paper money. State elections in the North in the fall of 1857 indicated that the strategy was working. In New York, Pennsylvania, and Ohio, the Democrats regained most of the ground lost since 1854.

Popular anger against banks was quite strong, but the backlash in favor of the Democrats was short-lived. The economy was simply too complex and the connections between Democratic politicians and bankers too intimate for the implementation of any coherent anti-bank policy. Although Buchanan, in his annual message of December 1857, railed against the banks and proposed an eventual elimination of all banknotes $50 and under in denomination, there was never a chance that Congress would approve such a radical restructuring of the country's currency. Currency and banking changes, if any, would be up to Democrats in the individual states, and here party unity broke down under the pressure of regional and business demands for preferred treatment.

Meanwhile, the resumption of banknote redemptions in the spring of 1858 diffused much of the anti-bank rhetoric. Public concern now focused on the business recession that followed in the wake of the panic. The sluggish economy in the North and the apparent Democratic mismanagement of the nation's finances reversed the political impact of the financial panic and handed the partisan initiative over to the Republicans.

In early 1857, before the panic, the federal treasury was enjoying a comfortable surplus, and the public debt had fallen to its lowest point since the end of the Mexican War. The economy was still booming, and the timing seemed perfect for another Democratic reduction in the tariff. The lower rates in the Tariff of 1857 had just taken effect when the economic recession sharply curtailed imports and hence the government receipts derived from import duties. Since public land sales, the government's other major source of income, also plunged in the recession, the treasury suddenly faced a shortfall in receipts. Raising the tariff to generate more income was out of the question in a Democratic- and Southern-dominated administration. So also was a retrenchment in federal expenditures. Public monies spent on post offices, navy yards, and customhouses created jobs for party workers and slush funds from which to influence elections and legislative votes. Thus, the secretary of the treasury, Howell Cobb, a Georgian, met his expenses by issuing short-term treasury notes; that is, he borrowed the money needed to run the federal government. In 1858 the treasury ran its highest deficit since 1847, and it remained in the red for the rest of the Buchanan presidency. Before Buchanan left office, the public debt more than doubled.

By the middle of 1858 the Democrats were in full retreat over their handling of the economy and federal spending. Fiscal retrenchment and a higher tariff were winning issues for the Republicans, especially in Pennsylvania, a doubtful state critical to the party's chances in 1860. The coal-mining and iron-and-steel industries in Pennsylvania were hard hit by the post-1857 recession. Owners and operatives alike blamed the Tariff of 1857 and its lower duties on British railroad iron, and they demanded protection from the pauperized foreign labor that presumably was costing American workers their jobs and decent wages. Tariff protection was the issue around which the anti-Democratic opposition coalesced in Pennsylvania, and the Democrats lost heavily in the state's industrial districts in the congressional elections of 1858. For the first time the Republicans made significant gains among voters who earlier had not been swayed by the party's Slave Power rhetoric. As an anti-Lecompton Democrat noted in explaining his party losses in Pennsylvania, the voters were

> for protection that will at least put our labor on fair terms with that of other countries. They hate negroes, and have no affection for slavery; they would leave it alone where it is, and not prevent its going where the people really wish to have it.[13]

Elsewhere in the North in 1858, the Republicans hammered away at the issue of Democratic corruption and fiscal recklessness. Here, they received an indirect boost from the religious revival of 1857–1858. Unlike earlier revivals that were usually centered in rural areas and small towns, this one was disproportionately a phenomenon of Northern cities. Strongest in the financial centers and interior industrial cities of the Northeast, the areas most directly affected by the panic of 1857, the revival fed off the traditional fear of American Protestants that God and mammon could not be served at the same time. The revival offered a release of guilt for businessmen who now blamed their economic misfortunes on their abandonment of God; it held out hope and solace for workers facing unemployment and poverty in the winter of 1857–1858; and it called upon all Americans to return to the true paths of righteousness and frugality. Democratic spending was anything but frugal, and the first of the many scandals that were to plague the Buchanan administration became public in 1858. The revival had heightened the political salience of the corruption issue, and the Republicans made the most of it.

The revival petered out in 1858 when the economy picked up. By now, the Buchanan Democrats could not shake the label of corruption, and the Republicans were fashioning an economic program that called for the destruction of the Slave Power on behalf of renewing Northern prosperity. Working with themes first developed by the Liberty party in the early 1840s, the Republicans charged that the Slave Power was the greatest threat to the moral and material progress of Northern free labor.

Southern opposition to a higher tariff was one link in the Republican chain of argument. As was summarized by a Republican editor, "We ask that the free laborers of the country shall be protected from competition with laborers who are bought and sold; but we ask this in no stronger terms than we demand that American laborers shall be protected against the pauper labor of Europe."[14]

Just as damning to the interests of Northern workers, said the Republicans, was the blockage of a homestead bill by Southern congressmen. Incorporating the ideas of George Henry Evans, a New York labor leader and reform politician in the Workingmen's party, the Republicans claimed that access to free land in the West would give workers in the East a chance to realize the American dream of economic independence. For workers who chose to remain in the East, wages would rise as the labor surplus was drained off to the West. Only the slaveholders' fear of an educated work force, charged the Republicans, could explain the Southern refusal to support grants of public land to the states for the founding of agricultural and mechanical colleges, institutions where workers and farmers could better themselves by learning practical skills. Finally, the Republicans accused the slave interests of stymieing economic progress by defeating legislation for land-grant Pacific railroads that would unleash the economic potential of the West and benefit the entire country.

In every session of Congress after the Lecompton crisis the Republicans returned to the same economic themes. The poverty, vice, and ignorance that were afflicting industrializing America could be alleviated, if not eliminated, by a positive federal program of economic assistance. This was a powerful message with which to attract Northern voters increasingly concerned that avenues of economic opportunity and independence were being closed off. By mid-century a majority of the Northern work force was no longer self-employed, and three in five adult white males held no landed property. The economy was generating plenty of wealth, but more and more of it was going to fewer and fewer. Wealth inequality increased markedly during the antebellum period. Whereas the richest ten percent of American families owned about fifty percent of the total wealth in 1800, their share had increased to over seventy percent by 1860. Although the 1850s overall were a decade of prosperity, the real income of workers and farmers was lower at the end of the decade. The cost of living rose twelve percent during the decade, but wages increased by only four percent and the price index of agricultural products fell five percent.

This context of a generalized sense of social and economic malaise both heightened Northern concerns over Southern political power and added to the attractiveness of the Republicans' economic proposals. First, the Republicans personalized the malaise in the symbol of the Slave Power. Then, they offered legislation touted to give all Northerners a fair chance to get ahead. When that legislation was blocked by Southern congressmen, the Republicans could claim that only the greed and corruption of the slave interests stood in the way of economic independence for all white Americans.

The Republicans' legislative program was the political expression of the united front on economic issues that had been forged by the 1850s between the Northeast and the Midwest. Until the railroads linked western farmers to eastern businessmen, western trade was more closely tied to the South then the Northeast. In the 1830s, most western pork, corn, and wheat were shipped southward along the river system of the Mississippi. By the 1850s, that trade had reversed itself in much greater volume, and it went East on a rail system that had no direct North–South connections. This rapidly growing exchange of agricultural and manufactured goods prepared the way for a regional political alliance in the North that backed higher tariffs, free homesteads, agricultural colleges, and transcontinental railroads.

This alliance radically altered the earlier sectional balance of power in which the Northeast, West, and South all vied with each other to secure legislation favorable to their own specialized economic interests. Until the 1850s, the South and the Old Northwest had tended to be allies against the Northeast on the issues of low tariffs and cheap land. Now, and rather suddenly, Southerners broke off that alliance out of their fear that the federal subsidies in the Republican program would speed up the development of a West that was thoroughly committed to free soil. Southern congressmen fell back on their last line of defense for slavery in the Union. They in effect vetoed legislation which they were convinced would only increase the majority power of the free-soil North. In turn, Northerners were ever more likely to interpret each veto as further evidence of a Slave Power conspiracy against the interests of free labor.

The combination of Lecompton and the panic of 1857 gave the Republicans the momentum that carried them to the presidency in 1860. Yet, that same combination also threw up a potentially major roadblock in the path of Republican victory, a new party of conservative Northerners and Southerners that sought to replace the Republicans as the major alternative for anti-Democratic voters. The Opposition party, as it was commonly called, was composed mainly of former Whigs and Know-Nothings from the Upper South. Fillmore, the American party candidate in 1856, had drawn 45 percent of the popular vote in the broad border area stretching from Maryland to Missouri, and his supporters were the backbone of the new party that formed in 1858 and 1859.

Led by John J. Crittenden of Kentucky and John Bell of Tennessee, the Opposition party assailed the Buchanan Democrats on their Lecompton policy and reckless federal spending and endorsed a higher tariff to help workers hurt by the Democratic recession. On state issues the party attacked the Democrats for failing to support internal improvements and reforms in taxation that would benefit the nonslaveholding majority of whites. Most critical to the party's hopes of attracting a national following was its self-proclaimed image as a moderating force that would preserve the Union from the sectional extremism of both the Republicans and the Democrats. On the all important issue of slavery in the territories, the party simply preached obedience to the Constitution and the Supreme Court.

In the state elections of 1859, the Opposition party picked up congressional seats in Kentucky, Tennessee, and North Carolina and ran a close second to Democratic candidates throughout the Upper South. The Republicans were right-fully concerned that the Opposition party would use that strong showing as a springboard to build a national party in 1860 of conservative ex-Whigs. Since the Republicans had to sweep the North in order to win in 1860, such a conservative party could easily cost them the election by depriving the Republicans of just a few Northern states. Thanks to John Brown, however, that conservative party barely got off the ground in the North.

John Brown's raid at Harper's Ferry on the night of October 16, 1859, reversed the recent momentum that sectional conservatives had been developing. In particular, Southern conservatives and moderates were immediately thrown on the defensive, and the hand of Southern radicals was strengthened just as a new Congress was about to meet and plans were being laid for the national nominating conventions in the spring of 1860. By confirming the worst nightmares of Southern whites, John Brown had raised sectional passions to a feverish pitch.

Any publicity that may have eluded Brown over his role in the Pottawatomie massacre was more than made up by the sensationalized notoriety of his raid at Harper's Ferry. This fifty-nine-year-old drifter and loner was the very epitome of the fanatical Yankee abolitionist. A stern, unbending Calvinist, he had convinced himself that he was God's appointed agent for unleashing divine wrath against the sin of slavery. The cause of antislavery became the sole purpose of his life. After leaving Kansas in late 1856, Brown spent the next three years drumming up support for a fantastic scheme. He proposed seizing the federal arsenal at Harper's Ferry, Virginia (now West Virginia), distributing the weapons to his followers, and raising the banner of revolt for slaves, who, presumably, would join Brown's band in launching guerrilla warfare against the slaveholders.

A small group of abolitionists centered in Boston, the Secret Six, funded Brown's scheme. Though hardly representative of all abolitionists in their open espousal of a violent overthrow of slavery, the Secret Six did reflect the growing frustration of abolitionists in the 1850s over such setbacks as the Fugitive Slave Act and the Kansas–Nebraska Act. As the decade progressed, a radical minority of abolitionists grew increasingly shrill in their demands for direct action against slavery. "We must make continual aggressions against slavery; resent its attacks; nay, invade slavery on any suitable occasion, and with any weapons that it is just, manly, and effectual to use,"[15] wrote the Unitarian minister, Theodore Parker, in 1853. Parker, one of the Secret Six, found his weapon of redemptive vengeance in John Brown.

As a military foray to spark slavery uprisings throughout the South, Brown's raid was a miserable, even ludicrous, failure, Brown did not bring along any food for his "army" of nineteen men. He did not reconnoiter the area and, hence, had no escape route. The first fatality was a black baggage master, inadvertently killed by Brown's men. Few, if any, slaves voluntarily joined Brown, who, in any event, had not informed them in advance of his plans. Within thirty-six hours, Brown and his men were surrounded and were either captured or killed by a force of marines commanded by Colonel Robert E. Lee and Lieutenant J. E. B. Stuart.

As pathetic and tragic as the episode turned out, it is easy to forget that Brown, a failure at virtually everything that he ever tried in his life, actually secured his first major objective. He seized the arsenal and the rifle factory and, until the mid-morning of the second day, October 17, had ample opportunity to escape with the weapons up into the mountains. Yet, what did he do? He sat there and did virtually nothing. He sent out parties to seize some hostages and remained immobilized while the trap around him closed. Incredibly, after having first stopped it, he permitted a Baltimore and Ohio express train to pass through in the early hours of October 17. Surely, Brown must have known that news of what he was up to would soon be flashing through the telegraph wires. As for the weapons in his possession, Brown refused to give them to the handful of slaves who had been brought in along with the white hostages. His stated reason was that slaves were too inexperienced with firearms to be entrusted with them. Pikes would be good enough for the slaves, Brown said.

Why then did Brown seize an arsenal to acquire weapons that he had no intention of giving to the slaves? Perhaps, as Governor Henry Wise of Virginia soon came to suspect, Brown intended the rifles for the local nonslaveholders whom he thought would be anxious to go into battle against the slavocracy. Assuming that Brown had any rational plan at all, this one at least helps explain the curious choice of Harper's Ferry for Brown's intended war against slavery. It was in the midst of a mountainous region with very few slaves but a long history of opposition to the domination of the Virginia government by the tidewater aristocracy. If Brown anticipated turning that opposition into pitched warfare against the slave interests, he was dead wrong. Yet, it should be noted, the white mechanics and canal workers in Harper's Ferry, many of whom were from the North, showed no great enthusiasm

The execution of John Brown in December 1859 worsened sectional tensions and created a martyr for the cause of abolitionism.

in crushing Brown and his men. They pretty much stood back and waited for the marines.

Brown's intentions at Harper's Ferry will never be definitively known, and it is tempting to dismiss his sorry performance there as the confused paralysis of an old man who was morally unbalanced, if not clinically insane. Yet, Brown was anything but confused and indecisive in the six weeks between his capture on October 18 and execution on December 2 by Virginia authorities for treason and conspiracy to incite insurrection. He refused to whine or play at being insane. With moral resolve and steadfastness he accepted responsibility for his actions and insisted that it was God's will that his life be sacrificed on the altar of human freedom. Even Governor Wise, Brown's chief adversary and the individual who could have stayed his execution, praised Brown for his sincerity and fortitude. He paid the old man the compliment of seeing that he quickly received the martyrdom he so earnestly wanted.

Although Northern politicians, and most notably the Republicans, scrambled to disassociate themselves from Brown and his actions, Southern whites were outraged by Brown's elevation to martyrdom by the abolitionists and some Northern intellectuals. The Black Republicans, as they were sneeringly called in the South, became even blacker, and Southern radicals had their most convincing evidence yet for the existence of an abolitionist–Republican conspiracy that was as fully frightening to Southern whites as was the Republican imagery of a Slave Power to Northern Whites. John Brown succeeded where Southern radicals had failed. He had popularized the idea of disunion in the South and turned secession from an abstract right to a visceral need for many Southern whites.

The gallows that hanged John Brown were to cast a very long shadow over the election of 1860 and any remaining hopes for sectional harmony.

THE ELECTION OF 1860

John Brown's raid badly shook the psychological self-confidence of Southern whites already bordering on paranoia over their declining political ability to protect slavery within the Union. Panic swept many rural communities, and suspicious outsiders were caught up in a reign of terror. Vigilance committees mobilized and dealt savagely with anyone who failed to proclaim complete support for slavery. Stories of floggings and lynchings filtered North, and when Congress met in December, three days after Brown's execution, Northern congressmen were primed to view their Southern colleagues as a bunch of terrorizing bullies.

Tense, armed to the teeth, and ready to vilify each other's section at the slightest provocation, the representatives in the House engaged in a war of words that paralyzed Congress for close to two months. The Democrats controlled the Senate, but no party had an absolute majority in the House, and a long deadlock developed over the election of the Speaker of the House. Real issues of power were at stake, for the Speaker made all the key committee assignments. Southern honor, however, was also involved. The Republican choice for the speakership, John Sherman of Ohio, had publicly endorsed Hinton R. Helper's *The Impending Crisis of the South* and its mass distribution as a Republican campaign document. Helper, a nonslaveholding white from North Carolina, had written *The Impending Crisis of the South* in 1857 as a scathing indictment of slavery. He blamed slavery for the impoverishment and ignorance of the bulk of Southern whites and urged the nonslaveholders to overthrow an institution that he argued was so clearly against their economic self-interests. Slaveholders denounced Helper as a Southern-born John Brown who fought with a pen rather than iron pikes, and Southern congressmen accused the Republicans of formenting disunion by publicizing his treasonous ideas. Finally, on February 1, 1860, a compromise was reached, and William Pennington, a conservative Republican–Know-Nothing from New Jersey, was elected speaker. Although he had no real qualifications for the post, Pennington was acceptable to both sides given his simultaneous support of both the Fugitive Slave Act and the prohibition of slavery in the territories.

As soon as the House had organized itself with Pennington's election, Senator Jefferson Davis introduced a set of resolutions that defined the strategy of the southern Democrats for their party's national convention in the spring. In what amounted to a sectional manifesto on behalf of Southern rights, Davis reiterated all the constitutional demands for the protection of slavery that were associated with Calhoun's bid in the late 1840s to build a united Southern front. His most controversial resolution called for a federal slave code. Citing the *Dred Scott* decision,

Davis argued that Congress had a positive duty to pass legislation protecting the rights of slavery in the territories whenever those rights were threatened or denied. Here was the South's answer to Douglas' heretical contention that a territorial legislature could prohibit slavery by simply not acting to protect it. And here as well was fair warning that unless Douglas recanted he was to be denied the party's presidential nomination.

As everyone knew, the Davis resolutions had no chance of passing Congress. Their purpose was to convert an extremist Southern rights doctrine into the party orthodoxy of all Democrats and, failing in that, to punish Douglas for abandoning the South on *Dred Scott* and Lecompton. It was this strategy of rule or ruin that southern Democrats would take to their national convention in Charleston, South Carolina.

Meanwhile, the gridlock in congressional politics tightened. The Republicans had a program to promote industrial development and the rights of free labor, but they were continually frustrated by their inability to get their legislature through Congress or past a presidential veto. Buchanan had virtually no domestic program, but he persistently pushed for plans of expansion into Cuba and northern Mexico. These plans raised Southern hopes for new slave areas that were quickly dashed by the resolute opposition of congressional Republicans. Tensions mounted in both sections, and it was an open question whether the election of 1860 would release those tensions or channel them into an explosion that would break up the Union.

As was the custom in antebellum politics, the Democrats were the first party to hold their national nominating convention. By the time they met at Charleston, South Carolina, in April 1860, there was no doubt that a majority of Southern whites felt they had been pushed to the wall by Yankee aggressions and that a minority was prepared to leave the Union if a Republican were elected president in 1860. Democratic politicians in the Lower South spoke for that minority, and they went to Charleston determined to make their last stand on Southern rights. Led by William Lowndes Yancey of Alabama, they demanded that the party endorse a federal slave code in its national platform. If their demand were rejected, they were prepared to bolt the convention.

Acceptance of this demand by Douglas would have destroyed his chances in the North of competing successfully against any Republican nominee in the fall. It also would have shattered the state organizations of the Democrats in the Midwest where the appeal of popular sovereignty was still strong. The Douglas Democrats had a majority of the convention delegates, though not the two-thirds required under party rules to nominate a candidate. They used their majority to turn back the demand for a slave code in the platform, and the delegates from the Lower South walked out.

Was this split of the Democratic party at Charleston, as the Douglas Democrats and moderates from both sections charged, the first step in a plot to break up the Union? Was it an attempt to create a pretext for secession by ensuring the victory of the Republicans, through the destruction of the only national party that stood a chance of defeating the Republican bid for the presidency? For some of the departing delegates and their supporters in the Lower South, the answers were undoubtedly yes. There was a hard-core radical element committed at any cost to securing an independent South. Yet, to label all the bolting delegates as conspiring secessionists is to oversimplify a complex and highly emotional situation in which most of the participants had no idea where their actions would lead. The sectional balance that Calhoun had stressed was the only guarantee of Southern rights in the Union had definitely shifted to the advantage of the free states. There were a number of options that possibly could swing that balance back toward the South. They included pressure on the Northern Democrats to make concessions for the sake of party unity; the creation of a Southern party that might draw enough votes to deprive any party of an electoral majority and thus throw the presidential election into the House, where the South would have more bargaining power; and the threat or reality of secession following a Republican triumph. All these options were open in the spring of 1860, and Southern Democrats were willing to try any or all of them.

Before the fractured Democratic party made separate nominations for the presidency in June, a new Constitutional Union party was formed at Baltimore in early May from a merger of Know-Nothings and die-hard Whigs. Although the party was new, its leadership was decidedly old. Its presidential nominee was John Bell of Tennessee, a lifelong Whig aged sixty-four, and his running mate was Edward Everett of Massachusetts, another Whig who was sixty-seven. The party's chief appeal was among Whigs of Clay's generation in the Border states who desperately wanted to stave off a dissolution of the Union that would find them, quite literally, in the middle of any armed conflict. The party's platform, such as it was, consisted only of a declaration of support for the Union and a love of the Constitution.

Although the party had no chance of winning the presidency, it influenced the outcome of both the Republican and the Democratic conventions. Southern Democrats, recalling the strong challenge of the Opposition party in the Upper South the year before, were more determined than ever not to accept Douglas. His free-soil brand of popular sovereignty was hated by nearly all Southern whites, and the Democrats did not want to give Southern voters an excuse to turn to Bell. Such a defection might well erode the power base of the Democrats in the state governments of the South. As for the Republicans, the Bell–Everett ticket maximized the party's need to find a moderate candidate who could attract the critical Whig–Know-Nothing vote in the lower North.

Meeting in Chicago a week after the Constitutional Unionists had adjourned, the Republicans rejected their pre-convention front runner, Senator Seward of New York, for Abraham Lincoln, a politician who had been out of office for more than a decade. Although shrewd bargaining by his convention managers and the lusty enthusiasm of the local hog-callers who packed the convention hall certainly helped his cause, the case for Lincoln's nomination was compelling enough on its merits.

Unlike Seward, who had coined the unforgettable phrase, "irrepressible conflict," in 1858, Lincoln was not popularly perceived as a radical. Still, Lincoln's antislavery credentials were impeccable. He insisted that Congress could prohibit slavery in the territories, and he never let up on the theme that what distinguished the Republicans as a party was their belief that slavery was wrong. In turn, Lincoln balanced this moral condemnation with an absolute recognition of the constitutional right of slavery to be protected in those states where it already existed. Lincoln detested nativism, but he never permitted himself to become identified, as had Seward, with political assistance to Catholics, especially on the volatile issue of using public funds to support parochial schools. Seward was also hurt by the issue of corruption. If the Republicans were to benefit from this issue, they had to be able to pin it exclusively on the Democrats. A Seward candidacy would have made this unlikely, since his chief political ally, Thurlow Weed, was notorious for running one of the most corrupt party machines in the North. It would have been hard for the Republicans to sell Seward as an "Honest Abe." Last, and most obviously, Lincoln had the best chance of carrying Illinois, a traditionally Democratic state that the Republicans needed to win in the fall.

Lincoln, an ex-Whig, was teamed with Hannibal Hamlin of Maine, an ex-Democrat. They ran on a platform designed to broaden the party's original antislavery appeal. The economic planks—a protective tariff, free homesteads of 160 acres for actual settlers on the land (including unnaturalized immigrants), and a Pacific railroad—promised better times ahead and exploited the lingering discontent in the North after the panic of 1857. Most important, the party reaffirmed its opposition to the spread of slavery into the territories, though in language considerably softened from that used in 1856.

The Douglas men in the rump convention in Charleston were unable to muster the two-thirds vote needed for a Douglas nomination. The convention adjourned and agreed to meet again at Baltimore on June 18. The bolting delegates, having failed to achieve their immediate objective of forcing the convention to nominate a compromise candidate acceptable to the South, now decided to hold a convention of their own at Richmond, Virginia, on June 11. They met, but most of the delegates quickly moved to Baltimore where they demanded to be admitted to the regular Democratic convention. It was Charleston all over again, only this time the split occurred over the seating of rival sets of Douglas and anti-Douglas delegates. This split was permanent. A predominantly Northern group of Democrats nominated Douglas at one convention hall in Baltimore. On the next day and at a different hall, the bolting Democrats nominated John C. Breckinridge of Kentucky, Buchanan's vice president, on a platform that called for a federal slave code.

As confirmed by the final Democratic rupture at Baltimore, the election was going to be a very sectionalized one. Lincoln was not even on the ballot in ten of the slave states. He and Douglas combined received less than fifteen percent of the popular vote in the South. In the North they accounted for nearly ninety percent of the vote. The sectional breakdown of the vote was almost the exact reverse for Breckinridge and Bell: eighty-five percent in the South and barely over ten percent in the North. Breckinridge carried the Lower South; Bell did quite well in the Upper South (Virginia, Kentucky, and Tennessee); and Douglas, the most national of the

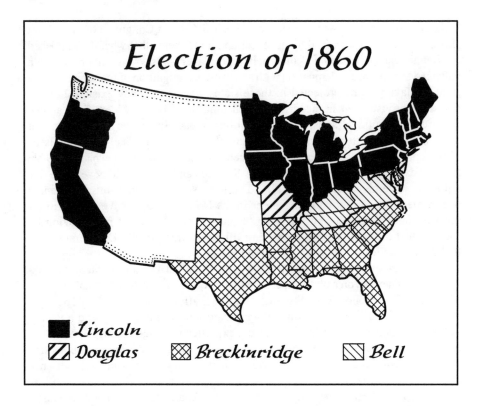

Election of 1860

Lincoln
Douglas   Breckinridge   Bell

candidates measured by the scattered distribution of his vote, won only Missouri and a share of the electoral vote in New Jersey.

Lincoln polled only forty percent of the popular vote, but he had a clear electoral majority because of his virtually clean sweep of the North. The animosity between the Buchanan and Douglas Democrats ran too deep for any effective fusion against Lincoln. Somewhat surprisingly, though, fewer than five percent of Northern voters were attracted to the Constitutional Union party. Northern conservatives were appalled at what John Brown had done, but many of them were nearly as outraged by his quick execution.

As expected, rural and small-town Yankees in New England and the upper Midwest strongly supported Lincoln with over sixty percent of their vote. The crucial returns were from the Mid-Atlantic and lower midwestern states. It was here that the election was won. In 1856, Frémont had carried only 43 percent of the vote in these states. Lincoln, by running exceptionally well among new, younger voters and cutting heavily into the former Know-Nothing party vote, gained a majority of fifty-three percent. Lincoln won the election where Frémont had lost it.

Republicans were overjoyed. The Slave Power had been met and defeated. Speaking for the party as a whole once the returns were in, William Cullen Bryant, a Republican editor, rejoiced to a friend that "the cause of justice and liberty has triumphed in the late election." He then added, "I am sorry, on their own account, that the people of South Carolina are making so much fuss about their defeat, but I have not the least apprehension that any thing serious will result from it."[16]

Bryant, of course, could hardly have more misread what was going on in South Carolina after Lincoln's election. Often threatened in the South, and just as often scoffed at in the North, secession was about to become a reality.

NOTES

1. Martin Van Buren to Moses Tilden, September 1, 1856, in John Bigelow (ed.), *Letters and Literary Memorials of Samuel J. Tilden,* vol. 1 (New York: Harper & Brothers, 1908), pp. 119–120.
2. *Charles Sumner: His Complete Works,* vol 4 (New York: Negro Universities Press, 1969 [1900]), pp. 262–263.
3. Quoted in Stephen E. Maizlish, "The Meaning of Nativism and the Crisis of the Union," in Stephen E. Maizlish and John J. Kushma (eds.), *Essays on American Antebellum Politics, 1840–1860* (College Station: Texas A & M University Press, 1982), p. 180.
4. Roy P. Basler (ed.), *The Collected Works of Abraham Lincoln,* vol. 2 (New Brunswick: Rutgers University Press, 1953), p. 323.
5. The speech is reproduced in *Charles Sumner: His Complete Works,* vol. 5, pp. 137–249, the source for all the quoted passages from the speech.
6. Richmond *Enquirer,* June 12, 1856, in *Charles Sumner: His Complete Works,* vol. 5, p. 279.
7. New York *Evening Post,* May 23, 1856, quoted in William E. Gienapp, "The Crime Against Sumner: The Caning of Charles Sumner and the Rise of the Republican Party," *Civil War History,* vol. 25, p. 232, 1979.
8. *Congressional Globe,* 35 Congress, 1 session, p. 941.
9. Basler, vol. 2, p. 467.
10. Ibid., vol. 2, p. 492.
11. Ibid., vol. 2, pp. 461–462.
12. Ibid., vol. 3, p. 29.
13. William H. Keim, quoted in Bruce Collins, "The Democrats' Loss of Pennsylvania in 1858," *Pennsylvania Magazine of History and Biography,* vol. 109, p. 522, 1958.
14. *Lebanon (Pa.) Courier,* May 3, 1860, quoted in James L. Huston, "A Political Response to Industrialism: The Republican Embrace of Protectionist Labor Doctrines," *Journal of American History,* vol. 70, p. 53, 1983.
15. Quoted in Michael Fellman, "Theodore Parker and the Abolitionist Role in the 1850s," *Journal of American History,* vol. 61, p. 675, 1974.
16. William Cullen Bryant III and Thomas G. Voss (eds.), *The Letters of William Cullen Bryant,* vol. 4 (New York: Fordham University Press, 1984), p. 185.

SUGGESTED READINGS

BORITT, G. S., *Lincoln and the Economics of the American Dream*. Memphis, Tenn.: Memphis State University Press, 1978.

CRAVEN, AVERY O., *The Growth of Southern Nationalism, 1848–1861*. Baton Rouge, La.: Louisiana State University Press, 1953.

CRENSHAW, OLLINGER, *The Slave States in the Presidential Election of 1860*. Gloucester, Mass.: Peter Smith, 1964.

DAVIS, DAVID BRION, *The Slave Power Conspiracy and the Paranoid Style*. Baton Rouge, La.: Louisiana State University Press, 1969.

DONALD, DAVID, *Charles Sumner and the Coming of the Civil War*. New York: Alfred A. Knopf, 1960.

FEHRENBACKER, DON E., *The Dred Scott Case*. New York: Oxford University Press, 1978.

FONER, ERIC, *Free Soil, Free Labor, Free Men*. New York: Oxford University Press, 1970.

GIENAPP, WILLIAM E., *The Origins of the Republican Party, 1852–1856*. New York: Oxford University Press, 1987.

HUSTON, JAMES L., *The Panic of 1857 and the Coming of the Civil War*. Baton Rouge, La.: Louisiana State University Press, 1987.

KLEIN, PHILIP SHRIVER, *President James Buchanan*. University Park, Pa.: Pennsylvania State University Press, 1962.

NEVINS, ALLAN, *Ordeal of the Union*. 2 vols. New York: Scribner, 1947.

NICHOLS, ROY F., *The Disruption of American Democracy*. New York: Macmillan, 1948.

OATES, STEPHEN B., *To Purge the Land with Blood: A Biography of John Brown*. New York: Harper and Row, 1970.

RAWLEY, JAMES A., *Race and Politics: "Bleeding Kansas" and the Coming of the Civil War*. Philadelphia, Pa.: J. B. Lippincott, 1969.

SEWELL, RICHARD H., *Ballots for Freedom: Antislavery Politics in the United States, 1837–1860*. New York: Oxford University Press, 1976.

SOLTOW, LEE, *Men and Wealth in the United States, 1850–1870*. New Haven, Conn.: Yale University Press, 1975.

SUMMERS, MARK W., *The Plundering Generation: Corruption and the Crisis of the Union, 1849–1861*. New York: Oxford University Press, 1987.

4

The Old
South and
Secession

"The crisis *must* come; and it seems to me there can never be a time more favorable than the present. Certainly, I shudder at the *possible* consequences; but if we seek to avoid them, at the expense of principle, we shall only prepare a worst crisis for our prosperity."[1] Thus did Lydia Maria Child, an abolitionist, steel herself in early January 1861 against any last-ditch compromise to keep Southern states within the Union during the secession winter of 1860–1861. For Child, and nearly all Republicans, talk of secession was one gigantic bluff, a desperate attempt by Southern hotheads to rob antislavery Northerners of the victory they had fairly won with Lincoln's election. "Rather than submit to another dishonorable *compromise*," thundered the Indianapolis *Indiana American,* "we would prefer to settle the question of equal rights by the sword if need be. If a fear of secession—rebellion, TREASON is to overawe us forever, then we are not freemen."[2]

Many Southern whites were equally loathe to hear any talk of compromise during the secession crisis. Rather than submitting to Lincoln's election, the *Independent South* in Waynesboro, Georgia, raged:

> Sooner let devastation and ruin spread over all the land—sooner endure bankruptcy with its disastrous consequences[,] aye rather *welcome* the bloodiest civil and most deadly internecine warfare than hear even, much less obey, the injunctions of base submissionists—the fears of dastardly and craven-hearted cowards....[3]

In the Lower South the mere fact of Lincoln's election was viewed as an overt act of aggression against Southern interests and honor that freemen could resist only by withdrawing their states from the Union.

These were the conflicting sectional attitudes that shaped the events that destroyed the antebellum Union within six months of Lincoln's election. However much most Southern whites feared and hated Lincoln, they would have agreed with him that "The tug has to come, & better now, then any time hereafter."[4] Secession occurred in two distinct waves. In reaction to Lincoln's election, seven states in the Lower South seceded between December 20, 1860, and February 1, 1861. Delegates from these states met at Montgomery, Alabama, on February 4, 1861, and created the Provisional Government of the Confederate States of America. In the meantime, voters in the Upper South rejected secession. The four states from the Upper South that joined the Confederacy did so in the spring of 1861 only after the firing on Fort Sumter and Lincoln's subsequent call for troops to put down the rebellion. At that point, the choice was no longer Union or disunion but rather one of fighting for or against fellow Southerners.

In addition to examining the sequence and process of secession, this chapter will present a framework for understanding why secession occurred when and how it did. Slavery, as the Confederate vice president, Alexander Stephens, put it, was the "cornerstone" of the Confederacy, and particular attention will be paid to the fears of the secessionists that the institution was threatened both from inside and outside the South. Convinced that they faced a dual threat to their power, slaveholders reacted by using the external threat of the hostile Republicans in the North to neutralize the internal threat of declining support for slavery within the South. An independent Southern nation, so hoped the secessionists, would unite all Southern whites behind the institution that the Confederacy was created to defend.

SLAVERY AND THE ROOTS OF SECESSION

No white Americans were more aware of the blunt realities of power than slaveholders. Their economic success depended on the power to control slaves through physical coercion; their social standing rested on honor, the power to command respect from others; and their political achievements were tied to their ability to portray themselves as the defenders of the personal liberties of all Southern whites from the power of tyrannical institutions and outsiders. By the same token, no class of white Americans more passionately feared the loss of power, for such a loss entailed nothing less than the degradation and humiliation of the black slaves, the presence of whom was a daily reminder of the horrors of powerlessness. Whether viewed as the basis of class position, the source of wealth, the means of racial control, or the symbol to whites of what it meant to be unfree, slavery was at the very core of Southern society and politics.

The Old South was not simply a society with slaves. It was a slave society, and the centrality of slavery to the Southern experience explains why contemporar-

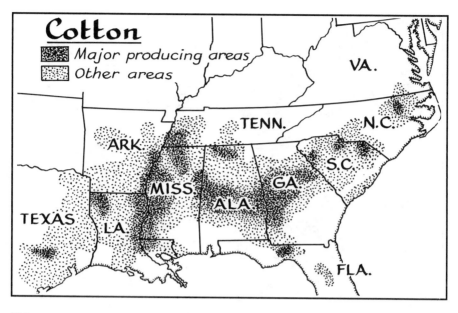

Major cotton-producing areas in the South in 1860.

ies and later historians often take the liberty of speaking of a "South." In fact, there were many Souths, and the geographic and social diversity of the region ranged from the near-subsistence lifestyle of a nonslaveholding family occupying a cabin in the Appalachian mountains to the lavish consumption of a planter's family living in an elegant mansion on the banks of the Mississippi. There were broad plantation belts with large concentrations of slaves where agricultural staples—tobacco, rice, sugar, and above all, cotton—were produced for world markets. In the pine barrens close to the coast and throughout the broad sweep of the Appalachian Highlands bisecting the interior of the South on an axis running from Virginia to Alabama, slaves were comparatively few; here, localized economies rested on the cultivation of foodstuffs, notably corn, and on the herding of livestock, especially the hogs that wandered at will in an open range. In these areas, and throughout the rural South, most nonslaveholders were not shiftless poor whites, as depicted by the abolitionists and Republicans, but rather small farmers who owned their own land.

Each state, as well as the South as a whole, was divided into regional economies with different crop specializations. In terms of value, though certainly not income generated by export sales, corn was the South's leading crop. The planters felt superior to many of the nonslaveholding poor, and they in turn resented the pretensions and arrogance of the planters. A wealthy planter in the lowcountry had more in common with the cultural values and standards of the Northern merchants who marketed his crops than he did with those of the local swamp-dwellers who were trafficking in stolen goods with his slaves.

Still, with the exception of the mountainous areas with their short growing

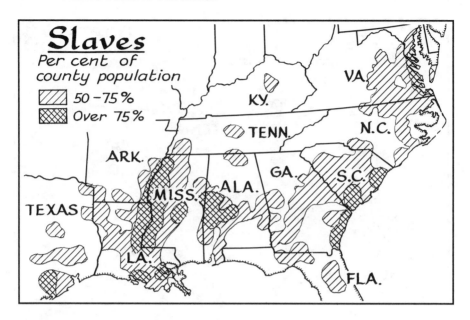

Slaves by percentage of county population in 1860.

seasons, cotton could be grown profitably virtually anywhere in the rural South, and the spread of cotton cultivation based on slave labor stamped much of the South in a common mold. The wide-scale presence of slaves, the wealth they produced, and the need of Southern whites to defend slavery as both an economic system of profits and a racial system of control from outside attacks did result, after all, in a region with sufficient unity to justify speaking of a South.

Contrary to the impression left by Northern and foreign critics, the economic benefits of slaveownership among whites were rather widely distributed. Throughout most of the antebellum period, about one in three Southern white families owned slaves, and they could expect to earn an annual return of eight to ten percent on their slave investment. The per capita wealth (including slaves) of Southern whites in 1860 was twice that of Northerners. The profits of Southern slavery were at least as high as Northern returns on capital, and the percentage of Southern families owning slaves in 1850 was over ten times greater than the percentage of American families owning corporate stock of an equivalent value a century later.

At the apex of the slaveholding pyramid, and the preeminent symbol of the wealth and power of the South, were the very wealthy planters owning forty or more slaves. Though representing but one percent of Southern white families in 1860, these planters owned nearly one-third of all the slaves. Just over ten percent of the remaining slaveholders were small planters owning twenty to thirty-nine slaves. Thus, about ninety percent of the slaveholders fell short of the planter class, and fully half of them owned only five or fewer slaves. However, despite the marked concentration of slaves in large holdings, a very broad range of white Southerners—small farmers, tradespeople, and professionals—were able to own slaves. A numerous, but unquantifiable, number of whites also rented out slaves on a seasonal basis. Thus, perhaps close to half of all white families had a tangible economic stake in slavery at some time or other in the middle of the nineteenth century. In addition, bonds of kinship, a common status as landowning farmers, and, above all, a shared and fervid commitment to maintaining white supremacy by keeping the blacks enslaved, tied many of the nonslaveholders to the slaveholders in a defense of the South's defining institution.

Slaves were found in all walks of Southern life; about one in ten were used in artisan or manufacturing work, but over half of the enslaved population was concentrated on plantation units with twenty or more slaves. Thus, although nearly three-fourths of slaveowners held fewer than ten slaves, most of the slaves were grouped together in relatively large units. The enslaved were neither the helpless, brutalized victims of Southern immorality, as depicted by the abolitionists, nor the happy, carefree children of Southern benevolence, as portrayed by the proslavery apologists. Instead, the slaves were a people in their own right with their own values and strengths. The need for self-survival taught blacks how to suppress their rage at being enslaved, but they simultaneously learned how to build a cultural world that enabled them to preserve their sense of human dignity and freedom.

As a result of the closing of the African slave trade in 1808, the vast majority of American slaves were native-born by midcentury. The slaves were not Africans; they were Afro-Americans. They spoke a common language, shared a common fate, and had a common self-interest in resisting an enslavement they were powerless to prevent. The culture they fashioned provided them with a means of resistance by sustaining their uniqueness as a people and their passionate belief that someday they would be free.

The core institution of the slave community was the family, and the family in turn was embedded in a network of overlapping kin relationships that had thickened after 1808 with the steady growth of a native-born population of blacks grouped together on plantations for the production of agricultural staples. Most slaves lived in family units in a social setting where most of their contacts were with fellow blacks and where blood relations were close by for mutual support. Slave marriages were not recognized in Southern law, though most planters encouraged them, if for no other reason than to promote an increase of their capital investment in human property. Close to one-third of slave marriages were broken up, usually by the sale or forced removal of the husband or father. Nonetheless, the slave family was amazingly resilient. Two-thirds of these families were headed by both parents. Apart from meeting deeply human needs for companionship, slave families did result in lasting, loving commitments that nurtured and socialized slave children as human beings in a system that legally treated them as chattel. Indicative of the strength of the slave family were the speed with which the freed slaves legalized their marriages after the war and the anguish with which they searched for loved ones separated from them under slavery.

In their music, folklore, and religion, the slaves expressed their yearning for freedom and belief in ultimate deliverance. The beat of their drums, the rhythms of their dances, and the chants of their spirituals were alien, even frightening, to whites because they were living reminders of an African heritage that was beyond the power of masters to eradicate. This heritage sustained a black pride in their separateness from whites, and, when fused with American Christianity, gave the slaves a strong spiritual sense of themselves as human beings. The slave religion the masters tried to foster was one of submission and docility. The religion fashioned by the slaves for themselves was one of liberation and pride. Jesus was a Moses-like figure for the slaves, and, for them, He had not forgotten His people.

The daily, inescapable reality of life for most slaves was hard, physical labor from sunup to sundown. Avoiding as much of this labor as possible was the most common means of slave resistance. The careless, shiftless, and seemingly slow-witted slave was a constant source of frustration and anger for the slaveowners. To be sure, some slaves did produce superior work, especially skilled craftsmen who were

One of the most important tasks of slaves on a plantation was the preparation of cotton for ginning.

permitted to hire out their time and retain some of their wages, but, in general, the slaves were not steady, efficient workers. After all, their labor and its rewards belonged not to them but to their masters. Thus, the crack of the whip, both the symbol and the reality of the master's legal monopoly on physical tyranny, was commonplace on the plantations of even the most benevolent owners. Slavery rested on fear and physical coercion. Even masters who promoted better work by offering incentives—easier jobs, extra rations, and perhaps some cash payments—readily admitted that only the fear of the whip kept most slaves in line.

In addition to stealing food and goods from the masters that they morally regarded as partly theirs by virtue of their uncompensated labor, blacks frequently resisted their enslavement by running away for a few days. Although these runaways were punished upon their return, they were now often able to bargain for concessions from the master in return for agreeing to work faithfully in the future. The chances of a permanent escape from the slave South were quite remote because of the surveillance of slave patrols and the necessity of slaves to have a written pass for travel beyond their home plantations. On an annual basis, fewer than 1,000 slaves (out of a slave population in excess of 3 million by the 1850s) succeeded in fleeing the South and making it to the Northern states or Canada. Contrary to the abolitionist-inspired legend of the Underground Railroad spiriting slaves away to freedom, fugitive slaves most likely would have been aided along the way by fellow blacks and not by friendly whites.

Throughout the antebellum years the slave population remained at about thirty-five percent of the total Southern population. Outnumbered two-to-one by whites, who, of course, also had all the firearms, the slaves were unable to mount successful, large-scale rebellions. Significantly, their attempts to do so fell off when the supply of young, African-born male slaves, always those most prone to rebel, was cut off with the end of the African slave trade.

There were three major attempts at open rebellion in the nineteenth century. The first two—Gabriel Prosser's rebellion in Richmond in 1800 and an extensive plot known as the Denmark Vesey affair in Charleston, South Carolina, in 1822— were betrayed and smashed before they got much beyond the planning stage. The third was led by Nat Turner, a slave preacher. Nat Turner's rebellion in Southampton County, Virginia, resulted in the butchering of about 60 whites in August 1831 before the rebels were in turn butchered or executed by the white authorities. About 200 slaves were killed.

Whites throughout the South lived in dread of a slave rebellion after the Turner uprising, and this revolt, coming in the midst of the emergence of an abolitionist movement in the North, was a key factor in both the softening and the tightening of late antebellum slavery. Many planters now tried to improve the living conditions of their slaves, and the material standards of slave life did rise after 1830 in terms of diet, clothing, and housing. To be sure, the slaves still had a lower life expectancy and significantly higher infant mortality rates than whites. Their basic food ration of cornmeal and fatty pork was nutritionally deficient, they had to make do on two suits of clothes per year, and they were forced to cram families of five or six into a slave cabin measuring about 15 square feet. Nonetheless, after 1810, the general health of slaves in the South was adequate enough to support a population increase by natural reproduction that was just below the levels reached by the white population.

After the Turner rebellion, masters also grew more conscious of the need to attend to slave needs in the areas of marriage, religion, and family rights. By mid-century, Southern legislatures had set down and enforced minimum legal safeguards for slaves accused of a crime or victimized by whites (though slaves could never testify in court against a white person). All the while, planters began to refer to slavery in paternalistic terms that portrayed the institution as part of the master's extended family of wife, children, and kin. Rarely heard in the eighteenth century, this language of paternalism held that the master, no less than the slave, was obligated to a mutual set of duties and responsibilities.

The planters hoped that the material amelioration of slavery would reduce the likelihood of a slave uprising, and, apart from enhancing their self-esteem as Christian masters, their ideological domestication of slavery into a family affair was also designed to deflect abolitionist criticisms. This softening of slavery, however, was simultaneously accompanied by a tightening of the controls necessary for the preservation of slavery. In the wake of the Turner insurrection, Southern law made it increasingly difficult for a master to free a slave through an act of manumission. Other laws prohibited teaching slaves to read or write. Free blacks, about five percent of the total black population in the South, were hemmed in by growing restrictions on their movement and rights of free assembly. Slave patrols were strengthened, and any criticism of slavery on any grounds was now likely to be violently suppressed by a mob of frightened white vigilantes. In short, the defense of slavery increasingly dominated the concerns of Southern whites, and that defense stood at the center of Southern politics.

Southern politicians erected many defenses for slavery, and they adjusted their arguments to meet new lines of attack on the institution. They were resourceful and resilient, but each position of defense was beset with its own contradictions that became more glaring as the antebellum period progressed. Finally, in opting for secession, the slaveholders admitted their belief that slavery could no longer be protected within the Union.

The first line of defense was political and constitutional, and it was written into the Constitution. Southerners constantly emphasized that slavery was the only property specifically recognized in the Constitution, and, through the three-fifths clause, the only property that was actually represented in Congress and the electoral college. The Constitution, Southerners insisted, created a federal union of co-equal states, not a unitary nation–state. The individual states had never relinquished their sovereign powers but had only transferred to the federal government certain limited and defined powers, they believed, and the states retained their sovereign right to decide on the constitutionality of any federal laws and, if necessary to protect the rights of their citizens, to reclaim their full sovereignty and withdraw from the Union. According to this compact theory of the Union, citizens were never the direct subjects of the federal government: They were equal co-partners in a government formed for their own use, and they had every right, indeed the duty, to resist any federal actions that deprived them of their individual freedoms.

For all the skill and tenacity with which Southerners threw up constitutional safeguards around slavery, the success of these efforts ultimately depended upon a sectional balance of power. Such an equilibrium had existed when the Union was formed. By the 1840s, and as Calhoun repeatedly warned, the growing population and industrial base of the free states had upset that equilibrium. Beginning with Iowa in 1846, the last five states that entered the antebellum Union were all free. On the eve of secession, the North outnumbered the South by three-to-two in total population and by better than two-to-one in free population. Frustrated by the continual dominance of the federal government by the South in the 1850s, Northerners demanded that their rights as the political majority be recognized. Those demands, especially when accompanied by bellicose free-labor rhetoric, convinced many Southerners that a new political tyranny, that of King Numbers, was about to breach the constitutional defenses for slavery.

Just as menacing to Southerners as the sheer numbers that bolstered the political power of the free states was the developing sense of nationalism in the North. Americans had always taken an immense pride in their country as the world's greatest republic of free men, and the Puritans had bequeathed the notion of America as the new Israel of God's chosen people. Nationalism existed in the early republic, but it grew primarily out of attachments to particular localities or states. The nation as something more than a collection of local identities had to await the communications and transportation revolutions of the second quarter of the nineteenth century. As electronic and steam technology shrank distances, it enlarged markets and the vision of what America could be. The social and economic basis of nationalism, the functional interdependence of individuals tied to a network of spreading market relations, was in place by midcentury.

Market relations were much more pervasive in the North than the South, and the pace of industrialization, urbanization, and public education, all indicators of a process of mass socialization in which cultural norms were gradually becoming more homogenized, was more rapid in the North. Consequently, the vast majority of Southern whites throughout the antebellum period continued to live in isolation on scattered farms and plantations. They remained locked into local subcultures regulated by face-to-face encounters and the values of blood, race, and honor.

Most Southern whites were yeomen, farmers who owned few, if any, slaves. They grew no cotton, or only a few bales. Rather than risk financial ruin by going in debt to purchase the slaves needed to expand production, they chose instead to preserve their economic independence by using their family labor to produce food crops. On the other hand, planters were the most involved of all Americans in the market economy at the point of production. However, there was a fundamental difference between their participation and that of Northerners.

The expansion of market production in the free states necessitated a transformation of the social relations of work through the substitution of wage labor outside the home for work previously performed in the household by family members or in the artisan shop under the personal supervision of the master craftsman. No such transformation occurred in the South. Market production could be expanded without a shift to wage labor because of the presence of slave labor. Market demand for Southern staples simply reinforced and froze into place the prior social relations of slave labor. Plantations and their surrounding rural areas approximated self-suffi-cient economic units, and this in turn helped perpetuate the cultural localism of Southern whites. Because they saw little need for the social and economic services that a centralized government can provide, Southerners rejected the growing eco-nomic nationalism of Northerners as a dangerous intrusion into the rights of the states.

Even more frightening to Southern whites was the emerging sense of moral nationalism in the North. This nationalism was implicit in the abolitionist demand for a common labor system based upon freedom. It was also nourished by the Northern evangelical vision of America as a redeemer nation whose history was the unfolding of God's plan for universal freedom and progress. The goal of this nationalism was a morally homogeneous America with a single standard of freedom and legal equality for all its citizens. Religious in its origins, this nationalism had a secular version for which the Republicans were the spokesmen. As expressed in an 1855 resolution passed by the party in Wisconsin, "the fundamental principles of the Republican party are based upon the equal rights of all men;...these principles are utterly hostile to the proscription of any on account of birth place, religion, or color."[5] To be sure, the Republicans often failed to live up to these ideals, but this declaration of America's moral purpose was very appealing to those Northerners who believed that the market economy had freed all men from personal dependency upon others and had thus made possible the self-governance on which freedom and prosperity were based.

Such a vision of America could be nothing less than horrifying to Southern whites. They found the very talk of legal equality for blacks to be morally offensive and a threat to their personal safety. Their America presupposed the existence of divergent moral principles and the unqualified right of local majorities to enforce those principles. Thus, it was no coincidence that abolitionism and nationalism were linked in the minds of Southern whites. For Jefferson Davis, the very source of abolitionism was the "political heresy that ours is a union of the people, the formation of a nation, and a supreme government charged with providing for the general welfare."[6]

Even when Southerners granted the religious source of abolitionism, they denied that it had any scriptural validity. Southern churches had always been defenders of slavery. Radical antislavery evangelicals in the Upper South were the major exception, but they were effectively silenced or driven out in the conservative reaction that set in after Nat Turner's slave uprising of 1831. Their silencing marked a critical stage in the evolution of Southern evangelicanism. Originally a backwoods phenomenon associated with poor farmers who attacked planters for their arrogant greed, unrepublican luxury, and un-Christian domination of fellow human beings, evangelicalism by the 1830s was the dominant form of religious expression in the South. In particular, the slaveholders were converted. The persecuted outsiders on the Virginia frontier of the 1770s were now the cultural and social insiders for the South as a whole. Evangelicalism became respectable, and it lost its antislavery edge.

In reaction to the abolitionist onslaught of the 1830s, proslavery Christianity became more pronounced and articulate. Southern evangelicals did more than simply reject the abolitionist view that slaveholding was a sin. In contradistinction to Northern evangelicals, Southern theologians, ministers, and lay Christians renounced any notions of universal rights and social perfection. Reflecting and confirming the inequality within Southern society, they pointed to the patriarchal authority of the husband over his wife, his children, and his slaves as the model of subordination upon which all Christian societies should rest. They argued that civilized societies were grounded in the servitude of the laboring classes. Rather than degrading white laborers by forcing them to perform menial work for a capitalist master, Southerners were said to be blessed with an institution that uplifted and civilized inferior African savages created by God to perform useful labor for white masters. While clothing the world in cheap cotton goods, slavery was spreading Christianity among heathen Africans. In a phrase, slavery was a positive good.

Proslavery Southerners might as well have been shouting in the wind for all the impact they had on public opinion in the North and the Western world at large. Once wage labor had replaced various forms of bound labor as the norm in Western societies (Russian serfdom was the major exception), ethical and moral appeals on behalf of slavery were doomed to failure. Free labor had assumed the moral high ground, and selective proslavery quotations from the Bible could not dislodge it. Most Northerners reacted with a mixture of anger and pity at the religious defense of slavery, and, in a defeat for slavery that must have been particularly galling to Southern church leaders, black abolitionists in Britain succeeded by the 1850s in having slaveholders barred from international religious conventions.

The religious case for slavery undoubtedly strengthened the commitment to slavery of all Southern whites who craved social stability. Yet, the argument for slavery as a positive good remained localized among the older, conservative elites along the Atlantic seaboard. Most Southern whites continued to view slavery as a necessary evil, and they justified it on grounds of alleged racial inferiority. As a Southern highlander told Frederick Law Olmsted, a Northern observer, in the 1850s, "there's hardly any one here that do n't think slavery's a curse to our country, or who would n't be glad to get rid of it."[7] That highlander personally disapproved of slavery, but, like nearly all Southern whites, he simply could not conceive of living in a society with a large free black population. Blacks were naturally lazy, it was held, and hence would be unable to support themselves when freed. With no master to take care of them, so the argument went, they would become vagabonds plundering and stealing from whites, and, even worse, as natural brutes unable to control their passions, they would lust after white women, and panic-stricken white males would have to exterminate them in order to save their wives and daughters from unspeakable degradation. There was no middle ground between slavery and bloody social chaos.

Claims of black inferiority had always been crucial to the defense of slavery. Until the 1830s, however, those claims were largely based on environmental factors. The debilitating tropical heat and supposed barbarism of life in Africa, combined with the obvious impediments of slavery itself, allegedly made blacks clearly inferior to whites in intelligence and ambition. By the 1850s, a full-blown theory of the inherently biological inferiority of blacks had developed. In part this shift in racial thinking was a response to the abolitionist challenge. If environmental factors explained the sorry condition of blacks, then the more temperate climate of America and the incentives for self-improvement held out by freedom would surely enable blacks to realize their God-given capacity of competing equally with whites. Defenders of slavery had to deny the basic premise of this emancipationist argument, and they turned to the theory of innate black inferiority to do so.

Another factor also influenced their thinking. White demands for political equality intensified in the South after the War of 1812. The newer slave states in the Old Southwest had constitutions as democratic as any in the Union, and in the 1820s and 1830s the call for democratization spread to the older and more politically conservative slave states in the Southeast. Nonslaveholders pressured planters to drop property qualifications for voting and officeholding and to equalize representation so that slave districts were not overweighted in the apportionment of legislative seats. Fearful of dropping these property defenses for slavery and thus entrusting the institution to the political good will of the nonslaveholding majority, the planters fought a rearguard action. They gradually and grudgingly conceded greater political liberalization, and they simultaneously reemphasized the racial defense of slavery. If all whites agreed that blacks must be assigned a position of permanent inferiority that could be guaranteed only by slavery, then planters could more easily contain any democratic challenge to the institution.

The racial defense of slavery was the standard one, and it seemed to meet the needs of slaveholders. Not only did it give nonslaveholding Southern whites a social stake in the institution, it also appealed to the racist strain that dominated the thinking of most white Americans regarding blacks. The condition of free blacks in the North was deplorable. Subjected to discriminatory legislation and the racial contempt of whites, they were trapped in poverty and could work at only the most menial jobs. With the exception of Massachusetts, rigid racial segregation was the rule throughout the North, and many midwestern states had black codes denying entry to free blacks unless they posted a bond for "good behavior." Unable to vote, serve on juries, or send their children to the public schools, blacks outside of New England were legally treated as distinctly inferior citizens.

What greater proof could there be, railed Southerners, of the utter hypocrisy of antislavery Northerners? Blacks in the North were treated as pariahs and had the freedom only to starve. Though less than two percent of the total population, they were feared and loathed by Northern whites. Southern blacks were housed, clothed, fed, cared for in old age, and paternalistically treated as dependent children. With arguments such as these, Southerners tried to absolve themselves of any guilt over slavery and turn the tables on their Yankee tormentors.

For all its persuasiveness in an American culture that was, after all, profoundly racist, the racial defense of slavery failed to reverse the growing commitment of the Republicans to racial equality, in and of itself an insufferable threat to slavery. The Republicans were decidedly not racial egalitarians in the modern meaning of the term. Very few Republicans favored complete social and political equality for blacks, and most probably agreed with Lincoln that colonization abroad offered blacks their only chance of escaping the intractable hostility of white Americans. Nonetheless, most Republicans did believe in the principle of equality before the law, one of the cardinal tenets of the liberal nation–state, and in the equal right of blacks to enjoy the rewards of their own labor. Moreover, they were far more likely than Democrats to support black suffrage. Republicans were predominately rural, native-born, and relatively prosperous Yankees. Secure in their status and immune from any practical threat of economic competition from blacks, they could support black suffrage without any sense of endangering their own social position. Whereas rural Republicans disliked blacks, poor, foreign-born Democrats in Northern cities viscerally hated them. These Democrats were the butt of the nativist backlash against immigrants and the bitter rivals of blacks for the lowest paying jobs. They feared that any step toward racial equality would erode the status they desperately valued as the racial superiors of blacks and hasten the day that they would lose their jobs to former slaves.

While northern Democrats fully supported the racial defense of slavery, the Republicans turned the logic of that defense inside out. As had the abolitionists before them, the Republicans stressed that even if the claim of black inferiority were true, this was scarcely a justification for enslaving them. To the contrary, they felt that it was all the more reason why the blacks should be freed and assisted by the stronger race to improve themselves and that any civilized society should be ashamed of invoking the law of the jungle to enslave the weak and the inferior. Besides, added the Republicans, slavery was polluting the very racial purity that Southern whites boasted it was defending. Racially mixed slaves could be found on every plantation, and at least ten percent of all slaves by 1860 were mulattoes.

Within the South, nonslaveholders accepted the racial defense of slavery so literally that the use of race to defend slavery had the ironic consequence of weakening the institution: If whites were the master race, then why should they have to compete against blacks, either as free men or slaves, for skilled jobs? Why should a planter even be permitted to teach his slaves the mechanical arts and thus take jobs away from white workers? Should not all remunerative labor outside the plantations be legally reserved only for whites? The very logic of the racial defense of slavery raised such questions, and that same logic posited that the demands of whites as a race should supersede the property interests of slaveholders as a class.

By the 1850s the bonds of white solidarity were cracking in Southern cities. Working-class immigrants were now the principal source of free labor in all the important port cities of the South. Even in the more isolated interior towns, they comprised about forty percent of the free work force. Compared to the North, the South received few immigrants, but they settled overwhelmingly in the cities where they could find work. At the same time, strong cotton prices in the 1850s created a rural demand for labor that pulled slaves out of the cities. The result was a striking demographic shift that, in the ten largest Southern cities, saw the slave population decrease by twelve percent and the immigrant population increase by seventy-six percent during the 1850s.

Slaveholders were understandably alarmed by this shift. Urban manufacturers and businessmen were becoming increasingly dependent upon a labor source of dubious political loyalty to the slaveholding regime. Although these workers were as racist as they could be, their demands for protection against slave labor inevitably impinged upon the rights of the slaveholders to the most profitable use of their property. Planters reacted by denouncing the workers as proto-abolitionists who would soon be raising the cry of labor versus capital. The Southern commitment to white democracy left the slaveholders powerless to deal with this threat of internal subversion by depriving white workers of the vote. Thus, the planters sought to minimize the threat by increasing the supply of slave labor. Some wanted to reenslave free blacks, but this would likely only drive free blacks out of the South and magnify the economic importance of immigrant labor. Others opted for a reopening of the African slave trade, a move that would flood the South with cheap labor and give workers an opportunity to acquire a direct economic stake in slavery.

The drive to reopen the African slave trade in the 1850s was intended to shore up the defense of slavery among both rural and urban Southerners. The issue was immensely divisive within the South itself and was cited by outsiders as further evidence of the South's moral depravity. By turning to this desperate expedient, the proponents of reopening the trade were virtually admitting that the economic defense of slavery had failed.

Ever since Nat Turner's rebellion of 1831 had sparked a remarkable debate in the Virginia legislature over slavery, proslavery ideologues realized that the defense of slavery ultimately had to rest on economic grounds. The opponents of slavery in the Virginia debate of 1831–1832 failed to push through a program of gradual emancipation, but their economic arguments on behalf of western farmers and eastern workers put the planters on the defensive and foreshadowed the Republicans' free-labor critique of slavery in the 1850s. At the core of this attack upon slavery was the charge that the institution was an economic curse on the nonslaveholding majority of Southern whites. They were unable to compete against planters for the best land. Deprived of employment by slave competition and taught that honest labor itself was shameful, they were, concluded these critics, forced to live out their lives in poverty and ignorance.

This was a powerful argument because it was aimed directly at the economic self-interests of the Southern political majority. It was made even all the more persuasive because the free-labor North stood as the model of a society that could confer greater material benefits on its citizens. The problem that Northern progress posed for the defense of slavery was cogently laid out by J. H. Taylor of South Carolina in 1850. After warning that the nonslaveholding poor had the vote and the political power to dismantle slavery, Taylor argued that appeals to white supremacy alone could not protect the institution.

> So long as these poor but industrious people could see no mode of living except by a degrading operation of work with the negro on the plantation, they were content to endure life in its most discouraging form, satisfied that they were *above* the slave, though faring often worse than he. But the progress of the world is "onward"...and the great mass of our poor white population begin to understand that they have rights....*It is this great upbearing of our masses that we are to fear, so far as our institutions are concerned.*[8]

In an effort to prevent that "upbearing," slaveholders fashioned an economic defense of slavery that promised all Southern whites freedom from the degradation of menial labor. It was this defense that explains why such a political champion of nonslaveholders as Andrew Johnson of Tennessee was a strong advocate of slavery. Slavery was an economic blessing to whites, Johnson insisted, and "I wish to God every head of a family in the United States had one [slave] to take the drudgery and menial service off his family."[9] Inequality, not equality, he thought, was the basic human condition, and far better that blacks, an inferior race, worked for whites than the degrading Northern spectacle of whites being forced to perform menial tasks for other whites. Thanks to slavery, argued Johnson, even common whites in the South could aspire to relief from mindless toil and enjoy a life of leisure.

This defense of slavery enabled hill-country Southern politicians to portray themselves as being both against the aristocratic pretensions of planters and in favor of slavery. Moreover, the argument that the ownership of just one slave could lighten the backbreaking load of farm labor did appeal to most slaveholders, three-fourths of whom owned fewer than ten slaves. However, in pushing this defense of the institution, slaveholders inevitably denigrated the labor of the majority of Southern whites who in fact did have to engage in physical labor. When Senator James Hammond of South Carolina delivered his highly publicized "mud-sill" speech in 1858, a speech in which he stigmatized free laborers in the North as white slaves whose physical toil was the foundation, or mudsill, for all the refinements of Northern society, he was immediately reprimanded by Johnson of Tennessee. How, asked Johnson, could the planters expect to retain the political support of nonslaveholders if they were insultingly labeled as slaves because they had to work with their hands? In scoring debating points for slavery against the North, Hammond was undercutting support for slavery within the South.

The economic defense of slavery created an inescapable dilemma, and there was only one way out. Nonslaveholders had to be assured that their "demeaning" labor was temporary. They needed incentives to work like "slaves" so that they soon could become masters and enjoy the leisure of the slaveholding class. Their chances of doing so, however, were sharply curtailed in the 1850s. High cotton prices during the decade increased the demand for slave labor. Slave prices nearly doubled, and, by 1859, a prime male field hand was worth about $1700 ($15,000 to $20,000 in current dollars). More and more Southern whites could not afford to purchase a slave, and during the 1850s the proportion of Southern families owning slaves fell sharply from thirty-one percent to twenty-five percent.

In an effort to reverse this politically alarming trend, proslavery ideologues agitated to reopen the African slave trade and thereby drive down slave prices and increase slave ownership. Yet, in trying to salvage an economic defense of slavery directed at nonslaveholders, they threatened the economic self-interest of all Southern whites who already owned slaves. A flood of cheap African imports would decrease the value of all slave property within the South. In addition, cheap labor would erode the wages of free white labor and further impoverish the non-slaveholders who already lacked the income to buy a slave.

Most Southern whites opposed the reopening of the African slave trade on both economic and moral grounds. Agitation over the issue succeeded only in dramatizing the dilemmas inherent in any concerted effort to fashion a defense of slavery. In the end, and as slaveholders had known from the beginning, the defense of slavery boiled down to a question of power. For this reason, Lincoln's election was guaranteed to produce a crisis within the South. A party that did not even legally exist in most of the slave states had captured the presidency. Slaveholders would not have been true to their class had they reacted with anything but a sense of enraged impotency.

SECESSION IN THE LOWER SOUTH

Lincoln's election triggered a secession movement in the Lower South that broke up the Union with astonishing speed. The actual mechanics of secession were fairly straightforward. State legislatures issued calls for special elections to elect delegates to conventions that would consider the question of secession. The calls went out, the elections were quickly held, pro-secession delegates were chosen, and the conventions individually withdrew their states from the Union. Within six weeks of South Carolina having kicked off secession on December 20, 1860, six other states in the Lower South left the Union in the following order: Mississippi, Florida, Alabama, Georgia, Louisiana, and Texas. Meeting at Montgomery, Alabama, in February 1861, delegates from the seven seceded states drafted a constitution for an independent Southern government and selected Jefferson Davis as its president. All this took place before Lincoln was even sworn in as president of the now divided United States.

Secession happened very fast and seemingly was very popular. At the seven state conventions, the average vote of the delegates in favor of secession was in excess of eighty percent. In short, secession seemed to have all the hallmarks of a popular revolution. That was certainly how secessionists portrayed the movement. It was 1776 all over again, they claimed, and true patriots had to live up to the memory of their illustrious forefathers and strike another blow for individual liberties against external tyranny. Lincoln and the Republicans replaced George

III and the British as the despotic tyrants, South Carolina emulated Massachusetts in launching the revolution, and another generation of patriots was about to be sired.

The invocation of the sacred American Revolution was a brilliant political stroke by the secessionists. It instantly legitimated their actions and cast them in the roles of innocent defenders of threatened Southern liberties. It also provided a rhetorical mask for the very real divisions over secession that existed even within the Lower South. Southern whites were nearly unanimous in their belief that Lincoln's election was an unconscionable insult and a provocative act that had to be resisted. Differences existed, however, over the means of that resistance.

Conditional Unionists, a very small minority in the Lower South, argued that the Union was now on trial. They conceded that Southern rights were clearly endangered but believed the South risked nothing vital by temporarily remaining within the Union on the condition that the Lincoln administration take no hostile steps against slavery. In the meantime, they insisted that additional demands guaranteeing the safety of slavery should be drawn up. The acceptance or rejection of these demands could then serve as a test of Republican intentions. Cooperationists more openly advocated secession but only in the form of a united Southern action. In unity was strength, they argued, and Southern rights could best be protected by a collective response that still might force the North to accede to Southern demands. Most radical of all were the immediate secessionists. The crisis was at hand, they cried, and any further delay would only strengthen the hand of the Republicans in crushing Southern liberties. They denounced the cooperationists as cowardly submissionists and insisted that individual states had to take the lead in leaving the Union.

Although the immediate secessionists had a clear majority only in South Carolina, they determined the political fate of the Lower South during the secession winter. They had several advantages over their more conservative opponents that they exploited to the utmost. Most of the immediate secessionists were Breckinridge Democrats. Throughout the presidential campaign of 1860 they had proclaimed the necessity for secession in the event of a Republican triumph. More important, the Breckinridge Democrats could back up their words. As the majority party in the Lower South, they controlled editorial opinion, the governorships, and the machinery of local politics. Thus, as soon as Lincoln's election was official, they were in a position to mobilize and direct public opinion. There was no delay in launching secession, and moderates and conservatives were immediately placed on the defensive.

Speed, as the secessionists well knew, was of the essence in winning support for secession. Any delay would cool the feverish sense of apprehension that had gripped the South during the presidential campaign. Wild stories of abolitionist plots and slave conspiracies swept the South, and many communities were close to emotional hysteria. Vigilance committees and roving mobs terrorized anyone suspected of abolitionist sympathies or, in what amounted to the same thing, disloyalty to the South. John Brown may have been dead, but the memory of what he had tried to do at Harper's Ferry in 1859 was still a living nightmare to Southern whites.

This hysteria, much of which was whipped up by the Breckinridge press, was a great asset to the secessionists. Southern whites were psychologically prepared for the worst in the aftermath of Lincoln's election, and the secessionists told them that the worst would soon happen unless they immediately withdrew from the Union. They charged that Lincoln and the other Black Republicans would forment slave uprisings, and no whites would be safe. Any one who dared to say otherwise was intimidated into silence by the "Minute Men" and other paramilitary groups organized by the secessionists to promote the cause of Southern independence.

By moving quickly the secessionists were also able to take advantage of the *de facto* vacuum of power that existed in the nation's capital. Until the 20th Amendment of 1933 moved the presidential inauguration up to January 20, the Constitution provided for a four-month period between the presidential election in early November and the inauguration in early March. Buchanan, a lame-duck president working with an outgoing Congress, still held the office, but he had lost the popular mandate to rule. Lincoln now had that mandate but no official power with which to exercise it. The confusion and uncertainty that reigned in Washington played right into the hands of the secessionists.

Finally, a speedy withdrawal from the Union would render irrelevant the most telling argument of the Southern opponents of immediate secession. Ironically, Lincoln's election had actually strengthened the bargaining position of the slave states within the federal government. The Republicans were a new and untested coalition that controlled neither Congress nor the Supreme Court. If they wanted to rule effectively, instead of just engaging in moral posturing, they would need the cooperation of Southern politicians both in Washington and within the slave states, where the Republicans had no organizational means of dispensing federal patronage. The Republicans would be under intense pressure to make concessions to the South, and their refusal to yield to that pressure could well brand them as disunionists who should be thrown out of office.

The longer that secession was talked about and not acted on, the greater was the likelihood that Southern public opinion would swing around to the position that the Republicans could be checkmated. Aware that time was on the side of their opponents, the secessionists moved before their opposition could organize and popularize the idea that the Republicans posed no immediate threat to Southern interests. The South Carolina legislature provided the model for this strategy of precipitate action with its decision on November 10, 1860, to hold elections within six weeks for a secession convention. The only state that still chose its presidential electors by the vote of its legislature, South Carolina was in the perfect position to launch secession since its legislature had assembled just before Lincoln's election in order to cast the state's electoral ballots.

The secessionists in the deep South never lost the momentum they had seized within days of Lincoln's election. Political common sense and cool logic favored their opponents, but the secessionists had the incalculable advantage of an ideological appeal based on phrases and symbols that evoked the most deeply held values of Southern whites. Southern manhood demanded an immediate, public defiance of any act or gesture that threatened independence and honor. Only cowards forever shamed by their slavish servility would refuse to act now, shouted the secessionists. They claimed that the Republicans denied Southern equality within the Union and would send abolitionist-fiends to arm the slaves for the rape and murder of Southern white women. Anything short of a manly assertion of Southern rights through the act of secession, concluded the secessionists, would only embolden the Black Republicans to treat Southern whites more contemptuously in the future.

Honor was closely attached to equality in the value structure of Southern white males, and both were directly related to the existence of black slavery. The presence of slaves exemplified for whites the horror of losing their honor and independence. And slaves, they thought, by performing the subservient tasks suited to their "inferior" condition, made equality possible among whites. "Where Capital rules, where there are no black slaves," explained B. F. Rice, a South Carolina secessionist, "there must be white ones. No Southern born [white] man would brush the boots...of his extortionate Master."[10] By portraying the Republicans as those "Masters" who would force Southern whites into the slavish dependency of wage labor, the secessionists were able to broaden their appeal to include all Southern whites who felt threatened by the economic changes within their own society.

Throughout the cotton South in the 1850s, and especially in areas opened up for cotton production and plantation agriculture by railroads, the number of farms was declining and the yeomen's share of the local wealth was dropping. Wage labor for whites was increasing within the South and, by the logic of their own belief system, whites were becoming slaves. The resultant tensions had produced the abortive effort to reopen the African slave trade, and those tensions had to be deflected onto outsiders if the shrinking minority of slaveholders was to maintain political control. The secessionists accomplished this by using the Republicans as a symbol for all the threatening changes brought about in reality by the economic consolidation of the slave system. The Republicans became, in secessionist rhetoric, the party of the factory owners and the aristocratic capitalists intent on economically enslaving Southern nonslaveholders. Most tellingly, the Republicans were depicted as the party that had blocked upward mobility for Southern whites. By keeping slavery out of the territories, the Republicans were accused of having deprived needy Southern whites of their chance to make a fresh start with a few slaves on western lands.

Now that the Republicans were about to assume control of the federal government, the secessionists insisted that the plight of nonslaveholders would dramatically worsen. According to the secessionists, slavery would be doomed under a Republican administration and economic opportunities would be closed off for common whites. Even if the Republicans refrained from fomenting slave revolts, their policy of containing slavery within its present limits presumably would deny the institution the room that it needed to prosper and survive. Then, argued the secessionists, whites would be hemmed into a confined space with a hostile and growing population of slaves. Within a generation, plantation lands would lose their fertility, slave labor would become unprofitable, and wealthy whites would flee the South to avoid the horrible consequences of the inevitable breakdown in racial controls. The remaining whites, those too poor to escape, would then be forced to wage to the death a war of racial extermination. All the while, warned the secessionists, this terrifying scenario would be speeded along by traitorous Southern whites who joined the Republican party after being corrupted by offers of federal patronage. With its will to resist sapped from within, the South would be an easy prey for any abolitionist schemes of the Republicans.

Who but a coward unworthy of his Southern heritage could counsel delay and patience when the South was faced with such future horrors under Republican rule, as depicted by the secessionists? Conditional Unionists and cooperationists had no effective response to this incessant charge of the secessionists, who pitched much of their appeal at this level of raw emotions. When added to their organizational weaknesses, this emotional handicap ensured the defeat of the opponents of immediate secession.

Despite all of the advantages enjoyed by the secessionists in the Lower South, their margin of victory in the elections for convention delegates was surprisingly thin. With the exception of South Carolina, the cooperationists polled about forty percent of the vote. In Georgia, Alabama, and Louisiana, they ran in a virtual dead heat with the secessionists. Also surprising, given the momentous issues involved, was the extent of voter apathy. Compared with the November presidential election, voter turnout was down by more than one-third. Hasty and sporadic campaigning, the running of uncontested delegates in some counties, the refusal of many candidates to take a clear-cut position, and the absence of traditional party labels undoubtedly accounted for much of this drop off. In addition, many Whig conservatives boycotted the elections out of fear of reprisals if they publicly opposed secession. Nonetheless, the secessionists had to be concerned that their crusade for Southern rights had not generated a stronger showing of direct political support.

If anything, the secessionists had pushed too hard and too fast. The upcountry yeomanry, the backbone of the Democratic party in the Lower South, deserted the Breckinridge–secessionists camp for the cooperationists. To be sure, many of these cooperationist yeomanry did ultimately favor secession, but they had not yet decided to go out, and they opposed the precipitate action of the slaveholder-dominated secessionists. In turn, the secessionists doubted the commitment of the yeomanry to Southern independence. After the cooperationist delegates agreed to vote for secession as a sign of Southern unity, the secession conventions pointedly refused to submit the question of secession to popular ratification. Texas was the lone exception, but by that time the Confederacy was being organized and the result was a foregone conclusion.

Slaveholders took the Lower South out of the Union. Four out of five counties in which slaves comprised a majority of the population backed immediate secession. Conversely, support for secession was weakest in the counties with the fewest slaves. The balance between secessionists and cooperationists was close enough for events in Washington to have influenced the outcome of their struggle. During a critical three-week span from mid-December to early January, six states held their elections for the secession conventions. Had a compromise package been worked out in Congress, the cooperationist leaders of the hill country and mountain yeomanry might well have gained the leverage they needed to break the momentum of the immediate secessionists. The absence of such a compromise gave the secessionists their final, and perhaps most significant, advantage.

Tired, discredited, and with such a literalist view of the Constitution that he argued simultaneously for the illegality of secession and the powerlessness of his office to prevent it, President Buchanan was in no position to offer decisive leadership. He felt that secession was the Republicans' problem; after all, their ceaseless agitation of the slavery issue had brought on the whole crisis. Unfortunately, Buchanan left exactly that impression in his annual message of December 3, 1860. By openly sympathizing with the South and blaming support for secession upon Northern interference with slavery, he forfeited whatever chance he might have had for acting as a sectional compromiser. His only proposal for dealing with the crisis was a call for a constitutional convention that he recommended should yield to all Southern demands on slavery, including the right of slavery to move into the federal territories. When that call was rejected, Buchanan's policy was a negative one of doing nothing to provoke a confrontation with any of the slave states. He desperately wanted to avoid a civil war and hold together as much of the

The secession crisis destroyed the political career of President Buchanan. Here, he is depicted as the cowardly watchdog of American liberties who ran away while the secessionist wolf culled out seven states from the Unionist flock.

Union as he could before the Republicans would have to deal with the problem upon Lincoln's inauguration.

Any resolution of the secession crisis would have to come out of Congress when it assembled in early December, and here, of course, the Republicans were the key. No compromise could arrest secession unless the Republicans strongly favored it. Yet, the Republicans were in no mood to compromise. Initially, they denied that there was any real crisis that required a compromise between the sections. Typical of the party's reading of the early stages of secession was the response of the Boston *Daily Atlas and Bee*. Let "a few hot-headed fanatics" rant and rave about secession, editorialized the paper on November 12. "There is in this nothing new, unexpected, or alarming. The truth is, the slave states have neither the right, the power, nor the inclination to secede—therefore they will not."[11]

When evidence mounted that at least South Carolina was dead serious about secession, Republican businessmen with close economic ties with the South joined with Northern Democrats in pressuring Lincoln and congressional Republicans to offer a compromise to the South. Still, the Republicans were adamant.

Republicans viewed secession as the dying gasp of the Slave Power recklessly trying to bully the Republicans into giving up the electoral prize they had just won. The most immediate fear of Lincoln and other party leaders was not the breakup of the Union but the destruction of the Republican party. The plain truth, as the Republicans saw it, was that any compromise on the expansion of slavery accept-able to the secessionists would involve a surrender of the very heart and soul of the Republican party, which was its opposition to the spread of slavery. In editorials, public meetings, and private correspondence, rank-and-file Republicans implored their leaders not to yield the great unifying principle of their party. If they cave in now, William Cullen Bryant warned Lincoln on Christmas day, 1860, "the Repub-lican party is annihilated."[12] Lincoln hardly needed any convincing. Two weeks earlier, when rumors of compromise first swept through Congress, Lincoln made it clear that the party had to stand firm. "Entertain no proposition for a compromise in regard to the *extension* of slavery," he instructed an Illinois congressman. "The instant you do, they have us under again; all our labor is lost, and sooner or later must be done over."[13]

In late December, Congress debated a compromise of sorts. The House had appointed a Committee of Thirty-Three (a member from each state) and the Senate a Committee of Thirteen, and it was this latter committee which offered a specific plan to save the Union. The Crittenden Compromise, named after Senator John J. Crittenden of Kentucky, the so-called heir to Henry Clay, was an omnibus package of six constitutional amendments and four resolutions.

In effect, the Crittenden Compromise followed Buchanan's advice of making major concessions to the South. Constitutional guarantees were to be given that the federal government could not interfere with the interstate slave trade or with slavery in the District of Columbia and any federal installations within the South. Slave-holders were to be indemnified for any fugitive slaves who were unrecoverable because of Northern defiance of the Fugitive Slave Act. The federal government was to be prohibited from ever moving against slavery in the states, and this guarantee could never be revoked by any future amendment. To the Republicans all of these amendments were highly objectionable but potentially negotiable. The one amendment they absolutely rejected was the key to the whole compromise package, which was an extension of the old Missouri Compromise line of 36°30′ to the Pacific. Slavery was to be recognized and protected south of 36°30′ in all federal territories "now held, or hereafter acquired." This amendment, like all the rest, could not be altered by any future amendments.

Taking their cue from Lincoln, congressional Republicans unanimously rejected the extension of the Missouri Compromise line. As long as slavery was confined to its present limits, the Republicans were convinced that the institution would wither and die. Just as important, Southerners agreed. Both sides also agreed that future American expansion was inevitable. Thus, the Republicans felt they had to slam shut the door to slavery's expansion or else the South would take advantage of the "hereafter acquired" clause in the Crittenden proposal and carve out a new empire for slavery in Mexico, the Caribbean, and Central America. The Republicans would not yield on the principle that defined them as a party and, as they put it, mortgage America's future to the Slave Power. Nor would they abandon their followers. For some Republicans, restricting slavery was a constitutional means toward the moral goal of ultimately destroying a sinful institution. For others, and probably the majority, restriction primarily served the economic self-interests of free labor. As one Philadelphia Republican aptly put it: "It is not a question of abolitionism in our section but a question whether the working and industrious classes shall have the repelling institution of slavery to compete with in the territories[.]"[14]

The Republicans killed the Crittenden Compromise and thereby eliminated any chance of stopping and then reversing secession in the Lower South. Of course, this consequence of the Republicans' action is much clearer in retrospect than it was at the time. There was no guarantee that the secessionists would call a halt or return to the Union on the basis of the Crittenden Compromise. Still, that is just what the most committed secessionists feared would happen. Throughout December and on into January, when most of the secession elections were held, the leaders of secession worried that all but the most fervid Southern radicals could still be enticed back into the Union or refrained from leaving by a Republican concession on the expansion of slavery.

This issue of expansion was, as it had always been, the nub of the sectional controversy. Whether measured in political, economic, social, or moral terms, the expansion or restriction of slavery was at the center of the power confrontation between the free and slave states. Slaveholders were hardly so foolhardy as to imagine that they could long retain their power within the South, let alone the Union, if the institution that was the basis of their wealth and status was confined to its limits of 1860. Even if the present generation of Southern whites remained loyal to slavery, a restriction on its growth meant that in the future the bulk of Southern whites inevitably would have to define opportunity in terms of free-labor principles.

Moving into the territories with a few slaves had been the traditional safety valve of the Southern yeomanry throughout the antebellum period. If such movement were shut off, and slave prices remained beyond the reach of most nonslaveholders, the yeomen would either leave the South and swell the ranks of the free-soil majority in the North or stay behind as a growing source of recruits for a Southern free-soil party.

Slaveholders in the Lower South had to look no farther than the Upper South for ominous signs of what happened to slavery when it was no longer a dynamic economic institution. Throughout the border region from Maryland to Missouri, political support for slavery was eroding. Most critically, it was here that the momentum for secession was broken. In February 1861, the voters in the Upper South rejected secession, and the crisis of the Union entered a new phase.

STALEMATE IN THE UPPER SOUTH

Southern radicals had long feared that the Upper South would be untrustworthy in any general crisis affecting slavery. They correctly sensed that in the Border South slavery was becoming an expedient, and thereby expendable, institution. The census figures bore them out. Eight of the fifteen slave states hung back from immediate secession. In these states, slavery lacked the overwhelming importance that it had in the Lower South as both an economic investment and a means of racial control. Slaveholders in the Upper South comprised twenty percent of all white families, and slaves were twenty-four percent of the population. In the seven states that made up the original Confederacy, these percentages were twice as high. More significantly, slavery was in decline throughout the Border South which abutted the free states. In all of these five states—Delaware, Maryland, Virginia, Kentucky, and Missouri—the percentage of slaves in the total population had dropped between 1830 and 1860. It was not a coincidence that these were the slave states in which the Republicans were on the ballot in 1860.

Time was working against slavery in the Upper South, and the trend was unmistakable. Only in Arkansas, a state whose southeastern section along the Mississippi offered planters a new frontier for plantation agriculture, and in eastern North Carolina, a region where new rail communications set off a boom in cotton production, was slavery still a thriving institution by the 1850s. In most of North Carolina and Tennessee, slavery was more or less holding its own. Elsewhere, along the entire northern rim of the South, slavery was giving way to free labor. The implications were obvious. "Those border States can get along without slavery," said Senator Alfred Iveson of Georgia during the secession crisis. "Their soil and climate are appropriate to white labor; they can live and flourish without African slavery; but the cotton States cannot."[15]

Iveson was right. With an intensity that picked up considerably in the 1850s, two ethical and economic systems were vying for supremacy in the Border South. One was based on slave labor and the other on free labor. Slavery was gradually losing out because as a system of organizing production it was incompatible with major structural changes that were occurring in the economy of the Upper South after 1820. Wheat was replacing or competing with tobacco as the region's major cash crop, and urban economies were shifting to manufacturing. Both of these shifts put slavery at a competitive disadvantage against free labor.

Unlike tobacco, wheat did not require the nearly continuous attention of a labor force. Cheap, seasonal labor, hired for wages at harvest time, met the needs of farmers or planters who were increasing wheat production in order to profit from the growing urban demand for foodstuffs in the lower North. Within the cities of the Border South, slaves were too expensive and too few in number to service the need of urban manufacturers for a cheap and abundant labor force that could be hired or fired at a moment's notice. Urban slavery weakened throughout the South after 1820, but the decline was sharpest in those cities in the border region that were experiencing a rapid growth in manufacturing underwritten by a heavy influx of foreign immigrants. St. Louis, Baltimore, and Louisville—all in the Border South— were the three leading manufacturing cities in the South as of 1860. Slaves comprised a miniscule one percent of the population in the first two of these cities and only seven percent in Louisville. To be sure, slaves could be and were profitably employed in Southern factories. Nonetheless, in most instances, urban manufacturers clearly favored immigrant over slave labor because of its cheapness and easy availability.

Economically, as well as geographically, the Border South was caught in the middle between the North and the South. The demand in the Lower South for slaves provided a major market for the sale of slaves from the Upper South. Profits from these sales in turn financed the agricultural diversification and industrialization that were slowly integrating the economies of the Border states into those of the Ohio valley and Mid-Atlantic regions. The result was a complex political economy that simultaneously generated support for and against slavery.

In general, Democrats in the Upper South represented planting interests who turned to states' rights as a bulwark against economic changes that were undermining popular support for slavery. The Whigs favored these changes but argued that economic diversification would protect slavery by freeing the South from its galling dependence on the North for manufactured goods. Yet, diversification was producing just the antislavery consequences that the Democrats had predicted. Under the leadership of Frank P. Blair, Jr., in St. Louis and John Minor Botts in Richmond, the Republicans were beginning to attract a working-class following. Although there was no immediate likelihood of emancipation, agitation for it had started in the cities. A wealthy class of businessmen with no direct ties to plantation agriculture was emerging, wage laborers were developing a class consciousness, and farmers were learning that they did not need slave labor in order to produce cash crops. These groups, when added to the subsistence farmers in the mountains who had long resented planter rule, were more than sufficient to block secession in the Upper South.

Unlike the Lower South, where the need to protect slavery had submerged all other issues and produced a one-party system in the 1850s, the Upper South still had competitive two-party politics at the time of Lincoln's election. This party competition was grounded in the region's more diverse economy and pluralistic social structure, and it offered voters in the Upper South a meaningful alternative to the extreme Southern rights' stance of the Democratic party. Thus, whereas Bell and Douglas had carried only forty-four percent of the popular vote in the Lower South, they won fifty-seven percent of the vote in the Upper South. This majority coalition, supported by local party organizations of Whigs that were much stronger than any still found in the Deep South, defeated the secessionists in the February elections of 1861.

Political sentiment in the Upper South during the secession crisis divided into three main camps. At the extremes were the immediate secessionists, slaveholders who had voted for Breckinridge, and the out-and-out Unionists, mostly isolated farmers in the mountain districts and antislavery urban mechanics. In the middle and attracting the most followers were the Conditional Unionists, the group that best captured the ambivalence of a region torn between ties to Northern markets and a free-labor economy on the one hand and still strong commitments to slavery as a way of life on the other.

The Conditional Unionists argued convincingly against joining the Confederacy of slave states then being formed. They declared that the Confederacy would be committed to free trade, cheap slaves, and an expansion of slave territory and that all of these policies would work against the economic interests of the Border South. Free trade would retard or destroy its promising beginnings in manufacturing, and cheap slaves, perhaps gained through a reopening of the African slave trade, would eliminate most of its profits in the interstate slave trade and so depress the wages of labor in the Upper South as to turn all white workers against slavery. They reasoned that the Confederacy would have to enlarge its slave empire so as to ensure the South's monopoly on the world's supply of cotton, and that this would benefit chiefly young planters in the Lower South. Meanwhile, land prices in the Upper South would plunge as whites left to settle in the new slave territories. Most tellingly, the Conditional Unionists insisted that secession would most likely lead to a war with the free states, a war in which the Upper South would suffer the most because of its central location. The federal government, they felt, heretofore a great defender of slavery, would destroy the institution before it conceded defeat in such a war.

Just as convincingly, the Conditional Unionists argued that the South required additional guarantees for its slave property were it to remain in a Union now headed by a Black Republican. These guarantees were written into the Crittenden Compromise. Although the Republicans defeated that compromise as an omnibus package, they absolutely rejected only the provision for the extension of the Missouri Compromise line. On all the other separate points of the compromise, the Republicans indicated a willingness to negotiate. The Republicans were pursuing a subtle strategy, and it worked well enough to strengthen the hand of the antisecessionists during the crucial month of February when the secession elections were held in the Upper South.

Throughout February, congressional Republicans encouraged moderates and conservatives in the Upper South to believe that the party was on the verge of making major concessions to the slave states. Prodded by Senator Seward, most Republicans agreed to at least formally support the so-called Peace Convention called by the Virginia legislature to meet in Washington in early February. Boycotted by some of the Northern states and all of the states that had already seceded, and dominated by elderly politicians whom no one took seriously as power brokers between the sections, the Convention was an exercise in futility. After three weeks of debate, the Convention finally approved an altered version of the Crittenden Compromise. Under the Convention plan, the extension of the 36°30′ line would apply only to territory then held by the United States, and a majority of senators from both the free and slave states would have to approve the acquisition of any new territories. Hours before Lincoln's inauguration, this plan, as well as the Crittenden Compromise, was voted down in the Senate, primarily because of Republican opposition. Although the Peace Convention accomplished nothing, it bought the Republicans a precious month of time during which the mere discussion of a possible sectional compromise helped stem the secessionist tide in the Upper South.

Before Congress adjourned in early March, the Republicans also made apparently conciliatory gestures regarding the territories. Three new territories—Dakota, Colorado, and Nevada—were organized without any reference to slavery. Technically, the status of slavery in these territories would be governed by the popular sovereignty clause in the Kansas–Nebraska Act. Douglas publicly claimed that he was finally vindicated, but the Republicans were little concerned. They would be appointing the territorial officers, and there was no chance of slavery moving into the territories.

In a potentially more significant concession, the House Committee of Thirty-Three, at the urging of a Republican, Charles Francis Adams of Massachusetts, sponsored a bill admitting New Mexico nominally as a slave state. The territorial legislature of New Mexico had passed a slave code, and a few slaves were in the territory (which included the present state of Arizona). Once again, however, the Republicans were yielding more in theory than in fact. They had received assurance that slavery would never flourish in New Mexico, and they fully expected the settlers to amend their state constitution and prohibit slavery.

The purpose of these Republican maneuvers was to drive a wedge between the Upper and Lower South. Border-state Southerners were offered concrete proof that the Republicans were not extremists on the slavery issue, and the secessionists in the Deep South could now be branded as the true extremists forced to admit that they would settle for nothing less than guarantees for the expansion of slavery into *future* territories. The strategy worked. More precisely, the Republicans held out the possibility of New Mexico as a slave state until the secession elections were over in the Upper South. Then, in late February, the Republicans killed the statehood proposal.

In the end, the Republicans made only one significant concession. Thomas

Corwin of Ohio, the Republican chairman of the House Committee of Thirty-Three, proposed a 13th amendment to the Constitution that would have forever prohibited the federal government from abolishing or in any way interfering with slavery in the states. The amendment had Lincoln's approval. Although most Republicans opposed such an ironclad guarantee for slavery, enough of them voted for it, about forty percent, to enable the amendment to pass both Houses of Congress by early March with the two-thirds majority required for its submission to the states for possible ratification.

This amendment came far too late to act as a moderating influence against secession in the Lower South, and it is very doubtful that it could have derailed secession even had it been passed in December before South Carolina decided to leave the Union. As the Southern radicals were acutely aware, the threat to slavery in the states came not only from outside the South, but from inside as well. To counter this internal threat, the secessionists were committed to building a white consensus behind an independent South that would have the freedom to acquire more slave territory to promote economic opportunities for the growing majority of nonslaveholders. For the states still wavering between secession and the Union, however, the amendment did serve a definite purpose. It helped hold the Upper South within the Union by strengthening the case of the Unionists that the Republicans could be entrusted, at least temporarily, with control of the federal government.

By the time of Lincoln's inauguration, many Republicans hoped that the worst of the secession crisis was over. Their belief in the Slave Power led them to the natural conclusion that secession was the product of a slaveholders' conspiracy. A fanatical minority had undemocratically driven the Lower South out of the Union and then had overextended itself in the Upper South where it met defeat, they felt. From these premises, it was easy enough to conclude that a Unionist majority controlled the Upper South and that a latent Unionist majority was still waiting to be mobilized on behalf of the Union in the Lower South. In short, secession had burned itself out, and a peaceful reunion was still a distinct possibility.

No Republican argued this position more forcefully than did William Seward, Lincoln's choice for secretary of state and the dominant influence on Lincoln's thinking through most of March. Seward's strategy, dubbed the policy of "masterly inactivity," sought above all to buy the time needed by Southern Unionists to begin the expected process of voluntary reunion. For that Unionist reaction to set in, and Seward estimated it would take no more than three months, the new Republican administration had to follow a middle road between acceptance of secession and forced reunion. Thus, Seward counseled Lincoln to uphold the utter permanency of the Union and simultaneously avoid any coercive action that might stampede the Upper South into joining the Confederacy. This was the position that Lincoln outlined in his Inaugural Address.

In this address, his first public statement on policy since his election, Lincoln revealed his political skill at holding in abeyance several possible courses of action while waiting for circumstances to dictate what course should be followed. The address balanced an aggressive assertion of the indivisibility of the Union with a defensive statement of the steps he would take to ensure that indivisibility. Although he assured Southerners that they had nothing to fear from his administration and indicated his willingness to support the recently proposed 13th amendment guaranteeing federal noninterference with slavery in the states, he flatly denied the constitutionality of secession and declared it "the essence of anarchy." He pledged to defend the Union and enforce all of its laws, but, in the most critical passage of the address, he maintained that:

> In doing this there needs to be no bloodshed or violence; and there shall be none, unless it be forced upon the national authority. The power confided to me, will be used to hold, occupy, and possess the property, and places belonging to the government, and to collect the duties and imposts; but beyond what may be necessary for these objects, there will be no invasion—no using of force against, or among the people anywhere.[16]

Here was a proposed course of action that pleased or displeased Americans of all political persuasions, depending on the intentions they read into Lincoln's carefully phrased ambiguity over just how and when he planned to uphold federal authority.

Lincoln was willing to prolong the stalemate that had existed between the Union and the Confederacy since early February in order to give Seward's plan of voluntary reunion time to unfold. The day after his inauguration, however, Lincoln received news from the federal garrison at Fort Sumter, South Carolina, that forced him to rethink just how long he could put off a confrontation with the Confederacy over the enforcement of federal authority. Within six weeks, such a confrontation erupted over Fort Sumter, and it destroyed any lingering hopes of a peaceful reunion.

THE FORT SUMTER CRISIS

On March 5, Lincoln learned from Major Robert Anderson, the commander at Fort Sumter, that dwindling food supplies would force an evacuation of the fort within four to six weeks. By a process of elimination, Fort Sumter had become a powerful symbol of federal resolve in dealing with secession. On setting up their own state governments, the secessionists had seized federal property and installations throughout the Lower South. With the exception of two isolated forts in the Florida Keys, only two forts were still in federal possession at the end of the Buchanan presidency: Fort Pickens in Pensacola harbor and Fort Sumter in Charleston harbor. Of these two, Fort Pickens was strategically more defensible and politically less explosive. Attention focused on Fort Sumter because South Carolinians loudly insisted that federal control of the fort was an insufferable affront to their sovereignty as an independent republic. South Carolina militia and shore batteries had opened fire on the *Star of the West,* a relief ship sent by Buchanan in early January, and a civil war was averted at that point only because Anderson, lacking explicit orders to do so, did not return the fire. Anxious to avoid a war before a new

Confederate government could be organized, secessionists outside of South Carolina urged restraint on the Carolinians. An uneasy truce upholding the status quo was worked out and readily accepted by Buchanan. There matters stood until Anderson's report in early March presented the incoming Lincoln administration with its first major crisis.

Lincoln initially responded to the crisis by trying to expand his options beyond the stark choice of either resupplying Fort Sumter or surrendering it. The sending of a relief expedition would most likely provoke an armed response from Confederate authorities that would touch off a civil war. Doing nothing and abandoning the fort would destroy the credibility of the Republicans as the defenders of the Union and subject the party to the same derision in the North that had mocked the dying days of the Buchanan administration. One possible way to avoid either of these disastrous choices involved a reinforcement of Fort Pickens. More accessible to the federal navy because of its location outside the Pensacola harbor beyond the range of Confederate artillery, Fort Pickens had the additional advantage of having escaped the public attention focused on Fort Sumter. Presumably, its reinforcement would entail less risk of precipitating a war but would still serve as a demonstration of Lincoln's determination to uphold federal authority even if Fort Sumter had to be surrendered. On March 12 Lincoln issued the orders for the reinforcement of Fort Pickens.

While awaiting the results of this relief expedition, Lincoln explored a second possible way out of the dilemma posed by Fort Sumter. He considered a withdrawal from Fort Sumter in exchange for a binding commitment from the Border states that they would remain in the Union. Seward strongly pushed this approach, and his case was strengthened by a report from the general in chief, Winfield Scott, that argued against the military feasibility of a successful reprovisioning of Fort Sumter. On March 15 Lincoln's cabinet went on record as opposing any immediate attempt to resupply Fort Sumter. For the next two weeks, Lincoln put off a final decision as he gave Seward's peace policy one last chance.

From the very beginning, Seward overplayed his hand. He was convinced that "masterly inactivity" would work if only a collision at Fort Sumter could be avoided. He was also convinced that Lincoln was a country politician out of his element in Washington and that he needed a prime minister who, in effect, would run the government. That was the role that Seward, rather blatantly, tried to assume in March.

On March 15, and behind Lincoln's back, Seward used an intermediary to pass on word to the three Confederate commissioners in Washington who were seeking a transfer of Fort Pickens and Fort Sumter to the Confederacy that a decision had been made to evacuate Fort Sumter. Seward assumed that an evacuation was a foregone conclusion, and he stated that assumption as a pledge in order to forestall negotiations that he could not undertake without officially recognizing the existence of the Confederate government. At the same time, and with Lincoln's knowledge, Seward was maintaining contact with members of Virginia's secession convention. Although that convention had voted against secession, it pointedly remained in session. Secession sentiment was still very much alive in Virginia, and the legislature had resolved in January that the state would resist any attempt to coerce a seceded state back into the Union. By dangling the surrender of Fort Sumter as bait, Seward hoped to convince the convention to adjourn and thus isolate the Confederacy within its original boundaries of just seven states. If the Confederacy were so isolated and faced with the united front of the Upper South and North against it, Seward was confident that its leaders would soon be willing to negotiate a peaceful reconstruction of the Union.

By late March Seward was boxed into a corner. Quite unintentionally, he had deceived the Confederate commissioners and the Virginia Unionists into believing that the evacuation of Fort Sumter was imminent. Their patience was wearing thin over what they regarded as Seward's duplicity, just as was Lincoln's over Seward's attempt to be a surrogate president. Meanwhile, Northern public opinion rapidly hardened on the Sumter issue. Democrats still opposed any intervention, but Republicans demanded an end to what seemed to be a shameful policy of endless drift and delay. Lincoln had to move quickly and decisively to maintain control of his party and his administration. Time had run out on Seward's conciliatory approach.

Assured by Gustavus V. Fox, a naval advisor, that Fort Sumter could be reprovisioned under cover of darkness, Lincoln now decided to prepare a relief expedition. He reconvened his cabinet on March 29 and swung them around to his position. Desperate to save his policy at any cost, Seward then sent Lincoln an incredible memorandum advocating not only an abandonment of Fort Sumter but a foreign war against the major European powers on trumped up charges of aggression in the Western Hemisphere. Such a war, argued Seward, would rekindle the patriotism of even the seceded Southerners and reunite the country. He ended by suggesting himself as the bold leader prepared to step forward as the savior of the Union. With masterful tact Lincoln spurned these recommendations and reminded Seward as to who had just been elected president.

Two factors were decisive in Lincoln's decision to challenge the Confederacy over the issue of Fort Sumter. First and foremost, Lincoln was convinced by late March that every day of further delay was reducing his administration's capacity for effective leadership. Any more temporizing would only demoralize his party, embolden the secessionists in the Upper South, and encourage foreign nations to regard the Confederacy as a sovereign power that deserved official diplomatic recognition. Second, Lincoln realized after a month in office that he had underestimated the popular strength of secession in the Lower South and overestimated the extent of unconditional Unionism in the Upper South.

On April 4 Lincoln met with a Virginia Unionist. There is no firsthand account of what was said, and it is unclear whether Lincoln made a final offer to surrender Sumter in exchange for an immediate adjournment of the Virginia secession convention. What is clear is that right after the meeting Lincoln went ahead with his Sumter plans and sent word to Major Anderson that a relief expedition was on the way. Apparently, Lincoln left that meeting convinced that Virginia Unionism came attached with too many demands on limiting federal power. If Lincoln wanted to negotiate from strength in any future talks with the Virginians, he would have to demonstrate the reality of that power at Fort Sumter.

The die was finally cast on April 6, the day that Lincoln learned that his orders to reinforce Fort Pickens had been botched. The relief expedition arrived, but the troops had not landed because the naval commander at Fort Pickens refused to enforce an order not signed by the secretary of the navy. Lincoln now moved swiftly. He sent a messenger to Charleston with the notification that "an attempt will be made to supply Fort Sumter with provisions only; and that, if such attempt be not resisted, no effort to throw in men, arms, or amunition, will be made, without further notice, or in case of an attack upon the Fort."[17] Thus, even to the very end, Lincoln kept open the possibility of maintaining the status quo over Fort Sumter. As he had pledged in his Inaugural Address, the Union would not use military force against the Confederacy unless first attacked. If the shaky truce in the Charleston harbor were broken, he had made certain that the Confederacy would bear the burden of having fired the first shot.

Confederate leaders readily accepted that burden as the price they had to pay to establish their claim to sovereign power. An independent nation did not permit a foreign power to hold a fort at the entrance to one of its major harbors. Nor would the leaders of such a nation allow themselves to be deceived into believing that the relief expedition on its way to the fort was not a cover for strengthening a hostile garrison. After all, reasoned the Confederate high command, the Lincoln administration had been sending signals for over a month that Fort Sumter was about to be evacuated. Why should Lincoln now be trusted when he professed only the most innocent of intentions?

Such considerations, along with incessant demands from South Carolinians for action to redeem Southern honor, heavily influenced Jefferson Davis' decision to meet Lincoln's challenge at Fort Sumter with military force. Equally significant was the political factor. Davis, like Lincoln, was under attack for failing to provide resolute leadership. In particular, he was criticized for sitting back and doing nothing to bring the Upper South into the original Confederacy. As long as the Upper South, and especially Virginia, stayed out, the Confederacy was but a cipher of a nation. Two-thirds of the South's free population was still within the Union in early April 1861, and without it the Confederacy was outnumbered ten to one by the manpower of the North. Most of the industrialization in the slave states was also in the Upper South. Without access to those factories, the Confederacy had but one-twentieth the industrial capacity of the North. That would be a crippling disadvantage if war ever came.

Aside from these basic demographic and economic factors, Davis also had to bring in the Upper South in order to squelch once and for all any talk of a peaceful reconstruction of the Union. This, not the possibility of war, was the greatest fear of the most committed secessionists. Despite the success with which the Confederacy had been launched, deep pockets of Unionism persisted within its borders. From northern Georgia in late March Senator Andrew Johnson heard from an old Clay

Whig who, along with his neighbors, had been "coaxed Flattered and Bullyed out of the union....Tell [Lincoln and his cabinet] they are makeing many *warm* friends in my country and did the people only dare to do so they would Huzaw for Lincolns conservitive Peacefull administration [sic]."[18] Cooperationists in northern Alabama were likewise hoping for a conciliatory policy from Lincoln that would give them a chance to bring their state back into the Union.

Down to the moment of decision at Fort Sumter, the Confederates had every reason to believe that Seward's approach of "masterly inactivity" was working in the Upper South. The compromises that Seward had championed, and most notably the proposed 13th amendment, gave Southern Unionists a powerful rallying cry for keeping their states in the Union. That cry more than neutralized the efforts made by the Confederacy to entice the Upper South into joining it.

The constitutional convention that assembled at Montgomery, Alabama, in February went out of its way to calm the fears and appeal to the interests of the slave states still in the Union. Aware of their image as firebrands who had rashly precipitated secession before a convention of all the Southern states could meet, the delegates denied positions of power to the fire-eaters, the hard-core radicals who had done so much to promote secession. Leading fire-eaters, such as William Lowndes Yancey of Alabama and Robert Barnwell Rhett of South Carolina, were pushed aside. The presidency went to Jefferson Davis, a late convert to secession, and the vice presidency to Alexander Stephens, a former Conditional Unionist from Georgia. The Confederate constitution was closely modeled after the federal charter of 1787, and it projected an image of conservative statesmanship seeking to preserve the best from the federal tradition. Its politically most significant clause, and one opposed by most of the radicals, prohibited the African slave trade. The Upper South was assured that its labor market for slaves would not be glutted in the Confederacy. Even when supported by the appeals of special commissioners sent to each of the states in the Upper South, these concessions were not enough to overcome the Unionism that Seward was banking on to arrest and then reverse secession. Even worse from the perspective of the Confederates was the emergence of a new political grouping in the Upper South that threatened to deal a crippling blow to the interests of slaveholders.

The February elections in Virginia, North Carolina, and Tennessee were a disaster for the secessionist cause. The reasons included not just the obvious one of defeat at the polls but also the mobilization of a large Unionist majority overwhelmingly based on the support of nonslaveholders. To a greater extent than in the Lower South, class lines polarized in these elections. In particular, large numbers of Democratic nonslaveholders deserted the secessionist, slaveholding wing of their party. In combination with the Whig yeomanry in the mountains, the Democrats formed an antisecessionist majority that threatened to unseat the slaveholders from their accustomed positions of power within their own states.

The nurturing of this temporary antisecessionist coalition into a permanent Unionist party open to the free-labor ideology of the Republicans was Seward's great hope in the early spring of 1861. Everything depended on avoiding a civil war.

For that very reason, secessionists in the Upper South bombarded South Carolinians with urgent requests to open fire on Fort Sumter and thus start the war that would force their states to commit themselves to the Confederacy. Such logic was just as compelling to secessionists in the Lower South. As an Alabamian said in late January, "South Carolina has the power of putting us beyond the reach of reconstruction by taking Fort Sumter at any cost."[19] In early April that power rested with the Confederate government in Montgomery.

News of Lincoln's notification to the governor of South Carolina that he was sending a relief expedition to Fort Sumter reached Montgomery on April 8. The message could not be sent directly to President Davis since Lincoln's government never recognized the legality of secession. The next day, Davis' cabinet ratified his decision to order General P. G. T. Beauregard, the Confederate commander at Charleston, to demand an immediate surrender of Fort Sumter. If Major Anderson refused, Beauregard was ordered to destroy the fort. Although Beauregard already had orders to repel any Union attempt to send a fleet into the Charleston harbor, Davis issued the new orders because he wanted Sumter in Confederate hands before the relief expedition arrived. In strict military terms this was a sound decision, for it eliminated the risk of having to fight two Union forces at the same time. In political terms, Davis could not have made a worse decision. He allowed himself and his cause to be cast as the aggressor that started the Civil War. He, more than Lincoln, unified the North behind a crusade to preserve the Union.

Anderson agreed to surrender within three days, but his response was so

The Confederate bombardment of Fort Sumter on April 12th and 13th, 1861, ignited the Civil War.

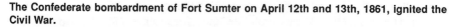

hedged that it was unsatisfactory. In the pre-dawn hours of April 12, 1861, Confederate batteries opened fire on Fort Sumter. The fort surrendered on April 14, and the next day Lincoln issued a call for 75,000 state militia to put down insurrectionary "combinations too powerful to be suppressed by the ordinary course of judicial proceedings, or by the powers vested in the Marshals by law."[20] Scornfully rejecting Lincoln's call for troops, and citing their duty to protect the liberties of their Southern kin from a federal invasion, Virginia, Arkansas, Tennessee, and North Carolina joined the Confederacy in the next five weeks.

As Confederate leaders had expected and predicted, Fort Sumter was the key to gaining the critical states of the Upper South. Fort Sumter was also the burning fuse that ignited a military explosion that destroyed the system of human bondage that the Confederacy was founded to perpetuate. "God grant that all the slave-holders may rebel, and remain in rebellion, till the emancipation of their slaves is accomplished!"[21] wrote the abolitionist Lydia Maria Child in June 1861. She got her wish.

NOTES

1. Lydia Maria Child to Francis Shaw, Jan. 8, 1861, in Milton Meltzer and Patricia G. Holland (eds.), *Lydia Maria Child: Selected Letters, 1817–1880* (Amherst: The University of Massachusetts Press, 1982), p. 369.
2. Indianapolis *Indiana American,* Nov. 21, 1860, in Howard Cecil Perkins (ed.), *Northern Editorials on Secession,* vol. 1 (Gloucester, Mass.: Peter Smith, 1964), p. 98.
3. Waynesboro (Ga.) *Independent South,* Oct. 31, 1860, quoted in Ollinger Crenshaw, *The Slave States in the Presidential Election of 1860* (Gloucester, Mass.: Peter Smith, 1969), p. 234.
4. Roy P. Basler (ed.), *The Collected Works of Abraham Lincoln,* vol. 4 (New Brunswick: Rutgers University Press, 1953), p. 150.
5. *Wisconsin State Journal,* Sept. 8, 1855, quoted in Michael J. McManus, "Wisconsin Republicans and Negro Suffrage: Attitudes and Behavior, 1857," *Civil War History,* vol. 25, p. 38, 1979.
6. Lynda Lasswell Crist (ed.), *The Papers of Jefferson Davis,* vol. 4 (Baton Rouge: Louisiana State University Press, 1983), p. 27.
7. Frederick Law Olmsted, *A Journey in the Back Country* (New York: Schocken Books, 1970 [1860]), p. 264.
8. *Debow's Review,* vol. 8, p. 25, 1850.
9. Leroy P. Graf and Ralph W. Haskins (eds.), *The Papers of Andrew Johnson,* vol. 3 (Knoxville: The University of Tennessee Press, 1972), p. 165.
10. Quoted in Lacy K. Ford, "Yeoman Farmers in the South Carolina Upcountry: Changing Production Patterns in the Late Antebellum Period," *Agricultural History,* vol. 60, p. 37, 1986.
11. Boston *Daily Atlas and Bee,* Nov. 12, 1860, in Perkins, vol. 1, p. 88.
12. William Cullen Bryant III and Lomas G. Voss (eds.), *The Letters of William Cullen Bryant,* vol. 4 (New York: Fordham University Press, 1954), p. 188.
13. Basler, vol. 4, p. 150.

14. Joseph W. Stokes to Andrew Johnson, Jan. 16, 1861, in Graf and Haskins, vol. 4, p. 175.

15. *Congressional Globe,* 36 Congress, 2 Session, p. 49.

16. Basler, vol. 4, pp. 266, 268.

17. Ibid., p. 323.

18. Clisbe Austin to Andrew Johnston [sic], March 29, 1861, in Graf and Haskins, vol. 4, pp. 448–449.

19. J. L. Pugh to William Porcher Miles, January 24, 1861, William Porcher Miles Papers, Southern Historical Collection, University of North Carolina at Chapel Hill.

20. Basler, vol. 4, p. 332.

21. Lydia Maria Child to Lucy Searle, June 5, 1861, in Meltzer and Holland, p. 383.

SUGGESTED READINGS

BARNEY, WILLIAM L., *The Road to Secession.* New York: Praeger, 1972.

BLASSINGAME, JOHN W., *The Slave Community: Plantation Life in the Antebellum South.* New York: Oxford University Press, 1972.

CROFTS, DANIEL W., *Reluctant Confederates: Upper South Unionists in the Secession Crisis.* Chapel Hill, N.C.: University of North Carolina Press, 1989.

CURRENT, RICHARD N., *Lincoln and the First Shot.* Philadelphia, Pa.: J.B. Lippincott, 1963.

FIELDS, BARBARA J., *Slavery and Freedom on the Middle Ground: Maryland During the Nineteenth Century.* New Haven, Conn.: Yale University Press, 1985.

FORD, LACY K., JR., *Origins of Southern Radicalism: The South Carolina Upcountry, 1800– 1860.* New York: Oxford University Press, 1988.

GENOVESE, EUGENE D., *Roll, Jordan, Roll: The World the Slaves Made.* New York: Pantheon, 1974.

GUTMAN, HERBERT G., *The Black Family in Slavery and Freedom, 1750–1925.* New York: Pantheon, 1974.

LEVINE, LAWRENCE W., *Black Culture and Black Consciousness: Afro-American Folk Thought from Slavery to Freedom.* New York: Oxford University Press, 1977.

OAKES, JAMES, *The Ruling Race: A History of American Slaveholders.* New York: Alfred A. Knopf, 1982.

POTTER, DAVID M., *Lincoln and His Party in the Secession Crisis.* New Haven, Conn.: Yale University Press, 1942.

STAMPP, KENNETH M., *The Peculiar Institution.* New York: Vintage, 1956.

STAMPP, KENNETH M., *And the War Came: The North and the Secession Crisis.* Baton Rouge, La.: Louisiana State University Press, 1950.

THORNTON, J. MILLS, III, *Politics and Power in a Slave Society.* Baton Rouge, La.: Louisiana State University Press, 1978.

WADE, RICHARD C., *Slavery in the Cities.* New York: Oxford University Press, 1964.

WYATT-BROWN, BERTRAM, *Southern Honor: Ethics and Behavior in the Old South.* New York: Oxford University Press, 1982.

5

The
Stalemated
War

"Civil war is freely accepted everywhere,"[1] declared a Bostonian a week after the firing on Fort Sumter. He, like countless other Northerners and Southerners, was swept along by an outpouring of such intense emotion and enthusiasm that, as a New York woman put it in early May, "the 'time before Sumter' seems to belong to some dim antiquity."[2] After the building of tensions throughout the 1850s and the agonizing suspense of the secession winter, the actual outbreak of war came as a relief.

Editorials, sermons, and private correspondence on both sides of the sectional divide were virtually interchangeable in the secular and religious reasons they gave for embracing war. Unionists and Confederates each spoke of a rebirth of patriotism, of finally having a cause and country for which they would willingly sacrifice their lives. Each believed they were embarking on a holy crusade for the righteousness of a Christianity they accused the other of profaning through corruption and greed. Whether colored Blue or Gray, Americans saw themselves as the worthy heirs of the Revolution, ready now to rededicate themselves to the principles of liberty and self-government. Duty, honor, and the need to prove oneself a man were the reasons cited by both Billy Yank and Johnny Reb for rushing to join their volunteer units.

Each side also widely believed that the war would be short and relatively bloodless. Indeed, much of the enthusiasm, even joy, which greeted the outbreak of the war was based on a romanticized image of a gallant little war that would be over by the fall of 1861. Instead, the war dragged on for four years and piled up casualty lists that would have been inconceivable in the innocent spring days of 1861. Almost as many Americans were to die in the Civil War than all our other wars combined.

This chapter will begin by examining the central features of the conflict that turned it into such a prolonged, bloody struggle. Because Confederate resistance was far more powerful and effective than anything initially envisioned by the Union, the first two years of the war resulted in a military stalemate. During this phase of the war, the official objective of the Lincoln administration was the restoration of the Union as it existed in 1860 with slavery intact. Under the political and military constraints imposed by that objective, however, the Union had achieved no better than a deadlock. In order to break that deadlock, Lincoln began to redefine the war aims of the Union in his Preliminary Emancipation Proclamation of September 1862. As abolitionists and blacks, both free and slave, had known all along, and as the Union army came to realize when faced with the tenacity of Confederate resistance, slavery would have to be destroyed if the Union were to defeat the Confederacy. The chapter concludes at the point where the war was becoming, in Lincoln's words, "a violent and remorseless revolutionary struggle."[3]

THE NATURE OF THE WAR

The Myth of the Lost Cause to the contrary, the Union and Confederacy were very evenly balanced combatants. The Union's decided edge in men and material was counterbalanced by the sheer size of the Confederacy and the advantages that accrued to the side that strategically was fighting a war of maintenance against an opponent's war of conquest. With a central government organized above an established structure of state governments and tremendous morale and unity at the start of the war, the Confederacy was in a very strong position to defend itself. After the war, General P. G. T. Beauregard forcefully argued that

> No people ever warred for independence with more relative advantages than the Confederates....The South, with its great material resources, its defensive means of mountains, rivers, railroads, and telegraph, with the immense advantages of the interior lines of war, would be open to discredit as a people if its failure could not be explained otherwise than by mere material contrast.[4]

The "material contrast" noted by Beauregard did indeed favor the North. Once the initial political lines of the war were drawn with the addition of four states in the Upper South to the Confederacy by the end of May 1861, the Union was left with a manpower pool for its armed forces of 3.5 million men (white males age eighteen to forty-five). The Confederacy had only 1 million white males available for military service. Other material measures just as one-sided favored the Union at the outbreak of the war. The Confederacy had but one-tenth the manufacturing output of the North and one-half the railroad mileage and draft animals (the horses

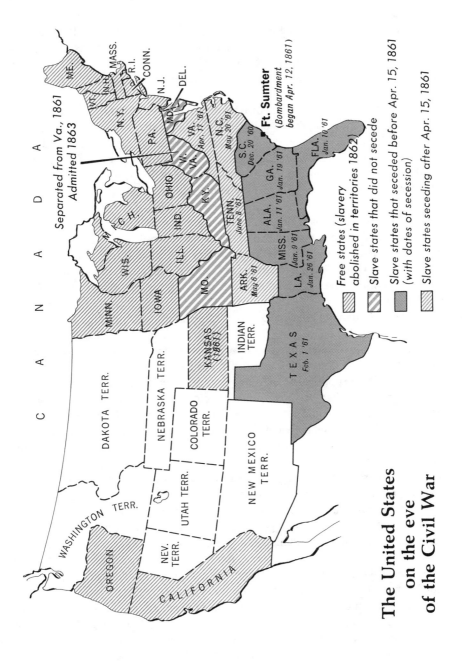

Separated from Va., 1861
Admitted 1863

Ft. Sumter
(Bombardment
began Apr. 12, 1861)

Free states (slavery
abolished in territories 1862)

Slave states that did not secede

Slave states that seceded before Apr. 15, 1861
(with dates of secession)

Slave states seceding after Apr. 15, 1861

ME.
VT.
N.H.
MASS.
R.I.
CONN.
N.Y.
N.J.
PA.
DEL.
MD.
W. VA.
VA. Apr. 17 '61
N.C. May 20 '61
OHIO
KY.
TENN. June 8 '61
S.C. Dec. 20 '60
GA. Jan. 19 '61
ALA. Jan. 11 '61
FLA. Jan. 10 '61
MISS. Jan. 9 '61
LA. Jan. 26 '61
MICH.
IND.
ILL.
WIS.
MINN.
IOWA
MO.
ARK. May 6 '61
KANSAS (1861)
INDIAN TERR.
T E X A S
Feb. 1 '61
DAKOTA TERR.
NEBRASKA TERR.
COLORADO TERR.
NEW MEXICO TERR.
WASHINGTON TERR.
UTAH TERR.
NEV. TERR.
OREGON
CALIFORNIA
C A N A D A

The United States
on the eve
of the Civil War

and mules needed to supply troops in the field). In the production of locomotives and firearms, the Union advantage was in excess of twenty-five to one. Whether measured by the size of manufacturing production, the ability to replace or replenish industrial equipment destroyed in the course of the war, such as the rolling stock of railroads, or the logistical means of transporting and supplying troops, the North's economic superiority appeared to be overwhelming. On top of all this, the Union began with a navy of ninety ships. The Confederacy had to build a navy from scratch.

What then were the sources of Beauregard's belief that the edge belonged to the South? The most important factor was the large size of the Confederacy. Its 750,000 square miles covered an area as extensive as western Europe and Great Britain combined. With the obvious example of the American Revolution in mind, Southerners were well aware that history had repeatedly demonstrated that countries far smaller than the Confederacy could successfully win or maintain their independence against invaders with larger armies and more material resources. George W. Randolph, the Confederate secretary of war in the fall of 1861, confidently stated, "There is no instance in history of a people as numerous as we are inhabiting a country so extensive as ours being subjected if true to themselves."[5] For this same reason, foreign observers in 1861 felt that it was only a matter of time before Lincoln's government was forced to recognize the independence of the Confederacy.

The second major advantage of the Confederacy was the defensive nature of the war it was called on to fight. The primary strategic task of the Confederacy was the defensive one of retaining control over most of the territory that it held at the start of the war. Unlike the Union, it did not have to wage an offensive war of subjugation for the political objective of restoring loyalty to a national government whose right to rule had been overturned. Victory or even stalemate on the battlefields most probably would have resulted in the survival of the Confederacy, at least into the indefinite future, but victory for the Union had to encompass more than just winning battles. Union armies had to penetrate into enemy territory, seize and hold it, and eventually break the resistance of Confederates to the reimposition of national authority. This war of conquest required far more troops than the war of maintenance pursued by the Confederacy.

As the invading and occupying forces, Union armies had to protect their supply lines in enemy territory, garrison key communication centers, and perform such pacification duties as administering loyalty oaths to the Union and protecting Southern Unionists from Confederate reprisals. All of these non-combat duties necessitated the detachment of more troops the farther Union armies pushed into Confederate territory. On average, the combined effect of these logistical and occupational demands reduced the front-line combat strength of the Union armies by one-third. In contrast, Confederate armies generally fought on their own soil, had shorter supply lines, and were free of any political responsibilities that would decrease the number of soldiers available for combat. Placed on the strategic defensive, Confederate troops usually held the interior lines of communication, that is, the distances they had to cover in order to shift and combine units were shorter than those facing Union forces strung out along a wide, attacking perimeter. In practical terms, this meant that under skilled leadership smaller Confederate armies could concentrate faster than the Yankees and attack with a surprising preponderance of strength at a weak spot in the Union position.

Defending troops had a tremendous tactical edge against their attackers in mid-nineteenth-century warfare. Tactics—the way in which a particular battle is fought—heavily favored the defense after the introduction in the 1850s of new rifled firearms as the standard weapon of infantry troops. For centuries the infantry had been equipped with smoothbore muskets. Accurate up to a distance of only about 80 yards, smoothbores were the standard weapon because of their reliability and speed in reloading. Rifles had far greater range and accuracy, but they had the crippling disadvantage of taking too long to reload under battlefield conditions. After each firing, a bullet had to be rammed laboriously down the barrel in order to fit tightly within its spiraled grooves. The spin imparted by these grooves gave the rifle bullet its accuracy and range. In the 1850s, an American adoption of a French invention produced the "minie ball," a conical bullet with a hollow metal base that expanded from the heat of the firing of the percussion cap to fit snugly into the grooves of the rifle barrel. This bullet represented a major technological breakthrough because its caliber was sufficiently smaller than the rifle barrel to permit relatively rapid loading and reloading. Defending troops armed with rifled muzzle loaders could now hold off an attacking force that outnumbered them three to one.

This dominant edge of the defense resulted from the five-fold expansion of the lethal zone of deadly fire from infantry troops. Rifles were accurate up to 400 yards. Frontal assaults in compact formations were now suicidal, and fewer than one in eight succeeded during the Civil War. Neither cavalry charges nor the wheeling up of cannon to pound the defender's position were of much help to the attacking troops because the horses and artillery crews would be killed before they got close enough to the defenders to make much difference. By the midpoint of the war, troops on both sides routinely entrenched their positions behind breastworks, and, under these conditions, the defense had an overwhelming advantage of five to one.

The Confederacy succeeded by the spring of 1863 in equipping nearly all of its troops with these new, long-range rifles. This was a remarkable achievement given the fact that the Confederacy began the war with virtually no industrial facilities with which to manufacture rifles or ammunition. In 1861 and 1862, imports from Britain and captured Union weapons supplied Southern armies with most of their rifled muzzle loaders. One of the most important duties of ordnance officers in Confederate armies was the systematic stripping or gleaning of battlefields. Anything that was salvageable was collected and shipped back to processing centers for recycling. By 1863, the Confederacy had created its own armaments industry. Southern factories, owned outright by the Confederate government or subsidized by it, were producing enough ammunition, weapons, and heavy ordnance in the second half of the war to make the Confederacy self-sufficient in the materials of modern warfare.

The third major factor that enabled the Confederacy to reduce the material odds against its armies was the presence of slavery. At the beginning of the war, one-third of the Confederate population were slaves. Southern whites boasted that these slaves were a decided military asset, and, at least for the first half of the war, they were correct. The Union general, Ulysses S. Grant, estimated that slaves contributed at least three times as much to the Confederate war effort as did an equivalent number of noncombatants in the North to the Union war effort. Once the South went on a wartime footing, slaves were more than ever the backbone of its economy. They produced the foodstuffs for its armies, mined the raw materials needed for its armaments industry, filled the unskilled jobs in its war plants, and dug and repaired fortifications for its defense. Slave labor freed up an extraordinarily high percentage of the South's white manpower for combat duty. At least seventy-five percent of Southern white males of military age served in Confederate armies. The comparable figure for the North was about fifty-five percent.

Thus, the actual disparity in the aggregate size of the Union and Confederate armies for most of the war was well under the greater than three-to-one edge held by the North in accessible white manpower. Although the Union put two and a half times as many men under arms, Union armies in the war's major battles were on average only thirty-seven percent larger than their Confederate opponents. The primary reason for this surprisingly small numerical advantage was the large numbers of Union soldiers continually being detached for non-combat duties.

The Union and Confederacy were too evenly balanced for either to force a speedy military resolution of the fundamental issue of sovereign power that was at stake in the war. The Union was fighting for the preservation of the Union that the Confederacy was fighting to destroy through the maintenance of its independence. Lincoln and Davis rejected each other's claims to sovereign power, and there was no middle ground that could serve as a basis for any negotiations. Nor was there any popular demand from civilians for a negotiated settlement that in the North stopped short of preserving the Union intact or in the South refused to recognize Confederate independence. The armies that began the fighting were overwhelmingly volunteer ones, and, as casualties started to mount, Union and Confederate civilians alike demanded that their fallen heroes be honored by fighting to the finish for the respective causes that had claimed their lives. Anything less than a total victory, it was felt, would dishonor the sacrifices of those who had already died. The war quickly developed a momentum that fed on itself, and that momentum in turn drove forward a war that neither side initially understood or was prepared to fight.

The Civil War is often called the first modern war because it marked the first time that the economic and technological advances of the industrial revolution directly influenced battlefield conditions and shaped the conduct of war. The essence of the industrial revolution was the production of more goods with fewer workers. During the Civil War this enhanced productivity generated the economic surpluses that made possible the raising, supplying, and reprovisioning of mass armies as large in size as a major American city. This was especially the case in the North where there were no slaves to maintain the production lost when the men left for the war. For most of the war, one-third of the North's agricultural work force was in the Union army, and, yet, agricultural production increased while they were off fighting. Women took up much of the slack, and they were assisted by labor-saving machinery. Sales of reapers and mowers tripled from 1860 to 1865, and the Civil War decade saw the second highest gain in agricultural productivity of any in the nineteenth century. As a result, no other army in history had ever been better fed than the Union army.

Once mobilized, the armies had a voracious appetite for armaments and such basic consumer staples as bread, meat, shoes, and clothes. Through the course of the war, 2.3 million Union soldiers and some 1 million Confederates had to be supplied on nearly a daily basis. Factory production in both sections expanded to meet this military demand. Animal-drawn wagons, riverboats, and railroads provided the logistical support for the massive problem of resupply. Every field army was dependent on a long lifeline of support that stretched over country roads back to a supply base located on a river or at a rail junction. Given the tons of goods and thousands of troops that had to be moved and deployed, the railroads were indispensable to the logistics of both armies. As long as the railroads funneled provisions and reinforcements to the military theaters, the armies could fight almost indefinitely. No matter how badly mauled it might be after a given battle, an army was ready to fight again in a few weeks, or even days, because it could be quickly resupplied. Thus, for all the unprecedented firepower concentrated in Civil War armies with their rifled weapons, defeats were less decisive than they had been for armies in the past. This in turn was a prime factor in the prolonged military stalemate of 1861–1862.

The telegraph was another new technological feature of the industrial revolution that played a major role in the Civil War. The telegraph began to revolutionize American business in the 1850s when the miles of line jumped from under 5,000 to 56,000. During the war, the United States Military Telegraph built an additional 15,000 miles of line. Hampered by a scarcity of operators and wire, the Confederacy added about 500 miles in military telegraph lines. Incredibly faster and cheaper than pre-electronic communications, the telegraph made possible the coordination of troop movements in a war zone the size of western Europe. Widely scattered armies could hardly have been concentrated into integrated campaigns without it, nor could Washington and Richmond, the respective political capitals, have functioned as the nerve centers of the war. Just as significantly, the mass armies could not have been so rapidly mobilized nor so effectively supplied in the field without the fast, long-distance communications network of the telegraph. It was the managerial key to raising the armies within a matter of months and systematizing the complex logistical operations they needed for their survival. Much like the railroads then, the very speed and efficiency of the telegraph contributed to the sluggish pace of a war in which huge armies fought one indecisive battle after another.

In terms of direct battlefield application, the rifled firearms of the Civil War were the deadliest result of the fusion of industrial technology and war. The mass destruction inflicted by these weapons was now the dominant tactical consideration in any battle, but most generals continued to order frontal assaults throughout the war. The result was mass slaughter. About sixty Union regiments, and an even greater number of Confederate ones, suffered battlefield casualties in excess of fifty percent in a single engagement. Many soldiers soon took the precaution of making out their own "identification tags" before they went into battle. On scraps of paper or cloth pinned to their tunics, they jotted down their names, next of kin, and home address. If killed, they at least stood a good chance of being buried next to loved ones at home.

Often criticized for their stupidity and callousness in repeatedly sending their troops on suicidal charges, the generals in fact had few other options open to them. They could not maintain a strictly defensive posture in the presence of a strong enemy force, for that would surrender the initiative to their opponent and expose their supply lines to a series of raids that would soon force them to retreat or attack. Even though the rapid resupplying of contending armies had robbed individual battles of their decisiveness and political significance, generals were still under tremendous pressure to win them. The massing of assault troops for a turning movement on an enemy's flank or a breakthrough at a supposed weak spot in the enemy's lines was the only way they knew of doing so and what military theory of the day told them to do. Such assaults almost always failed, and even when an army had tactically won a battle, it was too physically and psychologically battered to follow up its victory by pursuing its retreating opponent. Winners and losers alike averaged close to twenty percent casualties in the battles of the Civil War. These were roughly twice the casualty rates at which contemporary European armies were considered knocked out of action.

Each aspect of the industrial revolution that drastically enlarged the scope and intensity of the war—the factory system, railroad, telegraph, and rifle—was new to the military experience of generals trained in the pre-industrial age. Their approach to war was based on a strategic concept of a limited conflict fought for fixed objectives by small armies. Such a concept had successfully guided their thinking in the Mexican War, the prime source of the field experience that the generals brought to the Civil War. The American armies that fought the Mexican War were about one-tenth the size of Civil War armies. Attacking in massed columns against troops armed with smoothbore muskets, American soldiers were often successful in their frontal assaults. In short, most of what the Mexican War taught the generals was either inapplicable to the Civil War or murderously misleading.

The generals, no less than their civilian superiors in Washington and Richmond, were woefully unprepared to wage a conflict that evolved into a total war against mass armies, lines of communication, and the economic resources that fed into those lines. As Simon Cameron, Lincoln's first secretary of war, recalled at the beginning of the war: "...it was impossible to find a man who had any intelligent idea of the magnitude of the struggle. We were entirely unprepared to engage in war."[6] The preparation began as soon as Lincoln issued his first call for 75,000 troops after the firing on Fort Sumter.

THE BORDER SOUTH AND FIRST BULL RUN

The battle of First Bull Run on July 21, 1861, is easily the best known military engagement of the early part of the war. In a strategic sense, however, a series of obscure battles and political struggles in the Border South were of far greater significance in determining the outcome of the Civil War. The Union suffered a humiliating defeat at First Bull Run, but it emerged victorious in the crucial struggle for strategic control of the states along the northern rim of the Confederacy.

The secession of Virginia, Arkansas, Tennessee, and North Carolina between April 17 and May 20, 1861, made the Confederacy militarily competitive with the Union. These additional states doubled the white population of the original Confederacy and increased its food supply, livestock, and manufacturing capacity by fifty percent. Its frontiers were stretched to the Potomac within shouting distance of the Union's capital, its control of the vital Mississippi River corridor was strengthened, and it acquired in Tennessee a natural shield against a Union invasion of the Mid-South. Of incalculable importance for its later industrialization program, the Tredegar Iron Works in Richmond provided the Confederacy with its only factory capable of casting cannon and producing heavy machinery.

Had the Confederacy been able to duplicate these gains in Missouri, Kentucky, and Maryland, the Union war effort would have been placed in an untenable strategic position. Among the slave states, Missouri and Kentucky ranked first and third, respectively, in the size of their free population. A Confederate Missouri would have disrupted the Union's control of the upper Mississippi, isolated Kansas and the Pacific coast from contact with Lincoln's government, and exposed the lower Midwest to constant military harassment. Without Kentucky and uncontested access to the Ohio River, the Union would have been deprived of its chief logistical means for supporting its western armies. Had Maryland seceded, Washington would have been completely encircled by rebel territory and, in all likelihood, would have had to be abandoned.

The securing of Union control over Maryland was the most pressing strategic need of Lincoln's government in late April. Although slavery was of declining importance in Maryland, and Unionist sentiment predominated, Southern sympathizers were quite prevalent in Baltimore and along the Eastern Shore. On April 19, a pro-secession mob in Baltimore attacked the 6th Massachusetts Regiment on its way to Washington, and for the next week Washington was cut off from communications with the free states. Railroad bridges and telegraph lines north of Baltimore were destroyed. All rail traffic into Washington had to pass through Baltimore, and with the city under the control of Southern sympathizers, Washington was completely isolated. There was a real possibility that the secessionist minority—Baltimore businessmen with investments in the Southern market and tobacco planters in the southern counties and along the Eastern Shore—might stampede the state into leaving the Union. Southern Rights Democrats dominated the legislature, and Governor Thomas Hicks, though a Unionist, was wavering.

Hicks gave in to the demands of the secessionists and called the legislature into special session to consider an ordinance of secession. Lincoln lacked the military forces to force the issue of troop transit through Baltimore, and he negotiated a compromise with Hicks by which reinforcements from the North would be ferried across the Chesapeake Bay to Annapolis and thus bypass Baltimore. Meanwhile, Hicks had the good sense to convene the legislature in Frederick in the heart of the strongly Unionist section of western Maryland. Lincoln's approach of buying time paid off. The immediate pressure on Washington was relieved with the arrival on April 25 of the New York 7th Regiment, and Maryland Unionists rallied when Lincoln ordered reinforcements to Baltimore.

By the time the Maryland legislature met on April 29 to consider secession, it was a safe bet that Lincoln was prepared to use federal troops to storm Baltimore or any other secessionist stronghold in the state. Winfield Scott, the general-in-chief of the Union army, was under orders "to adopt the most prompt and efficient means to counteract [secession], even, if necessary, to the bombardment of their cities."[7] Faced with that threat, and the Unionist majority of yeomen farmers in western Maryland, the legislature rejected secession by a vote of fifty-three to thirteen.

Maryland was far too important to the Union war effort for Lincoln to take chances with its political loyalty during the war. Beginning with the crisis of April, 1861, he periodically suspended the writ of *habeas corpus* in Maryland and thereby deprived suspected disunionists of their right to be brought before a civilian judge and released from an unlawful arrest. On the eve of the Maryland elections in the fall of 1861, nineteen members of the legislature and the mayor of Baltimore were arrested and jailed. Pro-Union Maryland troops were given furloughs to go home and vote, while civilians thought to be Confederate sympathizers were arrested when they tried to vote. After that election, Maryland was firmly in the Unionist camp for the rest of the war.

The results in Missouri were equally favorable to the Union, though here the Unionists almost overplayed their hand. Measured by its vote of seventy-one percent for Douglas and Bell in the 1860 election, and seemingly confirmed by the overwhelming decision of its secession convention in March 1861 to remain in the Union, Missouri was apparently safe for the Union. In particular, its German–Americans of St. Louis under the leadership of Francis P. Blair, the brother of Lincoln's postmaster-general, were ardent Unionists. Planters along the Missouri River and Southern-born Missourians in the southwestern corner of the state, however, were just as fervently pro-Confederate. Their champion was the governor, Claiborne Jackson.

After contemptuously rejecting Lincoln's call for troops, Jackson quickly moved to maneuver Missouri into the Confederacy. With the support of the pro-secessionist legislature, Jackson gained control of the police and militia in St. Louis, the site of a federal subtreasury and arsenal. When Jackson organized and armed a pro-Confederate militia and encamped it near St. Louis, the Unionists rashly decided on a preemptive strike. Commanded by Nathanial Lyon, a militantly antislavery veteran of the earlier border skirmishes in the Kansas Territory, regiments of German–Americans overran the camp on May 10. When the captured militia men were brazenly paraded in the streets of St. Louis, pro-Southern sympathizers touched off a riot that left twenty-eight civilians dead. Moderation was now impossible, and Missouri was plunged into its own civil war. Lyon's precipitative action had done more to arouse Confederate sentiment in the state than all the schemings of Jackson.

Despite sharp setbacks at the battles of Wilson's Creek on August 10 and Lexington on September 20, Union forces gained strategic control of most of the state by the spring of 1862. The Missouri River, which bisects the state west to east on a line running from Kansas City to St. Louis, was a federal highway that prevented Confederates in northern Missouri from linking up with Jackson's men in the south. Logistical control of the Missouri River, plus the Mississippi and Ohio rivers flowing from the north and east, permitted a buildup of federal forces that the Confederates could not match. The Union victory at the battle of Pea Ridge, March 6–8, 1862, in the northwestern corner of Arkansas, broke the back of organized Confederate resistance in Missouri. In the fall of 1861, Richmond had recognized Governor Jackson's rump government as the official representatives of the twelfth state of the Confederacy, but it was a meaningless gesture devoid of any strategic importance. The Union had won the main prize. A Missouri secure for the Union protected the critical flank of the federal advance through Kentucky and Tennessee into Mississippi in the spring of 1862.

In Kentucky, the native state of both the war presidents, Lincoln patiently steered a middle course designed to give Unionists time to organize. Kentucky could not be militarily intimidated as easily as Maryland, and Lincoln wanted to give its secessionist minority no excuse to hand the Confederacy the strategic gifts of Kentucky's rich resources of livestock and control of the southern banks of the Ohio River. As in Missouri, Kentucky's governor, Beriah Magoffin, was a secessionist who spurned Lincoln's troop request. Magoffin, however, was not as headstrong as Jackson, and he did not openly oppose the Unionist majority that exerted itself in the legislature and a series of special elections held in the spring and summer of 1861.

The legislature officially declared Kentucky's neutrality on May 20, 1861. Too strategically important to be kept out of the war for very long, Kentucky maintained an uneasy neutrality throughout the summer only because Davis and Lincoln each refrained from sending troops into the state. Until August 16, Lincoln even sanctioned the open trading of Kentuckians with the Confederacy. The waiting game was over on September 3. The Confederate General Leonidas Polk ordered his troops into Columbus, Kentucky, in order to prevent a suspected Union occupation of the city and its commanding heights overlooking the Mississippi River. As was also true of the Confederate decision to fire on Fort Sumter, this was the militarily correct decision, but, once again, the Confederacy paid a heavy political price. Declaring that their state had been invaded, Kentucky Unionists now had a pretext to abandon neutrality. At the request of the legislature, federal forces under General Grant moved into Kentucky and began preparations for using the Tennessee and Cumberland rivers as invasion routes into Confederate Tennessee. As in Missouri, it mattered little that a splinter government proclaimed Kentucky out of the Union nor that Kentucky was admitted into the Confederacy in December 1861 as its thirteenth and final state. Kentucky in fact was safely Unionist for the rest of the war.

Kentucky was never the Confederacy's to lose, but the mountain counties of western Virginia were, and this made their loss by the fall of 1861 all the more galling. Appalachian Virginia, the one-third of the state west of the Allegheny Mountains, was anti-Confederate from the very beginning. The region was popu- lated overwhelmingly by nonslaveholders and small farmers who had closer eco- nomic ties to bordering Ohio and Pennsylvania than to the rest of their own state. They had long complained that they were overtaxed to support a planter-dominated legislature in Richmond that kept them physically isolated and politically un- derrepresented. As soon as news of Virginia's secession reached the mountain counties, protest meetings were held that quickly mushroomed into a separatist movement. Francis H. Pierpont, a Republican lawyer and coal dealer, directed the movement from Wheeling, an industrial city sandwiched in the Virginia panhandle between Ohio and Pennsylvania.

After a series of complex, irregular, and probably illegal maneuvers, a convention with delegates from thirty-four of the 150 counties in the state met at Wheeling in early August and designated itself as the loyal government for all of Virginia. This legal fiction was necessary in order to provide a constitutional cover for the *de facto* secession of western Virginia from the rest of the state. Under the U.S. Constitution, no state can be formed from another without the legislative consent of the state that is to be partitioned. The consent was given in May 1862 by a Unionist legislature elected under provisions set up by the Wheeling convention. West Virginia was admitted to the Union in early 1863 on the condition that it provide for gradual emancipation. Pierpont, claiming to be the governor of the rest of Virginia, was now heading a Unionist government in Alexandria, a city near Washington.

Confederate Virginia had been humiliated. Only prompt and effective mili- tary intervention in the spring and summer of 1861 could have headed off the separatist movement. The Confederacy did rush troops to the Virginia mountains, but General George B. McClellan's army from Ohio handily defeated them. As was the case in most Civil War campaigns, logistics was the key. McClellan's army had the inestimable advantage of an assured line of supplies over the Union controlled Baltimore and Ohio Railroad. Its main opponent, General Robert E. Lee's Confed- erate army, had a much harder time in reaching northwestern Virginia in the first place, and once there, they were hamstrung by their inability to resolve the problem of resupply over muddy, often impassable mountain roads. After failing to dislodge the Union army at Cheat Mountain in mid-September, Lee returned to Richmond, a temporary failure.

No major battles renowned in the lore of the Civil War were fought in the Border South in 1861. Yet, the outcome of the political and diplomatic struggles here between the Union and Confederacy was instrumental in determining the ultimate defeat of the Confederacy. Maryland, Missouri, Kentucky, and West Virginia supplied the Union with nearly 200,000 white troops, twice what they furnished the Confederacy. Another 50,000 black soldiers for the Union were raised in these states. Quite apart from this disproportionate strengthening of the federal armies, and an equal disparity in economic resources made available to the Union, the Border South provided the Union with what in effect were launching pads for the invasion of the Confederate heartland. By the end of 1861 the Union dominated the approaches to the Tennessee, Cumberland, and lower Mississippi rivers. Invasion down those rivers in 1862 opened the way for the eventual conquest of the Confederacy.

While Lincoln and Davis were sparring for strategic control of the uncertain border region, popular attention in 1861 was focused on northern Virginia. The 100 mile stretch between Washington, on the Potomac River, to Richmond, on the James, was destined to become the most famous and bitterly contested military theater of the war. This was the almost inevitable result of the decision of the Confederate Congress on May 21, 1861, to make Richmond the permanent capital of the Confederacy. Lack of accommodations in Montgomery and the sweltering heat were the practical considerations in the move, but the political and economic importance of recognizing the indispensable role of Virginia in making the Confederacy a viable nation was the overriding factor.

Whether this decision worked for or against the military defense of the Confederacy has been debated ever since. On one hand, it placed the Davis government in the best position to protect Virginia from the large Union armies being mobilized in Washington, and it strengthened the defense of the Tredegar Iron Works, the one industrial facility early in the war that the Confederacy could not afford to lose. On the other hand, it so exposed the capital to a Union attack that the defense of Richmond absorbed manpower and resources that could have been better spent in protecting the strategically vulnerable areas of the Confederacy west of the Appalachians. On balance, the move probably worked to the advantage of the Confederacy. Because Richmond was such a close, inviting, and seemingly easy target, the North was obsessed with its capture. In actuality, the half a dozen major rivers and tangled underbrush that lay astraddle the southward advance of Union armies marching overland from Washington provided an ideal defensive terrain that Confederate generals exploited to the fullest. More than half the battlefield deaths in the entire Union army occurred on the bloody ground between Washington and Richmond. "On to Richmond," however, was the rallying cry of the Union's Army of the Potomac, especially in the first half of the war. The Union lost a staggering amount of men and material in the Virginia theater, resources that might well have brought victory sooner had they been expended elsewhere in the Confederacy.

Take Richmond and bring the war to a quick, glorious end. That was the impatient demand of the North in the early summer of 1861. By then, three months had passed since the firing on Fort Sumter, and both governments were still in the rudimentary stages of equipping and training the enthusiastic volunteers who swelled the size of their armies. As yet, neither side had a coherent strategy for waging war. The Confederacy lacked the logistical support and manpower reserves necessary to fight an offensive war. Aware that they could win by maintaining control over the territory they already possessed, Confederate leaders were content to mass troops close to Washington and wait to counteract any possible federal invasion. The North had to invade in order to win, and the first strategic plan of conquest was proposed by General Scott on May 3. Scott's plan had three elements: a large eastern army to protect Washington and pin down Confederate troops in northern Virginia, a naval blockade to deprive the Confederacy of essential supplies from Europe, and a joint army–navy invasion down the Mississippi to split the Confederacy and cordon off its Trans-Mississippi region. Designed to minimize Union casualties and maximize economic pressure on the Confederacy, Scott's proposal was hooted down by the Northern press as the "Anaconda Plan," a clear sign that the impatient North was unwilling to wait for a slow economic strangulation of the enemy.

Even before he responded to the popular pressure for an immediate advance, Lincoln had shown that he would be a decisive war leader. Resting his actions on his constitutional mandate as commander-in-chief, he assumed sweeping powers in the weeks just after the surrender of Fort Sumter on April 14. On April 19, he proclaimed a blockade of Confederate ports, an act tantamount under international law to a declaration of war; on April 27 he suspended the writ of *habeas corpus* on the military line from Philadelphia to Washington; and on May 3, he expanded the size of the regular army and the navy and called for 42,000 three-year volunteers to serve in the war. All this was done without the authorization of Congress, and Lincoln himself admitted that his actions were of dubious legality. He was confident that Congress, which he had called into special session for early July, would ratify the decisions that he had already made, and he was correct.

As Congress was meeting, the first major battle of the Civil War was fought on July 21, 1861, at Manassas, Virginia, a rail junction twenty-five miles to the southwest of Washington. Lincoln ordered a reluctant General Irvin McDowell to move his raw army of 35,000 men out of its encampment near Washington and attack the 22,000 troops of General Beauregard's at Manassas. The decision was Lincoln's. He was anxious not to drain Northern enthusiasm by further inaction and fearful that many of McDowell's three-month enlistees were ready to pack up and go home. McDowell was about to become the first Northern general victimized by the political pressure in the eastern theater to win a decisive victory that would deliver Richmond to the Union.

The battle was a textbook example of the advantage of interior lines of communication to an army on the defensive. General Joseph Johnston's Confederate force of 12,000 slipped away from the Union army in the Shenandoah Valley and linked up via the Manassas Gap Railroad with Beauregard's force at Manassas. The arrival of Johnston's troops shifted the momentum of the battle and converted an apparent Union victory into an ignominious Union rout. The way was open to Washington, but the victorious Confederates were as disorganized as the defeated federals. They hung back rather than testing the strong outer defenses of Washington.

First Bull Run, as the battle was called in the North, was the Union's first moment of truth. It was now clear that the war was not going to be short and easy. While tens of thousands of Northern farm youth were streaming into Washington in May and June to get a touch of military glory before the war was over, nearly as many Southern youth were hoping for the same thing as they converged on Richmond at the same time. Two days after Lincoln's inauguration, the Confederate Congress approved an army of 100,000 volunteers, and by mid-April the Confederacy had more men under arms than the Union, which started the war with only the 16,000 scattered troops of the U.S. Regular Army. In early May, Davis was authorized to accept as many volunteers as he thought were needed. Perhaps as many as 200,000 had to be turned away because the Confederate War Department lacked the weapons to arm them. Nevertheless, for all the inefficiencies of the Confederate mobilization effort, Southern armies by the summer of 1861 were far larger and better equipped and commanded than the North ever thought possible back in the early spring. By mid-July the Union had about 250,000 troops, but most were greenhorns liable to crack under pressure, as shown at First Bull Run. More than the battlefield appearance of such troops would be necessary to win the war, and the Union now started to dig in for the long struggle ahead.

The rout of federal troops at 1st Bull Run in July, 1861, was an immense morale booster for the Confederacy, the victors in the first major battle of the war.

The repercussions of First Bull Run were felt immediately in Congress. The day after the battle, Congress authorized the enlistment of 500,000 volunteers to serve for up to three years. (The Confederate Congress responded by voting for an army of 400,000.) Also on July 22, the House passed a resolution introduced by John J. Crittenden of Kentucky that declared its support for a war "to defend and maintain the supremacy of the Constitution, and to preserve the Union with all the dignity, equality, and rights of the several States unimpaired."[8] In other words, the destruction of slavery was not to be a war objective. A similar resolution from Andrew Johnson of Tennessee, a Unionist Democrat, passed the Senate a few days later.

The Crittenden–Johnson resolutions were the broadest possible platform on which all Northerners could stand in support of the Union war effort. To be sure, the North had responded with one voice of outrage over the Confederate firing on Fort Sumter. The assumption was then unanimous that acquiescence in secession would inevitably result in anarchy and a breakdown in law and order. If malcontents and traitors in the Southern states could illegally and violently break up the Union, then what would prevent other factionists from destroying public order and respect for the law by breaking away for whatever reason from any county, town, or civic body? There could be no middle ground between ordered government and violent anarchy, insisted Senator Stephen Douglas, and before his death in June 1861, from overwork and an overindulgence in alcohol, Douglas had rallied northern Democrats behind Lincoln's efforts to suppress the insurrection. Still, much of the support of northern Democrats, and nearly all of it from the Unionists in the loyal Border states, was conditional upon a war fought solely to restore the old Union of 1860 with slavery left untouched. Now that the war was apparently going to be a long, hard one, the Republicans could not risk damaging Northern morale and unity by appearing to favor a war against slavery.

Most Republicans grudgingly voted for the Crittenden–Johnson resolutions and its pledge to leave slavery alone. Had they not, they would have been branded at this stage of the war as the dangerous anarchists and destroyers of a constitutional Union. For northern Democrats and southern Unionists, a party of emancipationists was a party of anarchists who would plunge the country into social turmoil as fully frightening as the havoc already unleashed by the secessionists.

If the long war foreshadowed by First Bull Run put a premium on maintaining Northern unity, it also guaranteed growing Northern frustration the longer the Confederacy put up a stiff resistance. By the summer of 1861, that frustration had not yet reached the point where conservative and moderate Republicans would back emancipation as a war measure designed to bring the Confederacy to its knees. After all, Lincoln's constitutional case for putting down the rebellion rested on the argument that the seceded states, though temporarily in the hands of individual rebels, had never legally left the Union and hence were still entitled to the protection of the Constitution for all their rights, including those in slavery. Northern blacks, abolitionists, and those Republicans whose uncompromising stand against slavery earned them the label of the Radicals responded that all this was pernicious nonsense, a coddling of traitors whose institution of slavery was the mainspring of the rebellion and its chief basis of support. The federal humiliation at First Bull Run began the conversion of more conservative Republicans over to the Radicals' point of view.

On August 6, 1861, and with the Democrats in nearly unanimous opposition, Congress passed the First Confiscation Act. Although this was not an emancipation measure, it was a beginning. The act provided for the confiscation or seizure of all property, including slaves, actively used in support of the rebellion. Union General Benjamin Butler had slyly set the precedent for this whittling away at slavery with his announcement at Fortress Monroe, Virginia, on May 23 that he would retain as "contrabands of war" the fugitive slaves who escaped behind his Union lines. This was at a time when Union commanders were under orders to return fugitive slaves to their owners.

Congress was moving too fast for Lincoln, and he never actively enforced the Confiscation Act. He also had to restrain one of his generals, John C. Frémont. On August 30, 1861, Frémont issued an order confiscating the slave property of Missouri rebels. Pointing out that such a measure would drive away southern Unionists and "perhaps ruin our rather fair prospect for Kentucky,"[9] Lincoln directed Frémont to redraft his order to conform to the First Confiscation Act. Lincoln's restraint did save Kentucky for the Union, and Lincoln was now confident that as long as Northern unity held a patient buildup and consolidation of Union forces would lead to victory in the spring of 1862.

Just after Bull Run, George McClellan, who was the first genuine Union war hero, was brought to Washington and given the mission of organizing the Army of the Potomac into the finest fighting force on the continent. Throughout the summer and on into the fall and winter, McClellan drilled and redrilled his raw recruits. Lincoln initially wanted a rapid movement down the Mississippi and into the mountains of staunchly Unionist East Tennessee, but McClellan counseled delay and convinced Lincoln to wait until the Army of the Potomac was in shape to take Richmond. While Lincoln was waiting, plans went ahead to put teeth into the blockade.

PORT ROYAL AND THE TRENT AFFAIR

Lincoln's proclamation of a naval blockade of Confederate ports was his first major strategic decision. It was a shrewd move in its immediate recognition that military and economic power would be interchangeable in the upcoming war. No matter how many men the Confederacy put into its armies, it would still need to import massive amounts of military supplies from Europe to equip them, especially early in the war. And those imports would have to be paid for with exports of Confederate cotton.

Although four blockading zones were soon established—two each in the Atlantic and Gulf of Mexico—as a means of coordinating ship deployments, the Navy in fact had too few ships in the spring of 1861 even to begin sealing off multiple entry points along a Confederate coast that stretched for 3,550 miles. An emergency program of procurement and construction, however, quickly fleshed out the blockading squadrons. By the summer of 1861, the Navy had doubled its warships in commission to eighty-two, and that number was tripled to 264 by the end of the year. Eventually, close to 700 Union ships did mount an effective blockade. How effective is a matter of dispute because the records are incomplete and notoriously unreliable.

There is no doubt that for the first two years of the war the blockade was run with impunity. Up to nine out of ten blockade runners were getting through. As late as 1864, Union fleets were capturing only one in three. However, blockade runners, out of necessity, were fast, light vessels with a very limited carrying capacity, and their success ratios in evading the Union navy can be quite a misleading indicator of the effectiveness of the blockade. Measured against the immediate pre-war period, the ocean trade of the Confederacy was cut by two-thirds in the last half of the war. The one undeniable success of the blockade was in keeping out heavy and bulky industrial equipment. By denying the Confederacy access to railroad machinery and rolling stock, the blockade played a major role in the deterioration of the Confederate logistical system. Southern railroads broke down or were captured faster than they could be maintained or replaced. As that rail system crumbled, so also did the ability of the Confederacy to furnish its soldiers and civilians with the supplies necessary to carry on the war.

The key to the effectiveness of the Union blockade was the capture of bases along the coastline of the Confederacy. Each blockading squadron needed access to a safe, major harbor that could serve as a base for refueling, repairs, and supplies. Most of the blockading vessels were steam powered, and, hence, they had the speed and mobility to maintain a tighter blockade than a fleet of sailing ships. Yet, for all its advantages, steam technology also bound the navy to immovable bases. Steam-powered vessels had complex machinery that necessitated frequent repairs, and their fuel requirements were enormous. Over 5,000 tons of coal per week were needed for the blockading squadron by the midpoint of the war. Four major bases, one for each of the blockading squadrons, were early Union targets for amphibious or combined army–navy expeditions. The first base secured for the Union navy was Port Royal, South Carolina.

Port Royal offered a magnificent offshore anchorage halfway between Charleston and Savannah. Its sheltered harbor, which was large and deep enough to float the entire Union navy, provided an ideal location for the supply base needed by the South Atlantic squadron. Commanded by Flag-Officer Samuel F. DuPont, an immense Union armada of seventy-seven ships entered Port Royal Sound on November 7, 1861, and in a matter of hours pounded into submission the two Confederate forts guarding the sea approach to the inlet.

Even before the forts surrendered, the local white population fled to the interior. When the first Union vessel arrived in Beaufort, a village up-river from Port Royal, the only Southerners there to greet them were the slaves. As was reported by Rear-Admiral Daniel Ammen,

> On the wharves were hundreds of negroes, wild with excitement, engaged in carrying movables of every character, and packing them in scows. As the gun-boats appeared, a few mounted white men rode away rapidly.[10]

This scene was repeated throughout the sea-islands from Charleston to Savannah when the 12,000 man occupation force that accompanied Du Pont's fleet fanned out and instituted Union control. Almost overnight the social fabric of this plantation district unraveled.

Port Royal was the first major Union victory in the war, and it set an ominous precedent for the future defense of the Confederacy. Whereas advances in military technology had given defenders a decided advantage over attackers in landed warfare, comparable advances in naval technology favored the invading forces. The steam-driven warships in Du Pont's fleet were maneuverable enough to stay out of the range of Confederate shore batteries or to present, at best, a moving target difficult to hit. Firing on the move, these warships were equipped with new shell guns. In contrast to the solid cannon balls of past naval armaments, the newer guns fired a hollow projectile that exploded on impact. The resulting shrapnel demolished targets, such as earthwork forts, that otherwise would have been all but impervious to damage from solid shot.

The coastal forts that the South seized in the winter and spring of 1861 were built for defense against navies of sail armed with cannon. After Port Royal, it was clear that such forts were militarily obsolete. For all intents and purposes, the Confederacy was now defenseless at the water's edge. As developed by Robert E. Lee, who commanded the South Atlantic coastal defenses of the Confederacy in the fall of 1861, before being made general of the army of Northern Virginia, defense from a seaborne invasion now rested on the use of a mobile reserve stationed inland at points where the tidal inlets were narrow enough to be obstructed. Such a reserve could be rushed to trouble spots whenever federal forces threatened to move inland. This defensive system kept the Union troops pinned along the South Carolina coast, but it could hardly prevent the Union navy from exploiting its Port Royal victory. Employing the tactics pioneered by Du Pont at Port Royal, Union naval commanders closed off one Confederate port after another along the South Atlantic coast and in the Gulf of Mexico. By 1864 only Charleston, South Carolina, and Wilmington, North Carolina, were still open to blockade runners along the Atlantic seaboard.

Overshadowed in the first year of the war by the publicity surrounding First Bull Run, the Union victory at Port Royal has also tended to be neglected because of the crisis in Anglo–American affairs that broke out on November 8, 1861, the day after Port Royal fell to the Yankees. This crisis, the *Trent* affair, pushed the Union and Great Britain to the brink of war and thereby offered the Confederacy its best chance of breaking the blockade through the armed intervention of a foreign power.

Captain Charles Wilkes of the *U.S.S. San Jacinto* precipitated the crisis when he stopped the *Trent,* a British mail steamer on a run from Havana to St. Thomas in the Caribbean, searched it, and removed two Confederate envoys bound for Europe, James Mason and John Slidell. The envoys were taken to Boston and imprisoned. Though an instant war hero in the North, Wilkes had violated interna-tional maritime law (Wilkes had every legal right to remove contraband from a neutral ship, but it was highly debatable if individuals could be counted as war goods) and insulted the world's greatest maritime power. Britain demanded the release of the prisoners and an apology from Lincoln's government. As the British waited for a response, they put their fleet on a war footing, sent reinforcements to Canada, and suspended the delivery of munitions to the North. The war crisis was a real one, but a compromise was worked out by the end of December. Slidell and Mason were released, and Secretary of State Seward issued a note explaining that Wilkes's actions had been unauthorized. Not anxious for a war with their largest trading partner, the British accepted Seward's terms and did not press for an official apology.

The Union's successful resolution of the *Trent* affair was a disastrous blow to Confederate foreign policy. The Confederacy had assumed that Britain, which imported eighty percent of its cotton supply from the South in the 1850s, would rush to its defense once the flow of cotton was cut off by the combined effects of the Union blockade and a voluntary embargo in the South on cotton exports. "The Yankees aren't such cursed fools as to think they can come here and whip us, let alone the British," reasoned a young Carolinian to a British war correspondent in the spring of 1861. "They are bound to take our part: if they don't we'll just give them a hint about cotton, and that will set matters right."[11]

Most Southerners were convinced that cotton was indeed a king whose economic sovereignty would force the British to intervene on behalf of the Confed-eracy in order to protect the jobs and profits in Britain's leading industry, cotton textiles. Such reasoning, as well as the determination of nonslaveholders that planters would not unduly profit from the war, resulted in a virtual halt of cotton exports from the South in 1861. Enforced by local committees of safety, this self-imposed embargo turned out to be a major blunder. It prevented the Confeder-acy from taking advantage of the very porous Union blockage of 1861 by shipping cotton abroad and thus acquiring foreign credits that could be used to purchase war goods or to support the price of Confederate bonds and currency. Moreover, the embargo failed to force Britain's hand. As an industrial society, imperial power, and maritime giant, Britain had far more to gain by remaining on friendly terms with the Union than it did by going to war with the Union over the issue of access to its prewar supply of cotton. From the Confederate perspective, this was the bitter lesson of the *Trent* affair.

When faced during the war with a choice between bread and cotton, the British chose the bread. It was the misfortune of the Confederacy that the outbreak of the Civil War coincided with a series of bad harvests in Europe. The British met this shortfall by drastically increasing their imports of Northern wheat. American exports of wheat skyrocketed from 17 to 58 million bushels between 1860 and 1863. Comparable increases in other food exports gave the Union significant economic leverage over the British, who were now dependent on the North for one-third to one-half of their basic food supplies. Without Northern imports to feed the factory workers, the British government would have been confronted with massive social unrest. As it was, economic suffering among laid-off textile operatives was considerable by 1862, but most of these operatives could not vote and their misery could be alleviated by increases in Poor Relief and private charity. Britain did not feel the pinch of the cotton famine until 1862 because of huge surpluses of raw cotton on hand in 1861 from the large Southern crops of 1859 and 1860.

As this backlog was worked down, alternative sources of supply were developed in British India and Egypt. When the pinch did come in 1862, it was already apparent that the American war was more of a stimulant than a depressant for the British economy. By accepting war orders from both sides, the British enjoyed a boom in their munitions, iron, and shipbuilding industries. Meanwhile, the slump in cotton textiles was counterbalanced by increases in linen and woolen production.

If economic logic dictated that Britain stay on the sidelines during the Civil War, so also did considerations of power politics. As the world's leading imperial power, the British hardly wanted to set a foolhardy precedent of supporting a war for political independence. In an irony that British statesmen thoroughly enjoyed, the Union was now attempting to enforce maritime demands concerning blockades and searches and seizures of neutral ships that the British navy traditionally had upheld. Indeed, the United States had fought the War of 1812 against the British in part for maritime doctrines that the Union openly rejected during the Civil War. As skilled practitioners of balance-of-power diplomacy, British officials were also concerned that a Confederate victory might so weaken the American republic as to create a dangerous vacuum of power in the Western Hemisphere, a situation that could touch off a generalized war if European powers rushed in to claim territory.

In the end, Britain was willing to grant the Confederacy no more than it had in the beginning. On May 14, 1861, the British government issued a proclamation of neutrality that granted the Confederacy the rights of a belligerent. This meant that the British recognized the legal right of the Confederacy to engage in a war through such actions as maintaining agents abroad, contracting for supplies, and outfitting privateers to prey on Northern shipping. This fell far short, however, of recognizing the Confederacy as a nation with full powers to make treaties or enter into foreign alliances. Since the British also acknowledged the legality of the Union blockade, the North probably benefited more from Britain's neutral stance than the South. If the Confederacy was ever to secure British recognition of its nationhood, it would first have to establish its political independence through a series of battlefield victories.

THE UNION OFFENSIVE THROUGH THE SPRING OF 1862

The fall and winter months of 1861 and 1862 were a time of preparation for the Northern war machine that was taking shape in the camps around Washington and throughout the lower Midwest. By the time that the second session of the 37th

Congress assembled in early December 1861, the Union already had put over 600,000 men into its armies and navies. Winning the war, however, would entail more than just amassing troops. Victory would necessitate a coordinated organizational effort by the federal government on a scale undreamed of before the Union's rude awakening at First Bull Run. Economic resources had to be mobilized to support the military apparatus and a financial system had to be devised to pay for a war that increased the annual expenditures of the federal government more than ten times over their levels in the 1850s. In the winter of 1861–1862, the U.S. Congress took the first steps toward the organizational transformation that would unleash the war making potential of the Northern economy. Those steps were fully as much a part of the Union's major offensive in the war as were the advances of its armies and navies.

Northern industry in 1861 was small in scale and very decentralized. The typical manufacturing establishment was capitalized at about $10,000 (the cost of five or six adult male slaves in the South) and employed only a dozen workers. This lack of consolidation, combined with the administrative inexperience of federal bureaucrats, ruled out any centralized program of industrial production during the war. Instead, the federal government secured the bulk of its war supplies by offering very profitable contracts to whoever promised to produce the needed goods. The result was waste, duplication, and widespread corruption, but the goods were procured. Paying for these goods, however, as well as other war-related expenses, required revolutionary changes in the monetary system. As the first war fought between mass armies in the age of industrialization, the Civil War produced a tremendous demand for goods and services. That demand could be met only by raising mass purchasing power through the creation of more currency.

On December 30, 1861, Northern banks and the Treasury suspended specie payments. As a consequence, the federal government temporarily stopped paying its soldiers and other creditors, and banks refused to redeem their notes in bullion. This specie suspension brought the Union's fiscal crisis to a head. From the beginning of the war the Treasury had been running large deficits and struggling with the problem of paying for the war on a specie basis when the amount of available gold and silver was simply inadequate for the Union's monetary needs. Congress was loathe to raise taxes, and the two pieces of tax legislation it did pass in August, 1861—a direct tax and an income tax—produced little in the way of immediate revenue. The direct tax, one levied in proportion to the population of each state (including the seceded ones), generated only $17 million throughout the war, and the income tax, the first in American history, did not take effect until 1863. Congress did authorize a $150 million bond issue, but Secretary of the Treasury Salmon P. Chase insisted on payment in bullion. The subsequent drain on the banks' reserves, coupled with the flight abroad of specie during the war scare with Britain over the *Trent* affair, set the stage for the specie suspension.

Congress responded to this financial crisis with the Legal Tender Act of February 1862, the first indication that the Republicans were prepared to restructure the economy to meet the demands of total war. Opposed by three-fourths of the congressional Democrats, and supported just as heavily by the Republicans, this act provided for the issuance of $150 million in non-interest-bearing treasury notes, commonly known as greenbacks. With the exceptions of customs duties and interest payments on the federal debt, these notes were legal tender for all public and private debts. The greenbacks were fiat money, that is, paper money decreed to be legal tender that was not backed by any explicit promise of redemption in gold or silver. For this reason, as well as the vast extension of federal authority it represented in a country that had never had a national currency, the greenback legislation was denounced by Democrats and fiscal conservatives in both parties as unsound, revolutionary, and, indeed, immoral. The prewar money of the country in effect had been gold, and most Americans believed that gold or silver could provide the only sound and "real" basis for a currency of uniform and lasting value. According to this view, paper money non-redeemable in specie was inherently dishonest because it represented no real value. The Republicans were able to push through the greenback legislation only because of the pressing need to meet the unprecedented costs of the war.

The greenbacks played a vital role in the Northern war effort. Eventually, over 400 million of them were issued, and they accounted for thirteen percent of the war's cost in the North. They resolved the immediate financial crisis in early 1862 by furnishing the Treasury with the money needed to pay its bills and permitting the banks to resume specie payments. By in effect democraticizing demand throughout the Union, the greenbacks were also instrumental in raising the mass purchasing power that made it possible to sell government bonds directly to the Northern public. Bonds could be bought with greenbacks, and about 1 million Northerners, or one in four families, acquired a financial stake in the cause of the Union by purchasing these bonds. Jay Cooke, a Philadelphia banker quickly hailed as the financier of the Union, ingeniously promoted and mass marketed the sale of the bonds.

As the Republican-controlled Congress was reorganizing the Union's finances to pay for the upcoming spring campaigns, it was also prodding Lincoln into viewing those campaigns as a weapon for emancipation. In March 1862, Congress prohibited the army from returning to their owners fugitive slaves who had come behind Union lines. This was a direct refutation of the army's official policy earlier in the war of enforcing the Fugitive Slave Act of 1850. In April, Congress passed a bill for compensated emancipation in the District of Columbia. In June, Congress prohibited slavery in all the federal territories and ratified a treaty with Britain for the joint suppression of the African slave trade. Northern public opinion was slowly but inexorably turning against slavery. The very success of Confederate resistance in what Northerners had assumed would be a short, victorious war was converting more and more whites to what had been the black position from the beginning of the conflict. As Frederick Douglass, the great black orator, put it: "The war now being waged in this land is a war for and against slavery; and...it can never be effectually put down till one or the other of these vital forces is completely destroyed."[12]

Lincoln both responded to and shaped this shift in Northern attitudes. He had signaled a dramatic shift in the approach of the federal government toward slavery in February 1862 when he refused to commute the death sentence of Captain Nathaniel Gordon, a Northern slave trader who was the first and only American citizen ever to be executed under a congressional act of 1819, that declared the importation of African slaves a capital offense. In March, Lincoln proposed a comprehensive program for voluntary and gradual state emancipation that included federal compensation of $400 per slave and funds for the colonization abroad of the freed blacks. This program was aimed specifically at the loyal Border states. Lincoln believed that their acceptance of his plan would bring a quick end to the war because the Confederacy would be deprived of any hope of ever winning over the most northern of the slave states. Although Lincoln's plan was rebuffed by the Border states, the future direction of the Northern war effort was unmistakable. Whether masters willed it or not, slavery was going to be a casualty of the war.

The looming threat of emancipation, as well as the sheer size of the Northern armies poised for invasion, created a crisis atmosphere in the Confederacy by the winter of 1862. "There seems to me to be a more general feeling of despondency prevailing at this time than ever before since the war began," noted Robert Kean of the Confederate Bureau of War in late January. Confederate hopes raised by the *Trent* affair and the recent bankrupt condition of the Union treasury had been dashed. Most alarming, according to Kean, was "the apathy of the people, their anxious desire to avoid military service, and the apparent cowardice of the legislature, which seems afraid to do anything worthy of the occasion."[13]

The most immediate cause of Kean's gloom was a series of Confederate military setbacks after the exhilarating victory at First Bull Run. In the fall of 1861, the Confederacy lost western Virginia, the sea-islands along the Carolina–Georgia coast, and Ship Island at the mouth of the Mississippi, an important base for the federal blockade and a staging area for a possible invasion of the lower Mississippi valley. On January 19, 1862, a defeat at the battle of Logan's Cross Roads forced the Confederacy to evacuate its troops from eastern Kentucky.

In the next two months, matters went from bad to worse for the Confederacy. In early February a Union amphibious expedition under General Ambrose E. Burnside overran Roanoke Island and thereby gained control of the approaches to Pamlico and Albemarle sounds, the outlets by sea for all of North Carolina's ports with the exception of Wilmington. The tidal districts of eastern North Carolina were now exposed to Yankee raiding parties. As Roanoke Island was being surrendered with the loss of over 2,000 troops, Richmond received even worse news from Tennessee. By mid-February the Confederacy suffered its first major strategic setback, and significantly it occurred in the West, the military theater where the Confederacy eventually was to lose the war.

In early 1862, General Albert Sidney Johnston, the top Confederate commander in the West, was attempting the impossible. He was trying to protect a long and porous 300-mile defensive line stretching across southern Kentucky from a numerically superior enemy that had fleets of gunboats to control the river systems. Johnston's troops were so dispersed that his posture of a passive defense virtually invited a Union concentration of forces against the most vulnerable points in his line. Those points were Fort Henry and Fort Donelson, two undermanned and poorly constructed fortifications just inside of Tennessee that commanded access to the Tennessee and Cumberland rivers, respectively. The Tennessee could be followed southward into northern Alabama and the Cumberland eastward into central Tennessee. Hence, both were tempting targets for the Union because they offered strategic corridors into the western heartland of the Confederacy.

Fort Henry fell on February 6, 1862, and Fort Donelson ten days later. The Union commander who engineered these first spectacular federal victories in the war was Ulysses S. Grant, a little known West Point graduate and veteran of the Mexican War. A failure in civilian pursuits and something of a problem drinker, Grant found himself in the war, and his U.S. initials instantly became famous when the Northern press played up his message to the Confederate commander at Fort Donelson that nothing less than "unconditional and immediate surrender" would be accepted. A superb military strategist and a daring tactician who was willing to seize the initiative, Grant strikingly exposed the strategic weakness of the Confederate position in the West. Able to dominate the water lines of communication with its

Campaigns in the West, 1862

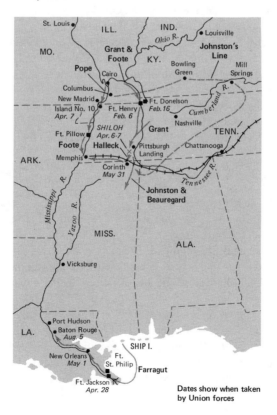

Dates show when taken by Union forces

ironplated and steam-powered gunboats, the Union could supply and concentrate their forces rapidly enough to outflank their Confederate opponents and compel them to retreat to more defensible positions. The loss of Fort Henry and Fort Donelson and the destruction of the Memphis and Ohio Railroad bridge just below Fort Henry cut off the logistical support for the Confederate armies in Tennessee. Those armies now had to retreat southward to Corinth, Mississippi. By February 23, Nashville, the capital of Tennessee, was in Union hands.

In March, the Confederacy's winter string of military reverses concluded with defeats at Pea Ridge, Arkansas, and Glorietta Pass in the New Mexico Territory. Pea Ridge cost the Confederacy its last chance for effective control in Missouri, and Glorietta Pass ended the Confederate dream of sending a column of Texas troops across the Southwest and into California to support an expected uprising of Southern sympathizers. Confederate possession of California conceivably could have turned the war around by depriving the Union of its major source of gold and by breaking the naval blockade. Only the unrelenting pressure of Union armies east of the Mississippi prevented the Confederacy from future attempts to gain access to the gold and ports of California.

The one bright spot in the late winter gloom of the Confederacy had been the spectacular initial success of the CSS *Virginia,* the armor-plated version of the captured Union steam frigate, the *Merrimac.* On March 8, the *Virginia* ventured out of Norfolk harbor and with its iron ram wreaked havoc among the wooden ships of the federal squadron in Hampton Roads. However, Confederate expectations of smashing the blockade were immediately quashed. Coincidentally, an experimental Union version of an ironclad, the *Monitor,* had just arrived in Hampton Roads. It fought the *Virginia* to a draw on March 9 and kept it bottled up in Norfolk. When the Confederacy was forced to evacuate Norfolk in May, the *Virginia* was scuttled. Most of the other ironclads the Confederate navy was feverishly building were lost when the ports of New Orleans and Memphis were captured by the Yankees in the spring of 1862.

On the eve of the spring campaigns of 1862, the Confederacy was in a desperate position. The war's heaviest fighting to date was about to begin, morale was slipping, and nearly two-thirds of Confederate soldiers were twelve-month volunteers whose terms of enlistment were set to expire. Casting a dark shadow over everything was the huge army in excess of 100,000 men that McClellan was preparing for a strike against Richmond. The reaction of Davis's government to this early crisis indicated for the first time that traditional Southern values of states' rights and individual liberties would be sacrificed in the cause of Confederate independence.

The most pressing problem was manpower. Following Davis's recommendation, the Confederate Congress passed the first national conscription act in American history on April 16, 1862. The act subjected all white males between the ages of eighteen and thirty-five (raised later in the war to the ages of forty-five and then fifty) to Confederate military service. Before the war was over, nearly one in five Confederate soldiers was a draftee.

Although intended in part to spur voluntary enlistments, the overriding purpose of the Conscription Act of 1862 was to retain in the armies the original volunteers whose terms of service were nearing expiration. These men were given no choice. They were kept in service, and three years were added to the date of their original enlistment. Five days later, Congress provided for a set of exemptions. Occupational categories were created by which bureaucrats, industrial workers, and some civilians, such as teachers, were exempted from fighting as long as their civilian service was deemed essential to the war effort.

The Conscription Act made possible a national army under the centralized control of the Richmond government. This invasion of states' rights and the civil liberties of individuals came six weeks after Congress authorized Davis on February 27, 1862, to declare martial law in Union-threatened areas and to suspend the writ of *habeas corpus*. Before March was out, Davis imposed martial law in parts of Louisiana and the major port cities of Virginia.

Congress acted decisively to deal with the problems of internal security and manpower, but it shrank from imposing the taxes that were needed to pay for the war without a ruinous spiral of runaway inflation. The first Confederate tax had been little more than a token gesture. In August, 1861, Congress levied a 0.5 percent tax on property. Without the administrative machinery to collect it, the Treasury officials relied upon the states to collect it for them. Nearly all of the states did so by the zero-sum procedure of borrowing money and issuing state bonds. Secretary of the Treasury Christopher Memminger tried to plug the revenue gap through loans. The Confederacy's first bond issue of $15 million in the spring of 1861 did sell well, but it drew in most of the available specie in the country. Produce loans, a pledge of planters of specified commodities, especially cotton, for the purchase of bonds, offered the promising alternative of substituting cotton for specie as a backing for Confederate debts. Once again, however, the Confederate Treasury was slow to create a collection agency, and planters were reluctant to surrender to government authorities a commodity that in effect was becoming white gold because of tremendous increases in the price of cotton. Out of authorized produce loans of $100 million, the Confederacy netted in depreciated currency barely one-third that amount.

Additional means of financing the war had to be found, and the Confederacy took the easy way out. It printed over $500 million in treasury notes, or paper money, in 1861 and 1862. By the winter of 1862, these notes were covering three-fourths of all Confederate expenses. Throughout the war, this paper money depreciated in value by an average of ten percent per month.

By simply holding onto their Confederate money, Southerners were being effectively taxed at a monthly rate of ten percent. Yet, no significant taxes on slaves and cotton, the two sources of Southern wealth that could have furnished the fiscal resources for a national currency, were passed in 1861 and 1862 when the Confederacy still had access to most of its original population base. Close to one-half of all Confederate congressmen owned more than twenty slaves, an economic status that placed them among the wealthiest three to four percent of all Southerners. They were not going to tax themselves to pay for a war being fought on behalf of their property interests in slaves. They also refused to run the risk of alienating the nonslaveholding majority by raising taxes on landed property. To have embarked upon such a program of taxation would have been tantamount in Southern political culture to a form of tyranny that hitherto had been attributed to the hated Yankees and the very Union that nonslaveholders had just been urged to leave. It was bad enough, at least for the time being, that those nonslaveholders had to be compelled to fight for the Confederacy through a national draft.

In the spring of 1862, Davis's government chose to ignore its mounting financial nightmare. If the Northern offensive could be stopped and Southern independence established, King Cotton would still have the time to assert itself and shore up the paper money of the Confederacy. That was the hope of Confederate leaders as they awaited the outcome of the spring battles.

In large measure because so much had been expected of it, McClellan's long heralded offensive against Richmond in the spring of 1862 was deemed a Union failure. Virtually commanded by Lincoln's War Order No. 1 of January 27, 1862, to come up with a plan and get moving by February 22, McClellan finally moved his military juggernaut out of Washington in mid-March. He avoided the overland route to Richmond by using his naval superiority to outflank the major Confederate

The Civil War in the East, 1861-1862

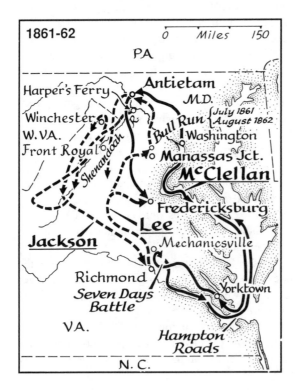

army in Virginia, which was under General Joseph Johnston. Union transports moved McClellan's force of 110,000 troops down the Potomac River and the Chesapeake Bay and landed it at Fortress Monroe at the tip of the Yorktown Peninsula between the York and James rivers. The Army of the Potomac was now within forty miles of Richmond, and its size was initially twice that of the Confederates opposing it. Had McClellan pushed his army quickly and decisively, the Confederate capital might well have fallen within a fortnight. Instead, McClellan dallied.

Deceived by reports of military intelligence that grossly exaggerated Confederate troop strength, McClellan wasted a month in front of the rebel fortifications at Yorktown. While his army stalled, McClellan pouted over Lincoln's last-minute decision to withhold from the Peninsula campaign the 40,000-man corps of General McDowell. Lincoln did so because he was worried over the threat posed to the Union capital and the Baltimore and Ohio Railroad by General Thomas J. (Stonewall) Jackson's campaign in the Shenandoah Valley. Outnumbered three to one by the federals, Jackson fought a brilliant campaign based on rapid marches and unorthodox tactics. He pinned down 60,000 Union troops and defeated them in five out of six battles.

While Jackson was running circles around Union armies, McClellan divided his army north and south of the Chickahominy River, a stream that bisects the Yorktown Peninsula. The northern wing was to protect McClellan's supply lines on the York River and cover the hoped-for arrival of McDowell's corps; the southern wing was to continue the advance on Richmond. This splitting of the Army of the Potomac gave the Confederates an opportunity to assume the offensive. First south and then north of the Chickahominy, the Confederates concentrated forces in an effort to destroy detached units of the Union army. The heaviest fighting occurred during the Seven Days' battles in late June. When the smoke had cleared, the main Confederate force in Virginia had a new name, the Army of Northern Virginia, and a new commander, Robert E. Lee, the replacement for Johnston who had been wounded at Fair Oaks on May 31. Most important, Lee had saved Richmond from being captured.

Although McClellan tactically had won most of the battles, he failed in his strategic objective of seizing Richmond. He compounded this failure by repeatedly accusing Lincoln of denying him needed support. When McClellan demanded 50,000 reinforcements in early July, Lincoln's patience ran out. He recalled McClellan's army to Washington. McClellan surely had been overly cautious, but it would be over two years before the Army of the Potomac was again as close to Richmond as McClellan had placed it during the Peninsula campaign.

The Union offensive in the West also ground to a halt by the summer of 1862. After its disastrous defeats at Fort Henry and Fort Donelson forced the evacuation of Tennessee, the Confederate command in the West reconcentrated its armies and surprised Grant's Army of the Tennessee in early April with a massive counterattack at Pittsburgh Landing on the Tennessee River. Named after a nearby backwoods church, the ensuing battle of Shiloh on April 6 and 7 was the first really bloody battle of the war. More Americans were killed at Shiloh than had died of battle wounds in the entire Mexican War. One of the dead was the Confederate commander, Albert Sidney Johnston. Before he was shot, his uniform had been riddled with bullet holes, the sole of a boot had been ripped off by a minie ball, and his horse had been hit in four places. The intense firepower of the armies resulted in 23,000 casualties, more than five times those killed or wounded at First Bull Run. This was a hellish baptism of fire for most of the troops, and many of them discovered, as one Confederate put it, that the glory of the battle "was all a glittering lie."[14] The survivors learned to inure themselves to such scenes of unimaginable horror as one described by a Union soldier. "I ate my dinner on Monday [April 7] within six paces of a rebel in four pieces. Both legs were blown off. His pelvis was the third piece, and his head and chest were the fourth piece."[15]

The Confederate objective at Shiloh was the annihilation of Grant's army before it was joined by General Don Carlos Buell's Army of the Ohio, which was moving southward from Nashville. A pell-mell attack along a three-mile front almost gave the Confederates a smashing victory on the first day of the battle. Grant's unentrenched army was caught unawares sipping its morning coffee and was nearly pushed back into the Tennessee River. However, the Confederate charge lost its momentum in the confusion of command after Johnston's death, the federals dug in at the river's edge, and Grant, who had been down river on a gunboat at the start of the battle, arrived and rallied his troops. That night, advanced elements of Buell's army reached Pittsburgh Landing, and the next day the federals took the fight to the rebels and forced them to abandon the battlefield and retreat back to their base at Corinth, Mississippi. As with subsequent Confederate counteroffensives in the West, the rebels had concentrated at Shiloh with barely too few men just a bit too late to achieve a decisive victory.

The top ranking Union general in the West was Henry W. Halleck. Half-convinced by reports (false, as it turned out) that the Union army had been caught unprepared at Shiloh because Grant was drunk the night before, Halleck assumed personal command of Grant's army after Shiloh. A very cautious general, who shared McClellan's proclivity for planning while he should have been marching, Halleck then proceeded to let the air out of the Union offensive. He moved his army of 120,000 against Beauregard's force of 70,000 at Corinth with all the speed of an advancing glacier. It took Halleck two months to cover the eighteen miles from Shiloh to Corinth that Johnston's army had marched over in three days back in early April on its way to Pittsburgh Landing. Halleck secured his objective of the rail center of Corinth, but by the time he arrived, Beauregard's army had slipped away. Contrary to Grant's wishes, Halleck then dispersed the huge Union army in the West. Some troops were sent to Arkansas; Grant took a bigger chunk with orders to protect Union supply lines stretched out along the Mobile and Ohio and Memphis and Charleston railroads; and Buell was sent east on a campaign to capture Chattanooga. The western armies of the Confederacy had been given a breathing spell and an opportunity to regain the strategic initiative.

In July, Lincoln called Halleck to the East, made him his top military adviser, and appointed him general-in-chief of all the Union armies. Although Halleck was not much of a fighter in the field, he was an excellent administrator and the Union had made major breakthroughs in the West while he was in command. Most significantly, with the exception of a short stretch from Vicksburg, Mississippi, to Port Hudson, Louisiana, the Mississippi River was under Union control by June 1862. Flag-Officer David Farragut had led an audacious naval assault up the Mississippi in early April, which culminated on April 25 with the capitulation of New Orleans, the largest city in the Confederacy and one of its major seaports. Halleck in turn coordinated the Union attacks that cleared most of the Mississippi of Confederate fortifications and delivered Memphis to the Union on June 6. If Halleck could repeat those successes in the East, Lincoln still hoped that the war might soon be over.

A NEW WAR AND CONFEDERATE COUNTERATTACKS: THE SUMMER AND FALL OF 1862

During a temporary lull in the fighting in July 1862, the war began to assume a fundamentally new character. On July 17 the Union Congress passed two acts that came close to confirming the worst fears of Confederate whites and realizing the deepest hopes of Union blacks. In the Militia Act, Congress authorized Lincoln to accept blacks into military service. This reversed a white-only policy for the militia that had stood since the War of 1812. Any blacks so enrolled, as well as their immediate families, who had been slaves of disloyal owners were declared free. In the Confiscation Act of 1862, Congress took a much bolder step against slavery than it had been willing to sanction in the summer of 1861. All slaves of rebel masters, regardless of whether they had actually been used to aid the rebellion, were now to be freed. The rationale for this limited program of emancipation was brutally simple. Slaves were property, and under the laws of war, the Union was entitled to confiscate any rebel property in order to bring the war to a successful end and punish the traitors who were pursuing it. In short, as more than one Republican congressman now insisted, it was time to take off the gloves and fight a real war.

This July legislation by no means satisfied abolitionists, blacks, and the Radical Republicans, and Lincoln made no real effort to enforce it. Lincoln initially did not recruit blacks for the military because he believed that Northern public opinion was not yet ready for such a step toward full black citizenship, and he himself doubted whether blacks would make good combat soldiers. He also questioned the constitutionality of the Second Confiscation Act and allowed it to become a virtual dead letter. Already infuriated by Lincoln's countermanding in May of General David Hunter's emancipation decree in the Department of the South (South Carolina, Georgia, and Florida), antislavery Northerners denounced Lincoln for his caution. Nonetheless, the abolitionist Lydia Maria Child had been correct when she noted back in February 1861, "The blind fury of the Secessionists have converted them into the most valuable Anti-Slavery Agents."[16] In particular, dogged rebel resistance converted the rank and file of the Union armies and many of their officers into agents of emancipation.

By the spring of 1862, the western armies were refusing to comply with orders for the release of fugitive slaves to loyal masters and harassing those owners who did try to reclaim their slaves. Some soldiers, to be sure, acted out of humanitarian reasons, but a far greater number were motivated by self-interest. They accepted the reality of the war for what it was: Most often the only friends they had in rebel territory were runaway slaves. Supposedly loyal Southern whites, the property of whom the army was ordered to protect, frequently turned out to be rebels at heart who betrayed the location of Union troops and fought as guerrillas under the cover of darkness. It was far easier to do away with any distinction between Unionist and rebel and simply take anybody's property that would help feed and shelter the army. The Union high command was coming to the same conclusion by the second year of the war. Orders went out to the generals to consume or destroy any property that could be of any use to the Confederate war effort. If that property included slaves, so much the better. Each slave behind federal lines was one less worker for the Confederacy and one more for the Union.

Runaway slaves proved to be invaluable to the Union military. Not only did they work as laborers in camps and on fortifications, they also acted as spies, scouts, and river pilots. In many campaigns they were the eyes and ears of the Union forces. For example, General O. M. Mitchel reported from northern Alabama in May 1862,

> I shall soon have watchful guards among the slaves on the plantations from Bridgeport to Florence, and all who communicate to me valuable information I have promised the protection of my government. Should my course in this particular be disapproved, it would be impossible for me to hold my position.[17]

When Congress did embark on a limited program of emancipation, it was only confirming what the soldiers already knew: Emancipation would be in the best interests of the Union army.

Emancipation was moving to the center stage of the war because slaves were pushing it there through their own actions. Many, perhaps most, slaves understood from the beginning that the outbreak of the war portended their freedom. It was their flight to the army camps, their refusal to be sent back into slavery, and their willingness to work and sacrifice for the cause of the Union that pressured the entire chain of command in the federal war effort to make emancipation an objective of the war. Slaves seized freedom whenever the opportunity presented itself. They risked being killed, mutilated, or savagely beaten if captured while fleeing to Union lines. Still, they continued to come. The presence of a federal force acted as a magnet to draw them out of their slave quarters. Slaveowners bewailed the aid and comfort their chattels gave to the enemy, and they were horrified at being driven off their own plantations by their own "loyal" slaves when the federals approached. Northern observers of these scenes immediately saw that the happy, docile slave described by Southern apologists for the institution was a myth. The slaves were enraged and embittered, and their anger was so frightfully evident that it provided one of the rationales for the formerly unthinkable Union policy of arming the ex-slaves as federal troops. A Northern reporter on the sea-islands in late December 1861 argued thus: "I have sometimes asked myself whether the time might not come when arming the blacks and regularly drilling them as soldiers under white officers might not prove the only means of averting the odious horrors of a servile insurrection."[18]

The slaves, as well as the army officials who channeled their demands and needs to Washington, were instrumental in redefining the Union's war aims to include emancipation. In July 1862, Lincoln made the decision to so redefine the meaning of the war. He decided to issue an emancipation proclamation that would be constitutionally based on his wartime powers as commander-in-chief of the armed forces. Only such powers, reasoned Lincoln, could legalize such a revolutionary overthrow of antebellum federalism.

Although Lincoln certainly believed that slavery was a moral evil, the existence of which was a major contributor to the surprisingly successful resistance of the Confederacy, he put off any final decision on slavery until the Border states were militarily secure for the Union and had had a chance to respond to his plan for gradual, compensated emancipation. These states were now firmly riveted to the Union, and their leaders had spurned his plan for emancipation. Meanwhile, Congress and the army were demanding a tougher policy against slavery. Finally,

As shown in this Civil War lithograph, Lincoln's decision in favor of emancipation rested ultimately on military logic.

McClellan's failure in front of Richmond and the subsequent need in July to call for 300,000 additional troops convinced Lincoln that a point of no return had been reached. To win the war he would have to strike directly at slavery.

Persuaded by Seward's advice to wait for a Union victory before issuing his proclamation, lest it appear as the desperate expedient of a floundering government, Lincoln postponed his proclamation. He waited. For the next two months Confederate counterattacks put Union forces on the defensive.

After absorbing the heaviest blows of the Union offensive in the spring, Confederate armies returned them in kind during the late summer and fall of 1862. In the East, Lee brilliantly exploited the confused and antagonistic command structure that Lincoln had created at the tail end of the Peninsula campaign. General John Pope, the conqueror of Island No. 10 in the Mississippi River, was brought in from the West to show the eastern armies how to fight. He was given command of the new Union Army of Virginia, an amalgam of units previously humiliated in the Shenandoah Valley by Stonewall Jackson. McClellan, whom Lincoln feared would never budge from his supply base at Harrison's Landing on the James River, was ordered to bring the Army of the Potomac back to Washington and combine it with Pope's for a landed offensive on Richmond from the north.

While McClellan took his own sweet time in preparing to reinforce the army of a rival general whom he considered an incompetent braggart, Lee also came to the conclusion that Pope talked a better battle than he fought. Correctly sensing that McClellan was content to just sit for a while at Harrison's Landing, Lee detached Jackson's corps and sent it north in mid-July to parry any southward thrust by Pope. Lee then capitalized on the snail-like withdrawal of McClellan's army from the Peninsula. Leaving behind a token force to protect Richmond, Lee wheeled the bulk of his army north to strike at Pope before McClellan could unite with him. The result was the second battle of Bull Run on August 29–30, 1862. This, like the first one, was a resounding Confederate victory. Though he had been ill-served by McClellan's near criminally slow effort to reach him, Pope compounded his problems by making a tactical fool of himself at Bull Run. He had difficulty in locating the Confederate troops and in determining what they were up to once he had. His troops, though fighting fiercely, fled the field, just as the federals had done during the First Bull Run battle. Pope was, obviously, not the general the Army of the Potomac needed, so he was cashiered and relegated to a minor post in the Midwest. His troops were placed under the command of McClellan, who now had the task of restoring the morale of the Army of the Potomac. When McClellan was seen riding toward the troops, cheers erupted, because the army's creator was back.

McClellan was barely back in charge when Lee again seized the initiative by marching his army into western Maryland. Unable to tackle the strong entrenchments in front of Washington, and unwilling to sit back passively while the Virginia countryside continued to be stripped of supplies by both armies, Lee launched his first invasion of Union soil. Lee went north primarily for logistical reasons. Since it had left Richmond in mid-August, his army had been subsisting on half rations of flour and meal, and Maryland offered a rich foraging area for fresh provisions. In addition, keeping the Army of the Potomac out of northern Virginia during the fall harvest of 1862 would help ensure the future supplies for Lee's army.

Political motives also influenced Lee's bold decision. If he could remain north of the Potomac throughout the fall, and perhaps even make a raid into Pennsylvania, he might so embarrass the Lincoln administration as to turn the Northern fall elections against it and embolden those Northerners willing to recognize Southern independence. Lee also hoped that the presence of a major Confederate army might still entice slaveholding Maryland into the Confederacy. In this he was soon disappointed. As one rebel soldier laconically noted, "...the citizens of Maryland did not greet us with the enthusiasm we anticipated."[19] Last, there was always the possibility that a Union mistake might give Lee an opportunity to win a decisive victory on Northern soil, a victory that could break the Northern will to persist in the war and gain for the Confederacy the elusive prize of foreign recognition.

Instead of Lee, it was McClellan who almost won a decisive victory in Maryland. Through a stroke of fate, Lee's orders for the splitting up of his army as it advanced fell into McClellan's hands. The orders had been wrapped around some cigars and, apparently, fell out of a Confederate officer's pocket. Union soldiers, who were shadowing the Confederates, were taking a breather in a field when one of them found the cigars. He was going to throw the wrapper away when he noticed that the wrapper was Special Orders 191 to Lee's generals. McClellan now had a golden opportunity to smash the dispersed columns of Lee's army before they could reunite.

As usual, McClellan moved too slowly. Lee, disdaining a retreat back into Virginia, had just enough time to draw up his army in battle formation along Antietam Creek near the town of Sharpsburg, Maryland. On September 17, 1862, the armies clashed in a single day's battle of unbelievable butchery. Over 20,000 maimed and dead bodies lay strewn along the battleground before night fell. Despite a two-to-one manpower advantage over the unentrenched Confederates, McClellan had refused to order an all-out assault. He held 20,000 troops in reserve and fought a battle of isolated, uncoordinated attacks. Potential breakthroughs were sealed by the desperate Confederate defenders, and the result was a bloody draw.

Tactically inconclusive, Antietam was nonetheless a very significant battle in strategic terms. Lee, having lost over twenty percent of the effective strength of his already outnumbered army, was forced to head back to Virginia without obtaining any of the political objectives of his Maryland campaign. And Lincoln, though bitterly frustrated by McClellan's inability to destroy Lee's army, read enough of a Union victory in Antietam to issue his Preliminary Emancipation Proclamation on September 22, 1862. Preliminary because it would not take effect until January 1, 1863, this proclamation declared free the slaves in the states or parts of states that remained in rebellion.

As Lee's army was swinging into Maryland, Confederate armies under generals Braxton Bragg and Edmund Kirby-Smith were rolling through Tennessee

Civil War battles took a sickening toll of human lives. Now bloated in death, these Confederate soldiers were killed at Antietam.

and on into Kentucky. Bragg, who replaced Beauregard after Corinth was evacuated, planned a daring offensive to gain Kentucky for the Confederacy and carry the war to the Yankees on the Ohio River. In the summer of 1862, the Union campaign of General Buell's against Chattanooga bogged down in northern Alabama. Taking advantage of this, as well as the stationary warfare imposed on the western armies of the Union by Halleck, Bragg divided his Army of Tennessee. He left generals Earl Van Dorn and Sterling Price behind in Mississippi with 32,000 troops to keep an eye on Grant, and, in an innovative strategic use of the railroads, he shipped his remaining 35,000 troops south to Mobile and then up to Atlanta and finally Chattanooga. He had gotten a jump on Buell and was now free to surge into Kentucky in a parallel move with Smith's smaller army coming out of eastern Tennessee.

Like Lee's offensive, the success of Bragg's invasion was heavily dependent on the assumed pro-Confederate loyalties of a Border state that the Confederacy felt was rightfully theirs. But in Kentucky, as in Maryland, the citizenry did not rise up and support the Southern forces. Although Bragg oversaw the inauguration of a Confederate governor in Frankfort, and Smith captured Lexington, civilians were more likely to treat their armies as invaders rather than as liberators. Moreover, those armies were in a precarious position as long as the tardy Buell was free to operate in their rear and against their lines of communications. Finally, and after much prodding from Washington, Buell caught up with the combined forces of

Bragg and Smith at Perryville on October 8, 1862. The battle was a tactical draw, but Bragg now had no choice but to retreat into middle Tennessee. The Confederacy just did not have the logistical means of supporting an offensive for very long, and Bragg's best hope for reinforcements had been lost when a Confederate attempt to break out of northern Mississippi failed in a counterattack at Corinth on October 3. After an auspicious beginning, Bragg's offensive wound up as another strategic failure for the Confederacy.

Antietam, Corinth, and Perryville marked the cresting of the high tide of the Confederate counteroffensives in the fall of 1862. Only the Union now had the fresh strength to begin new offensives before the onset of winter. While one formulated for Middle Tennessee did not culminate until the first days of January, the other two in Mississippi and Virginia were dismal failures in December.

Grant planned a two-pronged attack on Vicksburg, the major remaining Confederate stronghold on the Mississippi. Grant's overland approach from the north had to turn back after Confederates under Van Dorn destroyed his supply base in his rear at Holly Springs, Mississippi, and rebel cavalry in Tennessee under Nathan Bedford Forrest wrecked his railroad communications. Without the arrival of Grant's troops to draw off Confederate defenders from Vicksburg, the riverborne expedition led by General William T. Sherman collapsed when it met unexpectedly strong rebel resistance at Chickasaw Bluffs, just to the north of Vicksburg. Sherman's defeat came two weeks after the Virginia offensive had ended in a ghastly setback at Fredericksburg on December 13.

Lincoln relieved McClellan of his command on November 7 for his failure to pursue Lee's mauled army after Antietam. Ambrose Burnside, McClellan's replacement, was a competent corps commander who was now in over his head. Fully aware that Lincoln wanted an offensive as soon as possible, he produced a plan that was reasonable enough on paper. He would cross the Rappahannock River at Fredericksburg and steal a march on Lee by getting a headstart toward Richmond. It might have worked if the pontoon bridges needed to cross the river had arrived before Lee had time to consolidate his army in an impregnable defensive position on the heights overlooking Fredericksburg from the west. The pontoon bridges did not arrive on schedule, and Burnside lost the element of surprise while waiting for them. Still, Burnside forged ahead, or rather his troops did. In trying to storm the rebel lines on Marye's Heights, the center of Burnside's attack, they were simply slaughtered. The wonder of it all was that wave after wave of them continued to charge throughout the afternoon. The cost was 12,000 Union casualties.

Fredericksburg and Chickasaw Bluffs ended the Union war effort of 1862 on the worst possible note. The high promise of the spring campaign was now lost in the dark gloom of December. The Republicans had lost thirty-two congressional seats to the Democrats in the autumn elections of 1862, Lee was seemingly invincible, and Lincoln was under attack from all sides. The Radicals assailed Lincoln for being duped by such Democratic generals as McClellan and Buell and for being soft on the rebels. The Democrats condemned him for waging a war of military despotism and social upheaval. Well might a Republican congressman, William Parker Cutler, lament on hearing of the federal disaster at Fredericksburg that "God alone can take care of us & all his ways *seem* to be against us & to favor the rebels & their allies—the Democrats."[20] Much more fighting was in store before antislavery Republicans such as Cutler were to believe that God had returned to their side.

NOTES

1. George Ticknor in Henry Steele Commager (ed.), *The Blue and the Gray* (Indianapolis: Bobbs-Merrill, 1950), p. 41.
2. Jane Stuart Woolsey to a friend, May 10, 1861, in Commager, p. 43.
3. Roy P. Basler, ed., *The Collected Works of Abraham Lincoln* vol. 5 (New Brunswick: Rutgers University Press, 1953), p. 59.
4. G. T. Beauregard, "The First Battle of Bull Run," *Battles and Leaders of the Civil War* vol. 1 (New York: Thomas Yoseloff, 1956 [1887]), p. 222.
5. Quoted in Herman Hattaway and Archer Jones, *How the North Won: A Military History of the Civil War* (Urbana: University of Illinois Press, 1983), p. 18.
6. Quoted in William R. Brock, *Conflict and Transformation: The United States, 1844–1877* (Baltimore, Md.: Penguin, 1973), p. 241.
7. Basler, vol. 4, p. 344.
8. *Congressional Globe,* 37 Congress, 1 Session, p. 223.
9. Basler, vol. 4, p. 506.
10. Daniel Ammen, "Du Pont and the Port Royal Expedition," in *Battles and Leaders of the Civil War,* vol. 1, p. 688.
11. William Howard Russell, *My Diary North and South,* (New York: Harper & Row, 1954), p. 55.
12. Quoted in William L. Barney, *Flawed Victory* (New York: Praeger, 1975), p. 130.
13. Robert Garlick Kean, *Inside the Confederate Government,* (New York: Oxford University Press, 1957), p. 23.
14. Commager, p. 357.
15. Harold Elk Straubing (ed.), *The Fateful Lightning: Civil War Eyewitness Reports* (New York: Paragon House, 1987), p. 37.
16. Milton Miltzer and Patricia G. Holland (eds.), *Lydia Maria Child: Selected Letters, 1817–1880* (Amherst: The University of Massachusetts Press, 1982), p. 377.
17. Mitchel's report is cited in Don Carlos Buell, "Operations in North Alabama," *Battles and Leaders of the Civil War,* vol. 2, p. 703.
18. John W. Blassingame (ed.), *Slave Testimony: Two Centuries of Letters, Speeches, Interviews, and Autobiographies* (Baton Rouge: Louisiana State University Press, 1980), p. 360.
19. John Fisher (ed.), "The Travels of the 13th Mississippi Regiment: Excerpts from the Diary of Mike M. Hubbert of Attala County [1861–1862]," *Journal of Mississippi History,* vol. 45, p. 307, 1983.
20. Allan G. Bogue, "William Parker Cutler's Congressional Diary of 1862–63," *Civil War History,* vol. 33, p. 320, 1987.

SUGGESTED READINGS

COULTER, E. MERTON, *The Confederate States of America*. Baton Rouge, La.: Louisiana State University Press, 1950.

CROOK, DAVID P., *The North, the South, and the Powers, 1861–1865*. New York: John Wiley, 1974.

CURRY, LEONARD P., *Blueprint for Modern America*. Nashville, Tenn.: Vanderbilt University Press, 1968.

DONALD, DAVID, ed., *Why the North Won the Civil War*. Baton Rouge, La.: Louisiana State University Press, 1960.

HAGERMAN, EDWARD, *The American Civil War and the Origins of Modern Warfare*. Bloomington, Ind.: Indiana University Press, 1988.

HATTAWAY, HERMAN, and JONES, ARCHER, *How the North Won*. Urbana, Ill.: University of Illinois Press, 1983.

JIMERSON, RANDALL C., *The Private Civil War: Popular Thought During the Sectional Conflict*. Baton Rouge, La.: Louisiana State University Press, 1988.

LINDERMAN, GERALD F., *Embattled Courage: The Experience of Combat in the American Civil War*. New York: Free Press, 1987.

McPHERSON, JAMES M., *Battle Cry for Freedom*. New York: Oxford University Press, 1987.

McWHINEY, GRADY, and JAMISON, PERRY D., *Attack and Die: Civil War Military Tactics and the Southern Heritage*. University, Ala.: University of Alabama Press, 1982.

MITCHELL, REID, *Civil War Soldiers*. New York: Viking, 1988.

NEVINS, ALLAN, *The War for the Union: The Improvised War, 1861–1862*. New York: Scribner, 1959.

NEVINS, ALLAN, *The War for the Union: War Becomes Revolution, 1862–1863*. New York: Scribner, 1960.

ROBERTSON, JAMES I., JR., *Soldiers Blue and Gray*. Columbia, S.C., University of South Carolina Press, 1988.

THOMAS, EMORY M., *The Confederate Nation, 1861–1865*. New York: Harper and Row, 1979.

WILLIAMS, T. HARRY, *Lincoln and His Generals*. New York: Random House, 1952.

6

The Revolutionary War

"It is a war of extermination, and many openly declare it and are not ashamed to confess it, but glory in it."[1] By the spring of 1863, as Elizabeth Ingraham knew all too well after Union troops and slaves ransacked her Mississippi plantation, the war had entered a phase of mass destruction. She and countless other Southern civilians now bore the brunt of the North's application of total war.

In this first modern war, the mass mobilization of resources counted more toward victory or defeat than the individual heroism of the soldiers. For Union commanders victory became not so much a matter of winning battles but of destroying the resources of the Confederacy. Ultimately, the capacity of Confederate armies to wage war depended on the economic and psychological support they received from the civilian population. To win its war of conquest, the Union now targeted civilians as well as Confederate armies. To stave off defeat, the Confederate government increasingly demanded draconian sacrifices from those same civilians. It was now not a war of individual glory but of organized devastation. For all the talk on both sides of God still favoring their cause, perhaps the truth of the matter was best expressed by a surgeon in an Illinois regiment. "There is no God in war. It is merciless, cruel, vindictive, un-Christian, savage, relentless. It is all that devils could wish for."[2]

The Emancipation Proclamation of January 1, 1863, and its accompanying call for the arming of ex-slaves were the major strategic steps taken by Lincoln to break the military stalemate of the first half of the war. Cited by Jefferson Davis as additional proof that the Union was now waging the war for "no other purpose than revenge and thirst for blood and plunder of private property,"[3] the Emancipation Proclamation did in fact mark the point at which the Union focused the war against the property of planters. It also gave the Union cause a moral purpose in a war effort that earlier could be criticized as a naked grab for power. Friends of the Union in Europe received a tremendous emotional boost, and any chance of European recognition of the Confederacy was greatly reduced. And arming the freed slaves, as Lincoln predicted in March 1863, enabled the North to utilize "the great *available* and yet *unavailed* of, force for restoring the Union."[4]

Interpreted in the South as a declaration of total war, the Emancipation Proclamation had the effect of redoubling Confederate efforts to achieve by force of arms a total and irrevocable separation from the Union. In the spring of 1863, the Confederate Congress belatedly passed its first comprehensive program of taxation to finance the war, Union offensives in the West remained stalled, and Lee's Army of Northern Virginia appeared more invincible than ever after its victory at Chancellorsville, Virginia, in May. Yet, as this chapter will trace out, the pieces of the Union's victorious war plans had fallen into place by 1863. By simultaneously freeing and arming the slaves, the Union had gained the moral and military momentum in the war. Its strategy of holding in the East, winning in the West, and grinding away everywhere at the Southern social fabric left the Confederacy with neither the space, the material, nor the men it needed to maintain its independence. By the spring of 1865 the Union had bludgeoned the Confederacy into submission.

BREAKING THE STALEMATE: EMANCIPATION AND THE ARMING OF BLACKS

"It may have been indecisive, but our resources will stand the wear and tear of indecisive conflict longer than those of slavedom, and can sooner be repaired...."[5] This comment by the New Yorker George Templeton Strong concerning the battle of Murfreesboro (or Stone's River), fought on the last day of 1862 and the second day of 1863, was a shrewd assessment of the standoff in the first two years of the war and its future implications. The biggest battle in the West since Shiloh had just been fought, and the result was another bloody draw that further drained a diminishing Confederate resource base.

General William Rosecrans, the Union commander of the Army of the Cumberland, had replaced Buell after Perryville and was under orders to drive Bragg's Confederate army out of central Tennessee before the winter rains put an end to offensive campaigning. Determined to fight and gain a victory to salvage his Kentucky campaign, Bragg made his stand near Murfreesboro, Tennessee. After initially collapsing the federal right wing, Bragg's attack bogged down on the federal left. The armies rested for a day, and on January 2 Bragg ordered a senseless charge on a Union position east of Stone's River that was covered by the massed fire of the Union artillery. It was a ferocious battle. The sounds of the cannons could be heard twenty-six miles away, and Union soldiers later counted 150 bullets embedded in a two-foot diameter oak that was on the battle site. Yet, Bragg had gained nothing. He had lost one-third of his army killed and wounded, was out of supplies, and had to retreat southward to winter quarters in Tullahoma, Tennessee. Meanwhile, Rosecrans was quickly reinforced, and Middle Tennessee remained open to the federals.

Both before and after Murfreesboro, Rosecrans's army was plagued by Confederate raiders and guerrillas striking at its supply lines. This was a common problem of all Union generals, and it necessitated a huge deployment of troops that was out of all proportion to the amount of enemy territory actually secured by Union offensives. For example, to protect the federal enclave in northern Mississippi and west Tennessee early in 1863, 51,000 Union troops were needed to guard railroads and other lines of communication from a potential Confederate force of about 13,000. Similarly, 43,000 Confederates were able to pin down close to 200,000 federals in Missouri and Arkansas. Even at the end of 1862, at a time when the Union had regained from the Confederacy only the Carolina coast, west Tennessee, northern Arkansas, and the lower Mississippi Valley in the immediate vicinity of New Orleans, these demands for what was essentially garrison duty were already enormous. They could only intensify as Union armies pushed deeper into the South.

As Lincoln wrestled with the problem of emancipation in the last half of 1862, he also worried over how he could ever meet the spiraling demands on Union manpower for both combat and logistical duties. By linking emancipation with arming the ex-slaves, he hit upon one possible solution. The Emancipation Proclamation stipulated that, henceforth, freed slaves would be accepted by the Union military "to garrison forts, positions, stations, and other places, and to man vessels of all sorts in said service."[6]

As a moral document, the Emancipation Proclamation fell far short of a ringing declaration on behalf of human freedom. Critics immediately pointed out that the Proclamation freed slaves in areas where the Union had no authority and kept them enslaved in areas that were under effective Union control. Consistent with Lincoln's belief that emancipation was constitutional only under the war powers of the executive, the Proclamation declared free only those slaves in the Confederacy. Excluded from its provisions were slaves in the loyal states of the Border South and those in the Union-occupied areas of Tennessee, West Virginia, New Orleans and its surrounding parishes, and Norfolk and Virginia's eastern shore.

The Emancipation Proclamation did not free a single slave on the day it was issued, but that was never Lincoln's intention. The purpose of the Proclamation was to redefine the Union's war aims in such a way as to add to Union strength while subtracting from that of the Confederacy. Never forgetting that Union strength had to be defined in political as well as military terms, Lincoln deliberately cast his revolutionary decree in dry, legalistic language that substituted cool military logic for the warmth of moral ardor. Despite this language, Lincoln did disarm his critics

The above was a common scene in the latter part of the war: Black Union troops taking part in the liberation of slaves on a Southern plantation.

on the left by publicly identifying the cause of the Union with the principles of the Declaration of Independence; and because of that language, he assured his critics on the right that he was no wild-eyed radical, but a cautious military strategist who would augment the strength of the military while dismantling slavery.

There was no need to include the loyal slave states of the Upper South in the Proclamation because, as Lincoln repeatedly had told the planters there, the very wear and tear of the war was irreversibly destroying slavery outside the limits of the Confederacy. The Proclamation speeded up this process of disintegration by authorizing the enlistment of black troops. Within a year, efforts in the Border states to limit this recruitment first to free blacks and then to slaves of rebel owners collapsed as a result of the military's insatiable demand for manpower and the desire of nonslaveholding whites to fill their states' draft quotas with as many blacks as possible. In October 1863, the War Department officially sanctioned recruitment practices that had been going on for months. Now, the military could legally recruit all blacks in the Border states, and compensation was to be paid to loyal owners where slaves had enlisted without their permission. Late in the war, Maryland and Missouri provided for emancipation in their state constitutions. Kentucky and Delaware refused to face reality, and legal, as opposed to *de facto,* emancipation here had to await the passage of the 13th Amendment in 1865.

In its most immediate impact, the Emancipation Proclamation all but clinched the case against foreign recognition of the Confederacy. Reaction in Europe to the

Civil War loosely followed class lines. European aristocrats, for whom democracy was synonymous with mob rule and an end of legal privilege, generally sympathized with the Confederate cause as the noble effort of a conservative landed elite to break free from the radical excesses of American democracy. Workers, on the other hand, identified with the Union as the embodiment of those principles of liberty and equality that were at the heart of European liberalism and the workers' movement for greater political democracy. These workers embraced the Emancipation Proclamation as an affirmation of the Union's commitment to the rights and dignity of free labor throughout the world. They organized mass protest meetings demanding that their governments remain neutral in a war that could now be characterized as a great moral struggle against the evils of human bondage. Henry Adams, the son of Charles Francis Adams, the American minister to England, reported from London that the Proclamation was a "God-send" in rallying support for the Union.

> I never quite appreciated the "moral influence" of American democracy, nor the cause that the privileged classes in Europe have to fear us, until I saw directly how it works. At this moment, the American question is organising a vast mass of the lower orders in direct contact with the wealthy. They go our whole platform and are full of the "rights of man."[7]

Such talk of universal rights frightened European aristocrats the same way talk of emancipation terrified American slaveholders. To protect their privileged status at home, they pulled back from their espousal of the Confederacy. Led by Britain, Europe would remain on the sidelines barring a major Confederate breakthrough.

In longer terms, the Emancipation Proclamation was of critical importance in the meeting of Lincoln's manpower goals for the Union military. Although the first black troops were mustered into service in the fall of 1862, recruitment did not begin in earnest until the spring of 1863. Enlistment drives were organized in the Mississippi Valley and the sea-islands, the federally occupied areas with the largest concentration of slaves. Many Union recruiters virtually dragooned able-bodied black males into the army, but, generally, blacks welcomed the chance to fight for their freedom and for that of their families. As Solomon Bradley of South Carolina put it: "In Secesh times I used to pray the Lord for this opportunity to be released from bondage and to fight for my liberty, and I could not feel right so long as I was not in the regiment."[8]

In the North, free blacks enlisted at a rate three times higher than that of whites. Within the South the highest rates of black military participation (close to sixty percent of those eligible) occurred in the loyal Border states. Enrollment in the army brought the freedom that had not been included in the Emancipation Proclamation, and in March 1865 Congress conferred freedom on the families of the black soldiers. Eventually, 180,000 blacks served in the Union army, and four-fifths of them had been slaves at the start of the war.

The arming of the blacks was the logical culmination of a federal policy designed to resolve the problem of what to do with the massive numbers of fugitive slaves who sought the protection of Union armies and navies. By the war's end, half a million slaves had made it behind Union lines. Federal military authorities herded them into makeshift contraband camps. The lack of any federal tradition of responsibility for individual social and economic welfare, the resentment of Union commanders over being burdened with the care of a large class of noncombatants, and the brutal callousness of Union soldiers toward a race they deemed as inferior all contributed to the appalling conditions in these refugee centers. Crowded together in unsanitary conditions where epidemics took a heavy toll, the contrabands suffered mortality rates in excess of twenty-five percent.

Through a process of trial and error, a federal contraband policy took shape in 1862 and 1863. It aimed both at restoring the maximum military efficiency of Union armies and demonstrating to Northern voters that the unraveling of slavery would contribute to a Union victory. The core of this policy was the decision to put the black refugees to work. Battalions of blacks were organized for the heavy, physical work of chopping wood, hauling supplies, and building fortifications. Their wages, which were often late in being paid, were one-third to one-fifth of what black laborers could earn in civilian employment.

A far greater number of contrabands were put to work growing cotton. Virtually driven back to the plantations by army commanders, these blacks worked for loyal Southern planters, Northerners who leased abandoned plantations from the federal government, or for the government itself on land placed under the control of freedmen's aid societies in the North. Working conditions were best on the plantations operated by the Northern benevolent societies and their superintendents, but, in nearly all cases, the wages were so low that the freedmen wound up with little more than room and board in return for their labor. This was a free labor system that at the worst approximated slavery.

Still, in terms of the Union war effort, this policy of re-establishing the blacks as a rural work force in the occupied areas of the South was a success. Federal armies were freer to engage in military operations, the cotton-starved textile mills of New England were partially resupplied, and Northern reformers were able to proclaim that black labor could indeed be profitable without the coercive controls of slavery.

This contraband labor policy had the great political virtue of reassuring a worried Northern public that the freed slaves would be contained within the South. Although most blacks had no desire of moving to the North, the possibility of such a black migration and the competition it would touch off for jobs frightened many Northern whites. Sporadic anti-black riots in Northern cities and throughout the lower Ohio Valley in 1862 and 1863 convinced Lincoln that the political needs of his party and the avoidance of a racial explosion demanded a federal policy that would keep the blacks within the South. Ultimately, and as Lincoln so clearly saw by the midpoint of the war, the reservoir of black manpower drawn to federal armies in the South could best serve the Union cause as a source of combat soldiers. The mobilization of young black males into Union armies not only minimized any possibility of a war-induced migration of blacks into the North, it also hastened the day on which white Union soldiers in the South would be able to return to their homes in the North.

Defeated Confederates later insisted that the Union had never licked them in a fair fight but instead had to enlist the help of blacks in order to win the war. After allowances are made for the wounded pride of white Southerners, that argument stands as a pretty fair assessment of the impact of arming the blacks. The military contributions of blacks were a vital, if not indispensable, element in Union victory. One in eight federal soldiers at the war's end was a black man, and the number of blacks who fought for the Union was larger than the available manpower in Confederate armies as of January 1, 1865.

These numbers alone, however, tell only part of the story. Reliance on black troops helped sustain Northern morale and depress that of the Confederacy. Lincoln turned to black recruitment when white volunteering was at a standstill and a Union draft was about to be instituted in March 1863.

Under the procedures of the draft, each congressional district was assigned a quota of volunteers, and the draft would be implemented only if that quota were not filled within fifty days of each fresh call for troops. As the war dragged on, Northern localities increasingly filled their quotas with blacks recruited in the South by state agents. This substitution of nonlocal blacks for local whites as combat soldiers lightened the burden of the war in the North and thus boosted morale, which had become dangerously low by the spring of 1863. The reverse side of the coin was the demoralization that spread throughout the Confederacy as Southern whites realized that the North was tapping a huge manpower reserve in their former slaves and arming those slaves against them.

Much to the surprise of most whites, blacks quickly proved their effectiveness as combat soldiers in such battles as Milliken's Bend, Fort Wagner, and Petersburg. Nonetheless, and in line with Lincoln's original thinking on the deployment of black troops, blacks were used primarily for garrison and rear-guard duty. Their main role was to free whites for combat service, and they were often stationed in districts where white troops had been decimated by yellow fever and malaria. Such assignments, as well as the inadequate medical treatment that black troops received, largely accounted for a black mortality rate that was forty percent higher than that of white Union soldiers.

On top of their greater risk of dying in the war, black troops were also discriminated against in terms of pay and access to officers' commissions. White privates received twice the pay ($13 a month plus $3 allowance for clothing) than black soldiers of any rank ($10 a month minus $3 for clothing) until Congress equalized military salaries in June 1864, retroactive to the start of the year. With very few exceptions, commissions in the segregated black regiments were reserved for whites, a policy designed to raise white morale by providing opportunities for rapid advancement. If captured by Confederates, blacks ran the risk of being executed under Southern laws for inciting slave insurrections. Although this threat was rarely carried out, perhaps because Lincoln promised to retaliate in kind by executing Confederate prisoners of war on a one-to-one basis, blacks attempting to surrender were massacred by Confederates at Fort Pillow, Tennessee, and Plymouth, North Carolina, in 1864.

Blacks paid a heavy price in acting as their own liberators. More than one-third of the black soldiers died during their military service. The gains, however, were commensurately great. Blacks now had a claim on the Union that they could present in their demands for full equality and citizenship at the end of the war. After all, more than any other single factor, black military participation had tipped the scales against the Confederacy. Resorting to black troops was a revolutionary step in the white-supremacist culture of Civil War America. In taking that step on behalf of the manpower needs of the Union military, Lincoln was justifiably worried about a white backlash. Yet, as Lincoln sensed they would, even many of the rabid racists eventually conceded that black lives might as well be sacrificed along with white ones if it meant the preservation of the Union.

GEARING UP FOR TOTAL WAR: THE WINTER AND SPRING OF 1863

Soon after the Emancipation Proclamation, the Union Congress took three additional steps in preparation for total war. In February 1863 Congress passed a National Banking Act. As later amended in 1864, this Act created a system of national banks authorized to issue banknotes that soon became the nation's first paper currency of uniform value. The economic exigencies of total war accounted for this sharp break with the Jacksonian tradition of hostility to centralized banking.

The financing of the war required a stable, uniform currency and the successful marketing of government bonds. With the exception of gold and greenbacks, the Union's currency until 1863 consisted of over 12,000 different kinds of banknotes issued by 1,600 state banks. These banknotes were of very uneven value and could not be used to purchase government bonds or pay federal taxes. The greenbacks, though functioning as a national currency, were widely viewed as an emergency measure. Not convertible into gold and backed only by the good faith of the government, greenbacks also depreciated in value as measured against gold, still the monetary standard for international trade. In addition, when the fortunes of Union armies sank, so did the value of greenbacks in gold. What was needed was a national banking system that could both enlarge and standardize the currency. By rationalizing the chaotic money supply, such a system would provide the uniformity now demanded by the tremendously expanded role of the federal government in the economy. It could also be designed to serve as a ready market for government bonds.

These goals were realized in the National Banking Act, the core of which granted nationally chartered banks the right to issue banknotes for up to ninety percent of the value of their federal bonds in deposit with the Treasury. Secured by the bonds, the national banknotes were of uniform value. Bankers joined the system because they could earn profits on the interest from both their banknotes and bonds. A prohibitive tax on state banknotes in 1865 drove most of them out of circulation.

Congress also enacted in February 1863 the Union's first conscription law. This legislation served notice that the Union would fight the war to the finish.

Lagging enlistments and the scheduled mustering out in the spring of 1863 of a host of nine-month volunteers convinced the Republicans of the necessity for a national draft. All male citizens between the ages of twenty and forty-five were now liable for military service. As was noted earlier, the draft would take effect only in those congressional districts that failed to meet their quota of volunteers. Drafted men had the option of hiring a substitute or buying their way out of service for a commutation fee of $300. As a result of federal, state, and local bounties paid out to hire recruits to fill the quotas, the actual number of draftees was surprisingly low, about six percent of all enlistees. Still, the draft served its purpose. It spurred enlistments and added men to the armies.

Before it adjourned in March, Congress authorized Lincoln at his discretion to suspend the writ of habeas corpus for reasons of public safety. The Habeas Corpus Act, in confirming what Lincoln had been doing all along, made it clear that civil liberties in the North would be curbed under the wartime emergency. Although most Republicans intended the Act to set up judicial guidelines for the suspension of the writ, Congress in fact had accepted Lincoln's argument that dissent had to be stifled because the war zone extended beyond the battlefield to the Northern home front. In September 1862, Lincoln had issued a proclamation declaring that persons who discouraged enlistments or aided and abetted the Confederate enemy in any way were subject to military arrest. During the war, 15,000 such arrests were made in the North. Some of those arrested were Confederate spies or agents; others were guilty of no more than "disloyal" utterances. The most celebrated of these arrests concerned Clement L. Vallandigham, a Democratic congressman from Ohio.

In May 1863, General Burnside, who had been transferred after Fredericksburg to the Department of the Ohio, ordered the arrest of Vallandigham for antiwar statements he made while running for the governorship of Ohio. The arrest and the dilemma the arrest presented to the Lincoln administration climaxed the frustrations felt by many Republicans over the deadlocked war and the slippage in the party's political support at home. In the fall elections of 1862 the Republicans lost five states that Lincoln had carried in 1860: New York, Pennsylvania, Ohio, Indiana, and Illinois. The Republicans retained control of Congress only because the absence or proscription of pro-Southern voters in the Border region resulted in safe Republican majorities in what normally would have been Democratic states.

The situation in Illinois and Indiana was most alarming for the Republicans. Here, the Democratic-controlled legislatures threatened to pull their state troops out of the war unless Lincoln backed down on emancipation. Only the extraordinary actions of the two Republican governors, Richard Yates of Illinois and Oliver P. Morton of Indiana, prevented a serious crisis that could have crippled the Union war effort in the lower Midwest. Both governors exploited legal technicalities that enabled them in effect to rule without the consent of their legislatures. While Yates and Morton were acting to contain discontent in the Midwest, Union desertions rose sharply after Fredericksburg, and Democratic demands for an armistice intensified.

Of all the Democratic opponents of the war, known collectively as the Peace

Democrats, or in Republican parlance as Copperheads, none was as vocal or as desirous of a confrontation with federal authorities than Vallandigham. Whereas most Democrats supported the war in terms of the Crittenden Resolution, that is, a war fought solely to restore the old Union with slavery intact, Peace Democrats led by Vallandigham denounced the war itself as a wicked and unconstitutional affair that was sending the country down the road to revolutionary ruin and military despotism. When Vallandigham repeated these themes in a speech on May 1, 1863, Burnside's troops were there to arrest him. Burnside had acted without Lincoln's prior approval, and the arrest threatened to upset the alliance between the Republicans and War Democrats. Yet Lincoln, who was on public record as favoring the arrest of those whose talk undermined a whole-hearted support of the war, did not want to overrule Burnside. Nor did he want to make Vallandigham a martyr for the Democrats. By ordering Vallandigham to be sent behind Confederate lines, where he was something of an embarrassment to Confederate leaders with his talk of reunion, Lincoln succeeded in doing neither.

While the Union was cracking down on dissidents and centralizing its control over manpower and the currency, the significance of its new legislation was not lost on the Confederacy. It "indicates a truculent determination to crush us at every hazard,"[9] noted the Confederate official Robert Kean in March 1863. If the Confederate Congress needed any prodding to put the Southern economy on a war footing, the new measures of the Yankees provided it.

In the Impressment Act of March 1863, the Confederate Congress legalized and attempted to regulate the military seizure of private supplies of food crops and forage. Such seizures had become commonplace by the fall of 1862. Indeed, they were the chief means of subsistence for the Confederate armies. The loss of access to major food-producing areas in Kentucky and Tennessee early in the war, the shortage of salt for the curing of meat, and the refusal of farmers to sell their provisions to quartermaster and commissary officers when speculators offered them a much higher price on the open market all resulted in a staggering problem of securing food for the army. Inevitably, the military simply seized what it needed and wrote out credit certificates as payment. In an effort to bring uniformity and fairness to these seizures, the Impressment Act set up procedures by which prices were determined in arbitration between impressment agents and the private producers. Nonetheless, the Confederate bureaucracy had the upper hand. Government impressment prices were generally one-third to one-half the market value of the goods seized.

Rampant inflation lay at the root of many of the supply problems. At the start of 1863 a Confederate dollar was worth only 33 cents in gold, and prices measured in Confederate dollars had risen eightfold since the start of the war. Confronted with steadily rising prices for the goods they produced, Confederate farmers had every reason of self-interest to hold onto those goods while waiting for a higher price. Impressment was a clumsy and very unpopular method of acquiring goods for the army. Far better, argued top Confederate officials, would be a sharp reduction in the amount of redundant Confederate paper money in order to stabilize prices and encourage the voluntary sale of goods to the army. This was the intent of the Funding Loan Act of March 26, 1863.

The Act sought to reduce the currency in circulation by two-thirds through a voluntary exchange of non-interest-bearing treasury notes for interest-bearing bonds. Notes issued in the fall of 1862 and new ones of up to $50 million per month, which the Treasury was now authorized to issue, were eligible for the exchange. The response to the exchange offer was far below expectations. Prices shot up over 600 percent in 1863, and this inflation ate away at any income to be gained from the interest on government bonds. Meanwhile, the Treasury continued to print money to meet its daily expenses, and it actually reissued one-third of the notes that were exchanged for bonds.

Another attempt to dampen inflation was made in a very complex piece of tax legislation that the Confederate Congress enacted in April 1863. Designed to raise the revenue needed to support the price of the government's money, the Act slapped taxes on virtually everything but slaves and land, the main sources of Southern wealth. Permitting themselves to be hamstrung by a provision in the Confederate Constitution that prohibited any direct tax on land and slaves in the absence of a census to determine the proportionate amount that each state should be taxed, the Confederate Congress frantically tried to make up the revenue shortfall in other areas. License taxes were imposed on occupations, profit taxes on wholesalers, ad valorem taxes on farm produce grown in 1862, flat taxes on bank deposits and commercial paper, and graduated taxes on individual incomes. Finally, there was a ten percent tax in kind on agricultural goods and slaughtered livestock.

The agricultural tithe, or tax in kind, had the virtue of provisioning the army without the need for more paper money. Yet the tax was extremely difficult to administer and was unfair in that enforcement could take place only in areas within the reach of the tax agents. It enraged farmers, most of whom had paid very light taxes, if any, before the war. Tons of food supplies collected under the Act rotted because of logjams in the transportation system, and two-thirds of those supplies never reached the armies. What did get through to the soldiers, however, probably prevented the soldiers from starving. The cash taxes also produced disappointing results. In the first year they generated only $82 million in depreciated Confederate currency, a paltry sum relative to the $500 million in new notes issued by the Treasury during the same period.

For all the defects of the legislation on impressment, currency, and taxes, these new measures were vital to Confederate mobilization for total war. Confederate armies reached their largest size in 1863, about 250,000 men present for duty, and they were adequately supplied with arms and munitions from the South's own industries. In the military–industrial production basic to waging a modern war, the Confederacy achieved self-sufficiency in 1863. Each of the key military agencies, such as the Ordnance, Quartermaster, and Nitre and Mining bureaus, built or refitted the factories it needed for essential war production. Control was centralized at the top through the Army and Navy departments. Governmental assistance from Richmond, supplemented with aid from the states, force-fed manufacturing through the direct ownership of factories, loans to cover start-up costs, and guaranteed markets for the goods produced. Businesses with government contracts enjoyed high profits but had to accept a host of governmental regulations. Richmond controlled both their labor supply through policies on draft exemptions and their access to markets through the allotment of space on railroads that otherwise gave priority to military traffic.

The Confederacy had more than enough men and munitions in 1863 to wage a protracted war of defense in which the North might grow weary of the fighting and vote Lincoln's government out of office. What it lacked was the high level of civilian support it needed to drag out the war by basing its strategy on buying time rather than by seeking decisive victories on the battlefield. In raising, equipping, and feeding its armies, the Confederacy had stretched its resources and civilian morale to the breaking point. By the spring of 1863, morale on the home front was starting to break.

Economic hardships brought the war home to many Confederate civilians during the winter of 1862–1863. The economy could support a total war only at the expense of soaring prices and shortages of consumer goods. In April 1863, a bread riot broke out in Richmond, and it was quickly followed by others in Salisbury and High Point, North Carolina, and in Atlanta and Columbus, Georgia. The riots were touched off by working-class housewives protesting not so much the shortage of food but its exorbitant price. They simply could not afford to feed their families when industrial wages came nowhere near meeting the tenfold increase in the price of food during the first two years of the war. In the countryside, where the food was produced, farm families had suddenly been impoverished when they were unable to support themselves on the $11 monthly salaries that their husbands and sons were earning as privates in the Confederate army. As early as the fall of 1861, state governments passed laws staying the collection of soldiers' debts and providing some financial assistance to the indigent through special county taxes. These measures were insufficient, and, by 1863, the states were distributing food to the poor and spending millions on direct relief. Toward the end of the war, twenty to forty percent of Confederate white civilians were on some form of public relief.

The greatest cry of the swelling ranks of the Confederate poor was for reasonably priced food. There was enough food, though barely, for both civilians and the army. Public pressure from below, combined with state legislation that curtailed acreage put into cotton, did result in a marked shift from cotton to food production after the second year of the war. But much of the food was hoarded to keep it out of the hands of impressment agents and tax officials. The price of the food that did surface was bid up by speculators who profited by selling it at a large markup in urban markets where the Confederate elite could afford food at any price. Even when government authorities did acquire food supplies, the overburdened transportation system could not distribute them on anything approaching an equitable basis. The army always came first, and the rural and urban poor had to scramble as best they could for what was left.

The indifference of most nonslaveholders to secession and the Confederate experiment was turning into massive discontent by the midpoint of the war. In what amounted to a propaganda campaign, the secessionists had tried to convince the yeomanry that a Union under Republican control was incompatible with their individual liberties and economic independence. Now, the loss of those liberties was a reality, but the centralizing despot was the Confederacy itself. Impressment, heavy taxation, and wartime inflation were impoverishing the yeomanry, and the labor supply that was the basis of their economic independence, their menfolk, was being forced into Confederate service. What most angered the yeomanry was the belief that nonslaveholders were being forced to bear most of the sacrifices in a war fought to protect the property of slaveholders.

In the fall of 1861, when the burdens of the war were still relatively light, a north Georgian rhetorically asked,

> Is it right that the poor man should be taxed for the support of the war, when the war was being brought about on the slave question, and the slave at home accumulating for the benefit of his master, and the poor man's farm left uncultivated, and a chance for his wife to be a widow, and his children orphans?[10]

Two years of war had increased the numbers of widows and orphans at an alarming rate, and nothing symbolized better the class bias of Confederate policies than the so-called "Twenty Negro" law of October 1862. In response to pleas from plantation districts that both white security and economic productivity were threatened by the absence of adult white males to enforce discipline on the slaves, Congress granted draft exemptions for overseers on plantations with at least twenty slaves. Although the number of such exemptions was small—fewer than 1,000 for the entire Southeast at the end of 1863—no other single piece of Confederate legislation aroused as much hatred. Conscription had always been denounced in class terms because its impact fell heaviest on nonslaveholding families who were solely dependent on the labor of a husband or teenage sons for their economic survival. Planters' families had the labor of slaves to sustain them, and only they had the cash resources to afford the hiring of substitutes to serve in the army. Now they had the additional advantage of keeping their sons out of the army by classifying them as overseers. In January 1864, Congress repealed the provision for substitutes, but it lowered the overseer exemption to fifteen slaves. This more liberal exemption policy was justified on grounds of increasing food production for the military by requiring the exemptees to furnish the Confederacy with fixed amounts of provisions at prices set by the government.

In an irony that registered the extent of Confederate discontent by early 1863, the very slaveholders whom the yeomen accused of being the pampered pets of the Davis administration were also decrying the tyrannical powers of the Richmond government. Whereas impressment often deprived nonslaveholders of the draft animal or farm equipment needed to put in a crop, it wounded the pride and pocketbooks of planters by temporarily taking away some of their slaves.

Throughout the war, planters were notoriously reluctant to surrender their slaves as impressed laborers for the military. Voluntary recruitments had fallen off so much by the end of 1861 that first state and then national legislation was required to force planters to yield up slaves desperately needed for the war effort. Impressed slaves were overworked and harshly treated, and the compensation owed to their owners was rarely paid on time.

Apart from this infringement on their property rights and prerogatives as masters, planters objected most strongly to the suspension of the writ of *habeas corpus*. Centered in the person of President Davis, this power negated the states' rights and constitutional liberties that most planters had assumed the Confederacy was founded to preserve. When Davis's authorization to suspend the writ expired in February 1863, the Confederate Congress delayed for a year before renewing it. The same fear of centralized power, combined with a growing enmity toward Davis himself, also defeated a bill in early 1863 for the creation of a Confederate Supreme Court.

Mounting disaffection at home put additional pressure on Confederate commanders to seek a military resolution of the war in 1863. In turn, this led to an intensification of the very policies that had produced much of the civilian discontent in the first place. Efforts to impress goods and conscript manpower were redoubled in preparation for the spring campaigns. Symptomatic of the measures taken was the organization by General Braxton Bragg of his own recruiting bureau for volunteers and conscripts in January 1863. Operating outside of the legal channels of the Confederate Conscript Bureau, Bragg used cavalry from his Army of Tennessee to sweep up deserters, stragglers, and draft evaders hiding out in the mountains of northern Alabama. This military dragnet netted him 10,000 men for his army within a month.

Bragg applied a more drastic remedy than other Confederate generals, but all of them were plagued with manpower problems in early 1863. Enough men had volunteered or had been conscripted to replace those killed, wounded, and captured, but widespread absenteeism sharply reduced the numbers actually present for duty. At the start of 1863, absenteeism, or unauthorized absences, averaged thirty percent in the Southern armies. This was up from the twenty-one percent level at the end of 1861. At some point in mid-1862, absenteeism in Confederate armies rose above that in Union armies (about twenty-five percent), and the gap widened for the rest of the war. Certainly, the imposition of a Confederate draft, which forced men into the army who had less of a commitment than the original volunteers, had much to do with the growing tendency of rebel soldiers to leave the ranks. So also did the sudden realization after a battle like Shiloh that the battlefield was a slaughterhouse of death and suffering. Low pay, wretched provisions, and a structure of discipline that left many soldiers feeling as if they were being treated like slaves also played a role. But the most important factor by far was the spreading economic misery on the home front. Most men were fighting to protect their families at home and spare them from a Yankee invasion. When those families began sending letters to the army camps in which they described the economic ruin and possible starvation facing them, the husbands and sons increasingly concluded that their services were most needed at home. In short, as the Tuskegee Baptist Association explained, the soldiers began to fear that "the danger from the rear is greater than the danger in front."[11]

By 1863 the Confederate war effort was trapped in a vicious cycle that only got worse as the war continued. To be competitive against Union armies in manpower and material, the Confederate government had to resort to coercive, centralizing controls. But this in turn produced a counterproductive level of civilian discontent and deprivation that eroded the morale and combat strength of the very armies for whose benefit the controls were levied. Each bit of Confederate territory lost to the federals intensified this cycle by inducing soldiers to desert and search for their families and by forcing the Confederate government to squeeze harder for manpower and resources in the shrinking areas still under its control. When confronted with the dilemma of being able to maintain their armies only at the expense of declining civilian morale and diminishing resources, Confederate generals became impatient with a defensive strategy of simply holding off the Union forces while waiting for the Northern peace movement to oust Lincoln's government. Instead, first at Gettysburg in the East and then at Chickamauga in the West, they gambled on an offensive strategy aimed at winning decisive victories to bring the war to a quick end. They lost the gambles. These two battles, plus the Confederate loss of Vicksburg, turned the war's tide in favor of the Union in 1863.

THE WAR TURNS: THE CAMPAIGNS OF 1863

Lee had a new adversary in the spring of 1863. His last one, Ambrose Burnside, was replaced at the end of January by General Joseph Hooker. Morale in the Army of the Potomac, understandably low after the Fredericksburg debacle, sank to a point of near mutiny after the infamous "Mud March" in mid-January.

Determined to strike at Lee's army, Burnside ordered a movement up the northern bank of the Rappahannock River for a crossing operation designed to outflank the Confederates above Fredericksburg. Heavy rains turned the roads into a muddy glue, and rebel pickets had a good laugh watching the federals, many of whom were drunk from the whiskey rations Burnside had issued to bolster their spirits, trying to extricate themselves from the mess. Burnside, now the butt of his own troops' derisive jokes, had completely lost control of his army. Lincoln probably did him a favor by dropping him in favor of Hooker, a popular corps commander who was tagged with the nickname "Fighting Joe" during the Seven Days' battles.

Hooker soon restored the morale of the Army of the Potomac through a policy of liberal furloughs and extra rations. Like McClellan, he knew how to whip an army camp into shape and give the soldiers pride in their units. Unlike McClellan, however, he was not expected to capture Richmond. After the failure of McClellan and Burnside in 1862, Lincoln and Halleck concluded that Richmond was too difficult to reach and too well defended to serve as the focal point of a Union offensive. Even if Richmond could be placed under a partial seige, they reasoned

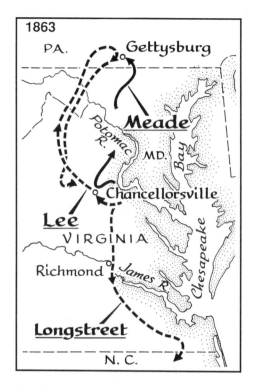

The Civil War in the East, 1863

that this would favor the Confederacy by enabling Lee to conserve his manpower behind entrenchments while sending reinforcements to the West or mounting politically dangerous raids toward Washington. Nor did Lincoln and Halleck favor a return to McClellan's approach via the Peninsula. Haunted by the memory of Second Bull Run, they feared that Lee would again take advantage of interior lines of movement and concentrate troops in northern Virginia for another raid into Maryland or beyond. Thus, Hooker's army was to move overland, and its primary objective was Lee's army, not the Confederate capital.

Hooker's spring offensive got off to a very good start. In late April he pulled off on a grander scale what Burnside had attempted in January. Leaving behind about two-fifths of his army at Fredericksburg to keep pressure on Lee's main army, he moved 70,000 troops upriver and crossed over to the southside of the Rappahannock River. He was now in a perfect position to turn Lee's left flank and smash through his army from the rear.

Lee was in a precarious spot, especially since he had already detached three divisions from General James Longstreet's corps to forage for supplies in southeastern Virginia and protect the rail link from Richmond to North Carolina from a threatened amphibious invasion. Lee's army was outnumbered better than two to one, and both its left and right flanks were in danger of caving in. A lesser general would have done just what Hooker expected, which was fall back to the next defensible position along the North Anna River. But Lee would not surrender his subsistence area north of Richmond without a fight. Undoubtedly aware of Hooker's reputation among Union officers as a great talker who lost his nerve when the chips were down, Lee sensed that Hooker could be bluffed out of the victory that he already assumed he had won.

Lee kept back 10,000 troops in the trenches above Fredericksburg and then shifted his army westward on May 1 to meet Hooker's main force. When rebel pickets clashed with Union troops moving eastward out of the Wilderness, a tangled area of woods and underbrush in the vicinity of Chancellorsville, Hooker called off his advance. Like a tortoise, he withdrew himself and his army into a defensive shell around Chancellorsville in the middle of the Wilderness. The initiative was now Lee's, and he seized it in a breathtaking gamble.

Betting that Hooker would keep his 70,000 troops on the defensive, Lee held the center of his own line with a mere 15,000 men while sending Stonewall Jackson with a force of 25,000 on a risky march across Hooker's entire front for a strike at the exposed right flank of the Union army. With this maneuver Lee outturned Hooker and caught him by surprise, and for the rest of the three-day battle he kept him in a state of paralyzed befuddlement. On May 4, Lee sent the bulk of his army eastward to check a federal breakthrough after the Confederate defenses at Fredericksburg had been overrun. On that day, as well as the preceding ones, all that stood between Hooker and victory was his order for a concerted Union drive against the separated and outnumbered Confederates. Hooker never gave that order, and when he withdrew his army back across the Rappahannock on May 5, he joined Pope and Burnside in the ranks of Union generals humbled by Lee.

Chancellorsville was another terrible blow to Northern morale, but the Union had lost nothing vital. The Army of the Potomac was still intact, and it emerged from the defeat proportionately stronger than the victorious Confederates. Whereas the 13,000 casualties suffered by the Army of Northern Virginia were twenty-one percent of its effective strength before the battle, the 16,800 Union casualties were but fifteen percent of the pre-battle size of Hooker's army. Even in victory, Confederate armies continued to bleed to death at a faster rate than the Yankees.

Chancellorsville also cost Lee his most daring lieutenant, Stonewall Jackson. Wounded by fire from his own troops while returning from a night reconnaissance patrol on May 3, Jackson died a week later from an infection that set in after his left arm was amputated. Jackson's death was emblematic of the incredible drain on the officer corps that was hampering the Confederate war effort by 1863. Compelled by their code of honor to charge into battle with reckless abandon, and aware that their soldiers respected and would follow only leaders who put their lives on the line, most Confederate generals were constantly exposing themselves to enemy fire. During the war, fifty-five percent of them were killed or wounded, a ratio of casualties that was three times higher than that for Union generals.

The Union defeat at Chancellorsville did not alter the stalemate in the East, and Lincoln was prepared to accept that stalemate as long as Union gains in the West continued to chew up sizable chunks of Confederate territory. The western prize that Lincoln wanted most in the spring of 1863 was Vicksburg. Within a few days after the Confederacy had begun to mourn the warrior Jackson and elevate him to the ranks of sainthood, Grant captured the city of Jackson, Mississippi, on May 14. This was the first indication that Grant's daring plan to invade Vicksburg from the back door of an eastern approach was on the verge of success.

Ever since the abortive offensives against Vicksburg in late December 1862, Grant had searched for a way to crack the Vicksburg defenses. Situated on a high bluff on the east bank of the Mississippi River, the city was protected on the west by the river and bayous and on the north by swamps and a well-guarded hilly terrain. The city was vulnerable to attack only from the east or south, but Grant's effort to use that approach in December had failed because his long supply lines were easily broken by Confederate cavalry. From his new base at Milliken's Landing on the west side of the Mississippi, Grant kept his army busy during the winter and early spring digging canals and probing water routes in an attempt to find a way to outflank the Vicksburg defenses from the north. Much of this was sheer busy work, and none of it got Grant anywhere. But it was better than going back to Memphis and starting the campaign all over again. Such a move would have been viewed in Washington as an admission of failure and well might have cost Grant his command. In April Grant found the key to unlock the Vicksburg defenses. He would attack from the east, and he would get there by marching his army down the west bank of the Mississippi and by using Admiral David Porter's fleet to ferry it across the river below the Vicksburg defenses. On the night of April 16, Porter ran his fleet past the Vicksburg guns. Two weeks later, Grant had 23,000 men on the dry ground east of the river at Bruinsburg, Mississippi.

Grant's move down the Mississippi to get at Vicksburg from the rear was one of the riskiest military maneuvers of the war. There was no room for error in the plan, and it meant plunging into enemy territory without any secure base of supplies and relying on the element of surprise to attack separate Confederate armies before they could concentrate against Grant's forces. Grant never looked back, and he was rewarded with the single most successful Union campaign of the war.

Grant did surprise and confuse the Confederates. He covered his initial move to Bruinsburg with a diversionary attack by Sherman's troops at Chickasaw Bluffs and a spectacular cavalry raid down the spine of Mississippi led by Colonel Benjamin Grierson. Once Grant started in motion, every weakness in the Confederate command structure in the West was exposed. Although Joseph Johnston now had overall command of Confederate armies between the Appalachians and the Mississippi, he was not a forceful strategist, and he downgraded the importance of Vicksburg relative to Middle Tennessee. The Confederate commander in Vicksburg, General John Pemberton, had little combat experience, and he still reported directly to Davis, not Johnston. The closest available troops for the support of Pemberton were in Arkansas in a separate military department, but their commander, General Theophilus Holmes, refused to cooperate with Davis' order to reinforce Pemberton. This awkward, uncoordinated command structure virtually invited a military disaster, and that is just what the Confederacy got.

Johnston was in the dark once Grant bypassed Vicksburg and crossed the river, and Pemberton then disregarded Johnston's order to break out of Vicksburg and link up with his smaller army for a joint attack on Grant. Davis had ordered Pemberton to hold Vicksburg at all costs. Reinforced with the arrival of Sherman's troops to a force of 44,000 men, Grant first brushed aside Johnston's desperate attempt to hold Jackson. Jackson was seized, and its rail communications to the east, the only logistical means by which Johnston could have mounted an offensive against Grant, were destroyed. Grant then turned to the west to meet Pemberton's army, which had ventured out of Vicksburg to protect its rail connection to Jackson. Grant's victories at Champion's Hill and Big Black River on May 16 and 17 sent Pemberton's army back into its prepared defenses at Vicksburg. After failing to dent the Vicksburg defenses, Grant placed the city under siege in late May and reestablished his supply base on the Mississippi. The siege was the only stationary aspect of a brilliant campaign based on lightning speed and deception.

Once Pemberton had locked his army inside Vicksburg, Davis had only two options that offered any hope of saving the city and its 30,000 defenders. He could send massive reinforcements to Vicksburg, but this meant stripping Middle Tennessee of most of Bragg's army, or he could relieve the pressure on the city by shifting troops from Virginia to Chattanooga, driving Rosecrans out of Tennessee, and invading Kentucky. Generals Longstreet and Beauregard strongly supported this second option, but it was even more strongly opposed by Lee. In the end, Davis wound up doing nothing because of Lee's decision to invade the North for a second time.

Had Hooker not retreated after the battle of Chancellorsville, Lee was prepared to attack him in order to drive the Army of the Potomac away from the Rappahannock River, the line that guarded his major supply region and his access to the provisions of the Shenandoah Valley via the Virginia Central Railroad. What Lee most wanted to avoid was being placed in a static defensive posture that gradually would force him back into the fortifications of Richmond in a never-ending struggle to protect the rail communications that were the life line of his army. Hooker's retreat, however, enabled Lee to regain his mobility and initiate the advance that finally culminated in early July at Gettysburg, Pennsylvania.

In early June 1863, Lee started moving his army northward through the Shenandoah Valley. By the end of the month the army had crossed Maryland into Pennsylvania. His goals in launching a second invasion of the North were much the same as they had been in the fall of 1862. Foremost was the logistical consideration of gaining access to a rich, untapped foraging area while simultaneously sparing the crops and livestock of central Virginia from the voracious needs of the Union and Confederate armies. Second, Lee wanted to free himself from the need to defend the Rappahannock line for the protection of his supply region. By drawing Hooker's army north of the Potomac, Lee felt that he would be in a much better position to dictate the terms of the next major battle.

After rejecting Hooker's advice to go after Richmond while Lee was heading north, Lincoln replaced Hooker with General George G. Meade in late June. A solid general, who made up for his lack of dash with his unflappability and thorough preparedness, Meade brought to the Army of the Potomac a careful stewardship that checkmated Lee's hopes for a decisive victory. Moving his army to block Lee from an unimpeded thrust toward Washington, Baltimore, or Philadelphia, Meade put Lee in a position where he had to attack or retreat. On June 30, two days after Meade's appointment, Confederates foraging for shoes clashed with advanced units of Union cavalry near Gettysburg. Lee had not planned on a battle at Gettysburg, but he did not have the luxury of waiting to choose the time and place. He was in unfamiliar territory, his army was living off the land, and his limited ammunition was dependent on a long supply line stretching back to the Shenandoah Valley. If he was going to fight, it would have to be very soon, and he rejected the option of withdrawing without a battle in the belief that that would be tantamount to a defeat after the high hopes of his campaign.

Lee's search for a climactic victory at Gettysburg ended in the costliest Confederate defeat of the war. The actual battle consisted of a series of Confederate assaults against a Union line just to the southeast of Gettysburg. In its shape, the Union line resembled the mirror image of a question mark. It ran along a slight ridge anchored in the northeast by Culp's Hill, in the middle by Cemetery Hill, and in the south by Little Round Top and Big Round Top.

Lee was able to concentrate his forces at Gettysburg faster than Meade, and the Confederate attack on July 1, the first day of the battle, almost secured a victory. The charges against the Union left and then the center on the next two days were more hopeless than heroic. The best known and most suicidal charge of all was led by General George Pickett of Virginia. Ever since, Pickett's name has been synonymous with the utter self-destructiveness that war defines as courage. Of the 5,000 men in Pickett's division who followed him to be slaughtered by Union fire as they marched in parade formation, seven out of ten were killed, wounded, or captured.

Total Confederate losses for the battle were 28,000, a staggering one-third of Lee's effective force. Although the 23,000 Union casualties were also huge, Meade lost only twenty percent of his army. As was usual in a major battle, it was the Confederacy that proportionately suffered the worst loss of manpower.

After waiting a day in the vain hope that Meade would order a counterattack, Lee began to retreat back to Hagerstown, Maryland, on July 4. Without a secure line of supply, and harassed in its foraging attempts by the Pennsylvania militia, Lee's army could not remain concentrated at Gettysburg for very long. Lee set up a strong defensive position on the north side of the Potomac River, and there was still a chance that his original goal of forcing the Army of the Potomac to assume the tactical offensive might be realized. But Meade refused to take the bait. Despite Lincoln's urgings to follow up Gettysburg with an all-out attack on Lee's army in an effort to destroy it, Meade did not go on the offensive. He permitted Lee to slip back across the Potomac in mid-July. Meade then shifted his army farther south, a move that eventually forced Lee back to a position south of the Rappahannock River not far from the spot where he had begun his Northern campaign two months earlier. For the rest of the 1863 campaign, the two armies remained in fairly stationary positions as each checked attempts by the other to outflank it.

Lee's Gettysburg campaign was a success in that it reprovisioned his army and scuttled any offensive plans of the Army of the Potomac. But its cost of 30,000 casualties was far higher than the dwindling manpower reserves of the Confederacy could afford to pay. Lee's frontal assaults at Gettysburg bled his army of most of its offensive power for the remainder of the war, and his foray into Pennsylvania had done nothing to reduce the pressure on Vicksburg and Pemberton's army.

Once trapped inside Vicksburg by the siege that Grant began on May 18, Pemberton's army was lost unless General Joseph Johnston could mount a relief expedition to break Grant's hold on the city. After collecting about 30,000 troops, Johnston got just close enough to Vicksburg to realize that an attack on Grant's forces would be foolhardy. With the inhabitants of Vicksburg on the brink of starvation, Pemberton surrendered the city and his 30,000 man army on July 4, the day that Lee withdrew from Gettysburg. Four days later, Port Hudson, Louisiana, fell to a Union expedition led by General Nathaniel P. Banks. One of the key war aims of the Union—control of the Mississippi—was now realized.

The Confederate defeats at Gettysburg and Vicksburg did not fundamentally alter the strategic situation in the East and West. Lee had gambled and lost, but his army was still strong enough to thwart any federal advances. Although the fall of Vicksburg was an immense blow to Confederate prestige, the losses a year earlier of New Orleans and Memphis had been more crucial in depriving the eastern Confederacy of logistical support from its trans-Mississippi region. Administratively and economically, the Confederacy had been cut in half since the spring of 1862. Nonetheless, Gettysburg and Vicksburg were devastating defeats in terms of manpower and morale. Nearly 60,000 troops had been lost, and they were virtually irreplaceable. At home, civilian and military confidence in the Davis administration was badly shaken, and in Europe the Confederacy lost its last chance for foreign recognition.

The mere fact that Lee could carry the war to the North, combined with Grant's initial failure to take Vicksburg, had raised the hopes of the pro-Confederate sympathizers in Europe in the spring of 1863. The wiliest of these sympathizers was Napoleon III of France. In Napoleon's plans for setting up a pro-French puppet regime in Mexico, he toyed with the idea of offering recognition to the Confederacy in return for a protectorate over territory in the American Southwest claimed by the Confederacy. However, fearing a war with Lincoln's government, Napoleon would not move unless Britain took the first step toward recognition. A resolution to that end was introduced in the British Parliament in late June 1863. Any slim chance of its passage was killed when news of the Union victories at Gettysburg and Vicksburg reached England. By convincing the British government that the Confederate cause was now all but hopeless, those victories were also instrumental in the British decision two months later to detain two powerful, blockade-busting rams that were being built in England for the Confederacy. Through loopholes in the British neutrality laws, Confederate agents had contracted for the construction of naval raiders to prey upon Union shipping. One of these, the *Alabama*, had a long and spectacularly successful career. The most formidable ships, however, were the two under construction at the Laird shipyards in Liverpool. Powered by steam, plated with armor, and equipped with underwater ramming spikes, they would have been fearsome weapons against the wooden blockading fleet of the Union navy. On September 3, 1863, the British Foreign Office detained the Laird rams and thereby ended the Confederacy's last hope for breaking the blockade.

In addition to Gettysburg and Vicksburg, Union arms secured two other significant victories in July, 1863. One of these was over Northern civilians, and it was hardly a skirmish by Civil War standards. It involved the use of some of the Gettysburg veterans in putting down the New York City draft riots. The first names for the Union draft were drawn by lottery in early July. Although there was sporadic resistance to the draft throughout the North, especially in the lower Midwest and Democratic districts with large numbers of immigrants, nothing came close to matching the outbreak of violence in New York City. A predominately Irish working-class mob of men and women poured out of the city's slums on July 13 and terrorized draft officials and blacks for the next four days. The mob had been egged on by the race-baiting Democratic press, which first blamed blacks for the coming of the war and then for the draft. Now, argued the Democrats, the poor would be forced to fight to free the blacks in a war that the Negro-loving rich could avoid by paying the commutation fee of $300 (a good year's wages for an Irish laborer) or by hiring a substitute (the going rate was about a $1,000).

The rampaging mob ransacked draft offices, attacked federal buildings, looted stores, and burned homes of the wealthy. Desperately fearful that ex-slaves would stream North and take away their jobs, the Irish workers unleashed most of their fury on blacks. After burning the Colored Orphan Asylum, they hunted down any luckless black found on the streets. A contemporary observed,

> If taken, he was pounded to death at once; if he escaped into a negro house for safety it was set on fire, and the inmates made to share a common fate. Deeds were done and sights witnessed that one would not have dreamed of, except among savage tribes.[12]

The arrival of troops from Gettysburg and the cannons that they leveled against the mob finally restored peace to the city. Many Republicans and Union soldiers had interpreted the riot as a testing of the federal resolve to win the war. The Lincoln administration met that test, successfully and brutally. About 150 people were killed in the riot, and two-thirds of them were rioters.

A week before the New York City draft riot, General Rosecrans won an important and uncharacteristically bloodless victory for the Union in Tennessee. For the first six months of 1863, the Tennessee front had been frozen as both Rosecrans's Army of the Cumberland and Bragg's Army of Tennessee rested after the battle of Murfreesboro. By late June, after Bragg's army had been weakened by the dispatching of troops to aid in the defense of Vicksburg, the initiative rested with Rosecrans. On June 23 Rosecrans began moving his army in a series of deft maneuvers that successfully turned Bragg's right flank. The subsequent threat to Bragg's rear position and communications was so great that Bragg was forced to abandon his base at Tullahoma in early July and retreat eastward to Chattanooga. In a campaign without a major battle, Rosecrans had cleared Middle Tennessee of Bragg's army and advanced four times as far as he had moved since Murfreesboro.

Chattanooga was far more strategically important to the Confederacy than Vicksburg. It was a key rail hub that linked Richmond to the Mid-South and the seaboard to the Mississippi River. Situated at the gateway to the mountains of northern Georgia, the city also guarded what has aptly been called the back door to the Confederacy. Beyond those mountains lay major Confederate centers of agricultural and industrial production in Georgia and Alabama. Despite a compelling need to defend Chattanooga at all costs, no massive reinforcements were rushed to Bragg's defending army. Finally, on September 7, Davis persuaded a reluctant Lee to send Longstreet's corps from the Army of Northern Virginia to join Bragg. By then it was too late to save Chattanooga.

In early September, Rosecrans once again outmaneuvered Bragg's army and forced it out of Chattanooga. After feinting to the northeast of the city, Rosecrans pushed his army across the Tennessee River to the southwest of Chattanooga and threatened the Western and Atlantic Railroad, Bragg's life line for supplies from Atlanta. Since Bragg could not hold the city without the railroad, he evacuated his army on September 9. The usually cautious Rosecrans now made a serious mistake. Assuming that Bragg was in full retreat, he divided his army and sent it in hot pursuit. But rather than retreating, Bragg was setting a trap. In a strategy reminiscent of Shiloh, the Confederate high command planned on a rapid concentration of forces for a surprise counteroffensive designed to destroy a major Union army in the West.

Rosecrans's recklessness gave the Confederacy an opportunity to act on Beauregard's ideas for a strategic offensive to regain the initiative in the West. Beauregard's plan called for Bragg's reinforced army to crush Rosecrans so that Bragg would be free to strike into west Tennessee, smash Grant's communications to the north, and force Grant to retreat out of Mississippi in order to protect his logistical base. Everything hinged on a decisive victory over Rosecrans. But, like Shiloh, such a victory was just beyond the grasp of the Confederates.

By mid-September Bragg's army was reinforced up to 70,000 men. Two divisions arrived from Johnston's army in Mississippi. They were free to join Bragg because Lincoln had rejected Grant's advice after Vicksburg to seize Mobile as a base for an invasion of central Alabama, an invasion that would have fully occupied Johnston's forces. Worried about French intentions in Mexico and the possibility that the Confederacy might cede Texas to Napoleon's regime in Mexico in return for recognition and economic assistance from the French, Lincoln instead opted for a Union invasion of Texas. While that expedition bogged down along the Texas coast and Grant's attention was focused on Arkansas and Louisiana, Johnston's divisions slipped away. Meanwhile, a Confederate defeat in East Tennessee freed up 9,000 troops to be sent to Bragg. The largest reinforcements came from

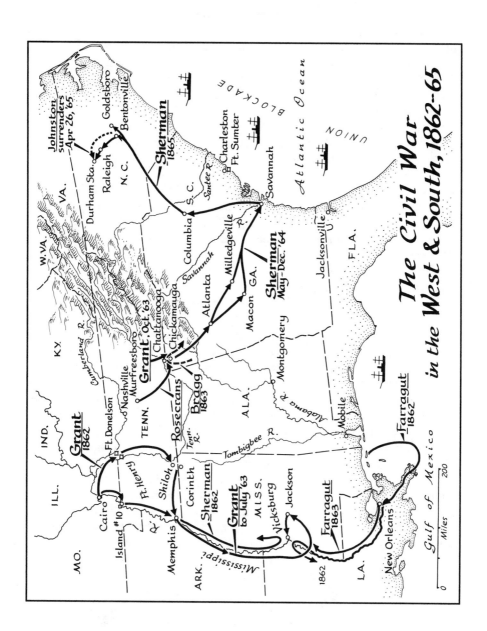

The Civil War
in the West & South, 1862-65

Longstreet's corps, which finally arrived on September 18 after a circuitous train ride via Charleston and Atlanta.

These reinforcements gave Bragg a rare luxury for a Confederate general, that is, numerical superiority over his Union opponent. However, even before Bragg's army reached its maximum strength, the best chance for an overwhelming victory had passed. Early in the second week of September, Rosecrans's army was scattered along a forty-mile front and conceivably could have been destroyed piecemeal. That was Bragg's intention, but his corps commanders had mistrusted his judgment ever since Murfreesboro. When ordered to attack on September 11 and 13, they hesitated, thereby giving an alerted Rosecrans time to reconcentrate his army. Even with this delay, the Army of the Tennessee almost secured a great victory when it finally attacked. A mix-up in Union orders on the second day of the battle created a huge gap in the federal right, and Longstreet's troops rushed through it. But Bragg failed to press this advantage, and a stubborn defense led by General George Thomas gave the Union army enough time to withdraw back to the safety of Chattanooga.

Named after a nearby creek, the battle of Chickamauga on September 19–20, 1863, was the bloodiest two-day battle of the war. Casualties totaled over 34,000, and 18,000 of these were Confederates, about thirty percent of the troops that Bragg threw into the battle. In noting that the ground had literally been soaked in blood, a Union soldier captured the horror of Chickamauga in an image of macabre beauty: "The painted butterfly took blood into the air upon the edges of its wings."[13]

In barely over two months Bragg completely squandered the tactical victory that he had purchased at such a heavy cost at Chickamauga. Rosecrans had saved his army by retreating to Chattanooga, but he had also put it in a trap. Bragg's army cut Rosecrans's major supply line, the railroad to Nashville, and trained heavy artillery down on the Tennessee River after occupying Missionary Ridge to the east of the city and Lookout Mountain to the immediate south and west. Cut off from rail and water supply routes, Rosecrans's army was in danger of being starved out. Rosecrans's normal caution was now closer to a dazed inactivity, and Bragg had a golden opportunity to still gain the strategic objectives of his Chickamauga campaign. Instead, he sat back while Lincoln and Grant bailed out Rosecrans.

In mid-October, when Rosecrans's army was at its weakest, Lincoln appointed Grant to overall command in the West and sent Hooker with two corps from the Army of the Potomac to Chattanooga. After replacing Rosecrans with Thomas, the Union hero at Chickamauga, Grant went to Chattanooga. He surprised Bragg on October 27 by sending a force past the Confederate defenses on Lookout Mountain and by seizing Brown's Ferry, a move that opened up a partial supply route on the Tennessee River for the besieged Union army. Then, an overconfident Bragg weakened his army by transferring Longstreet's corps to Knoxville, Tennessee. Although Bragg wanted to reopen a line of operations in East Tennessee, he was also motivated by the desire to rid himself of a lieutenant who had outspokenly criticized his handling of the army at Chickamauga. While Bragg's army was shrinking to 40,000, the Union army was expanding to 70,000 with the arrival of

Hooker's corps and Sherman's troops from Mississippi. With the numbers now on his side, Grant launched an attack on November 23.

The battle for Chattanooga seesawed for three days until Thomas's troops inexplicably stormed the entrenched center of the Confederate line on Missionary Ridge. No one ordered this frontal assault, and it defied all the odds for a Civil War battle. The Confederate guns on the ridge were sighted too high and fired over the heads of a wild melee of 25,000 bluecoats who charged up the steep slope, perhaps because that seemed preferable to remaining at the bottom like ducks in a shooting gallery. Its center suddenly broken, Bragg's panic-stricken army beat a hasty retreat to Dalton, Georgia. The gateway to Atlanta was now open.

Chattanooga was the most shocking defeat for the Confederacy in a year of dismal campaigning. To be sure, with the exception of Middle Tennessee, the Confederacy had lost little territory and had repelled Union attacks in Texas, Louisiana, and along the South Carolina coast at Charleston. Still, Pemberton had surrendered an entire army at Vicksburg, Lee's army had nearly been bled white at Gettysburg, and Bragg's army was humiliated at Chattanooga after suffering heavy casualties in its own "Gettysburg of the West" at Chickamauga. However much the actual strategic situation remained deadlocked in 1863, Southern losses in manpower and morale were enormous. Absentee rates in Confederate armies rose from thirty-five to forty percent in the last half of 1863. Battlefield defeats induced some soldiers to desert, but the major factor continued to be the growing discontent at home. "The women write to their husbands to leave the army and come home," noted Julia Gwyn of North Carolina in the summer of 1863, "and that's the reason that so many of them are deserting."[14]

Most Confederates were still committed to the goal of Southern independence, but, as war weariness set in, they increasingly turned against the Davis administration. Its coercive measures of centralization were seen by many as a betrayal of a promise to uphold the liberties of all Southern whites, and its failure to end the war resulted in strong peace movements in North Carolina, Georgia, and Alabama after the losses at Gettysburg and Vicksburg. The opposition to Davis scored major gains in the elections held in the fall of 1863 for the Confederate Congress and fell just short of forming an antiadministration majority. Their most telling charge against Davis was that he had not worked hard enough to gain a negotiated peace.

In the latter half of the war, any semblance of unity of purpose between the civilian populace and Confederate authorities completely broke down in much of the backcountry. Popular alienation from the Confederacy was greatest in a belt of counties in central North Carolina, a region of small farms where Quaker sects had maintained a tradition of strong religious opposition to slavery. This so-called Quaker belt had never favored secession. By 1863, it was home to the Heroes of America, a secret society that offered protection and an extensive network of civilian support for Unionists and Confederate draft dodgers and deserters. Confederate authorities sanctioned ever harsher measures against these disloyal Confederates and their families, and late in the war, after local troops of reserves had repeatedly failed to restore order, veteran units from Lee's army were sent in with orders to stamp out all opposition. Despite these efforts at pacification, this civil war within a civil war was still raging when the Confederacy collapsed.

As Confederate disaffection deepened, Union morale and confidence in the Lincoln administration correspondingly rose. The Republicans ran very strongly in the fall elections of 1863 in the North, and the backlash against emancipation and arming the blacks slackened when black troops repeatedly demonstrated their heroism in combat. Soon after the elections, Lincoln issued his Proclamation of Amnesty and Reconstruction on December 8, 1863. This was a plan designed both to encourage more discontent in the Confederacy and to calm the fears of conservatives in the North that emancipation would trigger a violent revolution. The plan provided that a rebel state could begin the process of returning to the Union as soon as ten percent of its voters in the 1860 presidential election had taken an oath of future loyalty to the Union. Acceptance of emancipation was made a precondition for readmission, and high-ranking Confederate officials were prohibited from taking the oath, but otherwise Lincoln's plan imposed no penalties for having been in rebellion. Here was a practical alternative to Confederate rule for Southern dissidents. The Davis government denounced the plan as another emancipation scheme and a mockery of the principle of majority rule. Nonetheless, Lincoln had shrewdly added a new dimension to the Union war effort that weakened the already declining resolve of many Confederates.

THE UNION OFFENSIVES OF 1864 AND THE END OF THE CONFEDERACY

Badly mauled but hardly defeated, the Confederacy was still a formidable military opponent for the Union at the start of 1864, the last full year of the war. The territory the Union had to conquer was still vast. The Confederacy retained control over nearly all of the Southeast, and its munitions-industrial complex in Georgia and Alabama was fully sufficient to churn out the materials of war. Save for the area around Norfolk and a thin strip of territory on the south side of the Potomac, the Union had been stymied in Virginia. Although the isolated Trans-Mississippi Department could provide little direct assistance to the war effort east of the Mississippi, it functioned successfully as a semi-autonomous region, and its commander, Edmund Kirby-Smith, had kept the Union at bay in Texas, southern Arkansas, and northern Louisiana. Conscription and some volunteering had kept up the numerical size of Confederate armies, at least on paper. The number of soldiers on the rolls was slightly higher at the end of 1863 (465,000) than it had been a year earlier (449,000). As a result of rising rates of desertion, however, the number of soldiers actually present for duty had fallen by 20,000 to 233,500.

This problem of absentee, if not outright deserting, troops would have been even more serious had it not been for the state welfare programs for soldiers' families implemented by the Confederate governors. Usually characterized as an obstreperous and backbiting lot who undercut the Confederate war effort by selfishly placing the needs of their states first, the governors in fact were ardent Southern nationalists, but, unlike the Richmond authorities, they realized that civilian fears of a military despotism had to be allayed. The most effective and allegedly anti-Confederate of these governors, Zebulon Vance of North Carolina and Joseph Brown of Georgia, projected themselves to the voters as tireless defenders of individual liberties against the tyrannical centralization of the Davis administration. Publicly and persistently, they railed against Confederate policies, especially conscription and the suspension of the writ of *habeas corpus*. These protests acted both as a safety valve for civilian discontent and as a smokescreen that masked the governors' very positive contributions to the Confederacy and their own programs of state centralization.

Georgia and North Carolina alone accounted for forty-two percent of all Confederate conscripts east of the Mississippi, and no state contributed a larger share of its manpower and resources to the Confederacy than North Carolina. Over half of Georgia's budget in 1864 was devoted to relief, and the funds for this aid to soldiers' families came from stiff progressive taxes that shifted the fiscal burden of the war onto the rich. By promising to shield their citizens from Confederate despotism and by enacting bold programs of economic assistance, Vance and Brown built up strong personal followings. This in turn gave them the political base they needed to draw heavily on the resources of their states for the support of the Confederacy.

In spite of the support of the governors and increasingly ruthless methods of impressment, the Confederacy continued to be plagued with problems of provisioning its armies throughout 1864. Civilians, the Richmond government, and state authorities were all desperate for supplies. At the same time, Northern speculators and officers and privates in the Union army were anxious to cut themselves into some of the immense profits that could be earned by dealing in cotton. Economic necessity on one side and greed on the other produced a makeshift solution to the Confederacy's provisioning problems—a vast network of illegal trade across the lines.

At the start of the war both governments officially banned trade with the enemy. As early as the summer of 1861, however, the Union Congress authorized Lincoln to issue licenses for trade with the Unionists inside the Confederacy. This policy was designed both to reward friends of the Union and to offer an economic incentive for winning over former Confederates to political reconstruction. Despite a host of subsequent regulations, this Union trade with the Confederacy was impossible to control, and it worked at cross purposes to the military side of the Union war effort. Union generals complained that the speculative mania in cotton demoralized their troops. Hordes of traders, unlicensed as well as licensed, brought out cotton in exchange for gold, greenbacks, and war goods, which were funneled to Confederate armies. The destruction of 2.5 million bales of cotton by Confederates under orders to keep them out of the hands of the Yankees, combined with cutbacks in production, jacked up the price of cotton late in the war to over $1.00

a pound in the North. Since that cotton could be purchased in the South for 10 cents a pound, and comparable markups prevailed for goods bought in the North for resale in the South, the profits in the cotton trade were enormous. More than enough cash was generated to bribe officials on both sides, many of whom participated in the trade themselves, to look the other way.

By 1864 the Davis government was grudgingly sanctioning trading with the Yankees on grounds of military necessity. The cost to Confederate morale was high, but there was no denying that Southern armies had become critically dependent on Northern goods for their survival. Ever since New Orleans and Memphis had been occupied by the Union in the spring of 1862, the illegal trade coming out of those cities was the major source of supplies for Confederate armies in the Mississippi Valley. In the last year of the war, the Confederate Quartermaster Department secured most of the meat for Lee's army by swapping cotton for Northern bacon. Eventually, the Confederacy sold about twice as much cotton to the North as it did to Europe.

While the Union was feeding the armies that it was fighting in 1864, the Southern whites displaced by its earlier advances were providing the Davis administration with the political support needed to exact yet more sacrifices from civilians to keep those armies in the field. As a result of refugees and soldiers being permitted to vote in the Confederacy, districts and even states that had been overrun by Union forces continued to be represented in the Confederate Congress. These displaced constituencies from areas outside of Confederate control returned solid majorities for the Davis administration throughout the war. Having already lost their homes and most of their property to the Yankees, the refugees demanded that other civilians should also be willing to sacrifice all for the Confederate cause.

Early in 1864 the Confederate Congress passed its toughest, most nationalist-minded legislation to date. Most of the representatives from the interior districts still within reach of the Confederate bureaucracy opposed these measures, but they passed because of the strong support of congressmen from Union-occupied districts. In an effort to make up for the manpower losses of 1863, a new draft law cut back on exemptions and expanded the military pool upward to the age of fifty and downward to seventeen. Although the fresh levies were intended primarily for local defense, the drafting of older men and younger sons hardly improved morale at the local level. Indeed, opposition to earlier drafts had become so intense that Congress now found it necessary to empower Davis once again to suspend the writ of *habeas corpus*. The draft of 1864 added about 5,000 conscripts a month to the Confederate armies early in the year and probably induced a comparable increase in volunteering. Still, these additions were more than offset by the continuous drain of desertion. By the summer of 1864 the present-for-duty numbers had shrunk another 30,000 to 200,000.

The other major Confederate legislation in February 1864 encompassed slaves, taxation, currency, and foreign trade. The War Department was authorized to impress up to 20,000 slaves if slaveholders did not voluntarily proffer them to the Confederate military for noncombat duties. The cash taxes of April 1863 were extended, and, setting aside its constitutional scruples, Congress imposed a new direct tax of five percent on land and slaves. An attempt was made to check inflation by shrinking the amount of the paper money. A Refunding Act obligated the holders of Confederate treasury notes to exchange them for either four percent bonds or new treasury notes at the rate of $3 in old money for $2 in new money. The penalty for failing to refund the old currency was an automatic monthly reduction of ten percent in its value until January 1, 1865, at which time it would be legally worthless. Foreign trade, hitherto controlled by private businessmen, was effectively nationalized. Exports of cotton and other agricultural staples now required a presidential permit, all imports save for essential military goods and medical supplies were prohibited, and one-half of cargo space on blockade runners had to be set aside at fixed freightage rates for governmental use.

As was also true of the draft legislation, the results of these new measures were disappointing. Any military gains in combat efficiency achieved through the impressment of slave labor were counterbalanced by the political loss of support from planters. The tax legislation repeated the familiar pattern of too little too late in Confederate finances. By the time Congress imposed taxes that would have raised significant amounts of revenue, inflation was already out of control, and the tax base that Richmond could tap was limited to the South Atlantic states. Even then, Congress taxed land and slaves at their 1860 value, a figure which was absurdly low in 1864 as a result of inflation. What taxes were collected in cash, and they amounted to less than five percent of Confederate revenue throughout the war, were paid in badly depreciated paper money, which yielded little in the way of real purchasing power. Although the Refunding Act of 1864 was briefly effective, it ultimately compounded the currency crisis. Confederates were slow to exchange their paper money, and inflation continued to soar as the old treasury notes lost their value and new ones were issued to meet the war's expenses. By partially repudiating its currency, the government succeeded only in destroying all confidence in its monetary system. Placing national controls over foreign trade did produce positive results in terms of increased supplies and a more efficient use of cotton as an economic weapon. Once again, however, Congress had acted too late to materially affect the outcome of the war. Although its measures early in 1864 enhanced the staying power of Confederate armies, the Union advantage in troops and resources was now on the verge of becoming overpowering.

At the start of the campaigning in 1864, the Union had three times as many men under arms and present with their units than did the Confederacy. On February 1, 1864, Lincoln issued a draft call for an additional 500,000 troops, twice the number of soldiers on duty in all the Confederate armies. This was also the year in which the Union began to reap the full benefits of enlisting black troops. As Lincoln put it with but scant exaggeration in the summer of 1864, "Take from us, and give to the enemy, the hundred and thirty, forty, or fifty thousand colored persons now serving us as soldiers, seamen, and laborers, and we can no longer maintain the contest."[15]

In terms of veteran, combat-hardened troops, however, the Confederate disadvantage was not as great as the sheer numbers would indicate. Whereas the bulk of the Union veterans, the three-year enlistees of 1861, were free to go home in the spring of 1864, the Confederate draft of 1864 extended the service of the veteran enlistees in the Southern armies for the duration of the war. These Confederate veterans ranked with the toughest and hardiest of any in the history of warfare. Under good leadership, they fought with a fanatical tenacity, and many of them had undergone an evangelical conversion in the religious revivals that swept through the Confederate armies after the winter of 1862–1863. The conversion experience helped steel them to the possibility of their deaths on the battlefield by offering the promise of eternal salvation, and it sustained their morale by assuring them that they could still control their own destinies by freely accepting Christ. Such veteran troops were more than a match for three times their numbers in fresh Union recruits.

Fortunately for the Union war effort, more than half of the three-year volunteers did reenlist in the spring of 1864. Lavish bounties and generous furloughs certainly influenced their decision, but the overriding factor seemed to have been their sense of duty. "I wont back out when the work is half done....I am solemnly impressed that it is my duty to help put this rebelion down,"[16] was how George Lennard of the 57th Indiana Volunteers explained his reenlistment decision to his wife in 1864. Enough of his fellow veterans agreed with this reasoning to enable the Union armies in 1864 to maintain their combat effectiveness.

In economic and logistical resources, as well as in manpower, the odds against the Confederacy had lengthened considerably by 1864. The wartime manufacturing production of the Union peaked in 1864, and ample rail and water transport permitted tons of supplies to be stockpiled for the Union armies. In addition to the work of government bureaus, the voluntary efforts of civilian agencies also filled the military pipeline with supplies. The largest of these agencies, the U.S. Sanitary Commission, was an outgrowth of women's relief societies. It coordinated relief activities throughout the North and shipped vast quantities of clothing, food packages, and medical supplies to the front. Much of its work also included policing sanitary arrangements in the army camps and maintaining soldiers' homes and convalescent centers for the wounded.

As exemplified by the Sanitary Commission and the active participation of some 200,000 women in Northern relief agencies, the mobilization demanded by total war deepened the involvement of women in public affairs and expanded the roles they could take on in Northern society. Former boundaries between a female private sphere and a male public sphere blurred, and women, under the strong leadership of Clara Barton and Dorothea Dix, broke down barriers against the employment of their sex in government service. For the first time, federal bureaus hired women as clerks and copyists, and, of some 20,000 women who served as nurses, over 3,000 were army nurses. Because of the absence of male workers, who enlisted in the military, 100,000 jobs opened up for women in private business. By 1864, women held down one-third of all the jobs in the manufacturing work force, a proportion that had risen from one-quarter at the start of the war. To be sure, women were paid less than the men whose jobs they replaced, and most of their

The demand for clerks in government offices opened up new employment opportunities for women in the North during the war. Shown above are female clerks leaving the Treasury Department.

employment gains did not survive the postwar return to civilian life of the demobilized male troops. Nonetheless, participation in the war effort had broadened the humanitarian concerns and organizational skills of thousands of women reformers and hastened the professionalization of nursing and teaching as careers for women. In addition, involvement in war-related services and jobs had raised the self-esteem of countless other women and had given many of them the self-confidence to take part in a postwar crusade to win the vote for themselves.

Southern women also assumed major new responsibilities during the war that were crucial to the support of their soldier population. They helped fill the rapidly expanding ranks of the Confederate bureaucracy at the clerical level, labored in the fields on farms stripped of a male work force, and staffed relief societies that collected food and clothing for the soldiers at the front. In the more traditional and family-centered society of the overwhelmingly rural South, where patriarchal authority based on male control of the land and churches remained stronger than in the North, the wartime volunteerism of women did not evolve into a broad-based movement on behalf of women's rights. Moreover, by 1864, many of the contributions made by Southern women to the cause of Confederate victory were being negated by the failure of the deteriorating rail system of the Confederacy to deliver needed supplies to the armies. That same logistical weakness now seriously hampered all Confederate efforts at fully utilizing their shrinking economic resources. This problem steadily worsened throughout 1864 as the Union increasingly resorted to massive raids in the implementation of its strategy of wrecking the communications and remaining economic base of the Confederacy.

Grant was the Union general most responsible for the strategic use of raids in 1864. He was appointed general-in-chief of all Union armies on March 9, 1864, and was promoted to lieutenant general, an exalted rank previously held only by George Washington. In consultation with Sherman, the other preeminent Union general in the Western theater, Grant evolved a strategy that made Confederate supply lines and logistics more of a target than the rebel armies themselves. Grounded in the recognition of the near impossibility of annihilating Confederate armies in the field, Grant's strategy was designed to resolve two problems that had hampered Union armies throughout the war. The first was the success of the Confederacy in using its railroads for surprise counteroffensives with concentrated armies against the federal forces. The second was the progressively greater drain on Union manpower for guard and garrison duties as Union armies advanced further into rebel territory. Massive Union raids alleviated both of these problems. They were directed against rebel railroads, telegraph lines, factories, crops, indeed any economic resource that might be used to support or move Confederate armies. Their purpose was to deprive rebel armies of their mobility and sustenance while simultaneously relieving Union armies of the need to detach troops to protect occupied areas and the supply lines leading into them.

Grant originally intended to launch the Union offensive in 1864 with two strategic raids. His plans called for the navy to land troops at Mobile, Alabama, and along the coast of North Carolina. The Mobile expedition was to move up the Alabama River, destroy factories and arsenals in Selma and Montgomery, and link up with Sherman's army moving south from Chattanooga for a move on Atlanta, Georgia. The ultimate objective was the communications complex in Atlanta, which provided the Confederacy with its major remaining East-West rail connections. The North Carolina raiders, in addition to gutting the supply region of eastern North Carolina and seizing the blockade-running port of Wilmington, were to smash the coastal railroads that shipped goods up to Lee's army in Virginia.

Neither of these raids made it off the drawing board. Lincoln and Halleck rejected the North Carolina landing because they feared that it would siphon off too many troops from what they felt should be Grant's overriding objective in the East, an attack on Lee's army. Lincoln also overruled Grant by postponing the Mobile expedition. The army of Nathaniel P. Banks that Grant intended to use in Alabama was instead ordered in March 1864 to move up the Red River in northwestern Louisiana. Lincoln hoped that this offensive would bring out huge quantities of stored Confederate cotton, complete the political pacification of Louisiana in time for the 1864 presidential election, and serve as a springboard for a Union conquest of Texas. Foremost in Lincoln's thinking was the desire to remove Texas as a bargaining chip for the Confederacy in its bid to win recognition from the imperial regime that Napoleon III was trying to establish in Mexico.

None of the objectives of the Red River campaign was achieved. Like most of the Union political generals who received their appointments because of the voting support they could bring to the Republican party, Banks was an inept commander. Virtually everyone in his army knew that Banks was after cotton for his textile constituency back in Massachusetts, and morale and discipline quickly broke down. By the time that Banks finally got his army safely downriver in May, Grant had been forced to abandon his plans for sending it on to Mobile.

Grant clearly did not have a completely free hand to shape Union strategy in 1864, but the offensive that began in early May retained an essential feature of his thinking, which was the coordinated movement of federal armies in the East and West so as to apply simultaneous pressure all along the Confederate line. While Union forces in Vicksburg, Memphis, Knoxville, and West Virginia were launching raids to distract rebel forces and destroy their communications and supplies, four offensives were set into motion. The two major ones were in Virginia and Georgia.

Meade's Army of the Potomac, which Grant accompanied and directed, attacked Lee's army. Its goal was to engage Lee so completely that he would be unable to send reinforcements to the West, where three combined armies under Sherman were driving toward Atlanta. Sherman's immediate target was the rebel Army of Tennessee, now commanded by Joseph Johnston. Once that army was smashed or outmaneuvered, Sherman would be free to go after his primary objectives of Atlanta and the resource base of central Georgia. Two supplementary

The Civil War in the East, 1864-1865

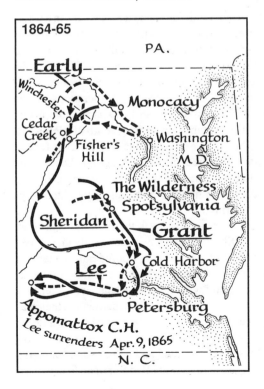

offensives in Virginia, one led by Franz Sigel up the Shenandoah Valley, and the other by Benjamin Butler up the James River toward Richmond, were designed to maximize the pressure on Lee and cut his rail lines to the west and south.

The grand Union offensive of May 1864 looked better on paper than it worked out in practice. The anticipated move of Banks from New Orleans to Mobile in support of Sherman's offensive, a key part of the original plan, never did get underway. Sigel and Butler, two political generals, were woefully incompetent. Sigel was forced to retreat from the Shenandoah Valley after his defeat at New Market on May 15, and the hesitant Butler allowed his army to become bottled up on a narrow peninsula between the James and Appomattox rivers by a rebel force one-fourth its size. Lee's rail lines were still intact, and reinforcements were rushed to him as he continued to hold off Grant.

When Grant sent the Army of the Potomac across the Rapidan River on May 4, he hoped to slide around Lee's right flank, get his army between Lee and Richmond, and force Lee to attack. But Lee, though outnumbered two-to-one, matched Grant's every move, and he counterattacked whenever he had the chance to catch Grant's army on the move. In two days of unbelievably savage fighting in the Wilderness on May 5 and 6, Lee pulled off a near replay of his Chancellorsville success. Grant, however, was no Joe Hooker, and he refused to accept defeat. Instead, he followed Lee, a move that won him the confidence of the Army of the Potomac, and he pushed south on May 7.

Grant continued to probe at Lee's right flank for the next five weeks in a series of battles—Spotsylvania Court House, North Anna, and Totopotomy Creek—which took a frightful toll of lives. Finally, after a frontal assault on June 3 at Cold Harbor returned a butcher's bill of 12,000 Union casualties (8,000 of them in the first eight minutes), Grant abandoned his attempts at turning Lee in a series of short-range maneuvers. Instead, he established a new base of operations on the James River in mid-June and used naval transports to shift his army completely around Lee's right flank and place it in Lee's rear at Petersburg, south of Richmond. For once, Lee was caught off guard, and an aggressive attack by the first federal forces to reach Petersburg would have captured the city. Although Lee's army arrived just in time to save the city, Lee's worst fears were now realized. He was forced into siege warfare, and for the next ten months Grant steadily tightened his grip on Petersburg and Lee's defending army.

Sherman began moving out of Chattanooga on May 4, the same day that Grant headed south to engage Lee. Like Grant, Sherman had a two-to-one advantage over the rebel army opposing him. Unlike Grant, he faced a Confederate general in Joseph Johnston who preferred defensive warfare over the risks of a tactical offensive. Johnston stuck to a deliberate policy of defensive maneuver that took advantage of the mountainous terrain in northern Georgia. Sherman, rather than attacking the strong rebel positions, repeatedly outflanked them and kept up a steady pressure on Johnston's rail link back to Atlanta. Johnston was thus forced into a slow retreat, but he always kept his forces concentrated and poised for a counterattack. This enabled him to conserve his army, and it compelled Sherman to take more

With defensive fortifications such as these, Johnston had hoped to keep Sherman out of Atlanta.

than two months to move from Chattanooga to the outskirts of Atlanta. Only once did Sherman lose his patience in what had become a campaign of nerves. On June 27, he ordered a frontal assault at Kenesaw Mountain that was easily beaten back with heavy casualties.

Sherman's frustration, however, was minor compared to that of Jefferson Davis's. Obsessed with the fear that Johnston would turn out to be another Pemberton and surrender Atlanta without a fight, and still smarting from criticism that he had retained for far too long the unpopular Bragg as head of the Army of Tennessee, Davis sacked Johnston on July 17 and replaced him with John B. Hood.

Davis's appointment of Hood was his second major mistake in the Atlanta campaign. The first had been his failure to order the 14,000 scattered Confederate cavalry in Alabama and Mississippi to concentrate for strikes against Sherman's very vulnerable rail supply line running north from Chattanooga to Nashville. Sherman's entire offensive against Atlanta was dependent on that railway. Hood was known as a very offensive-minded general, and he was under immediate pressure to attack Sherman and drive him away from Atlanta. Probably no Confederate general could have successfully carried out that assignment, but the impetuous Hood unfortunately hastened the fall of Atlanta when he quickly ordered a string of uncoordinated attacks that cost his army 20,000 men, one-third of its total, in the last week of July. Still, Sherman's initial failure to seize the city's rail lines to the south enabled the Atlanta defenses to hold throughout August.

Many Northerners felt by August 1864 that the major Union offensives had ground to a halt in front of Petersburg and Atlanta. Even more damaging to Northern morale were the 100,000 casualties that had been incurred since May. Grant's move from the Wilderness to Petersburg accounted for 60,000 of those casualties in little more than a month, and Grant's prestige suffered another blow when Lee sent Jubal Early with 9,000 men on a raid through the Shenandoah Valley in early July. Before Early turned back, he had defeated yet another federal army in the Valley, burned Chambersburg, Pennsylvania, and pushed to within sight of the Washington defenses. Though of little strategic value, Early's raid embarrassed the Lincoln administration and was cited by northern Democrats as proof that the Confederacy could not be vanquished.

War weariness was pervasive in the North by the late summer, and a discouraged Lincoln was convinced he stood no chance of reelection in November. His own party was divided by the charges of its antislavery leaders that Lincoln was too lenient in his reconstruction policy, and Democrats were damning him for unnecessarily prolonging the war by making emancipation a precondition for reunion. However, the Democrats provided an impetus for Republican unity when they nominated George McClellan for the presidency on a platform that called for a military armistice and a convention of the states to reunite the country. Most Democrats strongly opposed emancipation, and their platform implied that they would welcome back slavery along with the rebel states. Lincoln's Republican opponents, who had been pushing Secretary of the Treasury Chase for the presidency, now rallied behind Lincoln as their best bet to ensure that the Union did not renege on its commitment to end slavery.

While the presidential campaign was getting under way, a series of Union victories revived Northern morale and virtually guaranteed that Lincoln would be reelected after all. Mobile fell to Farragut's fleet in late August, and soon thereafter the North was thrilled by the news that Sherman had taken Atlanta. Hood had abandoned the city on September 1 when Sherman cut his last rail communications. Sherman's capture of Atlanta was perhaps the single most decisive Union victory of the war for it eliminated the political and psychological threat in 1864 that the Union war effort might collapse from within. And then, in the early autumn, the North finally received some good news from the Shenandoah Valley. Under orders from Grant to lay waste to the Valley and destroy it as a breadbasket for Lee's army, Phil Sheridan did just that. In the process he also soundly defeated Early's army in three separate battles.

This Union military surge, combined with a sharp drop in the casualty lists from the Army of the Potomac while Grant was slowly encircling Petersburg, helped Lincoln to clinch his reelection. As in past elections, Lincoln ordered the arrest of suspected Confederate sympathizers, and he dispatched federal troops to guard the polls, a move that undoubtedly kept some Democrats from voting. The Union army was also accused by McClellan's backers of favoring Republicans over

Democrats in issuing furloughs for soldiers to return home to vote in states that did not permit them to vote in the field. Still, regardless of the circumstances of the election, there is little reason to doubt that Lincoln would not have won. He received fifty-five percent of the popular vote and lost only Kentucky, Delaware, and New Jersey. Most important, the army was solidly behind him. Over eighty percent of the soldier vote was cast for Lincoln.

With the election safely out of the way, Washington cleared Sherman for his "March to the Sea," an unorthodox campaign of cutting loose from communications and living off the land that carried grave political risks if it backfired. As it turned out, the march was more of a lark than a strenuous campaign. Sherman had an unobstructed path to the sea because Hood had pulled his troops out of Georgia. Hood had decided to threaten the Union communications back to Tennessee in the hope that he could bait Sherman into following him. Sherman chased Hood for a month before tiring of the game. He dispatched two corps to deal with Hood and returned to Atlanta to pursue his primary goal of making the civilians in Georgia feel the pain of total war. As he explained, the purpose of his raid to the coast was "to demonstrate the vulnerability of the South and make its inhabitants feel that war and individual ruin are synonymous terms."[17]

After rendering homeless the civilians of Atlanta by the forced evacuation of the city back in September, and then ordering anything of military value to be burned on the eve of his army's departure, Sherman pulled out of the city on November 15 with 62,000 troops. For the next month he proceeded to make Georgians "howl." Smashing through Milledgeville and Macon in two wide swaths of destruction as they marched to Savannah, Sherman's veterans raised pillaging to an art form. Part of the some $100,000,000 in property damages they wracked up was repaired by the following spring, but the Confederacy never recovered from this shattering psychological blow to its morale. After ravaging the countryside, Sherman's army finished its Georgia campaign by capturing Savannah on December 20.

While Sherman was refitting his army in Savannah, the pathetic remnants of the once proud rebel Army of Tennessee were limping into winter quarters at Tupelo, Mississippi. With a complete disregard of logistical and manpower realities, Hood had embarked on a reconquest of Middle Tennessee in November. In the battle of Franklin on November 30, Hood's actions can most charitably be described as hurling his men to death in a useless charge against a strong Union position. Refusing to retreat, Hood attempted to lay siege to Nashville. On December 15, Thomas's army crashed through Hood's thin lines and all but destroyed his army as an effective fighting force. Of the 35,000 men Hood led into Tennessee, only about 15,000 were left to straggle into Tupelo.

By the end of 1864, the Confederacy had lost the war. However much its leaders chose to ignore this defeat, most of its soldiers were under no illusion that a military victory was still possible. Soldiers were deserting in droves, and absenteeism in the rebel armies rose from forty to fifty-three percent in the second half of 1864. At the start of 1865, the troops available for duty were down to 155,000.

More than half of the rebel armies had melted away. Unable to ignore this stark reality, the Confederate government now turned to the only source of manpower that offered it any hope of filling up the depleted ranks of the army. The arming and freeing of slaves, an absolutely unthinkable prospect at the beginning of the war, was now tentatively endorsed by the Confederate Congress.

While Duncan Kenner of Louisiana was in Europe in the winter of 1864–1865 on a vain mission to gain foreign recognition in return for Confederate emancipation, Davis was urging Congress to support the use of black soldiers. The issue had been raised a year earlier by commanders in the western armies, but Davis then had refused to consider it. The mere mention of such a measure ran the risk of completely alienating the planters and of exposing the Southern theory and racial defense of slavery as a sham. Yet, the need for additional troops became ever more pressing as the threat of Yankee subjugation became ever more real. For many Confederates the choice had seemingly boiled down to slavery for blacks or slavery for whites. This was the choice as laid out by Warren Atkin, a Confederate congressman from Georgia.

> We may (if necessary) put our slaves in the army, win our independence, and have liberty and homes for ourselves and children. But subjugation will deprive us of our homes, houses, property, liberty, honor, and every thing worth living for, leaving for us and our posterity only the chains of slavery, tenfold more galling and degrading than that now felt by our negroes.[18]

The Confederate debate over enlisting slaves in its armies inevitably forced Southern whites to confront the possibility of a general emancipation. Slaves would have fought for the Confederacy only in exchange for their freedom and that of their families. In turn, once a significant number of former slaves had gained military experience as combat soldiers, the internal security of slavery would have been irreversibly breached. Whites then would either have to abandon slavery or else watch it explode in a black war of liberation.

Southern whites, of course, clearly understood all this, and many of them who favored arming, and thereby freeing, the slaves also understood that the war had dramatically weakened slavery by eroding its control mechanisms and by providing the enslaved with new opportunities and responsibilities. There was no denying that large chunks of slavery had simply disintegrated as federal armies advanced and occupied areas of the Confederacy. This was especially the case by 1864 in the lower Mississippi Valley, and it was no coincidence that the Confederate debate over arming the slaves was initiated in Louisiana and Mississippi in late 1863. It was painfully obvious to Southern whites in this part of the Confederate West that their slaves lost to the Union were being used against the Confederacy as laborers and soldiers. If the Confederacy were to survive, argued these whites, it would have to arm its remaining slaves before the Yankees did. The same logic was used in early 1864 by General Patrick R. Cleburne of the Army of Tennessee, the first major officer in the army to come out in favor of arming the slaves.

The opposition to Cleburne's proposal was centered in the Southeast, a region where slavery was still largely intact well into 1864. But even here, where Union armies had not penetrated into the interior, slavery was undergoing fundamental changes.

Large numbers of seaboard slaves were moved back to the upcountry in order to prevent them from making contact with federal forces on the coast. These slaves correctly saw their forced removal as an act of weakness by their owners, an admission that the power of the masters was distinctly limited. When endangered by federal power, the masters had fled with their slave property. Usually strapped for funds, refugeeing planters cut back on the customary rations of food and clothing for their slaves and hired many of them out for additional income.

The refugeeing experience eroded the master-slave bond, just as did the employment in wartime industries of slaves no longer needed on plantations that had cut back on cotton production. As the war progressed, government shops and arsenals relied increasingly on slave labor. Whites became ever more dependent on factory slaves for essential wartime production, and this dependency gave the slaves a kind of power they had not had before, a power they used to gain concessions over their conditions of labor. Similar bargains were made in the countryside where Confederate masters, now predominately the wives or children of slaveowners off fighting, were forced to give the slaves greater freedoms to keep them on doing any kind of work.

Although the slaves behind the Confederate lines did not openly rebel, an act of defiance that would have been suicidal, they exploited every opportunity presented by the extraordinary wartime conditions to enlarge their personal liberties. They slackened off in their work, moved into managerial positions on the plantations, and controlled more of their daily activities. In the Confederate South, slavery was crumbling from within as a result of black initiatives and the dynamics unleashed by the war. It was this context of the ever weakening condition of slavery that made it possible for Southern whites, desperate to grasp at any expedient that might preserve Southern independence, to consider the previously heretical idea of arming and emancipating the slaves. Despite the undying opposition of many, probably most, planters, the Confederate Congress eventually sanctioned the use of black troops. By the time it did, however, the war was already a lost cause for the South.

Aided by the influential endorsement of Robert E. Lee, Davis secured authorization from Congress in early March 1865 to ask the states for up to 250,000 male slaves to be used in military service as Davis saw fit. This measure came far too late to have any impact on the military outcome of the war. No Confederate black troops were raised in time to serve in the war. If they had fought, they would have been free men. The War Department was willing to accept black recruits only on the condition that they were to be voluntarily freed by their owners.

The war ended before the Confederacy began freeing its slaves. In the early months of 1865 the Confederacy was defenseless against the hammering blows of Union raids. In the last major raid of the war, three cavalry divisions under General James Wilson demolished the remaining industrial base of the Confederacy by

Ten months after these Union soldiers were killed at Cold Harbor, Virginia, their remains were reburied in permanent graves. This photograph, taken in the spring of 1865, horrifyingly captures the war's macabre harvest of death.

razing ordnance and foundry centers in central Alabama and western Georgia. While this raid was still in progress, the two major rebel armies in the East surrendered.

On the verge of being completely encircled by Grant, Lee attempted to break free from the Petersburg trenches in early April for a juncture with Joseph Johnston's makeshift army in North Carolina. Johnston was awaiting the arrival of Sherman's army, whose move up through the Carolinas from Savannah had destroyed even more Confederate resources than its better known march through Georgia. Grant anticipated Lee's move and cut off his escape route. Rather than have his outmanned troops cut to pieces, Lee accepted the inevitable and surrendered to Grant at Appomattox Court House, Virginia, on April 9, 1865. Johnston, now about to be crushed between Grant to the north and Sherman to the south, surrendered his army to Sherman on April 29 at Durham Station, North Carolina. Confederate armies across the Mississippi had likewise yielded by late May.

Despite Davis's last-ditch proclamation of April 4 calling for a continuation of the war by guerrilla resistance, most Confederates no longer had the will to resist by the spring of 1865. Davis talked heroically of fleeing to the hills and fighting to the last man, but few of his erstwhile Confederates wanted any part of it. Far too much of their South had already been turned into a no man's land of near anarchy in which deserters, draft dodgers, and Unionists fought against those still loyal to the Confederacy in obscenely violent struggles. They had made incredible sacrifices for a dream of Southern independence that had become a nightmare. What they desperately wanted now was peace, and a chance to begin reestablishing their ties to the land and kin of their war-ravaged communities.

Davis was captured by the Union army on May 10 at Irwinsville, Georgia. As he had fled south from Richmond, his pleas for continued resistance fell on deaf ears. The war was over, but the devisive debate over its meaning was just beginning.

NOTES

1. W. Maury Darst (ed.), "The Vicksburg Diary of Mrs. Alfred Ingraham (May 2-June 13, 1863)," *Journal of Mississippi History*, vol. 44, p. 161, 1982.
2. Quoted in Joseph T. Glatthaar, *The March to the Sea and Beyond: Sherman's Troops in the Savannah and Carolinas Campaign* (New York: New York University Press, 1985), p. 174.
3. *Journal of the Congress of the Confederate States of America, 1861–1865*, vol. 3 (Washington, D.C.: Government Printing Office, 1904–1905), p. 7.
4. Roy P. Basler (ed.), *The Collected Works of Abraham Lincoln*, vol. 6 (New Brunswick: Rutgers University Press, 1953), p. 149.
5. Allan Nevins (ed.), *Diary of the Civil War, 1860–1865: George Templeton Strong* (New York: Macmillan, 1962), p. 287.
6. Basler, vol. 6, p. 30.
7. J. C. Levenson et al. (eds.), *The Letters of Henry Adams*, vol. 1. (Cambridge: The Belknap Press of Harvard University Press, 1982), pp. 338–339.
8. John W. Blassingame (ed.), *Slave Testimony: Two Centuries of Letters, Speeches, Interviews, and Autobiographies* (Baton Rouge: Louisiana State University Press, 1980), p. 372.
9. Robert Garlick Hill Kean, *Inside the Confederate Government,* (New York: Oxford University Press, 1957), p. 42.
10. Rome (Ga.) *Weekly Courier,* Sept. 27, 1861, quoted in Paul D. Escott, *After Secession: Jefferson Davis and the Failure of Confederate Nationalism* (Baton Rouge: Louisiana State University Press, 1978), p. 95.
11. Tuskegee (Ala.) *South Western Baptist,* Oct. 1, 1863, quoted in E. Merton Coulter, *The Confederate States of America, 1861–1865* (Baton Rouge: Louisiana State University Press, 1950), p. 465.
12. Joel Tyler Headley, *The Great Riots of New York 1712 to 1873* (New York: Dover, 1971), p. 207.
13. Theodore W. Blackburn, *Letters From the Front: A Union "Preacher" Regiment (74th Ohio) in the Civil War* (Dayton, Ohio: Press of Morningside House, 1981), p. 144.
14. Quoted in William Thomas Auman, "Neighbor Against Neighbor: The Inner Civil War in the Central Counties of Confederate North Carolina" (Ph.D. dissertation, University of North Carolina, Chapel Hill, 1988), p. 202.
15. Basler, vol. 7, p. 500.

16. Paul Hubbard and Christine Lewis (eds.), " 'Give Yourself No Trouble About Me': The Shiloh Letters of George W. Lennard," *Indiana Magazine of History*, vol. 76, p. 24, 1980.
17. Quoted in Herman Hattaway and Archer Jones, *How the North Won: A Military History of the Civil War* (Urbana, Ill: University of Illinois Press, 1983), p. 642.
18. Bell Irvin Wiley (ed.), *Letters of Warren Atkin: Confederate Congressman* (Athens, Ga.: University of Georgia Press, 1959), p. 33.

SUGGESTED READINGS

ASH, STEPHEN V., *Middle Tennessee Society Transformed, 1860–1870*. Baton Rouge, La.: Louisiana State University Press, 1987.

BERINGER, RICHARD E. ET AL., *Why the South Lost the Civil War*. Athens, Ga.: University of Georgia Press, 1986.

BERLIN, IRA, ET AL. (EDS.), *Freedom: A Documentary History of Emancipation*. New York: Cambridge University Press, 1982.

CORNISH, DUDLEY T., *The Sable Arm: Negro Troops in the Union Army, 1861–1865*. New York: W.W. Norton, 1956.

COX, LA WANDA, *Lincoln and Black Freedom*. Columbia, S.C.: University of South Carolina Press, 1981.

ESCOTT, PAUL D., *After Secession: Jefferson Davis and the Failure of Confederate Nationalism*. Baton Rouge, La.: Louisiana State University Press, 1978.

FREDRICKSON, GEORGE M., *The Inner Civil War: Northern Intellectuals and the Crisis of the Union*. New York: Harper and Row, 1965.

GERTEIS, LOUIS S., *From Contraband to Freedman: Federal Policy Toward Southern Blacks, 1861–1865*. Westport, Conn.: Greenwood, 1973.

KLEMENT, FRANK L., *The Copperheads in the Middle West*. Chicago, Ill.: University of Chicago Press, 1960.

MCPHERSON, JAMES M. (ED.), *The Negro's Civil War*. New York: Pantheon, 1965.

MOHR, CLARENCE L., *On the Threshold of Freedom: Masters and Slaves in Civil War Georgia*. Athens, Ga.: University of Georgia Press, 1986.

NEVINS, ALLAN, *The War for the Union: The Organized War, 1863–1864*. New York: Scribner, 1971.

NEVINS, ALLAN, *The War for the Union: The Organized War to Victory, 1864–1865*. New York: Scribner, 1971.

PALUDAN, PHILLIP S., *"A People's Contest": The Union and the Civil War, 1861–1865*. New York: Harper and Row, 1988.

ROSE, WILLIE LEE, *Rehearsal for Reconstruction: The Port Royal Experiment*. Indianapolis, Ind.: Bobbs-Merrill, 1964.

SILBEY, JOEL, *A Respectable Minority: The Democratic Party in the Civil War Era*. New York: W.W. Norton, 1977.

WILEY, BELL I., *Southern Negroes, 1861–1865*. New Haven, Conn.: Yale University Press, 1938.

7

The Shaping
of
Reconstruction

"*Peace* herself at last" rejoiced George Templeton Strong of New York in May 1865 on hearing of the surrender of the last Confederate armies in the Trans-Mississippi West. Just over four years had passed since the beginning of "the great tragedy," but Strong was surely correct when he added that "We have lived a century of common life since then."[1] The war had compressed time and emotions into a searing experience that forever set apart the generation that had lived through it.

Aside from this common bond of the war experience and the shared welcoming of peace, Americans remained deeply divided in the spring of 1865. Although nearly everyone agreed that the war had preserved an indivisible Union and destroyed slavery as an institution, there was no agreement on the other fundamental issues raised by the war or on the meaning of the war itself. Northern Democrats and most Southern whites held that the war had been fought to restore the Union of 1860. Slavery was a casualty of the war, but beyond the fact of emancipation, the postwar settlement should minimize change and adhere strictly to the traditional Democratic doctrine of states rights. Victory simply meant the restoration of the masses of Southern whites to their former loyalty to the Union. Republicans, and the majority of Northern whites whom they represented, believed that the immense cost and sacrifices of the war could be justified only through the creation of a more perfect Union. Their postwar America would be, in the words of George Julian of Indiana, "For the first time in her history, the model Republic of the world."[2]

Republicans differed sharply over the nature and amount of the change they would sanction in both the North and the South to create that model republic, but they remained united in their belief that a lasting and just peace required legal and political changes in the South sufficient to ensure the establishment of loyal state governments.

Reconstruction is usually associated with a cluster of Southern problems at the war's end. Who should exercise power in the postwar South, the majority of former Confederates or the minority of Southern Unionists? When should the ex-rebel states be readmitted to the Union? What should be the terms of their readmission, if any, and who should set those terms and control the process, the president or Congress? Above all, and central to all the other issues, was the status of the recently freed 4 million slaves. Were they to become citizens, and, if so, what rights of citizenship should they enjoy, and who would confer and protect those rights, the states or the federal government?

The attempts to find answers to these questions provoked a political struggle that defined Reconstruction as primarily a Southern issue. But Reconstruction also encompassed the North as part of a national phenomenon in which the Republicans sought to promote progress and equal rights through an extension of the governmental activism fostered by the Union's war effort. Although always keeping their main focus on the South, the Republicans nonetheless embarked on ambitious programs of social and economic reform in many of the Northern states after the war. These programs, like Reconstruction in the South, rested on the assumption that individual progress could best be advanced through positive governmental action on behalf of economic development and political democracy.

In addition to examining how a fixed policy of Reconstruction for the South gradually evolved between Appomattox and the passage of a congressional program of Reconstruction in 1867, this chapter will also look at the parallel commitment to Reconstruction in the North. Both of these movements were led by Republicans, and both drew heavily on the war legacy of an activist government. As early as 1867 a reaction against that legacy had set in, and the Republican coalition that had pushed for reform in both sections was starting to split. As a creative force for extending political democracy and civic equality, Reconstruction was nearly exhausted by 1868.

THE DEFEATED SOUTH AND PRESIDENTIAL RECONSTRUCTION

In the spring of 1865 Southern whites were militarily defeated, economically devastated, and politically expecting the worst from their Union conquerors. The human and economic losses they had suffered in the war were staggering. About three-fourths of all Southern white males of military age had served in the Confederate armies, and over half of them were killed or wounded. Uncompensated emancipation was the greatest act of confiscation in American history, and some

The ruins in Richmond, the former capital of the Confederacy, typified the war's destruction in the defeated South.

$1.5 billion in slave property, the largest capital investment in the antebellum economy, was wiped out. Gone too was the $500 million (measured in gold dollars) that Southerners had invested in the Confederate war effort. Land values were down by one-half, and they remained depressed because of labor shortages and massive losses in livestock and work animals. Crushed between two competing armies and governments, Southern whites readily admitted their defeat. This entailed no loss of honor because Southerners believed they had fought valiantly until overwhelmed by the superior numbers and material might of the Yankees. They had been overpowered, and, as many Northern observers noted in the months just after Appomattox, they fully expected the Yankees to claim the rights of a conqueror and dictate to them the terms of peace.

What those terms would have been, and how quickly they would have been imposed, had Lincoln lived, is, of course, a matter of conjecture. Conciliation and leniency seemed to have been the chief features of the reconstruction that he had tried to foster during the war. His program of amnesty and pardon rested on a single oath of future loyalty to the Union and excluded only high-ranking Confederate officials from its benefits. His ten percent plan aimed at a speedy restoration of the rebel states and, with the exception of slavery, said nothing about an economic and social reconstruction of the South. Indeed, Lincoln's plans initially excluded any black role and even included the suggestion that Southern whites resort to a system of "apprenticeship" in order to control black labor and lessen the economic disruptions of emancipation.

These were the central features of Lincoln's thinking on reconstruction at the midpoint of the war, but they were by no means immutable. The reconstruction that Lincoln pushed in Virginia, Tennessee, Arkansas, and Louisiana was a wartime measure and was defended as such. Its ultimate objective may have been to secure a national base for the Republicans by creating the core of a southern Republican party built around white Unionists and former Clay Whigs, but its immediate purpose was to weaken the Confederacy by depriving it of white support. As the war was winding down in March and April 1865, Lincoln made it clear that the whole context for a successful reconstruction policy was about to change and that the problem required fresh, hard thinking. According to Francis Pierpont, the Unionist governor of Virginia, Lincoln admitted the day after Lee's surrender that "he had no plan for reorganization, but must be guided by events."[3]

All along Lincoln had refused to be bound by any fixed position on reconstruction. Ever the pragmatist, he adjusted his thinking as circumstances warranted. Thus, in response to the demands of Republican radicals, and more specifically to the insistence of the antebellum free blacks of New Orleans that they be given the vote, Lincoln endorsed limited black suffrage for the South in his last public speech on April 11. He recommended that suffrage be extended to educated (literate) blacks and the much larger number who had fought as Union soldiers. As he had done before, Lincoln disarmed his more radical party opponents by staking out a position that met them more than halfway.

Up to the time that he was mortally wounded by John Wilkes Booth on April 14, 1865, Lincoln had failed to reach any agreement with Congress on an overall plan for reconstruction. Congressional opposition to Lincoln's approach had crystallized in the Wade–Davis bill of August 1864. Intended as a substitute for presidential Reconstruction, the bill had a host of provisions. It mandated that a majority of white voters, not just ten percent, would have to take an oath of future loyalty before reconstruction could begin; limited the actual electorate that could participate in reconstruction to those whites who could also swear to an oath of past loyalty; eliminated the role of the president and the army and replaced it with congressional tutelage of a civilian program; stipulated that the legal and civil status of blacks (with the exception of voting) be governed by the same state laws that applied to whites; and required new state constitutions providing for emancipation, political disqualification of leading rebels, and repudiation of Confederate war debts. Lincoln pocket-vetoed the bill, that is, he failed to sign it before the congressional session came to an end. He wanted to move his party toward the political center before the election of 1864 and preserve the Unionist governments he had nursed along in Louisiana and Arkansas. In turn, Republican radicals sharply criticized Lincoln in the Wade–Davis Manifesto for usurping the legislative prerogatives of Congress in his reconstruction policies and for failing to provide any safeguards against the resumption of political power by unrepentant rebels once the war was over.

Once the election was safely out of the way, the differences between Lincoln and Congress narrowed in the winter of 1864–1865. Lincoln supported a revised Wade–Davis bill, which recognized his reorganized governments in Louisiana and Arkansas and exempted them from its provisions. Only an unlikely alliance of radicals, who wanted universal black suffrage instead of the bill's call for limited black suffrage, and conservatives, who felt that the states should have a free hand in their reconstruction, prevented enactment of the revised measure. Most significantly, Lincoln and his radical critics worked together in January 1865 to secure the congressional passage of the 13th Amendment, which emancipated the slaves. This amendment was the crowning achievement of Lincoln's antislavery policy. It forever eliminated the possibility that his wartime measures against slavery could not be overturned by the courts or reversed by the actions of the Southern states after the war.

By the spring of 1865, Lincoln and Congress were in agreement on emancipation, limited black suffrage, and the need for antislavery Unionists to be represented in the reconstructed governments of the South. Booth's bullet deprived the nation of the opportunity to see whether this agreement could have laid the foundation for a reconstruction program that tempered leniency for the rebels with justice for blacks and white Unionists in the South.

Lincoln's successor, Vice President Andrew Johnson, had none of Lincoln's extraordinary political skills of tact, timing, and flexibility. Nor did he share Lincoln's sensitivity to slavery as a great moral wrong. A lifelong Jacksonian Democrat from Tennessee, Johnson rose from plebian origins of poverty and illiteracy to become a successful lawyer, politician, and slaveholder. Lincoln had similarly struggled upward, but in doing so he developed an empathy for the needs of others and a breadth of vision that were missing in Johnson's makeup. Embittered and suspicious throughout his life, Johnson shaped his career around an unending struggle against the political and social establishment that had sneered at him in his youth. He was the only senator from a seceded state who spoke out against secession and remained in the U.S. Senate after the outbreak of the war. Here, the needs of the public and private Johnson fused, for he blamed the rebellion on the same arrogant aristocracy of planters whom he felt had always wanted to lord it over common whites such as himself. Johnson championed the interests of these common whites, and his record as wartime governor of Union-occupied Tennessee seemed to indicate that he would make the rebel planters pay dearly for bringing on the war. So also did Johnson's highly publicized statement that "treason must be made odious, and traitors punished and impoverished."[4] An ardent southern Unionist from a rebel state, Johnson was a very valuable commodity to the Republicans in 1864, and he was chosen as Lincoln's running mate in 1864 in the party's continuing bid to build a base of bisectional support.

Lincoln's assassination suddenly made Johnson the most important political

In his physical bearing, as well as his style of political leadership, Andrew Johnson was stern and unbending.

figure in America. Congress had adjourned and was not scheduled to meet again until December. Johnson decided not to call it into special session, and for the next eight months he had virtually a free hand in shaping a reconstruction policy to meet the needs of the victorious North, the defeated South, and the suddenly freed blacks. Far from being up to the task, he badly mishandled it.

Part of Johnson's problem was a constitutional rigidity that converted states' rights into a fetish and that would brook no talk of a meaningful role for the federal government in Reconstruction. Also, as a political and social outsider in the Republican party, Johnson suspected the worst of his fellow Republicans, especially those who pushed for the extension and protection of black civil rights. In his list of political enemies he quickly substituted radical Republicans for haughty planters as the disunionists who had to be purged and punished. Most fundamentally, however, Johnson failed to exercise effective leadership because he was a Republican in name only. He was neither a Northerner nor, in any significant sense of the term, a Republican, and thus he simply could not understand what the war and the Union had come to mean for the majority of Northerners. Whereas that majority wanted a postwar settlement which would honor the sacrifices of their war dead with a more secure and morally just Union, Johnson thought only in terms of restoring the old Union. He ignored the demand of the North for proof and assurance of their victory from Southern whites after the war, and he was incapable of recognizing the legitimacy of the Northern insistence that the freed slaves should now be treated with a modicum of justice and fair play by Southern whites.

Although he falsely claimed only to have tolerated slavery before the war, rather than actively supporting it, Johnson did welcome the end of slavery. However, he did so not out of any belief that a great moral wrong inflicted on blacks had finally ended. Rather, he supported emancipation for breaking the power of the planter class that had deprived common whites of social and economic opportunities through its monopoly on the South's labor force. Johnson believed that Southern whites, not blacks, were the main victims of slavery, and he interpreted any move on behalf of black rights as class favoritism at the expense of whites. He was convinced that blacks as a race were utterly unfit for self-government, and any talk of black suffrage threatened his self-esteem as a Southern white. In his view, blacks were owed nothing upon being released from bondage, and any rights they should have could be entrusted to the constitutional safeguarding of the individual Southern states. All that he would offer the freedmen were lectures on the need to work for a living. "I want to say to them in candor," he told a campaign audience in 1864, "that freedom simply meant liberty to work and enjoy the products of their labor, and that was all there was of it."[5]

Johnson's program of reconstruction for Southern whites turned out to be about as narrow as his conception of freedom for Southern blacks. His restoration policy, as he insisted on calling it, took shape in two proclamations issued on May 29, 1865. The first offered a general pardon to most Confederates who would take an oath of future loyalty. This amnesty included a full restoration of political rights. Excluded from the pardon were the political and military leaders of the Confederacy and all former Confederates with taxable property worth more than $20,000. Individuals in the exempt categories had to make a personal appeal for a pardon from Johnson.

The other proclamation applied originally to North Carolina and then was extended to the other former rebel states where reconstruction had not been initiated during the war by Lincoln. This other proclamation appointed a provisional governor with the responsibility of registering voters in preparation for the election of delegates to a state constitutional convention. Despite Johnson's later insistence that Congress could impose no preconditions on what he argued should be a voluntary process of self-restoration by the rebel states, he himself set down what amounted to three demands. He made it clear that he expected each rebel state in its constitutional convention to nullify its ordinance of secession, recognize the legal end of slavery, and repudiate the debts that it had contracted in support of the

Confederacy. After calling these conventions, each provisional governor was then to supervise the holding of elections for new state and federal officers. Upon the completion of these elections and the ratification of the 13th Amendment by the state legislatures, reconstruction under Johnson's plan was virtually over. All that was left would be the formal readmission of the Southern states by Congress through its seating of their congressional delegations.

Presidential Reconstruction under Johnson's guidelines moved along very quickly, and Southern congressmen arrived in Washington in December. Johnson fully expected that they would be seated and that Reconstruction would thereby be completed. Yet, as indicated by the refusal of Congress to admit those Southern congressmen, Johnson had misread Northern public opinion as thoroughly as the radicals had misread Johnson's intentions back in the spring of 1865.

For all his talk of punishing individual rebels, Johnson had no intentions of reshaping the politics and society of the postwar South. He never shared the commitment of the Republican party to an expanded role for the federal government in a postwar settlement, and he was positively frightened by the demands of the radicals for extending legal and political equality to the freedmen. His racial and political instincts as a white Southerner and as a states rights' Democrat were the determining factors in his minimal policy of reconstruction designed to protect white supremacy, restore the South's traditional ruling class to power, and build a political base that would return him to the presidency in 1868. Because such a policy threatened the political future of the Republican party, precluded any role for Congress, save that of rubberstamping a program Johnson insisted was completed, and ignored the demand of Northerners that political power in the postwar South should be held only by loyal men, it was virtually guaranteed to be repudiated.

The initially broad but cautious support of Northerners for Johnsonian Reconstruction faded by the fall of 1865. By then it was clear that Johnson was unable or unwilling to use his pardoning power to shape a Southern electorate that met the Northern definition of loyalty. The number of Southern whites excluded from Johnson's original offer of amnesty was far larger than the group denied amnesty in Lincoln's wartime proclamation, and Johnson seemed to be implying that he would bar both the old planter elite and the former Confederate officials from a political role in reconstruction. In practice, however, Johnson was so generous in granting individual pardons for amnesty that he effectively handed over control of the postwar governments in the South to the same Southern whites whom he had loudly damned as traitors in the spring.

Undoubtedly, Johnson, an illiterate tailor's apprentice in his youth, received immense personal satisfaction from having the aristocratic planters, his old social and political enemies, now come to him for a pardon. But more than Johnson's ego was involved. A pardon conferred a full restitution of property, as well as political, rights, and, in granting pardons, Johnson was restoring wealth and status to individuals who would now have a very compelling reason to support him politically. These individuals were beholden to Johnson, but by the same token he had also become their political captive. When unpardoned rebels were elected to office,

Johnson could hardly avoid granting them an immediate amnesty without denying the legitimacy of the voluntary process of reconstruction that he had initiated in the South. For much the same reason, Johnson looked the other way when Mississippi refused to ratify the 13th Amendment and South Carolina repealed, rather than nullified, its secession ordinance. Yielding to pressure in August 1865 from William Sharkey, his provisional governor in Mississippi, Johnson even permitted the reorganization of the Mississippi militia, an all-white police force of Confederate veterans that Republicans correctly feared would be used to intimidate white Unionists and the freedmen. To many Northerners it now looked as if Johnson, far from asserting federal authority and demanding allegiance from the South, would do anything to cajole a rebel state back into the Union.

Southern postwar leaders in the Johnsonian governments were certainly not the die-hard Unionists whom the Republicans wanted to entrust with the reins of power. Such unconditional Unionists, Southern whites who had stood by the Union in the face of Confederate persecution, were numerous only in the Appalachian highlands and some of the central Piedmont counties in North Carolina. With the exception of Johnson's home state of Tennessee, they were simply too few in number to command the support of a white majority in any of the states that Johnson was trying to reconstruct. On the other hand, these Johnson politicians were also not the unrepentent rebels whom most Republicans saw lurking behind a facade of loyalty to the postwar Union. Instead, they were mostly Whiggishly inclined conservatives who had supported the Confederacy but not secession.

In the continuation of a trend that had set in by the midpoint of the war, Southern whites turned to former Whigs and antisecession Democrats for leadership in the Johnson governments. By the Southern definition of the term, and one that Johnson himself accepted in his criteria for selecting the provisional governors, these men were loyal Unionists. As men of honor and of integrity, they had worked for Southern independence once their neighbors and kin had decided on secession, but they had not favored breaking up the Union in the first place. Understandably, this distinction was lost on most Northerners. In their eyes, a rebel was a rebel, and they saw plenty of them in the Johnson governments.

As a result of both their Whiggish antecedents and the lessons they had drawn from Confederate defeat, the leaders in Johnson's provisional governments were ready and eager to promote industrialization and economic diversification in the postwar South. In most of the states they enacted ambitious programs of governmental aid for railroad development and business incorporations. In many respects these programs seemed to be a confirmation of Northern victory in that Southern legislatures were apparently embracing Northern doctrines of free-labor ideology and the positive role of the state in promoting economic change. Liberated from the economically enervating incubus of slavery and plantation agriculture, Southern whites now seemed eager to redeem themselves from defeat and poverty by building a prosperous society of independent farms and bustling factories. In fact, however, the postwar political economy envisioned by the Johnson governments did not rest on any fundamental acceptance by Southern whites of the North's free-labor ideology or its antislavery critique of antebellum Southern society. This became abundantly clear with the passage of the Southern Black Codes of 1865 and 1866, which were state legislature enactments necessitated by the need to define the legal rights of the emancipated blacks.

Nearly all Southern whites believed that the very idea of civil equality between the races was absurd and dangerous. The Black Codes were the legal expression of that belief. The codes did recognize certain minimal rights of the freed population, mainly the right to acquire and hold property, enter into legal marriages, make contracts, and sue and be sued. In general, as Southern whites were quick to point out, the codes did confer more rights than the antebellum South's legislation on free blacks. But there was no denying that the legal status of blacks was still inferior to and separate from that of whites. Blacks were barred from voting, holding public office, serving on juries, owning firearms, enlisting in the militias, or testifying in court cases involving whites. Restrictions were placed on their rights to assemble in public meetings and move about freely. Crimes by and against blacks were treated in special criminal codes that prescribed harsher penalties based on race.

Radical Republicans and abolitionists were outraged by the blatant manner in which the Southern Black Codes violated the principle of equality before the law. However, many of the features of these black codes, especially their prohibitions against voting, interracial marriage, and jury service, were also found in Northern statutes. To be sure, white supremacy still reigned in the North, but many Northern whites were nonetheless disturbed by the overt attempts of Southern whites to legislate racial discrimination in all areas of civil and criminal behavior. Blacks, after all, had proven to be the Union's most loyal friends in the South during the war, and Northern whites, who were otherwise quite racist in their thinking, believed that the freedmen should not be left to the mercy of Southern whites after the war. The war had broadened the Northern conception of loyalty to the Union, and that conception now included the willingness to support those who had come to the aid of the Union when rebels were attempting to destroy it. To do otherwise for Southern blacks would be to make a mockery of their freedom and the sacrifices of the Union soldiers who had died to achieve that freedom.

What particularly angered Northerners about the Southern Black Codes were provisions relating to labor and contracts that left the blacks with virtually no economic freedom save that of agreeing to work as a landless peasantry under labor terms set by their former owners. Southern whites had no faith in the ability or willingness of the freed blacks to work without coercive legal controls forcing them to do so. The myth of the inherently lazy black had been central to the defense of slavery, and it led to the inescapable conclusion that the blacks would interpret emancipation as a license to stop working, leave the plantations, and steal from whites in order to support themselves. While common whites feared for the safety of their property, planters were more specifically concerned with the problem of assuring themselves of a stable, docile supply of agricultural labor now that slavery was ended. Thus, regardless of class differences, Southern whites were unified in their belief that the coercive power of the state had to be substituted for the former legal prerogatives of the master as a means of disciplining a plantation labor force. That power was exercised in the sweeping vagrancy, apprenticeship, and contractual provisions in the codes.

These laws had the practical effect of defining as a vagrant any black who could not establish proof of gainful employment to the satisfaction of a local white magistrate. This proof usually consisted of an annual contract to work as a plantation laborer, and blacks without such a contract were to be arrested, fined, and bound over as an involuntary laborer to any employer willing to pay the fine. The apprenticeship laws were a thinly disguised legal cover for the seizure of black minors by planters as unpaid laborers. Local white courts were given complete authority to determine whether black parents were capable of providing adequate support for their children. Regardless of the parents' wishes, children in poor black families were handed over to white "guardians," usually planters who used the apprenticeship laws to regain control over the black children they formerly had owned. In the Upper South, where the practice was particularly notorious, as many as twenty-five percent of the newly freed children in some counties were bound over to their ex-masters.

The Southern Black Codes violated every central tenet of the North's free-labor ideology and confirmed the worst of Northern fears regarding the moral insensitivity of Southern whites toward blacks. More than any other aspect of Johnsonian Reconstruction, this legislation convinced Northerners that Southern whites simply did not understand the meaning of emancipation and the nature of a free economy in which workers were encouraged to improve themselves through access to equal economic opportunities and the protection of the law.

By the fall of 1865, Northerners, and most particularly members of the Republican party, were convinced that Southern whites were forgetting who had won the war. A minimal expectation of the North was that the former rebels should act as if they recognized their defeat. Instead, the state governments set up under the Johnson guidelines seemed to embody the same disloyalty and Southern white arrogance that Northerners believed had brought on the war in the first place. Rebels had been returned to power, and unrepentant Confederates were openly persecuting Southern Unionists and shutting them out of political offices. These same Confederates were insulting Union soldiers and harassing them with a battery of civil suits for interfering in black–white relations, especially in labor matters. And blacks, who had been returned to a status little better than slavery, were the daily victims of white violence and a legal system that denied them any justice. This was the composite picture of the South that military commanders and newspaper correspondents were sending North in the summer and fall of 1865. As summarized by Carl Schurz, a Republican whose reports from the South were influential in shaping Northern attitudes, "It is a stubborn fact that our truest friends are threatened and persecuted and that the negro is denied his freedom wherever the population has a chance to act upon its own impulses without immediately being checked."[6]

This was the dominant Northern image of Johnsonian Reconstruction by 1866. Northerners believed that Johnson had permitted unrepentant rebels to reduce Southern blacks to a condition little better than slavery.

However much Johnson and northern Democrats insisted that Southern whites were acting in good faith to prove their loyalty to the Union and protect the best interests of the freedmen, Northern public opinion had turned against Johnsonian Reconstruction before Congress convened in December 1865. The Republicans had all the mandate they needed to call a halt to Johnson's policy of restoration and to implement their program of reconstruction.

THE ENDANGERED REPUBLICAN PARTY

Implicit in Johnson's approach to reconstruction was an attempt to reorganize the national political parties after the war. This realignment threatened the very survival of the Republican party as it had existed in 1860, that is, a sectionalized party of Northerners that gained national power by running on an antislavery, anti-Southern platform. Isolated constitutionally and emotionally from this Republican party, Johnson tried to build a new one with himself at its head. Johnson's Republican party would be a bisectional Union party, a grand coalition of War Democrats, Southern whites, and moderate and conservative Republicans held together by its commitment to white supremacy and the restoration of the South to the Union under the minimal terms laid down by Johnson.

Johnson's attempt to fashion a new political center might well have succeeded had he been a more skillful politician. There was much talk in the spring of 1865 about the emergence of a new political era. Many observers predicted the breakup of Lincoln's Republican party now that its uneasy alliance of prewar Whigs and Democrats could no longer be fused together by the organizing principles of antislaveryism and the preservation of the Union. A precedent for reshaping the party also existed in the Union coalition of War Democrats, Southern white Unionists, and Republicans that had elected the Lincoln–Johnson ticket in 1864. In trying to revive and broaden that coalition, however, Johnson lost sight of the need to retain the support of the Republican moderates who comprised the great majority of the party. The major groups that rallied behind Johnsonian Reconstruction were either outside the mainstream of the Republican party or they represented a distinct threat to its interests and values.

The first of these groups was the white Southern constituency that Johnson had created through his pardoning powers and his dispensing of federal patronage. Thousands of federal jobs had to be filled in the postwar South, and Johnson's appointment of judges, attorneys, marshals, postmasters, and tax collectors ignored the ironclad test oath law that Congress had passed in 1862. This law stipulated that federal civil and military officials had to be able to swear to an oath of past as well as future loyalty to the Union. Johnson's defiance of the oath law thwarted Republican hopes of building local party organizations in the South around a nucleus of white Unionists and perhaps a few educated blacks. Instead, power at all levels in the Johnsonian South was held by men whom the Republicans viewed as unrepentant rebels, and they were using that power against the very Unionists and blacks whom the Republicans were pledged to defend and represent in any postwar settlement.

The major Northern group that joined the Johnsonian coalition in 1865 were the Democrats. The Republicans' wartime program of centralizing nationalism had intensified all the traditional concerns of the more localistic-minded Democrats. They rallied behind Johnsonian Reconstruction because it meshed neatly with the party's emphasis on states' rights and white supremacy. Moreover, by calling for the protection of the personal freedoms of Southern whites from encroaching federal power, the Democrats would quickly be able to reestablish their prewar dominance in the South. Indeed, having retained during the war a shade over forty-five percent of the electorate in the North, the Democrats could expect a rapid return to national power once they had a solid South behind them.

Conservative Republicans were the smallest, but strategically most important, component of the Johnsonian coalition. The Republicans who most strongly backed Johnson were ex-Democrats from the Border South. Led by the Blair political clan in Maryland and Missouri, they were stridently opposed to black suffrage or any other reconstruction policy that would force fundamental changes upon the South. The most racist of all the groups within the Republican party, they favored a strict segregation of the races and, if possible, the removal of blacks to a reservation-like setting in the Southwest. Racial separation, as Francis P. Blair, Sr., told Johnson, "would disarm the power of those men in the North who would disfranchise all those Southern States, in which the whites would not consent their Legislatures should accept new constitutions recognizing the political as well as personal equality of rights in respect to the two races."[7] Such political equality, of course, was not granted by the lily-white Johnson governments.

Johnson's other conservative Republican backers were drawn from the pre-war social and economic elite of the North, the interlocked class of wealthy merchants, financiers, shippers, and bankers who had a direct business stake in the Southern cotton trade. The appeal of Johnsonian Reconstruction to these Republicans was that it promised a speedy resumption of the export trade in cotton by minimizing any political agitation that might disrupt the re-establishment of plantation agriculture. In addition, and as stressed by Secretary of State William Seward, the leader of the pro-Johnson Republicans, Johnson's program offered conservative Republicans an opportunity to nationalize their party by reviving the prewar Whiggish alliance of Northern businessmen and Southern planters.

When Congress convened in December 1865, Johnson appeared to be in a commanding position, and most Republicans had every reason to fear for the future success of their party. To be sure, the Republicans had never been stronger in terms of congressional power. The party enjoyed better than a three-to-one edge in both the House and the Senate, and it had the incalculable advantage of being popularly identified in the North with the redeeming glory of having saved the Union. Nonetheless, the Republicans had yet to win a national election under normal political conditions. Lincoln had faced a badly divided Democratic party in 1860 and had won with less than forty percent of the popular vote. The party discarded the Republican label in 1864, and Lincoln won as the head of the Union party in an election in which the eleven Confederate states, of course, did not participate. Much of the party's wartime legislation, including its greatest accomplishment, the 13th Amendment, passed Congress only because of the Republican votes from the Union states of the Border South. Republican strength in these states rested on the mass disqualification from voting of rebels or rebel sympathizers, and that strength was likely to vanish once these ex-Confederates regained the vote after the war.

As for the immediate future, the Republicans faced the alarming prospect of suddenly being reduced to a political minority. It was no secret that Johnson's supporters in the South planned to align themselves with the Democratic party or with a new Union party in which only the most conservative of Republicans would be welcomed. And, now that the 13th Amendment had eliminated the three-fifths clause of the Constitution, the South would return to the Union with increased political power because its entire black population would count for purposes of apportioning seats in the House. The South stood to pick up an additional fifteen to twenty seats. Yet, as the Republicans bitterly complained, this hardly seemed fair given the refusal of the Johnsonian governments to extend the vote to the freedmen. Rebels, argued the Republicans, were being rewarded for their treason by generous presidential pardons, while blacks were punished for their loyalty by being denied any political rights in the Union they had fought to save.

Concerned over the future of their party, and convinced of the absolute necessity of implementing federal safeguards for the rights of white Unionists and blacks in the postwar South, congressional Republicans rejected Johnson's contention that the South had been restored to the Union by December 1865. The 39th Congress refused to seat the eighty Southern representatives and senators elected under the Johnson guidelines. Among these congressmen were ten former Confederate generals, nine ex-Confederate congressmen, and a bevy of lesser Confederate officials. The Republicans were united in their belief that the admission of such former rebels would have been tantamount to condoning treason and ignoring the legitimate demand of the victorious North for a more secure and just Union after the war.

The Republicans put Johnsonian Reconstruction on hold. A Joint Committee of Fifteen on Reconstruction, chaired by a respected moderate, William Pitt Fessenden of Maine, was appointed. The committee held hearings throughout the winter of 1865–1866 on the state of affairs in the South. The decision on readmitting the former Confederate states would await its recommendation. Meanwhile, it became clear that the Republicans had reached no consensus on a reconstruction plan of their own.

THE VICTORIOUS NORTH AND CONGRESSIONAL RECONSTRUCTION

The Republican radicals wanted a thorough restructuring of Southern society. They comprised about one-third of the party and were led in the House by Thaddeus Stevens of Pennsylvania and by George Julian of Indiana and in the Senate by Charles Sumner of Massachusetts. The radicals argued that the war had presented America with a providential opportunity to create a nation committed to equal rights for all its citizens. "For the sake of the whole country," insisted Sumner, and "for the sake of reconciliation, which can be complete only when justice prevails, we must insist upon Equal Rights as the condition of the new order of things."[8] The same national power that had destroyed slavery and upheld the Union was to usher in this "new order." According to the radicals, the rebel states had lost all their former rights and, having been militarily defeated, were now to be treated as conquered provinces or dependent federal territories. Before being admitted to the new Union, one purified of the aristocratic oppressions of slavery that had degraded the poor and the enslaved alike, the rebel states would have to undergo a revolution sponsored by the federal government. Such a revolution was necessary for the realization of the radicals' goal of a republic in which individual merit was the only mark of social distinction.

For Stevens and Julian, this revolution was to be primarily economic in nature. They believed that privilege and caste would persist in the South as long as the domineering elite responsible for secession continued to hold onto its plantation lands. Unless the laboring masses of the South, and most particularly the former slaves, became landowners, they would be deprived of economic, and therefore true political, independence, and the South would remain an impoverished social and intellectual backwater ruled over by a landed aristocracy. Thus, Stevens called for a federal seizure of the planters' land and its redistribution in forty-acre freeholds to each freedman. Julian would go even further and parcel out the land of rebel planters to Union veterans and poor Southern whites as well as the freedmen. This, and only this, he envisioned as the "basis of real democracy and genuine civilization" for the South. This is how he expressed that vision:

> Instead of large estates, widely scattered settlements, wasteful agriculture, popular ignorance, social degradation, the decline of manufactures, contempt for honest labor, and a pampered oligarchy, you want small farms, thrifty tillage, free schools, social independence, flourishing manufactures and the arts, respect for honest labor, and equality of political rights.[9]

In short, the South was to be made over into an idealized version of the free-labor North.

For Sumner, the postwar Southern revolution was to be primarily a political one grounded in the granting of the vote to the freedmen. Sumner's case was straightforward: Blacks needed the vote in order to protect their freedom and to exert any influence on power relations in the South. The cornerstone of any black equality before the law had to rest on the voting power of blacks. Moreover, as Sumner pointed out, the vote was at the top of the political agenda of the freedmen at the end of the war. Blacks had needed no whites to instruct them in the political meaning of freedom. In hundreds of meetings in the South throughout 1865, they claimed the vote as indispensable to the securing of their civil equality. Typical of these claims was the declaration by the freedmen of Alexandria, Virginia, in 1865 that

> each and every man may appeal to the law for his equal rights without regard to the color of his skin; and we believe this can only be done by extending to us the elective franchise, which we believe to be our inalienable right as freemen, and which the Declaration of Independence guarantees to all free citizens of this Government and which is the privilege of the nation.[10]

Sumner's stand on suffrage was much more compatible with Northern middle-class liberalism then the confiscation proposals of Stevens and Julian. Confiscation violated the sanctity of private property, the most basic tenet of the Northern middle class, and talk of confiscation frightened most Republicans as much as it did Southern planters. Sumner's position promised no revolutionary economic upheaval in the South, but it did threaten a revolutionary change in the balance of antebellum federalism. Suffrage had always been an issue left up to the individual states. Opposition on both constitutional and racial grounds kept Sumner and his followers in a minority position. In addition, the fact that three Northern states in 1865—Connecticut, Minnesota, and Wisconsin—rejected by popular vote state constitutional amendments to confer suffrage on black males hardly helped the Republican case for black suffrage in the South.

Unlike the radicals, who left no middle ground for an accommodation with Johnson, the moderate majority of Republicans was anxious to avoid an open break with Johnson. They felt that such a party rupture would benefit only the Democrats and deprive the party of any input into Reconstruction. Much more so than the radicals, the moderates approached Reconstruction as a practical problem that required careful negotiations and not as an ideological program that necessitated rejecting all that Johnson had done in order to embark upon a restructuring of Southern society. Rather than basing their Southern policy on notions of "state suicide," conquered provinces, or territorialization, the moderates accepted, as did Johnson, the indestructibility of the rebel states. These states, it was held, had forfeited some of their rights through the unconstitutional act of secession and consequently would have to accept federal supervision while they were held in the power of the "grasp of war."

In their political style and temperament the moderates reflected the pragmatism of politicians elected from congressional districts that were more competitive then those that sent radicals to Congress. Whereas the radicals tended to come out of safe Republican strongholds in New England and the belts of Yankee migration in the upper North, areas characterized by evangelical radicalism, persistent anti-slaveryism, and strident anti-Southernism, the moderates were more likely to be found in such states of the lower North as Ohio, Indiana, and Illinois. Here, the Democrats, by appealing to voters who had close personal and economic ties to the South, remained a formidable competitor for the Republicans, and the espousal of black suffrage was a distinct political liability.

Despite their differences, the radicals and moderates had more in common than Johnson was willing to recognize. Most fundamentally, both agreed that Congress had to have a meaningful say in Reconstruction. Both based congressional input on the clause in the Constitution (Article IV, Section 4) that guaranteed to each state a republican form of government. Largely ignored down to Reconstruction, and generally interpreted to mean that state governments had to rest on the voluntary consent of the white majority, the guarantee clause gave congressional Republicans a constitutional sanction for opposing Johnson's unilateral policy of executive Reconstruction. As a party, the Republicans now insisted that a republican form of government had to encompass the expanded definition of republicanism that had arisen during the war, that is, republicanism had to embrace both the end of slavery and the extension of legal equality to all citizens. And last, radicals and moderates were driven together by their common conviction that the future safety of the Union required the imposition of political penalties on leading ex-Confederates and an expanded use of federal power to protect the rights of the freedmen.

The moderates shaped the congressional Republican agenda on Reconstruction, and their first steps were designed to build a basis of cooperation with Johnson. In February 1866 Congress passed a bill extending the life of the Freedmen's Bureau, a federal agency created in 1865 to administer emergency relief for up to one year after the war to refugees and freedmen in the South. This bill was introduced by Lyman Trumbull, a Republican moderate from Illinois, and it received the support of nearly all Republicans as a measure to provide a modicum of federal protection for the freedmen.

As suggested by its official title, the Bureau for Refugees, Freedmen, and Abandoned Lands, the bureau was not intended to deal exclusively with blacks or to limit itself solely to the problem of relief. In fact, it dispensed more relief in the form of food and clothing to whites than it did to blacks. Moreover, it had responsibility for some 850,000 acres of confiscated and abandoned land in the South that had come under the military control of the federal government. This land was to be assigned in 40-acre plots to freedmen and loyal refugees for a rental period of up to three years. The lessees had the option to buy the land at its appraised value with whatever title the government could convey (this ambiguity reflected the fact that the heirs of rebels were contesting the government's legal title to the land). In addition to this land, the bureau at the end of the war also administered about half a million acres along the South Carolina–Georgia coast, which had been set aside by General Sherman in his Field Order No. 15 of January 1865 for exclusive settlement by blacks. Having issued the order to relieve his army of the burden of caring for the thousands of black refugees who sought its protection in Georgia, Sherman permitted black families to settle 40 acres under "possessory titles" that subsequently were to be regulated by Congress.

Any possible role that the bureau might have played as midwife to the creation of land-owning black yeomanry was scuttled by President Johnson. In the late summer of 1865 he overruled General Oliver O. Howard, the head of the bureau, and ordered the return of seized and abandoned land to all previous owners who had been pardoned. Within a year most of the arable land under the control of the bureau was back in the hands of its former owners.

Although the bureau did not serve as a catalyst for democraticizing land ownership in the postwar South, it did assume a number of unexpected responsibilities on behalf of the freedmen. In turn, these responsibilities convinced the Republicans of the need to put the bureau on a more permanent footing and to expand its jurisdiction. The bureau worked closely with Northern voluntary associations in sponsoring schools for the freedmen. Heavily dependent on private donations for its expenses, the bureau lacked the funds to establish and staff schools. Religious and black welfare groups supplied the money and teachers, while the bureau furnished the buildings and coordinated the educational activities of the relief agencies. By early 1866, nearly 100,000 blacks were enrolled in schools supervised by the bureau.

The bureau's most important function, however, was in the area of civil and legal relations between the races. Bureau agents, most of whom were military officers on loan from the army, were swamped with requests to provide standards for drafting labor contracts between the planters and the freedmen. Once the contracts were drawn up, they were frequently violated, especially by the planters who fired their laborers without any pay once the harvest was in. Bureau agents tried to adjudicate these labor disputes, as well as provide a court of last resort for blacks who were systematically being denied their rights in the Southern courts.

Both planters and freedmen turned to the local agent of the Freedmen's Bureau for the negotiation of labor contracts in the postwar South.

White Unionists, army officers, and Northerners who settled in the South after the war were likewise victims of harassment and discrimination in a legal system now controlled by ex-rebels. All these groups, plus the freedmen, of course, looked to the bureau to enforce equality of treatment by Southern legal officials.

Trumbull's bill for the Freedmen's Bureau extended its life indefinitely, provided it with a regular budget, and granted it jurisdiction in cases in which state and local officials denied blacks their civil rights on the basis of race. Counterbalancing this expansion of the bureau's legal responsibilities was a restriction on its capacity to distribute land to the freedmen. The bill confirmed Johnson's order of September 1865 that had returned land under the bureau's control to its pardoned owners. The effort of Stevens to add forfeited land of rebel planters to the bureau's holdings was overwhelmingly rejected. The bill sanctioned land reform only to the extent of setting aside 3 million acres of public land in the South for black homesteads and validating for three years the black occupation of land reserved for them under Sherman's Field Order No. 15.

Much to the surprise of the Republicans, who thought they had assurances from Johnson that he would go along with any reasonable congressional legislation, Johnson vetoed the Freedmen's Bureau bill on February 19, 1866. He followed that up a few days later with an extremely intemperate speech in which he attacked Stevens and Sumner as "traitors" who should be punished for delaying the readmission of the South. Still, the Republicans had high hopes that Johnson would support

Trumbull's Civil Rights bill, a measure that the party considered essential to any effective program of reconstruction.

The Civil Rights bill was meant to provide permanent, federal protection for the rights of the freed slaves. Written in response to both the Black Codes and the *Dred Scott* decision, which had ruled that blacks were not American citizens, the bill for the first time defined citizenship. Birth or naturalization in the United States conferred national and state citizenship (with the exception of Indians, who paid no taxes). The principle of equality before the law was also nationalized by extending its protection to all citizens. Cases in which any citizen was deprived of the full enjoyment of rights of person and property on account of race were to be transferred from state to federal courts. The bill was unprecedented not only in its nationalization of citizenship but in its declaration that the definition and protection of the fundamental rights of citizenship now fell under the rubric of national power. Those rights, as the abolitionists had insisted all along, and as the experience of saving the Union had taught other Northerners, now encompassed all Americans. The inalienable freedoms enunciated in the Declaration of Independence and specified in the Bill of Rights, as well as equal access to social services and economic opportunities, were the civil rights spelled out in the bill. The enforcement clause of the 13th Amendment had given Congress the power to enforce the intent of emancipation by passing legislation to secure the rights of the freed slaves. The systematic violation of those rights in the Johnsonian South convinced the Republicans of the need to act upon that power.

The Republicans were shocked when Johnson vetoed the Civil Rights bill on March 27. In vetoing this bill, as well as the extension of the Freedman's Bureau, Johnson virtually ruled out any possibility of future cooperation between himself and Congress. Grounding his position in doctrinaire states rights' rhetoric, and starting from the premise that Reconstruction had been completed under his policies, he argued that any legislation on the freedmen was solely a matter for the individual states. Furthermore, he held that any legislation affecting the excluded states was unconstitutional as long as these states were denied representation in Congress.

Johnson hoped that his vetoes would isolate the radicals from mainstream Republicans and prepare the way for the bulk of the party to rally behind his leadership of a new Union coalition. Instead, the vetoes isolated Johnson from his erstwhile party. The rigidity of his position forced an extraordinary unity on the Republicans. In order for the party to have any say in Reconstruction, it had to close ranks almost to a man. Otherwise, without the two-thirds majority needed to override a presidential veto or to pass constitutional amendments, Johnsonian Reconstruction would be left untouched. And, regardless of their deep differences over the extent of change they wanted in the postwar South, Republicans by the spring of 1866 were nearly unanimous in their belief that Johnsonian Reconstruction fell far short of securing the fruits of Union victory. Even most of Johnson's conservative backers in the party had voted for the two bills he vetoed.

In large measure because of his deep-seated racism and his expectation that a racially conscious North would support him in blocking federal protection for the freedmen, Johnson failed to grasp the dynamic by which the preservation of the Union had become tied to a broadening of liberties for blacks, that would have been politically unthinkable back in 1860. As long as the North felt that Southern whites were continuing to act as if the rebellion had never occurred, the Northern victory would not be secure.

In a continuation of the same logic that had taken root during the war, most Northerners now believed that a secure and loyal Union had to rest on an extension of meaningful rights to the freedmen. During the hearings conducted by the Joint Committee on Reconstruction, Senator Jacob M. Howard, a Michigan Republican, asked John W. Alford from the Freedman's Bureau the following question: "What other security does there exist at the south for the permanency of the Union and the government of the United States so great and so strong as the granting of civil and political rights to the black people?" Alford replied, "...that is our only hope."[11] Nearly all Republicans would have agreed.

In June 1866, the Republicans presented Johnson with one last opportunity to cooperate with the party. After months of deliberation, and a welter of proposals, the Joint Committee on Reconstruction completed work on the 14th Amendment. For most Republicans this amendment was in effect the Northern peace terms for the vanquished South. The 14th Amendment contained five sections. Its first section restated in more sweeping, nationalistic language the Civil Rights bill, which the Republicans had passed in April over Johnson's veto. This section placed into the Constitution the Republicans' interpretation of the war as one fought to establish the principle of the fundamental supremacy of the federal government in determining and protecting the rights of American citizenship. National citizenship now took precedence over state citizenship, and the federal government was empowered to protect the civil rights of all citizens when their rights were denied by the refusal of state and local courts to enforce equality before the law.

The second section was an awkward compromise on black suffrage, which satisfied no one. Suffrage was still left up to the states, but congressional representation would be proportionately reduced to the extent that a state denied the vote to its eligible male citizens. In practice this meant that the former rebel states, where over ninety percent of the black population lived, would not receive the advantage of more congressmen unless they correspondingly enfranchised the former slaves.

The most controversial and politically most important section was the third. It addressed Northern fears over a resurgence of rebel political power by disqualifying from state and federal office holding all individuals who had supported the rebellion after having taken an oath to uphold the Constitution. This bland language barred from political office the South's ruling class. Prewar military, federal, state, and local officials all would have taken this oath. They were all disqualified if they had aided the rebellion. The fourth section comprised the economic settlement. It reaffirmed that the Union war debt would be paid in full, repudiated the Confederate war debt, and voided the possibility of any monetary compensation to the slaveowners for their emancipated slaves. Congress was given the power to enforce the amendment in the fifth section.

The passage of the 14th Amendment by Congress in 1866 signified not a victory for the radicals but a distillation of the minimum terms the Northern public demanded of the defeated South. This Northern settlement did not force black suffrage on the South, disfranchise former Confederates, or confiscate the land of the planters. It left intact the structure of the Johnsonian governments but insisted that loyal Southern whites, those who had upheld the Union, be entrusted with political power until Congress saw fit to lift the office holding disqualification of former rebels.

In all probability Reconstruction would have been completed had the South accepted the 14th Amendment. That was the view of the Republican moderates, and they anxiously hoped that Johnson would support the amendment and its ratification. Instead, Johnson spurned the moderates and advised the still-excluded states not to ratify the amendment. Yet, there was no way that the 14th Amendment could receive the required three-fourths vote of approval from the states unless some of the former states of the Confederacy ratified it. The passage of the 13th Amendment in 1865 had established the precedent that all the states had to be counted for purposes of ratifying a constitutional amendment, despite the anomalous status of some of the states not being fully in the Union. This precedent now gave the South the power, at least temporarily, to say no to the Northern peace terms. Among the former rebel states, only Tennessee, the most Unionist of all the ex-Confederate states and one now controlled by Johnson's political enemies, ratified the 14th Amendment in 1866. All the others, plus Kentucky and Delaware, accepted Johnson's advice and opposed it.

Some of the Johnsonian leaders in the South believed, along with the president, that northern Democrats would rush to their defense and team up with Northern conservatives to inflict crippling losses on the Republicans in the congressional elections of 1866. Others were shrewd enough to realize that their political careers in the postwar South would be ruined if they publicly supported a constitutional change that most Southern whites felt branded the South with the stigma of war guilt. The third section was widely viewed as an unconscionable demand for a shameful surrender of honor on the part of Southern whites, an admission that they were wrong and at blame for the war. As Jonathan Worth, the North Carolina governor, pleaded, "no generous man ought to expect us to hasten to the whipping post and invite the lash in advance of condemnation."[12] Only slaves voluntarily submitted to their own self-degradation. Moreover, there were no guarantees that the Republicans would not make further demands on the South once the 14th Amendment was accepted.

Johnsonian Reconstruction had restored the self-confidence of Southern whites, and the moment had long since passed when the immediate shock of defeat had prepared ex-rebels to embrace virtually any peace terms that the Yankee conqueror offered them. If Southern whites were to accept the 14th Amendment, they would have to be forced to do so, and this was the purpose of the Reconstruction Act of March 1867.

The Republicans turned to a more coercive program of reconstruction after they felt they had been vindicated in their struggle with Johnson by the results of the congressional elections in the fall of 1866. To the extent that congressional elections can ever be a referendum on any national issue, this set amounted to a referendum on the 14th Amendment and the opposing position represented by Johnson. Still convinced that he spoke for the Northern majority, Johnson launched his formal bid for a new conservative party with the National Union convention at Philadelphia in August 1866. The new party, however, never got off the ground. Except for a handful of conservatives, Republicans by now had abandoned Johnson in the belief that he was surrendering the gains of the Northern victory and endangering the future safety of the Union by returning former rebels to power. The Democrats agreed with Johnson that the 14th Amendment was unjust and unconstitutional, but they refused to submerge their separate identity and goals in any new party.

Johnson used his patronage powers to remove Republican officeholders, and he took his case to the people in a politically disastrous speaking tour. The Republicans reacted to Johnson's declaration of war against the party by uniting against him, and Johnson was loudly rebuffed, first by hecklers during his speeches and then by the Republicans at the polls. With telling effect, the Republicans accused Johnson of deserting the party that had put him into power, of dishonoring the memory of the Union war dead by turning to disloyal Democrats for support, and of disgracing the office of the presidency by stooping to shouting contests with hecklers. Mob violence against freedmen and white Unionists in Memphis and New Orleans during the spring and summer confirmed for the Northern public the Republican charge that Johnson wanted to unleash unregenerate rebels against the only true friends of the Union in the South. The Memphis riots in May claimed forty-seven black lives, and the white mob in New Orleans killed thirty-four blacks in July.

The congressional elections of 1866 remobilized the emotional loyalties of the war, and a commanding Northern majority reaffirmed that the results of the war meant fundamental change. To get that change underway, and more specifically, to make the South accept the 14th Amendment, the Republicans resorted to the forceful measures of the Reconstitution Act of 1867.

Usually cited as the triumph of radical Republicanism, this act in fact was a cumbersome, almost desperate, compromise between the Johnsonian extreme of immediate, unqualified readmission and the radical extreme of declaring the excluded states to be territories subject to military rule for an indefinite period. A long and enforceable military occupation was out of the question. The army lacked the manpower and logistical services for such an occupation, and even attempting it would have been a politically unacceptable contradiction of the basic principles of civilian self-rule enshrined in American republicanism. These same principles also

White violence against blacks in the South, such as the Memphis riot in 1866, strengthened the Republican argument for a tougher policy on Reconstruction.

ruled out any large-scale disfranchisement of Southern whites. An enlargement of the Southern electorate, however, by extending suffrage to the freedmen would be in accord with republicanism. It would also create a loyal Southern majority that would accept the 14th Amendment.

Under the complicated provisions of the Reconstruction Act, black suffrage was now added to the ratification of the 14th Amendment as the price of readmission for the ten rebel states still out of the Union (Tennessee, having ratified the amendment, was back in the Union). The army was given supervisory authority to oversee a reconstruction process in which the ex-Confederate states were temporarily divided into five military districts. These states had to hold elections for constitutional conventions in which all male citizens, except those disqualified from political office by the 14th Amendment, were eligible to vote. Then, they had to draft and approve new state constitutions that provided for "impartial" suffrage. Finally, upon ratifying the 14th Amendment, they would be readmitted to the Union.

Although the Reconstruction Act made no provision for the confiscation of rebel estates, it was clearly a radical act in its overriding of state boundaries and especially in its enfranchising of the recently freed slaves. Nonetheless, Republican moderates supported the measure because it resolved the most pressing problem that had confronted the Republicans as a party since the end of the war two years earlier. Finally, here was a mechanism to normalize relations with the defeated South that did not endanger the majority status of the Republican party. The ex-rebel states would be speedily restored to the Union, but the feared resurgence of the Democratic party would be counterbalanced by a black Republican vote in the South.

THE CONSERVATIVE REACTION AND THE GRANT REPUBLICANS

Just as so-called Radical Reconstruction in the South was getting under way in the spring and summer of 1867, a conservative reaction against the Republicans in the North was setting sharp political limits on the amount of radical change in the South that the Republicans could favor in the future. Much of this reaction rested on fears that the Republicans were plotting a revolutionary reversal of the traditional priorities in American federalism and a destruction of the checks and balances within the federal system. Not only were they apparently running roughshod over states' rights, but, in the eyes of their growing critics, they were also seemingly intent on establishing a congressional dictatorship in which the presidency and judiciary were reduced to mere pawns of Congress.

A series of acts passed by the Republicans in 1867 and early 1868 to curb Johnson's power and to assert congressional authority over Reconstruction furnished the basis for these charges. Southern whites were unwilling to undertake any plan of reconstruction that included black suffrage. Thus, in order to initiate congressional Reconstruction, the Republicans passed a second Reconstruction Act on March 23, 1867, which specifically authorized army commanders in the South to register qualified voters and convene the constitutional conventions.

When Johnson's Attorney General, Henry Stanbery, issued a ruling severely limiting the authority of the generals in charge of the five military districts, congressional Republicans responded with a third Reconstruction Act in July 1867. Johnson's provisional governments were now clearly made subordinate to the rule of the army, and the generals were empowered to remove obstructionist civil officials and to bar from political participation Southern whites they had reason to believe had voluntarily supported the rebellion.

Finally, in March 1868, Congress closed the last loophole in its reconstruction program. Its legislation had originally stipulated that the ratification of a new constitution in a reconstructed state required the majority approval of all the registered voters. White conservatives in Alabama seized on this provision and organized a boycott of the ratification vote in February 1868. As a result, even though the new constitution was overwhelmingly approved by a vote of 71,000 to 1,000, it technically was defeated by virtue of the fact that only forty-three percent of the registered voters had turned out in the election. On March 11, 1868, Congress changed the rules of the game by decreeing that the new constitutions would take effect once they were ratified by a majority of the votes actually cast.

During this same period, Congress also passed four other acts designed to give it the upper hand in its ongoing struggle with Johnson over control of Reconstruction. The first of these in January 1867 called the new Congress (this would be the 40th Congress, elected in the fall of 1866) into special session as soon as the current Congress, the 39th, ended on March 4, 1867. The Republicans clearly feared that Johnson would undermine their program of Reconstruction unless they maintained checks on him during the long interval before the next Congress was regularly scheduled to meet in December. In an effort to strip Johnson of his control over patronage and the army, the Republicans passed a Tenure of Office Act and attached a special rider to an army appropriations bill on March 2. The former Act required Senate approval for the removal of any officeholder whose confirmation had required Senate consent, and the latter directed the president to route all military orders through the head of the army, General Grant. The Republicans trusted Grant, and they protected him by prohibiting Johnson to remove him from command without the consent of the Senate.

Having curbed Johnson, the Republicans then restricted the Supreme Court from intervening against congressional Reconstruction. The key issue here was the constitutionality of military tribunals in the postwar South with jurisdiction over civilians. In a wartime case arising from the military arrest and trial of an Indiana civilian for conspiring to aid the Confederacy, the Court ruled in *ex parte Milligan* that such an imposition of martial law was unconstitutional in peacetime when the civilian courts were open and there was no imminent likelihood of an enemy invasion. This decision was handed down in April 1866, and throughout 1867 the Republicans feared that the Court would use this case as a precedent with which to hamstring congressional Reconstruction. They felt most vulnerable in February 1868 when the Court agreed to hear an appeals case from Mississippi involving the denial of a writ of *habeas corpus* to one William McCardle. A rabid Negrophobe, McCardle was arrested by the military for publishing articles calling for the violent overthrow of Radical Reconstruction in Mississippi. If McCardle's appeal were successful, the legality of the entire structure of military rule in the South would have been called into question and perhaps overturned. The Republicans met this threat with a measure in March 1868 that deprived the Court of appellate jurisdiction in the McCardle case and in similar ones pending elsewhere in the South.

The Court, headed now by Salmon P. Chase, a former radical in Lincoln's cabinet and a staunch advocate of black suffrage, acquiesced in this congressional action. After all, as Chase noted, Congress was explicitly authorized in the Constitution to regulate the Court's appellate jurisdiction. Nor did the Court subsequently choose to challenge Congress over Reconstruction. In *Texas v. White* (1869) the Court in effect declared that Reconstruction was fundamentally a political question that was extraconstitutional in nature since the affected states never could have legally left the Union in the first place.

The Court backed away from a constitutional confrontation with Congress over Reconstruction even though Northern conservatives joined President Johnson and Southern whites in 1867 in raising a storm of protest over the congressional despotism they alleged the Republicans were trying to force on the nation. Democrats warned of a dark plot against the rights of all capitalist property, a plot first hatched in the decision to destroy the property holdings of slaveholders through forced emancipation. Well-bred and well-born Republicans, such as the Adams brothers of Massachusetts, decried what, in their view, was an unconstitutional descent into mob rule. If blacks, patently unfit by their standards to be entrusted with the vote, were put into power in the South, what then, they asked, would stop the radical Republicans from pandering to the wishes of the uneducated and poor immigrant masses in Northern cities? Business and financial interests were alarmed by the continuing demand of some Republicans for land confiscation and redistribution in the South. If the property of the South's landed aristocracy could be taken away by the government, then all so-called aristocratic wealth was in danger of expropriation. "This mode of argument is two-edged," noted the Boston *Daily Advertiser,* a moderate Republican newspaper. "For there are socialists who hold that *any* aristocracy is 'fatal to the advance of liberty and equal rights'....It is dangerous to prove too much."[13]

The barrage of criticism leveled against the Republicans in 1867 boiled down to the argument that governmental centralization had overstepped its constitutional bounds in the South and was now a threat to property rights and democratic home rule in the North. This criticism was all the more damaging to the Republicans because it confirmed the growing doubts of many Northerners over the centralizing programs of institutional and social reform that the Republicans had embarked on in several Northern states at the end of the war.

Several factors flowed into the Republican commitment to reform at the state level. Implicit in the party's free-labor ideology was the assumption that social harmony and progress would be the inevitable result of governmental action to remove barriers to individual progress. This belief had fueled the ideological drive against both slavery and the conferral of equal rights on the emancipated slaves. As a result of the war and its preservation of the Union through a successful application of expanded governmental power, the Republicans now had a popularly endorsed model of political centralization that seemingly could be applied to a host of social and economic problems at the state level. As Richard Yates of Illinois phrased it in his gubernatorial message of 1865, "The war has not only, of necessity, given more power to, but has led to a more intimate prevision of the government over every material interest of society."[14] The war had enhanced the vitality of government at all levels of the federal system in the North, and the Republicans confidently predicted at the end of the war that the states could now be vehicles for an agenda of reform expanded to include public health, education, and welfare.

The final element that pushed the Republicans toward reform was the need to find a unifying element for the party in state politics now that the causes of antislavery and the Union had been fought and won. To a great extent Johnson's defiance of the party over Reconstruction provided just such a cohesive force. As long as Republicans feared a neo-Confederate revival under Johnson's leadership, they remained united. But Johnson's actions, by eliminating any middle position that Republican moderates could take in opposing him, also strengthened the hand of the radicals both in Congress and in the Northern legislatures. Also, Johnson's use of patronage against the party gave Republican state organizations an added incentive to promote programs of institutional reform that would generate partisan jobs for loyal Republicans.

Massachusetts, Michigan, and New York launched the most ambitious reform programs in the North. The first two were very secure Republican states, and, in New York, the radicals had quickly been shut out of federal patronage as the result of an alliance between Johnson and the conservative Republican leaders, Thurlow Weed and William Seward. In 1865, Massachusetts passed the nation's first law banning racial discrimination in public accommodations. In the same year the Massachusetts legislature created what in effect was the nation's first state police force. This constabulary was to enforce all state laws, but it was intended primarily to suppress prostitution, gambling, and the illegal liquor traffic, vices that the rural-dominated Republican party blamed on the ignorance and depravity of the foreign born in the cities of the commonwealth. A child labor law of 1866 prohibited the employment of children under the age of ten and limited to ten hours the working day of employed children between the ages of ten and fourteen. A State Board of Health and a Bureau of Statistics of Labor were chartered in 1869 and charged with collecting and disseminating data on health and working conditions. All the while Massachusetts Republicans endorsed lavish state subsidies for the development of railroads.

The new order of reform in Michigan was to be ushered in by a revised state constitution in 1867. The constitution provided for both black and women's suffrage, increased the salaries and terms of state officers, replaced biennial legislative sessions with annual ones, and authorized cities and townships to borrow against their property valuations for financial aid to railroads. Although the voters rejected this constitution, Michigan Republicans nonetheless established a significant reform record. The legislation appropriated funds for a major expansion of state facilities for orphans, the mentally ill, and the deaf, dumb, and blind. Racial segregation in Michigan schools was made illegal in 1867, and public education became truly free in 1869 with the elimination of rate bills or fees for the common schools. In 1871 the legislature passed the state's first compulsory school-attendance law. The creation of a state board of health and extensive penal reforms, especially concerning the treatment of juvenile offenders, rounded out the Republicans' efforts in social welfare.

The most far-reaching Republican program of reform was enacted in New York between 1865 and 1867. In rapid succession came the Fire Department Act of 1865, the Metropolitan Health Act and Normal School Act of 1866, and the Tenement House Act and Free School Law of 1867. On top of this legislation, the Republicans chartered New York's first State Board of Charities and a state school for the blind. The common thread running through this spate of legislative activity was the imposition of centralized reform from above through the gubernatorial appointment of state administrative boards. Just as the Southern states, according to the Republicans, required national tutelage in self-government, so also did

Northern cities now need the firm guidance and control of state authorities. The Republicans believed that problems of health, housing, and fire protection in New York, the nation's largest and most crowded city, were immeasurably worsened by the corruption and inefficiency of the Democratic party. The Chicago *Tribune,* the leading radical newspaper in the Midwest, in arguing the case for reform in New York City, insisted that "the great Copperhead metropolis" stood indicted along with the ex-rebel states as proof of the fact that "incapacity for self-government arises out of, and is coextensive with, sham Democracy."[15]

Thus, much of the Republicans' reform legislation in New York was directed against the patronage base of the Democratic party and the ideological commitment of the Democrats to local autonomy. The Metropolitan Fire Department Act replaced New York City's volunteer fire companies, a key source of patronage for Tammany Hall, the Democratic machine that controlled city politics, with a professional department under the direction of a state board in Albany. The Board of Health created as part of the new Municipal Sanitary District in 1866 was empowered not only to collect statistics but also to regulate public health in such areas as the issuing of liquor licenses. By setting down minimum housing standards in the Tenement House Act, and by rationalizing and professionalizing the problem of public health, the Republicans hoped to produce a cleaner, healthier city. As part of their approach to reform, they also tried to break the Democratic stranglehold on the awarding of liquor licenses and street-cleaning contracts. Ultimately, the Republicans believed that their goal of honest, efficient government could be achieved only through the support of an informed citizenry. To that end, they established eight new state teachers' colleges in the Normal School Act and put public education on a fully tax supported basis in the Free School Law.

The high tide of radical reform in the Northern states was the effort to give blacks the vote. This was the issue around which the conservative and Democratic opposition coalesced and the one that broke the back of the radicals' momentum in Northern politics. Ohio, Kansas, and Minnesota all had black suffrage amendments on their ballots in 1867, and the issue of black political equality also figured prominently in the state elections of that year in Pennsylvania, New Jersey, and New York. The Democrats mounted viciously racist campaigns that highlighted the black issue as the most frightening evidence that the Republicans were seeking to destroy the prerogatives of local home rule by white majorities. Although a majority of Republicans favored black suffrage, their support could not overcome the united opposition of Democrats. Across the board, Republicans suffered losses as a result of the pronounced white backlash against black equality, and the huge Republican majorities of 1866 were reduced by about three-fourths. The most critical defeats were in Ohio, Pennsylvania, and New York, large electoral states that had never been safely Republican.

Ohio was the home state of the two leading radical candidates for the Republican presidential nomination in 1868, Senator Benjamin F. Wade and Salmon P. Chase, who was Secretary of the Treasury under Lincoln and then Chief Justice of the Supreme Court. Their candidacies and the radical cause as a whole suffered a major setback when the Republicans lost both houses of the legislature and carried only three of nineteen congressional districts in the Ohio elections of 1867. The constitutional amendment for black suffrage, which was coupled with the disfranchisement of deserters from the Union army and of those Ohioans who had aided the Confederacy, was easily defeated. In Pennsylvania a Republican majority of 17,000 votes in 1866 was reversed to a deficit of 1,000, and the Republicans barely retained control of the legislature. Voters in New York, the bellwether state of radical reform, returned the Democrats to the assembly and gave the Democrats a sweep of all state-wide offices up for election in 1867. Although black suffrage was not on the ballot in New York, the Republicans were thoroughly identified with the issue. They had called a state constitutional convention in the summer of 1867 with the intention of eliminating the clause in the 1846 constitution that required a property qualification of $250 for prospective black voters, a discriminatory measure that virtually excluded any black vote in the state. Immediately confronted by a storm of protest, the Republicans backtracked and adjourned the convention in September without proposing a new constitution. They temporarily abandoned their call for black suffrage, but the political damage had already been done.

The elections of 1867 involved mostly state and local offices, and the Democratic comeback in the North reduced rather than eliminated the large Republican majorities. Although the Republican losses did not seriously damage the party, the elections were nonetheless highly significant for reversing the ascent of radicalism within the party. Power now shifted to the moderates and conservatives, Republicans who read the election returns as a warning that the party was pushing too hard and too fast for fundamental change in both the South and the North. Any chances for a bill confiscating rebel land were effectively killed, and the party backed away from the proposals of Charles Sumner for a national law on impartial (i.e., black) suffrage in all the states and for a federal ruling mandating the Southern states to provide free public education for both races. Similarly, the party pulled back from its advocacy of black suffrage in the North.

Conservative Republicans, such as former Governor Andrew J. Curtin of Pennsylvania and New Yorkers William Seward and Thurlow Weed, had protested all along that the race issue would hurt the party in the North, and they now stood vindicated. They argued convincingly in 1868 that the party had to downplay talk of civil and political equality and repudiate its outspoken radicals. Their blueprint for national victory in 1868 called upon the party to turn to a nonpartisan hero who would offer the country moderation and stability after the turmoil of the Johnson administration. Such a hero was readily at hand in General Ulysses S. Grant, probably the nation's most popular man at the end of the war.

Grant had never been a favorite of the radicals. Their doubts regarding his political reliability were confirmed when the New York Republicans, looking for a winner after their defeat in the state election in 1867, followed the advice of Thurlow Weed and kicked off the state endorsements for Grant's presidential nomination. Apolitical, and hence suspect in the eyes of the radicals, Grant was nonetheless shrewd enough to realize which way the political winds were blowing. He cooperated very effectively with Lincoln on the controversial war measures of emancipation and raising black troops, and he supported Johnson up to the point that he became convinced Johnson was using him as a shield against the radicals.

The break between Grant and Johnson came while the general was serving as acting Secretary of War. In August 1867, Johnson suspended Edwin Stanton and replaced him with Grant. Stanton was an open friend of the radical cause and a steady source of information for the radicals on the deliberations within Johnson's cabinet. Johnson had long wanted to get rid of him, and he did so when Congress was not in session. This was legally permissible under the Tenure of Office Act, but final approval of the dismissal would be dependent on the Senate's action once Congress reconvened in December. Grant accepted the appointment out of loyalty to the army, not to Johnson. Many of the army commanders in the South were his professional and personal friends, and he hoped to protect them from Johnson's interference.

Against Grant's advice, Johnson removed Phil Sheridan and Daniel Sickles from their commands in Louisiana and the Carolinas for ousting too many ex-rebels from office. Had the fall elections not resulted in Republican reverses, these removals might well have resulted in an impeachment motion against Johnson once Congress assembled in December. Indeed, that was the recommendation of a Republican-controlled impeachment investigation set up under the House Judiciary Committee back in January 1867. However, most Republicans refused to go along with the recommendation. An impeachment trial carried the risk of splitting the party and making a martyr of Johnson, and it was simply too great a burden for the party to assume on top of the proven unpopularity of its championing of black suffrage.

No sooner had the House voted against impeachment in December 1867 than Johnson revived the entire issue. Believing that public opinion in the North had finally rallied behind him, he intensified his obstruction of the clear intent of congressional will in regard to Reconstruction. In late December he removed two military commanders in the Southeast and replaced them with decidedly more conservative generals. More ominously, and with no authorization or input at all from the Senate, he tried to create an entirely new army command in the East, the Department of the Atlantic, with General Sherman heading it at a rank equal to Grant's. Rumors of a possible military coup d'état swept through Republican ranks, but Sherman had the good sense to ignore Johnson's offer. He refused to be a party to politicizing the army into presidential and congressional factions. Having already emboldened Southern whites to defy Congress, Johnson, it seemed to the Republicans, was now intent on doing the same with the army.

The tensions between Congress and the president came to a head when Johnson openly defied the Tenure of Office Act. In January the Senate refused to confirm the suspension of Stanton, and Johnson responded on February 21, 1868, by having Stanton physically expelled from the office which Grant had vacated in obedience with the Senate's wishes. A shaky Lorenzo Thomas, hung over from a party the night before, was installed in Stanton's place. It was a messy affair made even more sordid by a public exchange of charges and countercharges between Grant and Johnson. The president accused Grant of having broken a promise to retain the post of Secretary of War, regardless of any congressional decision to the contrary, and Grant responded that he had never agreed to be Johnson's pawn in a power struggle with Congress. The two departed as bitter personal enemies, and the infuriated Republicans reversed themselves on impeachment. The House, in a strict party vote, levied impeachment charges against Johnson on February 24, 1868.

The actual impeachment trial on these charges, as stipulated in the Constitution, was held in the Senate, and here the Republicans came within one vote of a conviction that would have removed Johnson from office. The crucial vote was taken on May 16, and the tally of thirty-five to nineteen was just short of the two-thirds majority required for conviction. Seven Republicans had broken party ranks and voted for acquittal. Given the weaknesses in the Republicans' case against Johnson, the vote for conviction was surprisingly strong. Nine of the eleven articles of impeachment concerned the Stanton affair.

The formalistic nature of these charges gave Johnson's defense managers ample room to fall back on legal technicalities, not the least of which was the argument that the Tenure of Office Act could not legally apply to Stanton since he was a holdover from Lincoln's cabinet whom Johnson had not appointed in the first place. Only the eleventh article specifically dealt with Johnson's defiance of Congress, the issue that had precipitated the trial. Thus, the Republican trial managers were forced to engage in legalistic shadowboxing, and the trial revolved around the issue of whether Johnson was guilty of an indictable offense. On this point the evidence was ambiguous enough to win Johnson an acquittal.

Despite the closeness of the vote, much of the drama was contrived. If necessary, pro-conviction moderate Republicans would have switched their votes in order to save Johnson. The trial lasted two months, and before it ended the major goal of the moderates—the protection of congressional Reconstruction—had apparently been achieved.

Johnson pointedly did not interfere in the Southern elections during the spring of 1868 in which six new state constitutions were approved by a biracial electorate. In the meantime, the Supreme Court indicated that it would not invalidate congressional policy in the South. The Court refused to hear petitions from Mississippi and Georgia against the constitutionality of the Reconstruction Act of 1867, and it acceded to being deprived of jurisdiction in the McCardle case.

The moderates were willing to go along with the radicals in humbling a president whom they also had come to despise, but they had no desire to unseat Johnson. His replacement would have been the radical Benjamin Wade, who, as president pro tempore of the Senate, was next in line for the presidency. Wade was already endangering the party's prospects in the election of 1868 with his loose talk of confiscation in the South. Nor did the moderates want to damage, perhaps irreparably, the office of the presidency by decreeing that a president could be removed from office for disagreeing with Congress. They feared that such a precedent might upset the institutional balance of federalism and undermine the very stability of national governance for which the Civil War had been fought.

A chastised but unconvicted Johnson did honor his implicit agreement with the Republicans not to interfere with Reconstruction during the remainder of his term. In the end, however, the radicals had been humbled more than Johnson. Their gamble of putting Wade into the White House backfired when moderate opinion in the North concluded that ideological zeal had gone too far and that the radicals would have to be curbed in the interests of national stability. More than ever, the Republicans were convinced that victory in 1868 required a campaign of unifying moderation. Already on the rise, Grant's political stock in Republican circles soared during the impeachment proceedings. He handily won the party's presidential nomination in late May.

The breadth of Grant's appeal was best summarized by Edward Pierrepont, a New York City Democrat. "I cannot conceive how any intelligent man, who does not wish the Rebels returned to power, the Nation's faith violated, its debt repudiated, its name dishonored, its prosperity destroyed, its patriots insulted, and the 'Lost Cause' restored, can vote against Grant."[16] Pierrepont had close ties to merchant and finance capital in New York, and his support for Grant was echoed by other conservative businessmen in the North, including many former Democrats. In both Southern affairs and fiscal matters, a Grant presidency promised these conservatives the stability that they craved. Although unenthusiastic regarding congressional Reconstruction, and initially quite opposed to black suffrage, these Northern businessmen now felt that any attempt to undo Reconstruction in the South would plunge the country into a political turmoil that would delay indefinitely a full economic recovery from the postwar downturn during the Johnson years. Such an attempt to overturn Reconstruction was just what the Democrats promised in 1868.

Grant's Democratic opponent was Horatio Seymour, the wartime governor of New York who repeatedly had denounced Lincoln as a military despot. The Republicans never let the voters forget that Seymour had referred to the New York draft rioters as "my friends," and his candidacy reinforced the Republicans' self-proclaimed image as the party of patriotism and loyalty. Seymour's running mate, Frank P. Blair, Jr., of Missouri, had a fine war record as a Union general, but this former Johnson Republican scared off Northern voters by talking as if he were ready to start fighting in another civil war. He argued in a widely circulated public letter that Reconstruction was entirely unconstitutional and even suggested that the army should be used to break up the new Republican regimes in the South. Blair felt that power had to be returned to the whites, who, in his view, were the rightful rulers in the South, and, as he told Samuel J. Tilden of New York, the Democrats had to "rally to our standard all the zealots for the instant overthrow of the corrupt military despotism that now lords it over the land."[17] The advocacy of such bold action frightened many Northern voters, and it was all the more unsettling when juxtaposed against the Republican campaign slogan of "Let Us Have Peace." All but three of the ex-Confederate states had been readmitted to the Union by the summer of 1868,

As portrayed by the Republicans, the election of 1868 pitted Grant, the just conqueror of the rebellion, against Seymour, the enemy of the Union who had befriended the New York draft rioters.

and Northerners were hoping that the issue of Reconstruction could finally be laid to rest.

In basing their campaign on a blanket condemnation of Reconstruction and what they referred to as "negro supremacy," the Democrats rejected an alternative approach to the election of 1868 that had emerged from the western wing of their party. This approach dealt with the currency and was popularly known as the "Ohio Idea." It was associated with George H. Pendleton, a former Peace Democrat and party leader in Ohio.

The economic legislation of the Republicans during the war had consolidated control of the nation's finances in the hands of northeastern bankers. At the same time, the financial demands of the war had moved the economy into uncharted territory. The federal debt ballooned from $2 per capita in 1860 to $75 in 1865, and the nation's supply of currency doubled with the introduction of greenbacks and national banknotes. As soon as the war was over, eastern bankers and commercial interests demanded that immediate steps be taken to pare down the debt and contract what they viewed as a redundant and inherently inflationary paper currency. Johnson's secretary of the Treasury, Hugh McCulloch, followed just such a policy. In particular, he began a gradual contraction of the greenbacks. This policy coincided with an economic slump in 1866–1867 when business conditions were no longer stimulated by war production. Although McCulloch's deflationary initiatives were only partially responsible for this slump, all those groups that had prospered from the ready availability of cheap money now came out for a reinflation of the currency.

Pendleton's plan for doing so was seemingly a moderate one. He called for the redemption of the government's 5-20 bonds (the numbers referred to bonds paying five percent interest and maturing within twenty years) in greenbacks. Under law the interest on these bonds had to be paid in gold, but no specific provision had been made regarding the payment of the principal. The war debt had been contracted in depreciated currency, and, hence, argued Pendleton, it was only fair that it be paid back in the same greenback currency. Some inflation would result, he conceded, but that would contribute to a moderate expansion of the economy. Also, over the course of time, Pendleton stressed that greenbacks would gradually replace national banknotes and thus weaken what western Democrats saw as the bloated power of the eastern bankers, the traditional energy of agrarian Democrats since the days of Jackson.

Bankers and most businessmen in the Democratic and Republican parties alike were horrified by Pendleton's plan. Close to half of the federal debt was represented by the 5-20 bonds. Fiscal conservatives and most of the 1 million Northerners who had purchased the 5-20s in Jay Cooke's mass marketing campaign, asserted that national honor, the memory of the war dead, and the stability of the economy all demanded that the bonds be paid off in gold. In short, they equated greenback redemption with a repudiation of both the debt and the sanctity of the war itself. The self-interest of the large financial institutions that held most of the 5-20s was also at stake. They had a vested interest in the National Banking System and the issuance of banknotes secured by federal bonds. Moreover, wealthy financiers who were creditors had every reason to oppose an inflationary policy that would result in their debts being paid back in dollars of depreciating value.

Before the Democrats met and nominated Seymour, a staunch opponent of Pendleton's plan, business interests received assurances from the Republicans that a Grant presidency would be safe on the money question. Republican approval of greenback redemption was largely limited to a handful of radicals led by Thaddeus Stevens of Pennsylvania and Benjamin Butler of Massachusetts. Stevens spoke for manufacturers and entrepreneurs who wanted cheap credit, and Butler was trying to build a labor constituency by citing the need for more greenbacks as a means of breaking what he decried as the monopolistic power of the private bankers. Mainstream Republicans, however, wanted nothing to do with anything that smacked of repudiation, and the Chicago platform in 1868 emphatically endorsed the full payment of the debt in gold. The same platform also retreated from the radicalism of 1867 by stipulating that black suffrage in the North was a matter best left up to the individual states.

In the election of 1868 Grant carried twenty-six of the thirty-four states and swamped Seymour in the electoral vote by 214 to 80. Yet, Republicans were rightfully concerned that this margin of victory actually masked a deterioration in their party's popularity. Compared with the Lincoln vote in 1864, Grant ran marginally poorer in all the major regions of the North with the exception of New England. In the unreconstructed states of the Upper South, the Republican vote fell sharply from fifty-four to forty-two percent. Seymour carried three of these five states, three more in the North, including New York, the major electoral prize, and the two reconstructed states of Louisiana and Georgia, where white Democrats intimidated and terrorized blacks into staying away from the polls. The Southern white Democracy was making a comeback, and, nationwide, Seymour probably received a slight majority of the total white vote cast in the election.

Republicans were disappointed and even alarmed over Grant's inability to make a stronger showing against a Democratic party that was hampered throughout the North by its identification with a reckless crusade to reopen all the wounds of Reconstruction. Many concluded that the party that had saved the Union had still not saved itself from the threat of being unseated from power by a resurgent Democratic party whose ranks would be swelled by unrepentant rebels. The case for extending the vote to blacks in the North and the unreconstructed South in order to enlarge the electoral base of the Republicans now became a compelling one, and the 15th Amendment on suffrage would open a new chapter of Reconstruction in the early days of the Grant administration.

NOTES

1. Allan Nevins (ed.), *Diary of the Civil War, 1860–1865 George Templeton Strong* (New York: Macmillan, 1962), p. 601.
2. George W. Julian, *Speeches on Political Questions* (New York: Hurd and Houghton, 1872), p. 290.
3. Cited in La Wanda Cox, *Lincoln and Black Freedom: A Study in Presidential Leadership* (Columbia, S.C.: University of South Carolina Press), pp. 142–143.
4. Leroy P. Graf and Ralph W. Haskins (eds.), *The Papers of Andrew Johnson*, vol. 7 (Knoxville: The University of Tennessee Press, 1972), p. 398.
5. Ibid., p. 226.
6. Brooks D. Simpson, Leroy P. Graf, and John Muldowny (eds.), *Advice After Appomattox: Letters to Andrew Johnson, 1865–1866* (Knoxville: The University of Tennessee Press, 1987), p. 122.
7. Graf and Haskins, vol. 7, p. 293.
8. *Charles Sumner: His Complete Works*, vol. 12 (New York: Negro Universities Press, 1969 [1900]), pp. 368–369.
9. Julian, pp. 269–270.
10. Philip S. Foner and George E. Walker (eds.), *Proceedings of the Black State Conventions, 1840–1865*, vol. 2 (Philadelphia, Pa.: Temple University Press, 1980), p. 262.
11. *Report of the Joint Committee of Reconstruction at the First Session Thirty-Ninth Congress* (Westport, Conn.: Negro Universities Press, 1969 [1866]), Part II, p. 249.
12. Quoted in Michael Perman, *Emancipation and Reconstruction, 1862–1879* (Arlington Heights, Ill.: Harlan Davidson, 1987), p. 53.
13. Boston *Daily Advertiser*, June 13, 1867, cited in Michael Les Benedict, "The Rout of Radicalism: Republicans and the Election of 1867," *Civil War History*, vol. 18, p. 337, 1972.
14. Quoted in Philip D. Swenson, "Illinois: Disillusionment with State Activism," in James C. Mohr (ed.), *Radical Republicans in the North: State Politics During Reconstruction* (Baltimore, Md.: The Johns Hopkins University Press, 1976), p. 105.

15. Chicago *Tribune,* March 4, 1866, cited in James C. Mohr, "New York: The Depoliticization of Reform," in Mohr (ed.), p. 68.
16. Quoted in David Montgomery, *Beyond Equality: Labor and the Radical Republicans, 1862–1872* (New York: Alfred A. Knopf, 1967), p. 353.
17. Frank P. Blair to Samuel J. Tilden, July 15, 1868, in John Bigelow (ed.), *Letters and Literary Memorials of Samuel J. Tilden,* vol. 1 (New York: Harper & Brothers, 1908), p. 241.

SUGGESTED READINGS

ANDREANO, RALPH (ED.), *The Economic Impact of the American Civil War.* Cambridge, Mass.: Schenkman, 1962.

BELZ, HERMAN, *Reconstructing the Union: Theory and Practice During the Civil War.* Ithaca, N.Y.: Cornell University Press, 1969.

BENEDICT, MICHAEL L., *A Compromise of Principle: Congressional Republicans and Reconstruction, 1863–1869.* New York: W. W. Norton, 1974.

BROCK, WILLIAM R., *An American Crisis.* London: Macmillan, 1973.

CARTER, DAN T., *When the War Was Over: The Failure of Self-Reconstruction in the South.* Baton Rouge, La.: Louisiana State University Press, 1985.

CURRY, RICHARD O. (ED.), *Radicalism, Racism, and Party Realignment: The Border States During Reconstruction.* Baltimore, Md.: Johns Hopkins University Press, 1969.

FONER, ERIC, *Reconstruction: America's Unfinished Revolution, 1863–1877.* New York: Harper and Row, 1988.

HYMAN, HAROLD M., *A More Perfect Union: The Impact of the Civil War and Reconstruction on the Constitution.* New York: Alfred A. Knopf, 1973.

JAMES, JOSEPH B., *The Framing of the Fourteenth Amendment.* Urbana, Ill.: University of Illinois Press, 1956.

MCKITRICK, ERIC L., *Andrew Johnson and Reconstruction.* Chicago, Ill.: University of Chicago Press, 1960.

MCPHERSON, JAMES M., *The Struggle for Equality: Abolitionists and the Negro in the Civil War and Reconstruction.* Princeton, N.J.: Princeton University Press, 1964.

MOHR, JAMES C. (ED.), *Radical Republicans in the North.* Baltimore, Md.: Johns Hopkins University Press, 1976.

PERMAN, MICHAEL, *Reunion Without Compromise: The South and Reconstruction, 1865–1868.* New York: Cambridge University Press, 1973.

SHARKEY, ROBERT P., *Money, Class, and Party.* Baltimore, Md.: Johns Hopkins University Press, 1959.

8

The
Unwinding
of
Reconstruction

"The world is out of joint, and Hamlet was a damned fool for trying to set it right instead of trying to make money on it." On that sour note in 1867 Henry Adams proclaimed to his brother Charles Francis his disgust with the policies of the radical Republicans and his intention of limiting his investments to the safest of gold-bearing securities. From the perspective of Adams, a member of New England's most famous nineteenth-century family and a conservative antislavery Republican before the war, everything was going wrong in postwar America. The country "had turned a back somersault. I find the pure northern Congress, just such a one as we prayed for twenty years ago, violating the rights of minorities more persistently than the worst pro-slavery Congress could ever do."[1] Because of alleged Republican misrule, Adams was expecting a financial crash in 1867 and an end to American credit abroad. The crux of the problem was obvious enough to Adams.

> The idea that democracy in itself, by the mere fact of giving power to the masses, will elevate and purify human nature, seems to me to have now turned out one of those flattering fictions which have in all ages deluded philanthropists. The great problem of every system of Government has been to place administration and legislation in the hands of the best men. We have tried our formula and find that it has failed in consequence of its clashing with our other fundamental principle that one man is as good as another.[2]

Adams was far too wealthy, elitist, and snobbish to be a representative

American of his generation, and much of his alienation from Grant's America was of a highly personalized nature. In rejecting their "best men" for leadership, his fellow Americans had rejected, of course, men such as himself. Nonetheless, his pessimism accurately reflected the pervasive retreat in the 1870s from the demand for equal rights and political democracy that had set so much of the agenda for American politics in the 1860s.

There were, to be sure, in Adams's phraseology, idealistic "damned fools" in the Grant administration intent on making a reality of biracial democracy in the South and extending the egalitarian promise of radical Reconstruction to all segments of Northern society. Republicans in 1870 succeeded in securing the ratification of the 15th Amendment, which nationalized black voting, and they passed a series of enforcement acts in 1870–1871 to protect the voting rights of Southern blacks from the violence of the Ku Klux Klan. Some Republicans actively supported the attempts of Northern workers to secure labor's most pressing demand after the war, legislation establishing eight hours as the appropriate working day, and a minority of Republicans came out in favor of woman's suffrage. Still, the Grant administration is hardly remembered for its idealism and reforming zeal. Its image has remained pretty much as described by Adams in 1869. He reported from Washington that "from what I see here I suspect that our people may be properly divided into two classes, one which steals, the other which is stolen from...."[3]

The politics of money characterized the Grant years, and the reform coalition that pushed Reconstruction to its most radical limits broke up between 1868 and 1872. Always under pressure because it was too radical for Southern whites and Northern conservatives and not radical enough for Northern labor and women, this coalition collapsed when the Republicans rejected the vote for women and the extension of social Reconstruction to Northern workers. Ironically, the political struggle over the passage of the 15th Amendment, the capstone of congressional Reconstruction, accelerated this Republican retreat from equality.

After examining the struggle over the vote and the labor issue in Northern politics, this chapter will move on to the class and racial tensions that rapidly undermined the Republican governments set up in the South under congressional Reconstruction. The failure of Reconstruction in the South was in turn related to a pronounced conservative reaction in the North against the forces of centralization and reform unleashed by the Union war effort. That reaction fed upon cries of political corruption and inefficiency that eroded confidence in an activist government at all levels of the federal system. Although the Republicans easily carried the election of 1872, radicalism was now spent as a coherent political force.

THE 15TH AMENDMENT AND THE EIGHT-HOUR DAY

The first order of business for the Republicans after the election of 1868 was the drafting and passage of a constitutional amendment nationalizing black voting rights. For many Republicans, such an amendment would be a fitting culmination to their party's commitment to expand the concept of equality to include Afro-Americans. Although only Minnesota and Iowa had joined the New England states prior to 1869 in granting blacks the vote on the same terms as whites in the North, rank-and-file Republicans consistently had supported black suffrage in constitutional referendums. Also, as Charles Sumner eloquently reminded his fellow Republicans, there was a natural progression from the conferral of black freedom in the 13th Amendment, to black citizenship and equality before the law in the 14th Amendment, and to the vote for the protection of the black rights of citizenship in the proposed 15th Amendment. Party idealism, that is, the desire to do what was morally right for America's blacks, certainly motivated many Republicans to back the nationalization of the black vote, but party expediency was even more important. After having failed to push for black suffrage in the North during the presidential campaign of 1868, the Republicans did an apparent about-face after the election because they were now convinced that a national black vote was necessary for the continuance of the party as the majority power in national affairs.

If the Republicans were ever to become a national party, as opposed to the sectional one they had remained from their beginning, they had to secure permanently the black vote. Quite rationally, blacks who could vote overwhelmingly backed the Republicans, the party of emancipation and black civic equality. In 1868 nearly all of this black vote rested on the extraordinary legislation of 1867, which mandated black suffrage in ten former Confederate states. This legislation could be repealed or declared unconstitutional. Once states had been readmitted to the Union, revived Democratic majorities in the South might well rewrite their state constitutions and disfranchise the freedmen. Indeed, the success in 1868 of white Democrats in Georgia and Louisiana in drastically limiting the black vote was a stark reminder to the Republicans of just how precarious the voting base of their party in the South was.

Outside the reconstructed South, the largest concentration of blacks was in the loyal Border states. Reconstruction legislation did not apply here, and, consequently, there was no black suffrage. What strength the Republicans did have in the Upper South was contingent on state legislation that temporarily disfranchised many former Confederates. This explains why Grant was able to carry West Virginia and Missouri in 1868. White disfranchisement was also the key to Grant's victory in Tennessee, a state that escaped congressional Reconstruction by virtue of having ratified the 14th Amendment in 1866. Such victories would be highly unlikely in the future unless the Republicans were able to counterbalance the returning Democratic votes of ex-Confederates with the new vote of black Republicans.

To hold on to the gains they had made in the Upper South, and to build a lasting foundation for the party in the Lower South, the Republicans needed to place black suffrage in the Constitution. In the North, where blacks comprised less than two percent of the population, the potential Republican gains from a black electorate were clearly much smaller than in the South. Still, the possibility of tipping the party balance to their favor in the very evenly contested and electorally large Northern states of New York, Pennsylvania, and New Jersey gave the Republicans an added incentive for backing a suffrage amendment. Grant had carried only Pennsylvania among these states in 1868, but his victory there, as well as his defeats in New York and New Jersey, were by razor-thin margins. By enfranchising the blacks, the Republicans hoped to gain a winning edge in these key swing states.

The Republicans moved very quickly on suffrage once the lame duck session of the 40th Congress convened in December 1868. They had to, or else their opportunity to act on suffrage would have been lost indefinitely. The party had not retained its two-thirds majority in the Congress elected in the fall of 1868, and such a majority was the required minimum needed for congressional approval of a constitutional amendment. With only a simple majority in the upcoming 41st Congress, the Republicans would not have been able to overcome entrenched Democratic opposition to any extension of the vote to blacks. In February 1869, Congress approved the 15th Amendment. For all the speed with which the Republicans moved, they also acted quite cautiously. The version of the amendment that passed was easily the most conservative of the three under debate. The most radical and nationalistic proposal was an unequivocal and positive affirmation of the right of all adult males to vote. More conservative was a version that prohibited the states from disfranchising males on grounds of racial, nativity, educational, or property disqualifications. The 15th Amendment, as approved, was negatively worded and cited only "race, color, or previous condition of servitude" as grounds upon which a state could not deprive a male of the vote.

Political reality dictated the Republicans' caution. Party moderates could be won over to a suffrage amendment only if Northern states were left free to shape their own voting standards. In the Far West the Chinese were not permitted to vote, and in the Northeast several states at the behest of Republicans imposed property, tax-paying, or literacy requirements on suffrage that held down the number of potentially Democratic voters from among the poor and foreign born. Republican moderates also insisted that all references to the right of blacks to hold political office be dropped from the proposed amendment. Having already seen the party lose the vote of anti-black Northern whites in 1867, these moderates did not want to compound the political hemorrhaging within their state organizations by being pinned with a Democratic label of favoring black officeholders. By catering to the moderates in Congress, the Republicans also increased the odds on the 15th Amendment's being ratified by the requisite three-fourths of the state legislatures. The Republicans were assured of the support of New England and of the ten states in the reconstructed South, all of which were controlled by either the party or the military. Thus, the crucial struggle over ratification was in the Mid-Atlantic and Midwest states. Here, the Republicans just did squeeze the amendment through, primarily because of the nearly unanimous support of Republican state legislators anxious to settle the vexatious issue of black suffrage.

Within a generation, and as the radicals had predicted in the debates over suffrage in the 40th Congress, Southern whites exploited the loopholes in the 15th Amendment that permitted the denial of the vote ostensibly on grounds other than race. By the beginning of the twentieth century, Southern blacks were disfranchised on a massive scale. They then joined women as the only class of Americans systematically denied the right to vote.

Women reformers had campaigned for the 15th Amendment with the expectation that the reconstructed nation which emerged from the Civil War would now extend political equality to women, as well as blacks. First formally asserted as a demand at the Seneca Falls Convention in 1848, women's suffrage was the linchpin in the feminist effort to secure the full political equality of women. Only the vote, argued these reformers, would give women the power and protection they needed to redress the wrongs inflicted on them. Modeled after the Declaration of Independence, the Seneca Falls Declaration catalogued those wrongs and put women's disfranchisement at the top of the list. Other grievances included taxation without representation; exclusion from the professions; legal prohibitions against married women holding property, earning their own wages, or entering into contracts; and discriminatory divorce and guardianship laws that deprived mothers of custody over their children.

Suffrage directly raised the issue of the individual right of every woman to self-assertion and economic independence. For that reason the demand for woman's suffrage was met with outrage and scorn by most males, who felt that a woman's proper and God-ordained place was in the home where she naturally would be dependent on her husband. This was the fundamental cultural assumption regarding women in mid-nineteenth-century America. Shaped into an ideology by the sermons of ministers, the tracts of popular writers, and the teachings of many women's groups themselves, this assumption took the form of what has been called the "cult of domesticity." This ideology sharply divided life into public and private spheres segregated by sex. Woman's place was in the private sphere of the home because only there, it was believed, could she nurture the virtuous, Christian family necessary to protect the republic from the unrestrained pursuit of self-interest by males in the public sphere of politics and business.

In challenging the cult of domesticity, women reformers drew on the natural rights philosophy at the heart of the Declaration of Independence. As petitioners and organizers in the abolitionist movement, they also learned how ideas of equality and individual rights used to condemn slavery could be applied to issues of male oppression in their own lives. After a period of intense legislative activity in the 1850s aimed at securing more liberal divorce laws and greater control for women over their property, the feminists suspended their drive for civil and political rights during the Civil War. In addition to relief work for Union soldiers, they focused their energies on the cause of emancipation. In 1863 the National Women's Loyal League was formed under the leadership of Elizabeth Cady Stanton and Susan B. Anthony. It was instrumental in organizing a massive campaign of popular support for a constitutional amendment ending slavery. To that end the Loyal League collected 400,000 signatures on a petition in support of the 13th Amendment. This petition campaign was the greatest single success of the feminist–abolitionist alliance.

Emancipation was always part of a larger goal for the women's rights leader. As they expressed it, they wanted "A NEW CONSTITUTION in which the guarantee of liberty and equality to every human being shall be so plainly and clearly written as never again to be called into question."[4] Such a goal seemed within reach in the midst of the constitutional experimentation surrounding Reconstruction, especially once the Republicans began to give constitutional sanctions to the principle of equal rights. Feminists now expected male abolitionists and congressional radicals to support them in a push for universal suffrage. Having worked so hard and so effectively for emancipation during the war, these women felt they had fully earned that support. They were bitterly disappointed. They suffered their first defeat when the 14th Amendment put the word "male" into the Constitution for the first time. By specifically referring to "male inhabitants" and "male citizens," the amendment in effect legally authorized discrimination by sex. A more crushing setback occurred when the 15th Amendment retreated from natural rights philosophy by prohibiting only racial discrimination in voting. Both universal and black suffrage were politically unpopular, and, faced with a choice between the two, the Republicans rejected the claims to equality by women in order to maximize their chances for constitutionally securing the black vote.

The feminists understandably felt betrayed by male abolitionists and radical Republicans, their former allies in the cause of antislavery. The radical wing of the women's rights movement now abandoned the coalition politics of reform.

In 1869 Stanton and Anthony founded the National Woman Suffrage Association, an organization exclusively for women and controlled exclusively by women. Not only did this step mark a final rupture of the former feminist alliance with the freedmen and male reformers in the Republican party, but it also signaled a dramatically conservative shift in the argument for women's suffrage. Prior to the 15th Amendment, women had staked their claim to the vote on grounds of individualism and equality. Now, rather than asserting that the vote was an inalienable natural right regardless of sex or race, they argued that suffrage was a privilege that should be granted to women because, as women, they would strengthen and purify the nation by extending their moral guardianship of the family into the sphere of public affairs. In other words, Stanton and Anthony now accepted the notion of inherent differences between the sexes and turned it on its head in an effort to win the vote. They also vented racial and class prejudices that earlier had been suppressed in their commitment to egalitarianism. The National Woman Suffrage Association repeatedly emphasized that the educated and propertied women of the white middle class should be enfranchised in order to protect the nation from the allegedly harmful efforts of giving the vote to "lowly" immigrants and "ignorant" blacks.

Issues of class, as well as gender, broke apart the Northern reform coalition in the late 1860s. For women, suffrage was the key to ending gender slavery; for labor the eight-hour day was the indispensable reform that would end wage slavery and thus secure meaningful freedom and equality for American workers. When the Republicans refused to rally behind legislation limiting the work day to eight hours,

Susan B. Anthony and Elizabeth Cady Stanton fought for women's suffrage with the same fervor that they had devoted to the cause of emancipation.

they alienated labor reformers fully as much as they had the feminists when they drew the line at black suffrage.

Much like the women reformers, workers in the North emerged from the Civil War with the sense that they had subordinated their own special interests in the cause of Union and emancipation. The war economy generated nearly full employment, and skilled labor in industries with government contracts probably saw an increase in their real wages, but most workers experienced a drop in real income. Wages rose, but not as fast as prices. Real wages in the North fell by seventeen percent between 1860 and 1864 before rebounding slightly in 1865. Economic discontent was partially defused by a revived labor movement that rebuilt many of the trade unions destroyed in the depression of 1857.

Strike activity picked up considerably after 1863, and the federal government used troops to smash strikes or block organizing drives by unions in the key war industries. In July 1864 the War Department seized and operated the Philadelphia and Reading Railroad after striking railroad workers had shut down the flow of anthracite from northeastern Pennsylvania to transportation centers in Philadelphia. This was the first instance in American history of the presidential seizure of private property in the midst of a strike. The strikes were generally led by workers whose skills were in heavy demand in the war economy, but most workers were unskilled and so divided by sex, nationality, and religion that they could not organize any effective protest actions. One-quarter of the nonagricultural work force were women in desperate need of higher wages to increase family income while their husbands and sons were away fighting.

Despite the burdens placed on them, Northern workers remained loyal to the war effort. As a group, only professionals contributed a higher proportion of their numbers to the Union armies. The source of this loyalty was the belief of labor that the cause of the Union was the cause of free labor the world over. Victory meant the destruction of the aristocratic and hereditary system of slavery that degraded free labor and the perpetuation of the world's greatest democracy that gave all men an equal chance to succeed. In words very similar to those that Lincoln would use, Peter Welsh, an Irish Catholic carpenter, wrote in 1863 that the war was "the first test of a modern free government" based on "equal laws." If we fail, he told his wife, "the old cry will be sent forth from the aristocrats of europe that such is the common end of all republics[.]"[5]

At the end of the war, labor reformers embarked on a program to transform the position of the worker in Northern society. These reformers insisted that labor receive a fairer share of the wealth it created and more political benefits from the free institutions it had defended during the war. In their view the wage-labor system was tantamount to wage slavery. No individual could be truly free whose hours of work were dictated by another, they felt. Just as chattel slavery had to be destroyed as a necessary step in the creation of an America of equal citizens under the law, so also did the injustices of wage slavery demand radical reform, and labor reformers cited the principles of equal rights that the Republican radicals invoked to reconstruct the South as a justification for reconstructing social relations in the North. "So must our dinner tables be reconstructed," resolved the Boston Labor Reform Association in 1865, "...our dress, manners, education, morals, dwellings, and the whole Social System."[6]

Labor focused on two major reforms just after the war. One involved the establishment of consumers' and producers' cooperatives owned and operated by workers and their families. Such cooperatives, it was held, would restore to labor control over its own economic activities and break the monopoly of private capital, which was concentrating wealth and production in the hands of a new monied elite. These associations of workers were a long-range goal. Of more immediate concern was the securing of the eight-hour day, a demand that mobilized a mass movement among Northern workers by 1866.

Regardless of their skills or industrial affiliation, workers united behind the eight-hour movement because they wanted to relieve themselves of the drudgery and hardships of a ten-hour working day. A sixty-hour work week was the norm throughout the North, and for most workers such long hours smacked of slavery. As the labor reformers pointed out, work or starve was the iron rule of survival for most wage workers, and they had to accept whatever hours were offered by those who had capital or productive property. Consequently, the reformers argued that it was only morally fair that the state should step in and set legal limits on what constituted a just day's work. Once the eight-hour limit was set, then labor would have the leisure time for the moral and cultural self-improvement that would make them better informed and more active citizens. Workers then would have regained some measure of their personal liberty that had been enslaved by the tyranny of capital, and they could truly proclaim themselves as free men of the republic.

According to the vision of the eight-hour ideologues, the economy as a whole would benefit from a shorter work day. They reasoned that a reduction in hours would soon lead to an increase in wages, which would necessitate a more rapid introduction of labor-saving machinery by businessmen. As industrial technology became more sophisticated, then the need for better educated workers would correspondingly grow, and these well-paid workers would have the purchasing power to consume the goods produced in a constantly expanding economy. Much as the Republicans had attacked chattel slavery as a drag on national progress because it stifled technological innovation, so also did the labor reformers indict the long hours of wage slavery as an impediment to economic growth.

Although progress, self-improvement, and equal rights were positive concepts in the value structure of both the Republicans and the labor reformers, most Republicans, including such leading radicals as Stevens and Sumner, were indifferent or hostile to the eight-hour movement. The very notion of state interference with the hours or conditions of labor violated the self-regulating harmony between capital and labor at the center of their free labor ideology. The profits of capital, it was asserted, were returned to labor in higher wages, and any imbalance in favor of capital could be only a temporary one that would naturally be corrected by the law of supply and demand. Workers striking for the eight-hour day might succeed for the moment, conceded the conservatively Republican *Commercial and Financial Chronicle* in 1866, "but being against reason, and opposed to that community of interest which Providence has instituted between the workman and the employer, they must in the end bring the sure penalty that attends every infraction of natural law."[7]

In pledging to uphold the presumedly divine sanctity of the freedom of contract from the equally presumed heresy of the eight-hour movement, the ex-Whig manufacturers and industrial leaders in the Republican party were of course protecting their own economic self-interests. They expected a flat and deflationary economy once wartime markets dried up and prices fell with the return of peace, and their worst fears were realized.

A depression hit many sectors of the manufacturing economy from 1866 through 1869. Northern business failures in the late 1860s were running four times above the level of 1865, and the amount of capital lost in bankruptcies in 1867 was the greatest since the outbreak of the war in 1861.

What worsened the economic downturn was the attempt of businesses to maintain their market shares by lowering prices. But in doing so they could have maintained their profit margins only had they been able to slash their labor costs. However, food prices were falling more slowly than those for industrial goods, and labor fiercely resisted any wage cuts. In what the *Commercial and Financial Chronicle* decried as "a war of classes,"[8] labor walkouts in 1867 and 1868 hit the building trades in New York City and Brooklyn, the coal mines in Pennsylvania, New Jersey, and Illinois, and the steel factories in Pittsburgh. Labor was able to hold the line on wages, and in addition it demanded its former ten-hour wage for a new eight-hour day of work. This was sheer economic lunacy to most businessmen, and they mounted a united front against the eight-hour movement.

Despite intense business opposition and only lukewarm support from the Republicans, eight-hour laws were enacted by the legislatures of seven Northern states just after the war. Most of the Republicans who favored the legislation did so in the hope of detaching immigrant workers from their traditional political home in the Democratic party. They also wanted to protect their party from Democratic charges that the Republicans favored the factory slavery of whites in the North while hypocritically boasting that they ended the legal slavery of blacks in the South. Businesses were placated by provisions that guaranteed the freedom of contract.

These provisions, along with the absence of any enforcement machinery, vitiated the whole intent of the legislation as far as labor was concerned. Citing their freedom to set the terms of employment, businessmen refused to honor the eight-hour day unless workers agreed to a proportionate reduction in their wages. When forced to choose between shorter hours or higher wages, most workers chose the wages. On the average, an unskilled Northern worker had an annual wage income of $500, and this could meet only about sixty percent of the living costs for a family of four. Already living on the edge of economic survival, most Northern workers could not afford a cut in their pay. In the Pennsylvania coal miners' strike of 1868, the first major test of that state's eight-hour law, the miners dropped their demand for a shorter work day and settled for a wage increase.

The disappointment of workers over the pro-business policies of the Republicans was greatest in Massachusetts, the most industrialized of all the Northern states. Here, the issue of labor reform badly split the labor–radical coalition within the Republican party. After earlier rejecting eight-hour legislation, the Republican-controlled legislature in 1869 refused the application of the Knights of St. Crispin, a union of shoemakers that was the largest labor organization in the state, for a charter to establish workers' cooperatives. The Republicans based their refusal on an antilabor reading of trade unions as coercive instruments of class control that immorally and illegally interfered with the rights in private property of an employer. Under the leadership of a renegade Republican, Benjamin F. Butler, the unions responded by launching their own independent Labor Reform party. Its program—women's suffrage, the eight-hour day, taxation on federal bonds, and support of workers' cooperatives through an inflationary expansion of greenbacks to make money more abundant and thus to lower the cost of credit—was anathema to most Republicans, including many of those who were radicals on Southern Reconstruction. Independent labor tickets attracted ten to fifteen percent of the Massachusetts vote in 1869 and 1870, two-thirds of which was siphoned off from the Republicans.

Whether measured in terms of gender or class, entrenched inequalities in the power relationships of Northern society posed insurmountable barriers to the extension of equal rights to all Northerners. The passage of the 15th Amendment without women's suffrage and the token legislation in favor of the eight-hour day marked the outer ideological limits of radical Reconstruction in the North. Once those limits were reached in 1869 and 1870, labor reformers joined feminists in leaving the reform coalition of Republicans who had pushed for radical change in the postwar South.

To be sure, labor's support of congressional Reconstruction had always been tenuous, and much of it was based on a defensive strategy of granting enough rights to the freedmen to ensure that they would remain in the South where they would not be a threat to the jobs of Northern workers. And Northern trade unions most emphatically did not open their doors to blacks after the war. Nonetheless, there was a wing of the labor movement that was genuinely radical on racial issues, and it did enthusiastically support the Republicans on congressional Reconstruction. When that support was not reciprocated in kind with pro-labor legislation, this radical wing was left isolated and embittered. From its perspective, labor had helped the Republicans to destroy and humble the planter aristocracy, and, in return, the Republicans now upheld what William Sylvis, the president of the National Labor Union, described in 1869 as "the most infamous monied aristocracy on the face of the earth."[9] The destruction of that aristocracy, and not the plight of the Southern blacks or the success of Reconstruction, was labor's major concern heading into the 1870s.

Thus, just as congressional Reconstruction in the South was getting under way in the late 1860s, the radical coalition within the Republican party already had splintered, and much of the reform zeal of the party had been dampened. Mainstream Republicans had rejected efforts to broaden the party's constituency in the North on behalf of equal rights. By so doing, they served notice that Reconstruction in the South would be similarly circumscribed by a conservative approach aimed at preserving, not extending, the program that was in place by 1870. Indeed, the commitment of most Republicans to Reconstruction as a source of progressive change toward equality in the South ended with the ratification of the 15th Amendment in 1870. The conferral of black suffrage had apparently settled the last of the great issues raised by the war. The Union dead had been honored, the rebels had been made to recognize their defeat, and a constitutional settlement had been hammered out in which a more perfect Union had arisen from the ordeal of fratricide. And, all the while, the Republicans had maintained their status as the majority party holding national power.

The Republicans had always stressed legal, not political, social, or economic equality, and, by the logic of their middle-class liberalism, Southern blacks now had the same chance as other Americans to make good in a competitive economy in which all had an equal opportunity to succeed. It was time, the Republicans concluded, for politics as normal to determine the ultimate place of blacks in Southern society. But politics in the reconstructed South were anything but normal, and the crusade for Reconstruction that was over in the North had barely begun in the South.

RADICAL RECONSTRUCTION IN THE SOUTH

Writing from Grayson county, Texas, in the spring of 1867, Mattie Potts informed a brother who had migrated after the war to California that "if you are a good rebel and I almost know you are, you would not be satisfied here as man is not his owne here. Yankey's and Negroes carry the day here."[10] Radical Reconstruction had come to Texas and nine other Southern states, and for most Southern whites it was indeed a humiliating experience in which they believed their rights of self-government had been prostituted before an unholy alliance of ignorant, barbarous blacks and thieving Yankee conquerors. Nothing in Southern culture had prepared whites for the sudden emancipation of the slaves, let alone the political empowerment of

Black suffrage was the most radical feature of Congressional Reconstruction and that part of the congressional policy which was most objectionable to Southern whites.

those ex-slaves. What earned congressional Reconstruction the undying hatred of Southern whites, and what made it radical, was the conferral of political rights on the recently freed blacks.

As inherently radical as were the southern Republican parties that were dependent on the black vote for their very existence, these parties were almost pathetically conservative in their approach to governing in the reconstructed South. They neither perceived themselves nor acted as if they were a revolutionary vanguard. Instead, they went out of their way to conciliate their white opponents, and they tried to function as legitimate parties engaged in the normal political activities of building coalitions among the voters in order to win elections. However, this fundamental strategy of pursuing politics as usual was tantamount to committing political suicide, for most Southern whites never accepted the legitimacy of the southern Republican parties, that is, their right to govern or even to participate in any meaningful way in Southern political life.

Once the Republicans gained control of the reconstructed state governments in 1867 and 1868, Southern whites viewed them as an occupying army of outside mercenaries and alien elements within Southern society that had to be expelled at all costs. Republican efforts at conciliation were interpreted as a sign of cowardly weakness, and harsher coercive measures were seen as confirmation of the unconstitutional tyranny that Republicans were trying to force on the South. Thus, the southern Republicans had all the political weaknesses and none of the strengths of being identified with a program of revolutionary change that they themselves refused to push vigorously.

The first indication of the subdued radicalism that would characterize the southern Republican parties came in the state constitutional conventions called under the terms of congressional Reconstruction during the winter of 1867–1868. Without a doubt, the new constitutions did incorporate liberal and democratic changes. Property qualifications for office holding were reduced or eliminated, and more offices were made elected rather than appointed. Universal male suffrage was established and explicit guarantees for black civil and political rights were set forth. Following the Northern model of activist state governments, most of the constitutions expanded the responsibilities of the states in the areas of social welfare and public services. Most significantly, the constitutions provided for the first state-supported systems of public education in Southern history. Entering through the back door of male economic necessity, married women's rights to their own property were also recognized. Family property was in the husband's name, and because so many men were hard pressed by their creditors after the war, the constitutional conventions granted a form of economic relief by legalizing the transfer of family assets to women in order to protect that property from the claims of creditors.

All of these changes pointed the South in the direction of a more progressively democratic society, but the conventions refused to endorse the truly radical changes demanded by a minority of the delegates. On issues of land for blacks, the vote for ex-Confederates, and integrated schools for both races, most southern Republicans assumed a conservative posture that they hoped would make them respectable in the eyes of Southern whites. The demands of the radicals were rejected in favor of the first of many appeals to a political center of Southern white opinion that simply did not exist.

Although the confiscation of the land of planters for redistribution to landless blacks was brought up in all the constitutional conventions, measures calling for it were easily defeated. Not only were the Republicans anxious to attract a nucleus of former Whig planters, but they also rightfully feared that any provisions on confiscation would be set aside by Congress. The most radical step taken on the land issue was the creation of a state land commission in South Carolina. Funded with state securities, the commission bought up land at its market value for resale to the poor on liberal credit terms. Corruption and inadequate financing prevented it from having much of an impact.

On the emotionally charged and politically divisive issue of race relations, the conventions backed away from setting legal guarantees for integration in the public schools and equal access to public accommodations. Blacks themselves were split on this issue. Any access to public institutions and white-owned facilities represented an improvement over the status they had known as slaves, and many blacks worried that their children would learn from white teachers to accept the white culture's stereotypes of black inferiority.

Whereas black Republicans usually favored the more radical position on land confiscation and civil rights, white Republicans took the hard line on the crucial question of disfranchising former Confederates. Most of these Republicans were native Southerners who had been Unionists or bitter opponents of the Confederacy during the war. They came from upcountry districts that had been wracked by the most vicious fighting in the inner civil war festering within the South by 1863. Having given and received no quarter in their conflict with Confederate authorities and rebel neighbors, they turned to the Republican party after the war as a vehicle to strip former rebels of the vote and to protect themselves from rebel reprisals. This demand for political proscription was heavily tinged with resentment against the planters for having plunged the South into the war, and the low country planting elements in the party naturally resisted any program of disfranchisement that called into question the highly suspect nature of their own Unionism during the war. In addition, most blacks were opposed to any backsliding on the principle of universal male suffrage that was so central to their political hopes.

This unlikely Republican alliance of planters and blacks blocked any significant or lengthy disfranchisement of ex-rebels. Six of the ten reconstructed states imposed no political penalties for wartime loyalty to the Confederacy. The Virginia and Mississippi constitutions tried to do so, but for that reason they were rejected in the voter referendums. At the insistence of Congress the disqualification provisions were separated from the constitutions and voted on separately. Subsequently, the constitutions were approved but not rebel disfranchisement. In 1870 Alabama lifted its restrictions on Confederate voting, and Arkansas followed suit in 1872. Thus, almost from their inception, nearly all of the Republican state governments in the South committed themselves to a self-defeating policy of enlarging the voting base of a political opponent pledged to their destruction.Moreover, the decision to court the vote of rebels, which was implicit in this policy, inevitably weakened the party's position as the champion of black interests and pushed it toward the political right where the Democrats already had staked out and monopolized all the winning issues.

At their birth in 1867 and 1868, the southern Republican parties were able to command real majority support. Blacks comprised about forty percent of the population in the reconstructed South, and their solidly Republican vote, when added to the twenty to twenty-five percent of the native whites who joined the party, left the Republicans representing most Southerners. This majority, however, was quickly lost. The Democrats regained power by 1874 in all but four of the former Confederate states. Significantly, the remaining four were those with the heaviest concentration of blacks: South Carolina, Mississippi, Louisiana, and Florida. They were lost by the Republicans in 1876 and 1877. Congressional Reconstruction, on average, lasted only about six years, and nowhere did it survive for as long as a decade.

The most critical factor in the rapid collapse of the southern Republican parties was the crisis of identity that plagued them from the very beginning. As was illustrated by their actions at the constitutional conventions, the Republicans wanted to be liberals but not radicals, friends of the blacks but allies of the blacks' former masters, and supporters of the fierce Unionism of upcountry whites but placators of the rebels who were the inveterate enemies of those Southern Unionists. This confusion over who they were and what they stood for made them an easy prey for the militantly united Democrats. A patchwork of otherwise antagonistic racial and class elements thrown together by the upheaval of war and the extraordinary political circumstances that dictated the instant development of new parties in the postwar South, the southern Republicans lacked the internal unity and ideological coherence that were the minimal prerequisites for any lasting party success.

The freedmen supplied the mass voting base, the Northerners controlled most of the key offices, and former southern Whigs and Unionists provided the indispensable link to the native white communities. This was the basic framework of functional power and influence within the southern Republican parties. It was inherently unstable because each of the major social elements brought very different expectations and needs to Reconstruction. When these groups began to struggle against each other for the party influence they needed to implement their vision of Reconstruction, party factionalism soon became self-destructive.

For blacks, Reconstruction was an opportunity to achieve levels of equality and independence that they hardly were able to dream of under slavery. No later than 1863 Southern blacks sensed, as one Union officer reported, "that it was a war for their liberation; that the cause of the war was their being in slavery, and that the aim and result would be their freedom."[11] In large measure because the slaves through their own actions and services forced Union officials to define the war's objective as nothing less than total emancipation, the war did bring freedom. And,

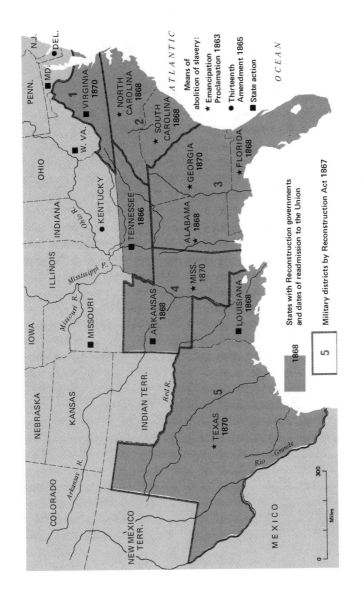

Reconstruction in the South.

Means of
abolition of slavery:
★ Emancipation
  Proclamation 1863
● Thirteenth
  Amendment 1865
■ State action

States with Reconstruction governments
and dates of readmission to the Union

Military districts by Reconstruction Act 1867

1868

5

PENN.
N.J.
MD.
DEL.
VIRGINIA
1870
NORTH
CAROLINA
1868
SOUTH
CAROLINA
1868
W. VA.
OHIO
GEORGIA
1870
FLORIDA
1868
ATLANTIC
OCEAN
KENTUCKY
TENNESSEE
1866
ALABAMA
1868
INDIANA
ILLINOIS
Ohio R.
Mississippi R.
MISS.
1870
ARKANSAS
1868
LOUISIANA
1868
IOWA
Missouri R.
MISSOURI
NEBRASKA
KANSAS
INDIAN TERR.
Red R.
TEXAS
1870
COLORADO
Arkansas R.
NEW MEXICO
TERR.
Rio Grande
MEXICO
Miles
0
300

at its end, the emancipated slaves had their own agenda for making that freedom meaningful.

Blacks immediately seized freedom as the opportunity to build an autonomous black community anchored in the values and institutions that had given them the cultural resiliency to maintain their self-esteem in the bondage of slavery. The core institution was the family. As the fugitives had shown so strikingly during the war, when they organized their escapes along family lines, the first objective under freedom was the strengthening of the black family. Despite the prime importance of family ties under slavery, thousands of black families had to be reunited in 1865. Many had already been broken up before the war. Slave marriages were never recognized under Southern law, and one-fifth to one-third of them ended with the sale or forced removal of one of the partners. The war years then brought on massive family disruptions when masters relocated their slaves to keep them away from the Yankees, and Union and Confederate officials competed for able-bodied black labor. All during 1865 countless blacks left the plantations in search of family members. By physically moving around in an effort to reknit their families, the freedmen were also attempting to remove themselves psychologically from that direct white supervision that had been basic to slave discipline. They demonstrated this desire for their own cultural space by laying claim to full control over the key community institution of slave society, the black church.

Driven by racial pride and their own sense of community, the freedmen pushed for separate black churches once the deliverance prophesied in their religious faith finally came. The religion that had sustained them as slaves was now drawn on to inform their self-definition as a freed people. Blacks used the disciplinary structure of their churches as a community-controlled judiciary system that operated like a small-claims court in moral and economic matters. Here, free from white interference and prejudice, the freedmen set down and enforced the ethical standards they valued as a people. Here, organizational skills were learned, family disputes were settled, social gatherings were planned, political meetings were held, and lessons in literacy were offered for children and adults. In the rural South, blacks made their churches synonymous with their communities.

Another key institution for the freedmen was the school. The basic black demand of education for their children had unmistakably been set forth by the actions of the freedmen during the war. Fugitive blacks quickly grasped the importance of their labor to the Union war effort, as well as the urgency with which federal officials wanted to establish that free black labor could be as profitable and disciplined as slave labor. Using the only weapon they had—their labor—freedmen behind Union lines often refused to work until they were assured that their children would receive an education. The Union army responded by establishing an organized system of black elementary education, notably in southern Louisiana in 1864.

Because as one black Mississippian put it in 1869, "I consider education the next best thing to liberty,"[12] the freedmen were passionately committed to education after the war. They equated ignorance with a continuation of their bondage, and they prized education as being essential for self-advancement. In an incredible display of self-sacrifice, they somehow scraped together some $1 million from their own meager resources for black schools by 1870. Meanwhile, the Freedmen's Bureau, white Protestant denominations in the North, and such black denominations as the African Methodist Episcopal Church combined their resources to launch a mixed system of private and public schooling in the postwar South. Then, despite opposition from Southern whites, the reconstructed state governments provided the tax dollars for a public system of schools open to both races. Black illiteracy, which was over ninety percent in 1865, was cut in half by 1900.

By knitting together family ties separated by slavery and war, regulating their own affairs with their own institutions, and sacrificing for the education of their children, blacks largely reconstructed their own lives in the aftermath of emancipation. In common with recently freed slaves throughout the rest of the Western Hemisphere, they also realized that the full measure of freedom could come only with economic independence secured through the ownership of land. As was noted by Sidney Andrews, a Northern newspaper correspondent who traveled throughout the South in 1865, the freedmen "seemed to think the ownership of land and a horse or mule made men of them at once."[13]

At the war's end, the freedmen immediately pressed their moral claims to a share of the land they had worked as slaves. In the moral economy of the freedmen, part of that land was rightfully theirs by virtue of their uncompensated labor under slavery. Black sweat and unrequited toil had made that land valuable, and now blacks demanded their share of it. Expectations for land reached millennial heights in the spring and summer of 1865, but they were soon dashed when President Johnson ordered that confiscated and abandoned lands in the South were to be returned to the pardoned ex-Confederate owners. In the meantime, federal commanders in the occupied South sided with the planters in disputes over land. Typically, when a planter complained that former slaves refused to work unless they were given their own plots of land, the army stepped in and forced the protesting freedmen to accept the labor terms set down by the planter. Army attitudes were well summarized by an officer in Gordonsville, Virginia, in the summer of 1865. After a local planter had called upon federal troops to put an end to a work stoppage on his plantation, the officer summoned the striking workers, pointed to the slave cemetery on the estate, and warned the spokesmen for the strikers, "The only land you will get, or any of you, will be 6 × 3 feet in that lot, and if you do not behave yourselves properly you will get your share very quickly."[14]

Of course, the vast majority of freedmen lacked the cash to purchase land. Not surprisingly, those Southern whites who could have granted them the long-term credit to buy land refused to do so. It was in the self-interest of the former slaveholders, as well as Northern commercial interests who had a direct stake in the revival of the Southern economy, to keep blacks on the plantations as landless laborers for the production of the agricultural cash staples that had generated such large profits for both sections before the war.

Barred from claiming the land and often pushed off at the point of federal bayonets from the plots they did seize, the freedmen nonetheless did force basic changes in plantation agriculture. The planters, supported by the coercive authority of the Southern Black Codes, initially attempted to structure working conditions under freedom as closely as possible to the labor regime under slavery. The freedmen were organized into labor gangs, directly supervised by an overseer or resident planter, provided rations from the employer, and housed in the old slave quarters. The main difference from the centralized controls under slavery was now the contractual obligation of the planter to pay fixed wages for the ex-slave's labor. However, this wage system of 1865 and 1866 soon broke down. The Freedmen's Bureau suspended the most discriminatory sections of the Black Codes, and the freedmen rejected the personal dependency and coercive controls of the slave system that had reemerged in the guise of free labor.

Blacks overwhelmingly wanted to work for cash wages at the end of the war. But their preference was for short-term contracts, which would enhance their labor mobility and pay them a regular, monthly wage. Over time they hoped that those wages might provide them with a capital fund from which to rent or purchase their own land. Instead, they were forced to accept annual contracts that were openly violated by the planters and a system of controls that left them feeling like slaves all over again.

In opposing this wage–labor system, the freedmen declared that their entire families would no longer work like slaves, and they pulled their wives and children from the fields. They flooded the Freedmen's Bureau with complaints of being cheated by employers who dismissed them without their yearly wages once the harvest was in. Capitalizing on the mobility that came with emancipation, they moved in search of better working conditions. Many sought out jobs in the towns and cities, but most of the moves were local rural ones. They forced the planters to bid for their services by creating temporary shortages of labor that they then exploited for a better contract. By 1870, the typical contract was not for cash wages but for a share of the crop. Under this arrangement the planters divided their estates into small family plots that were worked by the croppers. In proportion to the amount of food and farm supplies provided by the planter, the cropper was paid a wage based on a fixed share of the crop.

As it first evolved, sharecropping offered blacks real advantages over what the planters originally had tried to fix on them. Unable to acquire land of their own, blacks still sought the economic independence and social freedom that they associated with the ownership of land. Sharecropping eliminated overseers, gang labor, and the daily supervision of whites. The freedmen now not only had more control over their time, working conditions, and family life, but also more freedom to choose between work and leisure. Like the white yeomanry of the antebellum South, they opted, wherever possible, for self-sufficiency, a reduced work load for the family, and more leisure time for hunting and fishing.

Sharecropping as a system for producing cash crops represented a compromise between black demands for autonomy and a white shortage of capital and credit. Nearly all planters were strapped for working capital after the war, and the failure of the plantation economy to revive quickly left them scrambling for credit.

Despite their concerns that sharecropping left the freedmen with too much independence, planters recognized the advantages in a labor arrangement that conserved their scarce capital by not requiring that it be spent on wages.

Even before congressional Reconstruction got under way in 1867, Southern blacks had already made significant gains in organizing their lives since emancipation. The eagerness and enthusiasm with which the freedmen now registered to vote, and the speed with which a new political class of blacks arose out of the grassroots organizations of local Republican clubs, the Union Leagues, were the best evidence that the freedmen realized that these gains could be protected and extended only through political mobilization.

If land could not be acquired by the freedmen, then the legal protection of their right to a share in the crops they produced became an even more vital political objective. Agricultural credit in the postwar South took the form of advances secured by a lien upon the crops. To ensure that the sale of the crop would cover their advances, plus interest, planters and merchants competed with one another to establish a superior legal claim on the crops. The freedmen insisted that their claims for wages or shares should take legal precedence. This struggle to establish their rights under the crop–lien system shaped much of the freedmen's political agenda. Other major goals included public tax support for schools, adherence by Southern courts to black equality before the law, and the securing of enough political power to serve as a shield against the violence of local whites.

Although the freedmen supplied over eighty percent of the vote for the Southern Republican parties, they held only fifteen to twenty percent of the political offices. At the federal and upper echelon of leadership, black politicians were well-educated men drawn primarily from a Northern-born professional class of ministers, lawyers, and teachers. Out of this group came most of the sixteen blacks who served in Congress during Reconstruction. Blacks who held state and local offices were predominately ex-slave ministers and artisans, individuals who had been in positions of leadership and trust in the slave community. Freedmen straight from the ranks of the field hands probably played their greatest political role in mobilizing the plantation workers and leading protests against white efforts at intimidating blacks into subservience.

The freedmen furnished the votes, but white Republican politicians held the power. With the exception of South Carolina, where blacks had a majority in the lower house from 1868 to 1874, and some scattered areas in Mississippi, blacks did not come close to filling offices in proportion to their numbers in the population. Consequently, the realization of black political goals were dependent on the Northern and Southern whites who monopolized the leadership posts within the new Republican parties. Relations between these whites, however, were always strained, and they were further exacerbated by divisions over how to respond to black political aspirations. Thus, the harder that blacks pushed for their political agenda, the more they divided the white leadership of the Republicans.

Especially in the beginning, Northern-born whites were the driving element in the Southern Republican parties. Their voting strength was minuscule—about two percent of the party total—but they held over half of the Republican governor-ships, half of the party seats in Congress, and one-third of the elected Republican offices in the South. They controlled the committees in the constitutional conventions that reported out the Republican program for education, civil rights, and the vote. As Northerners, they had access to the federal patronage that all Republican politicians in the South desperately wanted. Patronage jobs offered Republicans one of their few sources of prestige and reliable income in the midst of hostile Southern whites who villified them as their sworn enemies. The black vote was the other factor that gave the northern Republicans such disproportionate influence in the party. When given a choice between voting for a Northern or a Southern-born Republican, the freedmen usually favored the former, whom they naturally identified with their freedom and citizenship. Besides, the freedmen simply did not trust Southern whites. South Carolina, Mississippi, Louisiana, and Florida, the reconstructed states with the largest percentages of blacks, were those in which the party power of the Northern Republicans was the greatest.

A major strength that these Northerners brought to Reconstruction was their capital. Portrayed by Southern whites as "carpetbaggers," greedy political adventurers who stuffed their scant belongings into a carpetbag and rushed to the prostrate South to loot the section, these Republicans in fact carried badly needed capital into the South. Most of them were former Union officers who remained in the South after the war. They were young and well-educated entrepreneurs who invested their modest stakes of capital in the local economies.

In combination with the Yankee missionaries and teachers who staffed the freedmen's schools, these entrepreneurial Republicans also had a clear vision of what they wanted the South to become under Northern guidance and leadership. Their vision was that blend of materialism and moralism that the Republicans had always promoted as true Christian progress. The Republicans believed that slavery, by degrading labor and removing incentives for self-improvement on the part of most Southern whites, had stunted the development of schools, churches, factories, and internal improvements. Once the withering force of slavery was removed, the South presumably would enter a golden age of prosperity, and Republicans from the North would show the way with their program of education, legal equality, and economic opportunity.

In supporting black civil rights, the Northern-born Republicans emphasized the conservative, producer side of their racial ideology. They argued that equality before the law did not mean an end to white superiority. They believed that in a free-labor society, all classes, spurred by an equal chance to benefit from the fruits of their labor, would improve themselves and that because the freedmen were starting at the bottom, they would remain below whites. Blacks would need equal access to education in order to improve themselves, and on this point the Northerners preached that educated labor would be more productive labor that would learn the value of work and the need to replace ignorant, superstitious beliefs with the rational, efficient tenets of the modern age. Educated labor would also help stabilize the Southern social order. Like the immigrants in the Northern cities, the freedmen would be taught the values of thrift, self-reliance, and temperance, which would cure them of their seeming licentiousness. Black revolutionary schemes for land confiscation were labeled a product of ignorance. Schooling, it was held, would replace such wild ideas with the self-restrained virtues of an obedient, productive citizenry, who would seek only fair compensation for their labor.

If the capital and free-labor beliefs of the so-called carpetbaggers gave them a strong material and ideological stake in the success of southern Republicanism, it also left them wide open to being depicted by Southern whites as the hated agents of Yankee imperialism. On average, the wealth of Southern whites was reduced by one-half as a result of the destruction during the war. For planters, who received no compensation for their capital investment in slaves, the plunge was on the order of seventy-five to ninety percent.

Ethnic Yankees were now often the wealthiest group in Southern communities. Their wealth, though usually modest, was bitterly resented. Meanwhile, and quite apart from the racial factor, their value system aroused the same hostility in most Southern whites as it had in 1860. Where a Yankee Southerner saw progress in the bridges, railroads, and schools to be built with state assistance, a native Southern white saw higher taxes and growing indebtedness. Where Yankees praised the material benefits of industrialization, their rural Southern counterparts damned the loss of economic independence that would come when workers were ordered around by factory owners.

The Republicans from the North were never able to shake their image as outsiders, and they absolutely had to create a lasting alliance with at least a minority of native whites if the Republican party were to perpetuate itself as a vital political force in the former Confederacy. The Southern whites who joined the Republican party were known as "scalawags," contemporary slang for a no-good scoundrel. As used by the enemies of congressional Reconstruction, the scalawag label conveyed an image of sleezy and mean poor whites who betrayed their race for a chance to profit from the plight of the defeated South. The label stuck because it was so politically valuable to the southern Democrats in regaining and holding power in the 1870s and after, but it was as intentionally misleading as was the carpetbagger label.

About twenty percent of Southern whites became Republicans in the late 1860s. Although most of them had been antisecessionists or Unionists during the war, they were almost as divided among themselves as they were from the majority of Southern whites. The bulk of these Republicans were small farmers from the hill country and mountainous interior of the South, a region bounded in the north by West Virginia and in the south by the foothills of the Appalachians in northern Alabama. Before the war, these yeomen farmers had distrusted and opposed the rule of the planter elites in the black belts. The disastrous war transformed that distrust into a commitment to the Republicans. Not only had Lincoln's party smashed the power of the slaveholding aristocracy who were blamed for the war, but its emphasis on free homesteads and the dignity of labor was inherently popular in the egalitarian Appalachian society of small property holders.

The leadership of the native Republican faction, however, came to the party from quite a different direction. These Republicans were planters and businessmen, and they were drawn from the former class opponents of the yeomanry in the plantation districts. As conservative men of capital, they had little sympathy for the program of economic relief and greater political democratization voiced by the upcountry majority of native Republicans.

These upper-class southern Republicans were Whiggish in their politics, and they had been reluctant secessionists. They supported the war effort out of a need to maintain political and civic influence, but they were concerned not so much with the attaining of Southern independence as they were with the goals of economic development and social order. They turned to Republicanism after the war in an effort to achieve these goals. They had internalized enough of the paternalistic ethos of slavery to think that the freedmen would naturally turn to them, their former masters, for political guidance, and they were ambitious enough to believe that they could emerge as the economic leaders of a New South by gaining access to Northern capital through the Republican party. By making an accommodation with the victors in the war, they hoped both to replace the Democrats in power and to fulfill the economic goals of their antebellum Whiggery.

THE FAILURE OF THE RADICAL PROMISE

From its inception the coalition comprising the southern Republican parties threw together strange political bedfellows who were always on the verge of falling out among themselves. Party unity and morale were also constantly weakened by the refusal of most Southern whites to grant the Republicans the right to exist as a legitimate political party. Clearly, if the southern Republicans were to survive, they had to give whites a reason to join or remain within the party. Simultaneously, they had to find a way to prevent their shaky coalition from splitting along racial and class lines.

Two basic strategies for survival were open to the party. The first, and the riskiest one for the party leaders, would have embraced and extended the revolutionary changes in Southern political life embodied in the very existence of the southern Republican party. This was the approach favored by the blacks, the more radical Northerners, and the economically strapped yeomanry in the party. It would have offered blacks protection for their civil rights, adequate tax monies for schools and social services, lien laws, local offices, and perhaps a chance to rent or acquire land. The white farmers would have received debt-relief legislation, stay laws for delaying the collection of back taxes, exemption of homesteads from debt collections, and protection from rebel reprisals for their wartime Unionism. This strategy was rejected by most of the party leaders because it highlighted the divisive race issue and directly challenged the propertied white Southerners whom they were trying to entice into the party.

Instead of using radicalism as an organizing principle to appeal to all the disaffected elements in Southern society, white as well as black, the party leadership chose to stress the theme of respectability. The cornerstone of their strategy, and the issue on which they staked the future of the party, was the promotion of prosperity through state aid to railroads. Here, after all, was a program of economic development that conservative Southern whites had tried to implement under the Johnson governments. If the Republicans could now revive and diversify the shattered Southern economy, the political benefits would be enormous. Postwar prosperity keyed to spreading markets opened up by railroads would have generated the tax revenues to fund social programs demanded by blacks, restored the economic fortunes of the white yeomanry, and given planters a profitable interest in the continuance of the Republican party.

If the Republicans' program of economic modernization were ever to succeed, then the individual state governments under their control had to be able to attract outside capital. Military defeat and the emancipation of the slaves had cost the South some $5 billion in capital, and, as a region, the South was starved for investment capital after the war. Since the Republicans in Washington had ruled out any infusion of federal funds into the postwar South, that capital would have to come from private Northern financiers. But there were plenty of profitable investment opportunities in the North and West, and these financiers were quite reluctant to risk their capital in the highly uncertain political environment of the reconstructed South. Consequently, what little Northern capital did flow into the South drove a very hard bargain, and, in meeting the demands of Northern investors, southern Republicans were forced to abandon much of their commitment to the needs of the bulk of the party's supporters, the agrarian poor of both races.

Apart from seeking protection from their rebel neighbors, most of the white farmers who joined the Republican party did so in search of economic relief. The war had been disastrous for the subsistence family economy of the Southern yeomanry. They depended on family labor for their livelihood, and the war losses of able-bodied males—twenty-five percent of all white males between the ages of twenty and forty—were irreplaceable. Moreover, the war destroyed not only the planters' capital in slaves, but also destroyed much of the yeomen's capital in the form of livestock. Per capita supplies of hogs, cattle, and livestock in the South fell by one-half in the 1860s. The consequences were less food for the family, shortages in the animal power needed for agricultural production, and growing economic dependency. A drop of fifty percent in per capita food production now forced a formerly independent class to become dependent on outside sources for food.

Just as the capacity of the yeomen to supply their own family needs declined, claims on their property and cash increased. Property damage inflicted by the war had to be repaired, and credit was needed to resume production. The public debts of the Confederacy were repudiated in the terms of readmission to the Union, but private debts, many of which had been contracted at highly inflated Confederate prices, remained legally binding in most states. As personal bankruptcies soared after the war, common white farmers were hard pressed to hold on to their land. James Alcorn, the Republican governor of Mississippi in the early 1870s, estimated that farm tenancy among whites in his state had doubled since the war.

Protection for the rights of property against lower-class agitation was a minimal precondition that had to be met before any Northerners would consider investing in the South. This in turn sharply limited the ability of the Republicans to deliver on their promises of economic relief for the upcountry farmers. Any decisive action in favor of debtor stay laws and a scaling down or abolition of debts would frighten off Northern investors with images of dishonest Southerners turning to the courts to avoid paying their just debts.

Also dampening Republican enthusiasm for economic relief were the party divisions that occurred on this issue. The freedmen, who had no debts to pay, and the planter–business interests in the party, many of whom held the debt that was crushing the yeomanry, were opposed to debtor relief. Thus, the white farmers were denied the economic relief which they had been told would be the top priority of the new Republican party. Especially in Georgia, Alabama, and North Carolina, such promises had been the prime factor behind what native white support the Republicans initially received. To be sure, and with the sole exception of Louisiana, the new Republican constitutions did provide for an exemption of homesteads from seizure by creditors. But these exemptions were designed to protect the holdings of small planters as much as they were aimed at the impoverished yeomanry. On the crucial issue of debt relief, the upcountry white Republicans lost out. Only Georgia passed a measure abrogating pre-1865 debts, and this relief clause in its constitution was disallowed when Congress readmitted Georgia to the Union.

Of all the aid that Southern Republicans showered on railroads when they took office, none was as financially important as the endorsement by the state governments of bonds for railroad construction. In effect, the Republicans loaned the credit of the states to the private railroad corporations. There was nothing unusual in this procedure, for it was the standard way in which state governments in the nineteenth century enlisted private capital for the financing of quasi-public enterprises. However, the Southern Republicans had staked so much on the rehabilitation and modernization of the Southern economy that they threw all caution to the wind. Despite the fact that they inherited state treasuries tottering on bankruptcy, they nearly doubled the indebtedness of the states under their control from 1868 to 1871. Three-fourths of this increased debt was in the form of state-endorsed railroad bonds. The debt service, or interest changes on these bonds, was a huge financial burden. Half expecting that Democrats in the future would repudiate state debts incurred by their Republican predecessors, Northern financiers demanded and got annual interest payments as high as fifteen to twenty percent on the money they loaned the Republican governments for the bonds. On top of that, Southern governments that were considered a particularly bad credit risk were able to market their bonds in Northern money markets only at large discounts to their face value. In the case of South Carolina, this meant that the Republicans received in actual cash only about one-third of the value of bonds that they were obligated to pay back in full.

In addition to pledging tax monies as collateral for the payment of railroad bonds, the Republicans tried to attract Northern investments in a host of other ways. Prospective owners of factories and mines, as well as the railroad barons, were granted exemptions from taxation on their corporate property. Public land originally designated for the public school funds was donated to railroads as a construction subsidy. To reassure investors that the reconstructed South was hospitable to a healthy return on capital, usury laws that had set a cap on interest rates were repealed. In Georgia, Alabama, and Louisiana, cheap labor was made available through the leasing of convicts. Local governments, anxious for the benefits of new markets, bought up large amounts of railroad stock in companies they were courting. All of this was intended to usher the South into the economic promised land. As argued by the Jackson (Mississippi) *Pilot* in 1871, governmental promotion of railroads "will prove to the thinking people that the great Republican party is one of progress, of energy, of principles founded upon good, sound common sense."[15]

The progress never came, and in seeking a party identity anchored in business interests, the Republican politicians neglected the needs of the poor constituency that had voted them into office in the first place. Plagued by widespread crop failures in 1866 and 1867, and falling cotton prices throughout the period of Republican rule, the Southern economy did not revive after the war. For all the ballyhoo about railroads as an economic panacea, they provided no instant solution to structural problems of low-population density and a weak tax base that had inhibited economic development in the prewar South. There simply was not enough freight traffic to support all the railroads projected by the Republicans, especially when those railroads were promoted without any thought to regional planning or fiscal responsibility.

Most of the Northern investors were interested more in quick profits and in gaining financial control of individual railroads than in building a rail network tied in to a healthy diversification of the Southern economy. The railroads did not spark an industrial boom. With but few exceptions, their economic impact was limited to the opening up of backcountry areas for the cultivation of cotton.

The Republicans could take credit for rebuilding the South's railroads and for increasing its mileage by forty percent between 1868 and 1872. But most of this new rail construction was concentrated in just two states, Texas and Alabama. In the meantime, before the rail craze ended in 1872, nearly all the reconstructed states were burdened by a mountain of debt that threatened financial ruin.

Where the leaders of the party saw nothing but common sense in lavishing aid on corporations, rank-and-file Republicans increasingly saw class favoritism to the wealthy that impoverished, rather then enriched, their local communities. What made common sense to the typical black Republican, an agricultural laborer, was party support for the right of plantation laborers to organize on their own behalf for better wages and working conditions. Such efforts at unionization were denounced by party officials as a foolhardy and revolutionary attempt by labor to dictate terms to management. Believing that the South had to attract, not scare off, capital, party leaders refused to recognize their own class bias in catering to the needs of capital. To pay for their railroad program, they diverted funds and scarce economic resources that had been earmarked for public schools and other social services desired by the black poor. Their tax-exemption incentives for industry reduced the tax base that the rural poor wanted the state governments to draw on as a fund for the acquisition of land for homesteads. Blacks quickly became disillusioned with the party's economic program, but they had too much invested in the success of the party to consider joining the Democrats. Native white Republicans had no such stake in the party, and they soon bolted over its handling of the economy.

In the absence of any meaningful economic relief, the Republican yeomanry hoped at least that their economic position would not deteriorate under Republican rule. It did, and the main culprit in their eyes was the sharp increase in taxation. Property taxes soared when the Republicans were in power. On average, the tax rate on land rose three to four times over the levels prevailing in 1860. This hike in taxes was as predictable as it was large. Farmers in the antebellum South had been very lightly taxed. Prewar governments served the needs of only the white race, provided little in the way of social services, and raised about forty percent of their tax revenue from a tax on slaves. All this changed after the war.

The Republican governments assumed responsibility for social programs, notably the new system of public education, to meet the needs of both whites and blacks, and simultaneously they had to replace revenue lost by the elimination of the slave tax. The burden of taxation now fell almost exclusively on land. Because land values had fallen by one-half in the aftermath of the war's destruction, assessments on land, that is, the rate at which it was taxed, had to rise dramatically to generate the revenue needed by the Republicans for their expanded social programs.

Steeped in a political tradition that associated taxation with tyranny, Republican farmers hit with a sudden jump in their taxes were now prepared to accept the Democratic party denunciation of the Republicans as an inherently corrupt and despotic alliance of greedy carpetbaggers, vile scalawags, and ignorant blacks. Many of the Democratic charges of corruption were unfounded, and nearly all of them were wildly exaggerated. Moreover, many leading Democrats had voted for or were implicated in the railroad schemes that produced the most flagrant corruption in the reconstructed South. Nonetheless, the Democrats succeeded in making corruption a partisan issue that badly damaged the Republicans.

Southern whites were predisposed to expect the worst of the Republicans, and enough undeniable corruption did occur under various Republican administrations to make the charges stick. Scorned by most whites and denied financial backing from the local business community, some Republican politicians did view their party service as a chance to make money in a hurry. They accepted bribes, engineered kickbacks, speculated in state bonds, and used their administration of the railroads as patronage machines. That such corruption was more prevalent in

Northern cities and state legislatures, was occurring in Congress where much larger sums of money were involved, and was continued under the Democratic successors to the Republicans in the South was, of course, beside the point in terms of undermining the credibility which the southern Republicans so desperately needed to establish for themselves.

Particularly because the widespread benefits from the Republicans' sponsorship of economic development turned out to be empty promises, the Democratic charges of corruption were unanswerable. Property values fell, rather than climbed, and only outside corporate interests tied to the Republican party seemed to be prospering. The yeomen who had broken racial ranks by joining the Republican party soon felt they had been betrayed. The Republicans, far from giving them an economic incentive to remain in the party, gave them an economic reason to leave it.

Economic tensions that quickly surfaced in the native white–black alliance of Republicans also hastened the white exodus from the party. Whereas white farmers demanded relief from taxation, the freedmen wanted access to the revenue derived from taxation. Emerging from slavery with little, if any, property, the black forty percent of the population paid less than ten percent of the state taxes. Yet, if the freedmen were to acquire property and hence be in a position to pay more in taxes, they had to acquire the literacy and educational skills that could be made available only through public schools funded by taxes on those Southerners who did own property, namely, the whites.

In order to gain security in their daily lives and the equality under the law promised them, blacks also had to gain political offices. But in pushing for political power within the Republican party, the freedman only gave native whites another reason to leave the party. For whites, already convinced that they were being crushed by taxes to support a propertyless class racially inferior to themselves, such demands added a racial insult to an economic injury.

The white exodus from the Republican party soon restored the Democrats to power in those Southern states in which the Republicans had been most dependent on the support of native whites. By 1871, these states—Virginia, Tennessee, North Carolina, and Georgia—were either back under Democratic control or ruled by a coalition of conservative Republicans and Democrats. In Virginia and Tennessee the Democrats formed fusion tickets with disgruntled Republicans drawn from that wing of the party that was most anxious to accommodate Southern white opinion. The basic terms of fusion called for Democratic acceptance of black voting in return for a Republican agreement to drop voting disqualification for ex-Confederates. By aligning themselves with pro-business Republicans, the Democrats employed this strategy so skillfully in Virginia that they were never shut out of power during Reconstruction. Factionalism within the Republican party and the recently restored vote of ex-rebels returned the Democrats to power in Tennessee in 1869, and the next year the Democrats won back the state legislature in North Carolina.

Republican rule in North Carolina had been discredited almost immediately by the failure of the railroads in 1868 to meet interest payments due on their state-backed bonds. Then a surge of violence by the Ku Klux Klan produced a sharp drop in the black vote in 1870. When William Holden, the Republican governor, declared martial law in an effort to stamp out the Klan, he was impeached and forced to flee the state. In Georgia the conservative leaders of the Southern white Republicans were always alienated from the party's Northern and black wing. In 1868, they had attempted to unseat black state legislators on the grounds that blacks were ineligible to hold office under the new constitution. This blatant attempt to reject a political role for blacks delayed the readmission of Georgia to the Union until 1870 and starkly revealed why the Democrats were able to defeat the divided Republicans just one year later.

By 1871, the southern Republicans were under intense pressure even in those states in which they still held power. This pressure was exerted in its most vicious form by the Ku Klux Klan and a host of other paramilitary organizations. The Klan, the best known of these groups, originated as a fraternal organization of Confederate veterans in 1866. Once congressional Reconstruction was in place, the Klan grew rapidly, and it began to operate as the military arm of the Democratic party and as a terroristic weapon of labor discipline on behalf of local planters. The targets of violence and assassination could be any active Republican, but the freedmen were singled out, both as voters and as workers. Night riders whipped and brutalized the freedmen and raped their women. Political murders became commonplace, and blacks had every reason to fear for their lives or the safety of their families if they continued to vote Republican. On the other hand, and as related in the congressional

The terrorism of the KKK was directed mainly against blacks active in the Southern Republican party.

testimony of Granville Bennett, an Alabama freedman, local whites told the blacks that "if we should vote the democratic ticket, they would insure us Ku-Kluxism would be done with, and there would be no more of it."[16]

The Klan's terror was a savage testimonial to the early successes of political reconstruction in the South. Unwilling to offer the freedmen any meaningful rights of equality that could wean them from the Republicans, and infuriated by the efforts of the freedmen to secure the best possible labor arrangements for themselves as renters and croppers, the planters resorted to violence to regain the control they had lost after emancipation. Klan activity was especially rampant in the South Carolina upcountry, and here the planters used the Klan to prevent the freedmen from renting land and to force them into surrendering part of their wages to help pay the land tax.

Like all successful guerrilla movements, the Klan had widespread community support in the countryside. Planters could count on embittered white farmers to turn with a vengeance on blacks, especially in politically contested and racially balanced areas in which common whites were losing their land and becoming tenants. In short, the Klan also represented a response to the economic failure of Reconstruction. As their debts mounted and their hold on the land weakened, whites increasingly feared blacks as competitors for the landed resources needed for economic independence. Thus, it was no accident that freedmen who had achieved a measure of economic success were often singled out for special retribution from the Klan.

Most of the Southern Republican governments failed in their attempts to protect themselves and their black voters from Klan violence. The Republicans dreaded the possibility of touching off a race war by enrolling and calling out black militias to combat the Klan, and they were worried that any forceful military response would totally alienate the whites they were still trying to conciliate. Only in Tennessee, Arkansas, and Texas, states where the Republicans could rely on a largely Unionist white base of party supporters to join the militias, was the Klan effectively suppressed without federal intervention. Elsewhere, the Republican governors were reduced to pleading for military assistance from Washington. Congress did respond in 1870 and 1871 with a series of enforcement acts, legislation based on the enforcement clauses of the 14th and 15th amendments. The first act prohibited state officials from interfering with a citizen's right to vote on grounds of race, and the second established federal machinery for the supervision of congressional elections in large cities (this was aimed primarily against Democratic city machines in the North). The third Enforcement Act of April 1871 was known as the Ku Klux Klan Act. It outlawed the Klan and other conspiratorial organizations that sought to deprive citizens of their civil and political rights under the Constitution. In restoring law and order in areas which he declared to be in a state of insurrection, the president was empowered to suspend the writ of *habeas corpus* and send in federal troops.

Armed with this legislation, the Grant administration was able to break the back of, if not destroy, the Klan. The federal crackdown hit hardest in South Carolina, when Grant revoked the writ of *habeas corpus* in nine upcountry counties.

Federal marshals and grand juries were also quite active in North Carolina and Mississippi. All told, some 3,000 indictments were handed down, and about 600 convictions were obtained. The government's basic strategy was to offer suspended sentences in return for information leading to the conviction of the Klan's local leadership. Despite the relatively small number of convictions, the organizational structure of the Klan was significantly weakened, and the level of violence in the South dropped markedly in the immediate aftermath of the Klan cases.

At least in the short run the success of the federal offensive against the Klan made it safer for Southern blacks to exercise their constitutional rights. The badly shaken confidence of the southern Republican parties was also momentarily restored. Still, there was no denying that the Klan had glaringly exposed the inability of these parties to protect the lives and property of their supporters without resorting to outside intervention. It was now obvious that their existence, let alone their success, was utterly dependent on the willingness of northern Republicans to come to their assistance. Yet, and in large measure because of the unprecedented extension of federal jurisdiction over criminal activity encompassed in the Ku Klux Klan Act, several northern Republicans had already come to the conclusion that their party had gone too far in broadening national authority.

The most prominent of these Republicans was Lyman Trumbull, the author of the Freedmen's Bureau bill and civil rights legislation of 1866. He would soon join other Republicans who formerly had supported congressional Reconstruction in founding a new third party, the Liberal Republicans. Republican unity over their Southern policy was breaking down. As it did, Republican rule in the South lost the Northern support that was indispensable to its survival.

THE GRANT REPUBLICANS AND THE POLITICS OF MONEY

Northern Republicans always viewed their Southern counterparts as something of an embarrassment to the party. At best, they approached the southern Republicans as junior partners in a party whose national power rested on electoral majorities in the Northern states. Precisely because the perceived radicalism of Reconstruction was eroding the party's voting base in the North by 1867, most Republicans had favored the enfranchisement of blacks as a means of relieving the party of an additional responsibility to intervene in Southern affairs. After the passage of the 15th Amendment in 1870, nearly all Republicans agreed that federal intervention to restructure the Southern polity was now over. As for the new Republican parties in the South that rested on the black vote, the national leaders of the party had no great confidence that they would survive for very long. The northern interests of the party, not its poor cousins in the South, always came first in formulating party strategy, and those interests in the Grant administration were overwhelmingly economic in nature. Tariffs, taxation, currency, and subsidies comprised the agenda of the politics of money, and the Republicans in the South were largely shut out of the federal largesse that would have aided them immeasurably in establishing their credibility among Southern voters.

In addition to ignoring the pleas of southern Republicans for organizational support in terms of outside speakers and campaign funds, the dominant northern wing of the party rejected their calls for economic assistance. The war-shattered Southern economy was in dire need of financial aid. Capital was needed to rebuild the levees along the Mississippi River, dredge and clean harbors, repair and extend the railroads, and finance the restoration of the cotton export economy. The South's economic problems were all the more acute because of a severe shortage of credit. The abolition of property in slaves had eliminated the major source of credit for commercial agriculture, and land, the only other significant source of collateral, was too abundant and depressed in value to serve as a basis for loans.

Although the South's need for outside financial assistance was obvious, the northern Republicans refused to meet it. Indeed, they pursued economic policies that undermined from the very beginning the political position of the southern Republicans. During Reconstruction the South received but fifteen to twenty percent of the federal funds available for internal improvements. Northern Republicans persisted in viewing the South as a source of cheap raw materials for the Northern economy, and they had little sympathy for the attempts of the party in the South to promote industrial diversification.

When the Republicans in 1868 repealed a special tax imposed at the end of the war on cotton sold outside the South, they made it clear that they wanted to keep cotton prices low so as to benefit textile manufacturers in New England. In the meantime they retained a stiff excise tax on liquor, which aroused the opposition of isolated farmers in the Southern upcountry, a key constituency for the southern Republicans. For many of these economically strapped farmers, distilled grain was their major cash crop and source of income.

Most important, northern Republicans continued to favor a fiscal policy that exacerbated the South's chronic shortage of credit and currency. During the war the South had lost some one billion dollars in banking capital, and all the money invested in Confederate bonds and currency had become worthless. After the war the South had but a very small share of the national banknotes and greenbacks, the new currency of the war years that now made up the primary supply of money after a prohibitive tax of 10 percent slapped on state banknotes drove this prewar form of money out of circulation. When the national banking system was set up, the total amount of national banknote currency (the paper money that could be issued against federal bonds as security) was limited by law at $300 million to keep inflation in check. Preference in the original allocation of this currency was given to established state banks willing to join the new federal system. This policy virtually guaranteed that the bulk of the national banknotes would be concentrated in the northeast, a capital-rich region with the most developed banking system in the country. Thus, when Southern banks applied for national charters after the war, there was very little of the national banknotes left to be distributed to them. New York and New England alone had received close to sixty percent of the total allocation of the currency. In

1866 the per capita circulation of national banknotes in these states was $33.30; in ten states of the former Confederacy it was $1.10. A similar regional imbalance existed in the circulation of greenbacks, the other paper money issued by the North during the war.

If the capital-starved Southern economy were ever to revive under Republican rule, it needed both a redistribution and an expansion of the nation's money supply. It received neither. Banking and commercial interests in the northeast blocked efforts to modify the national banking system on behalf of Southern needs, and the national leaders of the Republican party adamantly opposed any expansion in the authorized amount of greenbacks. Because the greenbacks were not explicitly backed by gold, and hence had no intrinsic value, they could be exchanged for gold only at a steep discount to their face value. Any significant expansion of the greenbacks, the Republicans feared, would ignite runaway inflation by further cheapening the value of the dollar relative to gold, the money of international exchange.

The northeast had plenty of circulating currency and it also had most of the creditors and bondholders who worried that a glut of greenbacks would drive down the purchasing power of the dollar and the value of the debts owed to them. In the Public Credit Act of 1869, the first legislation signed into law by President Grant, the Republicans reassured bondholders by promising that the federal debt would be paid in gold. The Public Credit Act of 1870 called for the eventual redemption of the greenbacks in gold and pledged in the meantime not to contract further the supply of greenbacks. This act did allow for an additional $10 million in greenbacks, but this was far short of the amount of monetary inflation needed to pump life into the Southern economy.

Parsimonious when it came to Southern needs, congressional Republicans were lavish to the point of recklessness in responding to the wishes of businessmen and private interests in the North. The greatest amount of government aid went to the railroads. In the decade after 1862 the Republicans subsidized the construction of the transcontinental railroads with nearly 100 million acres of public land. Over $60 million in government-backed credit was also provided. These railroads—the Union, Central, and Northern Pacific—serviced the Northern economy. The only transcontinental railroad projected for the South received a relatively small land subsidy in 1871. It then soon became enmeshed in the empire-building schemes of Tom Scott of the Pennsylvania Railroad. This road, the Southern Pacific, finally lost out on the subsidy and was not built until the 1880s.

Northern manufacturers and special interest groups received a host of benefits. Citing first the need to raise revenue to pay for the war and then the fairness of compensating industrialists for high wartime taxes, the Republicans had raised the average tariff rate from nineteen percent to forty-seven percent during the war. Northern factory owners were given a virtual monopoly in the domestic market. Although the business taxes were lifted after 1865, the tariff wall remained. The Wool and Woolens Act of 1867 and the Copper Act of 1869 were written to meet the particular needs of these two industries. The National Mining Act of 1869 was a bonanza for the mining industry. In effect, it handed over to private developers the mineral resources of the public domain. In the decade after the Civil War, the successful lobbying efforts of commercial and transportation interests resulted in a ten-fold increase in congressional appropriations for rivers and harbors aid over the levels of the 1850s. No special interest group was more vital to the political success of the Republicans than the Union army veterans, about one-third of the total Northern electorate after the war. They were rewarded with sizeable pensions which, by 1880, accounted for twenty percent of the spending in the federal budget.

Much of the Republicans' program of government beneficence was initially quite popular with Northern voters. After all, the Republicans had used the public domain to subsidize agriculture and public education as well as the railroads and mining interests. The absence of Southern congressmen during the war enabled the Republicans to pass the Homestead Act of 1862, granting 160 acres of public land to citizens who would occupy it for five years. The Morrill Land Grant Act of the same year gave 30,000 acres of public land per congressman to states establishing public agricultural colleges. All classes in the North, the Republicans believed, would benefit from the new political economy of federal largesse. Very quickly, however, revelations of government scandals besmirched the entire program of government aid. Grantism became synonymous with corruption, and the Republicans were thrown back on the defensive.

The corruption of the Grant years is legendary. Public officials at every level of government and in every region of the nation were all seemingly corrupt or corruptible. "If any one doubts the actual decay of public morality and of public faith," editorialized the *Commercial and Financial Chronicle* in the spring of 1870,

> he has but to watch the journals for a day; and he will scarcely fail to find in them charges that Congressmen, Senators, members of the Cabinet, kindred and friends of the very highest officers of the government, the directors and managers of corporations and of public institutions, the courts of law of a great city or State, and even entire legislative bodies, controlling the interests of millions of people, have sold their votes, influence and power for money, or that which can be exchanged for money.[17]

This remarkably sweeping indictment of political corruption was made, it should be stressed, before the really major scandals of the two Grant administrations hit the country. The most infamous of these involved the Crédit Mobilier, a "dummy" corporation chartered in Pennsylvania to receive construction contracts from the federally chartered Union Pacific Railroad. The same individuals who controlled the Union Pacific controlled the Crédit Mobilier, and they used the Crédit Mobilier to gain windfall profits by awarding themselves construction contracts at highly inflated costs. Oakes Ames, a Republican congressman from Massachusetts and a director of both corporations, peddled cheap stock in the Crédit Mobilier to congressmen as a means of gaining influential political friends for the scheme. The scandal broke in 1872, and several top-ranking Republicans were implicated.

In terms of the number of individuals who took part, the most pervasive

By 1872, Northern reformers were depicting the Grant administration as an orgy of corruption in which the venal politicians had sold out to special interest groups.

scandal in the Grant years involved the Whiskey Rings, which operated in St. Louis and other cities where large amounts of whiskey were distilled. The federal excise tax on whiskey, originally a special wartime tax, was retained after the war and raised to $2 a gallon in 1866. Since the production cost of whiskey was only about 20 cents a gallon, whiskey was taxed at an effective rate of 1,000 percent. Indeed, the tax was so prohibitively high that it virtually invited distillers to find a way to avoid paying it. Distillers did so by offering bribes and kickbacks to federal tax collectors and local Republican party officials. Such corruption was cost effective for the distillers and a source of campaign funds for the Republicans.

There was nothing new about political corruption in the Grant era. The politics of the 1850s were filled with outcries against it, and bribes, kickbacks, selling of votes, and influence-peddling had been facts of political life since at least the creation of the mass parties in the Jacksonian period. Measured as a percentage of federal funds stolen or embezzled, corruption by one estimate actually declined in the generation after the Civil War. However, because so much more money was now involved in the larger federal budgets, the dollar amount of corruption undoubtedly did soar. The postwar budgets remained at a level five times greater than federal expenditures in the late 1850s.

As first had become evident when the budget exploded during the war, public officials suddenly had wide discretionary powers over the dispersal and awarding of increasingly large sums of public money. Even by the lax standards of the twentieth century, the line between private gain and public service was very blurred in the nineteenth century. Otherwise honest politicians saw nothing wrong with accepting money or special favors from business interests in return for granting them preferential treatment when it came to legislation or government contracts. During and after the war these mutually accommodating and long-standing relationships merged into an informal business–political alliance that spawned most of the era's corruption.

The postwar municipal, state, and federal governments were ill-equipped to deal with the deluge of demands placed on them by businesses and other private interest groups. Typical in this regard was the situation in Congress. At any given time about half of its members were freshmen. Turnover rates were very high, and congressmen lacked any professional staffs to call on in the drafting of legislation and any formal system of rules or seniority to guide them in bringing bills up for a vote. The demands on their time were enormous, especially from office seekers clamoring for a patronage job and veterans or their widows trying to get a pension. Meanwhile, the territorial expansion of the Union between 1850 and 1870 had resulted in the admission of seven new states and the creation of nine new territories, and hence there was a corresponding increase in the demand for federal services in the areas of law courts, Indian policy, and post offices. The proliferation of government aid to railroads, telegraph companies, and steamship operators involved congressmen in endless negotiations with competing business groups anxious to cut themselves in on the economic expansion underwritten with federal funds. On top of all this were the unprecedented political and social responsibilities assumed by Congress in its Reconstruction policy. In other words, the system of governing was overloaded, and this was the political setting in which corruption flourished.

Overworked congressmen, struggling to cope with a legislative agenda of bills four times heavier than that of the 1850s, were the natural allies of businessmen or their lobbyists struggling to call the attention of the same congressmen to bills they wanted enacted or contracts they wanted granted. Deals were repeatedly struck and cash often changed hands. This was the basic pattern of corruption in Congress, state legislatures, and city councils, and it persisted because it enabled an overburdened system to meet widespread demands for rapid economic growth and a generous distribution of benefits.

THE LIBERAL REPUBLICANS

Corruption was cited by the dissident Republicans who established the Liberal Republican party in 1872 as just the most blatant evidence of the ways in which their former party had abused the public trust under Grant's leadership. The liberal reformers were appalled by Grant's attempt to annex Santo Domingo (now the Dominican Republic) in 1870. This scheme, which brought together land speculators, naval officers in search of a base in the Caribbean, a tottering dictator hoping to be bailed out by the Americans, and a president with a sincere, but misplaced, desire to improve the lot of blacks on Santo Domingo, drove a wedge between Grant and such future Liberal Republicans as Charles Sumner and Carl Schurz. Sumner, the chairman of the Senate Foreign Relations Committee, successfully blocked the ratification of the annexation treaty. He feared that the annexation of Santo Domingo would be but a prelude to the American occupation of the neighboring country of Haiti, one of only two black-controlled republics in the world. Schurz and most of the other Republicans in opposition were worried less about the political independence of blacks and more about the chicanery and corruption they saw lurking behind the strained arguments in favor of the treaty. Indeed, the case against annexation was based primarily on the racist assertion that blacks were unfit for the responsibilities of self-government.

In opposing the Santo Domingo treaty, the liberal reformers also made clear their growing dissatisfaction with Reconstruction. In both instances they stated that the Grant Republicans were endangering the safety and stability of the republic by misusing governmental power in an attempt to incorporate into political citizenship an ignorant and poverty-stricken race of blacks who were incapable of assuming the full responsibilities of citizenship. The Liberal Republicans had overwhelmingly supported the causes of antislavery and black suffrage. They still clung to their original reformist goals throughout Reconstruction, but they insisted that the limits of using public power to attain those goals had been reached in the 13th, 14th, and 15th amendments. The Slave Power had been broken, and blacks, now equipped with the principle of equality before the law, would have to pursue their own self-interests without any additional federal assistance if they wished to advance themselves.

From the perspective of the Liberal Republicans, continued federal intervention on behalf of Southern blacks was not only unnecessary, but was also a positive deterrent to the restoration of good government in the postwar South. They charged that such intervention under the Grant Republicans was inherently counterproductive because it attempted to prop up the political power of a poor agrarian class that lacked the intelligence and self-discipline required to make informed political decisions. At the same time, the South's "natural" leaders, its men of property and cultivated intellect, were excluded from holding power by the political disabilities imposed by congressional Reconstruction. The inevitable result, according to the Liberal Republicans, was a corrupt-ridden mockery of the democratic process. Although conceding that the Klan was occasionally guilty of violent excesses, the reformers explained these actions as the outcry of a white race suffering under an unconscionable tyranny.

The reformers' critique of Reconstruction also reflected their estrangement from the new organizational style of politics that was becoming dominant in the Republican party during the Grant years. Second-generation Republicans, most of whom were young professionals who climbed rapidly in party ranks as a result of their war records as commissioned officers, led the party shift from a politics of ideological intensity to one of organizational blandness. They downplayed ideological issues of public policy and relied instead on federal patronage and business support as props for the institutional strength of the party. After all, the ideological battles that had given birth to the Republican party were apparently all settled once the party's policy of Reconstruction was in place, and the efforts of some state leaders to push for extensive reform in the North had backfired when the Democrats seized on the issue of black suffrage to discredit them. These newer Republicans, and the business-oriented older Republicans who joined them, were dubbed the Stalwarts. What mattered most to them was the party organization itself, not its ideals; compromise, not principled opposition; and careers, not causes. They became the dominant power in the party after 1867 as the ideological cohesion of the radicals broke down once the party agreed on a political settlement with the defeated Confederate South.

Nearly all of the Liberal Republicans had lost out to the Stalwarts in terms of party influence and power. The result, in their eyes, was a party bloated with corruption that cynically exploited the Reconstruction issue to divert Northern attention from the reform measures the country desperately needed. Everything about the organizational politics of the party regulars reeked of corruption or class favoritism to the reformers. The Grant Republicans manipulated patronage to reward party supporters, and they assessed the salaries of office holders to build up a financial war chest for election campaigns. They tailored protective tariffs to meet the needs of specific industries, and they showered benefits on corporations whose monopolistic powers were already squeezing out the independent entrepreneur. They talked of restoring stability and honesty to the nation's finances by returning to a specie basis for the currency, while in fact they refused to take the greenbacks out of circulation. The reformers accused the Grant Republicans of polluting the democratic process throughout the nation by catering to the demands of the ignorant and irresponsible lower classes. The crusade for equal rights had gone too far for the Liberal Republicans. As Charles Francis Adams, Jr., lamented in 1869, "Universal Suffrage can only mean in plain English the government of ignorance and vice."[18]

Liberal Republicanism was as much a revolt against the whole concept of the activist state as it was a reaction against any specific policies of the Grant administration. Their definition of reform entailed a scaling back, not an extension, of government activism. They denigrated the new mass electorate of blacks in the South and immigrants in the North as a source of corruption, and they wanted to limit its impact on government policy by concentrating power in the hands of educated gentlemen of property. They promised to bring back honest, efficient government through a program that included a full restoration of political rights to all Southern whites and an end to federal interference with their domestic affairs; a sharply lower tariff; a return to the gold dollar; and the implementation of civil service reform to root out incompetent and corrupt party hacks and replace them with nonpartisan appointees who were awarded their government jobs on the basis of merit. At the state level the reformers pushed for lower taxes, and they argued that the pernicious effects of universal suffrage could be reversed only by imposing property and educational qualifications on voting.

When the Liberal Republicans met at their national convention in Cincinnati in 1872, it seemed as if everyone on the political outs with the Grant administration was present. Disgruntled professional politicians, disillusioned idealists, disgusted New England patricians, and disaffected former Democrats from Republican organizations in the Border South all jostled each other on the convention floor. The party they formed was hopelessly confused from the very beginning. Political insiders controlled the convention, and they settled on Horace Greeley, the popular, but eccentric, Republican editor of the New York *Tribune,* for the party's presidential nomination.

No friend of a lower tariff, currency deflation, or civil service reform, Greeley was in the anomalous position of heading a party whose platform he repudiated. Still, he had broken with the Grant administration over its alleged subversion of self-government in the South, and this made him attractive to a Democratic party anxious to establish a new image of moderation as a party willing to accept the results of the war and to work for sectional peace. Under the rubric of this New Departure, as it was called, the Democrats endorsed Greeley for the presidency.

The Democrats coopted the Liberal Republican movement, and the hybrid party suffered a resounding defeat in 1872. Greeley was unpopular with southern Democrats because of his earlier stands against slavery, and northern Republicans shunned him as a party renegade. Meanwhile, the Republican regulars were united behind Grant. The economy was back on a prosperous footing in 1872, and the Republicans had adroitly covered their political flank on the issue of sectional reconciliation. In May 1872 the Republicans passed an Amnesty Act, which lifted political penalties for all but a few ex-Confederates. Grant swept the North and lost only six Southern states in 1872. His fifty-six percent share of the popular vote was the highest of any presidential winner between 1828 and 1904.

The New Departure of the Democrats did not return them to power, but it did accelerate the flight of native whites out of the southern Republican parties. Throughout the South in 1872 the Democrats ran fusion tickets with dissident white Republicans, and these tickets served as a halfway station for the return of these Republicans to the Democratic party. In the North as well as the South, the strength of the Democrats was greater than that indicated by the election returns alone. As a consequence of the New Departure, the Democrats could no longer be branded by the Republicans as closet rebels who rejected the political and constitutional settlements that had emerged from the Civil War and Reconstruction. The Democrats had moved back toward the political center of Northern public opinion, and Northerners had backed the Republicans in spite of, not because of, the party's stand on Reconstruction.

The strong suit of the Republicans in 1872 was an economy that was booming once again. When the economy skidded into a depression during the financial panic of 1873, the postwar era of Republican dominance would be over. The stage was then set for the final overthrow of Reconstruction.

NOTES

1. J. C. Levenson et al., (eds.), *The Letters of Henry Adams,* vol. 1 (Cambridge: The Belknap Press of Harvard University Press, 1982), pp. 520, 509.
2. Ibid., vol. 2, p. 19.
3. Ibid., vol. 2, p. 15.
4. Quoted in Ellen Carol Du Bois, "Outgrowing the Compact of the Fathers: Equal Rights, Woman Suffrage, and the United States Constitution, 1820–1878," *Journal of American History,* vol. 74, p. 844, 1989.
5. Lawrence Frederick Kohl and Margaret Crossé Richard (eds.), *Irish Green and Union Blue: The Civil War Letters of Peter Welsh* (New York: Fordham University Press, 1986), pp. 65–66.
6. Quoted in David Montgomery, *Beyond Equality: Labor and the Radical Republicans, 1862–1872* (New York: Alfred A. Knopf, 1967), p. 9.
7. *Commercial and Financial Chronicle,* vol. 2, June 23, 1866.
8. Ibid., vol. 7, July 18, 1868.
9. Quoted in Bruce C. Levine, "Immigrant Workers, 'Equal Rights' and Anti-Slavery: The Germans of Newark, New Jersey," *Labor History,* vol. 25, p. 49, 1984.
10. Frances Mitchell Ross (ed.), " 'A Tie between Us that Time Cannot Sever': The Latta Family Letters, 1855–1872," *Arkansas Historical Quarterly,* vol. 40, p. 46, 1981.
11. Quoted in Leon F. Litwack, *Been in the Storm So Long: The Aftermath of Slavery* (New York: Alfred A. Knopf, 1979), p. 27.
12. Ibid., p. 472.
13. *Report of the Joint Committee of Reconstruction, at the First Session Thirty-Ninth Congress* (Westport Conn.: Negro Universities Press, 1969 [1866]), Part III, p. 174.
14. This incident is related in Robert Garlick Kean, *Inside the Confederate Government* (New York: Oxford University Press, 1957), pp. 209–210.
15. Quoted in Michael Perman, *The Road to Redemption: Southern Politics, 1869–1879* (Chapel Hill: University of North Carolina Press, 1984), p. 34.
16. *Reports of Committees of the House of Representatives for the Second Session of the Forty-Second Congress, 1871–72,* vol. 3 (Washington: Government Printing Office, 1872), p. 1739.
17. *Commercial and Financial Chronicle,* vol. 10, May 7, 1870.
18. Quoted in Michael E. McGerr, *The Decline of Popular Politics: The American North, 1865–1928* (New York: Oxford University Press, 1986), p. 46.

SUGGESTED READINGS

ABBOTT, RICHARD H., *The Republican Party and the South, 1855–1877.* Chapel Hill, N.C.: University of North Carolina Press, 1986.

DU BOIS, ELLEN C., *Feminism and Suffrage.* Ithaca, N.Y.: Cornell University Press, 1978.

DU BOIS, W. E. B., *Black Reconstruction in America.* Cleveland, Ohio: Meridian, 1962.

GILLETTE, WILLIAM, *Retreat from Reconstruction, 1869–1879.* Baton Rouge, La.: Louisiana State University Press, 1979.

JAYNES, GEROLD D., *Branches Without Roots: Genesis of the Black Working Class in the American South, 1862–1882.* New York: Oxford University Press, 1986.

KOLCHIN, PETER, *First Freedom: The Responses of Alabama's Blacks to Emancipation and Reconstruction.* Westport, Conn.: Greenwood, 1972.

LITWACK, LEON F., *Been in the Storm So Long: The Aftermath of Slavery.* New York: Alfred A. Knopf, 1979.

MONTGOMERY, DAVID, *Beyond Equality: Labor and the Radical Republicans, 1862–1872.* New York: Alfred A. Knopf, 1967.

MORRIS, ROBERT C., *Reading, 'Riting, and Reconstruction: The Education of Freedmen in the South, 1861–1870.* Chicago, Ill.: University of Chicago Press, 1981.

OLSEN, OTTO H. (ed.), *Reconstruction and Redemption in the South.* Baton Rouge, La.: Louisiana State University Press, 1980.

OUBRE, CLAUDE F., *Forty Acres and a Mule: The Freedmen's Bureau and Black Landowner-ship.* Baton Rouge, La.: Louisiana State University Press, 1978.

PERMAN, MICHAEL, *The Road to Redemption: Southern Politics, 1869–1879.* Chapel Hill, N.C.: University of North Carolina Press, 1984.

SEIP, TERRY L., *The South Returns to Congress.* Baton Rouge, La.: Louisiana State University Press, 1983.

SUMMERS, MARK W., *Railroads, Reconstruction, and the Gospel of Prosperity.* Princeton, N.J.: Princeton University Press, 1984.

THOMPSON, MARGARET S., *The "Spider Web": Congress and Lobbying in the Age of Grant.* Ithaca, N.Y.: Cornell University Press, 1985.

9

America
at the
Centennial

"I am no alarmist; far from it; but the next great contest...in this country is to be between capital and labor. Unless the servants of the people act wisely, it may be precipitated."[1] Such warnings as this one from Senator George W. Wright, an Iowa Republican, were commonplace when the 43rd Congress assembled in December 1873. The longest economic depression in American history, one that would persist for the next five years, had hit with frightening speed in the fall of 1873. The depression reduced Reconstruction to a nagging headache for most Northerners and focused public concerns on class issues relating to labor and capital. By touching off waves of industrial unrest and agrarian protests that propertied classes in the North viewed as a fundamental challenge to the rights of property, the depression also paved the way for the final reconciliation between the North and the South. Most significantly, the Republican party now conceded that rebellious Northern workers had replaced rebellious Southern whites as the gravest threat to the stability of the Union.

The remaining Republican governments in the South did not long survive the onset of the depression. The shaky railroad projects so heavily promoted by southern Republicans collapsed, and debt-ridden state governments were forced to sell their rail investments to Northern financiers at bankruptcy prices. The political stock of the southern Republicans also plummeted. Most of the Northern planters who had survived the labor disorganization and poor crops of 1866 and 1867 now permanently left the South. With their political base reduced almost exclusively to poor blacks, southern Republicans were more dependent than ever on outside assistance from northern Republicans. Little support was forthcoming.

The Republican majority in the North quickly became a political casualty of the depression. The Democrats, having already eliminated the Republicans' two-thirds majority in Congress in 1870, regained control of Congress in 1874 for the first time since the late 1850s. The Republicans, the party caught in power when the depression hit, were now fighting for their political lives. As part of their strategy for holding onto the presidency for 1876, they abandoned the Republican parties in the South. Those parties had become an albatross around the neck of the Grant Republicans and a powerful symbol of the political corruption, fiscal extravagance, and misguided government activism that business and propertied interests in the North blamed for the coming of the depression. In the minds of the Northern middle class, black field hands in the South were now linked with immigrant factory workers in the North as members of a swelling mob of the poor who threatened civic order and the rights of property.

The depression intensified the reaction against the egalitarian, activist side of the Republicans' free-labor ideology and thus was instrumental in bringing an end to Reconstruction. After exploring these themes, this chapter will focus on the centennial election of 1876 and the way in which it marked an end to a cycle in American history that had begun with the sectional crisis of 1850. The old Civil War–Reconstruction issues that had divided political and economic elites along sectional lines for the preceding quarter of a century were finally laid to rest. These elites closed ranks in what is known as the Compromise of 1877, a political and sectional agreement that settled the disputed election of 1876. In return for recognizing the Republican Rutherford B. Hayes as president, southern Democrats received assurances that the Republicans would abandon any attempts at using federal power to enforce the rights of blacks in the South and to sustain the southern Republican parties that were dependent on the black vote. Reconstruction was over. Its continued support was politically counterproductive for the Republican party and its propertied interests. Republicans now agreed with Southern planters that lower-class demands for democratic change, whether by blacks in the South or farmers and workers in the North, were a threat to social order and an impediment to an economic recovery from the depression of the 1870s.

THE PANIC OF 1873

The first Grant administration coincided with an economic boom. The cyclical postwar contraction gave way in 1869 to four years of spectacular growth. The manufacturing and mining sectors of the Northern economy, both of which enjoyed increases in excess of fifty percent in the value of production, were the chief beneficiaries of the renewed prosperity. At the height of the boom in 1872, industrial production had climbed thirty-five percent above the stagnant levels of 1868. In combination with a steady drop in the general price index after the inflationary period of the war, the strong demand for industrial labor resulted in an increase of about one-third for the real wages of nonfarm employees between 1866 and 1872.

The railroads spearheaded the boom, and their tremendous expansion illustrated how the war had acted as a catalyst for the maturing of America's industrial economy. During the war the Northern railroads utilized their full carrying capacity for the first time. The prodigious demands on transportation facilities to move the troops, munitions, and supplies swallowed up in the Union war effort doubled the freight tonnage carried by rail. Although freight rates generally declined as the railroads competed for business, the volume of traffic was so great that the first substantial earnings and stock dividends of many lines were by-products of the war years. The major lines generated enough income to embark on programs of technological modernization and to build up capital reserves for postwar expansion. They standardized gauges, double-tracked heavily used east–west thoroughfares, built larger and more efficient terminals at transshipment points, and switched to more powerful coal-burning locomotives. Under the aggressive leadership of Thomas Scott, whose managerial talents were tapped by Lincoln for the post of Assistant Secretary of War, the Pennsylvania Railroad completed the first through trunk line between Chicago and the Atlantic coast when it acquired the Pittsburgh, Fort Wayne, and Chicago railroad.

Total rail mileage doubled within eight years of the end of the war. The frantic pace of construction was spurred both by the massive federal subsidies for the transcontinental lines and the expansionist plans of rail tycoons anxious to emulate the Pennsylvania Railroad by acquiring monopolistic control over highly profitable east–west rail corridors. This burst of rail construction drove forward the development of the entire economy. The railroads opened up the settlement of the trans-Mississippi West, expanded the range of marketing opportunities for both farmers and manufacturers, and sparked an upsurge in the output of coal, iron, and steel. They were at the cutting edge of innovations in industrial technology and corporate organization, and the national market that they began to develop in the decade after the Civil War was the single most crucial factor in the emergence of the United States as the world's leading industrial power by the end of the nineteenth century. However, for all this spectacular growth, the postwar transition from agrarian to industrial capitalism occurred within a cycle of booms and busts, and the first and the longest economic downturn came in the fall of 1873.

The depression of the 1870s was set off by the failure in September 1873 of Jay Cooke & Co., one of the nation's largest and most respected banking firms. Cooke, the great financier of the Union war effort, had become overextended in railroad securities. The postwar expansion of the railroads created a virtually insatiable demand for capital to finance new construction. Some $2.5 billion was sunk into railroads between 1867 and 1873, a sum greater than the expenditures of the federal government during the same seven-year period. By the early 1870s, when railroad financing had become a speculative mania, investors began to shy away from any new investments. Public confidence was shaken by the Crédit

Moblier scandal, Congress was cutting back on its subsidies, and railroads as a whole had all the earmarks of an overbuilt industry. As a result, Cooke, the financial underwriter for the Northern Pacific, was unable to sell that railroad's construction bonds. When the bills came due for the construction costs of the Northern Pacific, Cooke paid them with loans drawn on the short-term deposits of New York City banks. The unmarketable bonds were the collateral for these loans, and when a financial crash hit Europe in the spring of 1873, Cooke lost his gamble that he would be able to sell the bonds in Europe.

Cooke was now strapped for funds, and so were the New York banks when the harvesting of the fall crops produced the seasonal demand for the return of money on deposit in New York needed for the purchasing of the crops. The bankers were unable to honor calls for deposits they no longer held, and on September 18, 1873, Cooke & Co. suspended business. Two days later, the New York Stock Exchange closed. The whole economy was now short of money or, more precisely, financial liquidity. The result was a financial panic that, in the words of James Garfield, the Republican chair of the House Committee on Appropriations, "fell with unparalleled weight and suddenness, and swept like a tornado, leaving destruction in its track."[2]

The worst of the panic was over within a month. The Treasury pumped funds into the money markets by purchasing $20 million of government bonds and reissuing $26 million of previously retired greenbacks. Although banking reserves and deposits were rising again by the late fall, the effects of the panic lingered through five years of a depressed economy. Business failures, which stood at 5,830 in 1874, the first full year of the depression, peaked at over 10,000 in 1878, the year the stagnant economy finally turned around.

This prolonged depression was part of a world-wide deflationary trend that was not reversed until the late 1890s. The long boom of the mid-nineteenth century for America and the industrializing nations of western Europe came to a grinding halt in a glut of overproduction. Regional, national, and then international markets had been created through the simultaneous spread of railroads, steamships, and the telegraph. As new farming areas and manufacturing techniques were developed to expand production for these enlarged markets, the financial burdens and disruptions of a series of major wars—the American Civil War, the Austro-Prussian War of 1866, and the Franco-Prussian War of 1870–1871—forced governments into inflationary programs of deficit-spending that expanded the supply of capital available to finance economic growth. When the overextended structure of international credit showed signs of cracking as financial panics swept through Europe and the United States in 1873, frightened governments responded by turning to deflationary monetary policies and recommitted themselves to the belief that the major currencies had to be freely convertible into specie, and most preferably into gold. Money was tight after the panics, and this fiscal conservatism made it even tighter. Production continued to outstrip a money supply tied to a metallic standard. Prices fell, and profit margins were eroded. Farmers, workers, and businessmen throughout the industrialized western world were pitted against each other in a ruthless

The panic of 1873 was portrayed in this cartoon as a giant scavenger cleaning out the financial garbage from Wall Street.

competition to maintain their shares in markets unable to absorb profitably all the goods being produced.

The brunt of the depression in America, as well as Europe, fell on industrial workers. Wages fell by fifteen percent, though the overall decline in prices kept the drop in real wages to about eight percent. More devastating was the massive unemployment. Under normal conditions, one-third of the male labor force in the postwar economy was out of work for three or four months out of the year. Now, even highly skilled mechanics previously in great demand were laid off. There are no uniform, reliable statistics on unemployment for the nineteenth century, but by the end of 1874 contemporaries were estimating that the panic had cost one million jobs. This estimate would translate into an unemployment rate of close to fifteen percent. When swelled by the numbers of irregular, seasonal workers, the resulting army of unemployed looking for jobs during the slack winter months in the mid-1870s was at least one-quarter of all available workers.

Workers in the railroads and their subsidiary industries were hit the hardest. Within a year of the panic, over 100 railroads were in default of interest payments on half a billion dollars worth of bonds. Unable to market bonds to cover their capital outlays, the railroads drastically slashed their construction budgets, and new rail construction fell by two-thirds between 1873 and 1875. Close to 500,000 rail jobs were lost by the fall of 1874, and a comparable number of coal miners and iron and steel workers were let go. The output of coal and pig iron production fell in tandem with the losses in their rail-related markets. As early as the spring of 1874, forty percent of the pig iron furnaces were closed. Over 100,000 steel workers were suddenly without jobs when half of the rolling mills shut their doors. Prices in all the basic industries plunged in 1874, and they kept falling until late in the decade. The depression fed on itself as the layoffs reduced the annual wages of labor by $200 million and consumers cut back on their purchases by twenty-five percent.

Workers fortunate enough to hold onto their jobs suffered hard times when employers repeatedly slashed wages. Labor resisted in a series of long, bitter strikes that the business community and most property holders shrilly denounced as labor's declaration of class warfare against capital. The rail strikes of 1874 were followed in 1875 by walkouts among textile workers in New England, coal miners in Pennsylvania and the Midwest, and iron workers in the industrial region around Pittsburgh. With the exception of some victories won by the Brotherhood of Locomotive Engineers, labor was defeated in most of the major strikes. Management hired strikebreakers from among blacks and recently arrived immigrants, deployed their own private armed forces of company police, and patiently waited until the striking workers were forced to choose a job at reduced wages over outright starvation. Workers' cooperatives and trade unions were decimated. As a share of the overall labor force, union membership fell by ninety percent after the panic, and, by 1880, fewer than one in a hundred workers belonged to a union.

Despite falling prices for foodstuffs, uncounted numbers of the unemployed were unable to afford the necessities of life for themselves or their families. They congregated in the major Northern cities looking for jobs that simply were not to be had. Bread lines and soup kitchens appeared, and the most desperate cases received some private charity. But demands for public employment on new construction projects were rebuffed, and when the unemployed mounted mass protests for "bread or work," rattled city authorities broke up the gatherings with the armed force of the police.

As the depression deepened, business and middle-class attitudes toward labor turned increasingly ugly and mean. In 1875, Benjamin F. Nourse, a member of the very conservative National Board of Trade, admitted that the surge in unemploy-

Part of the unemployed army in the depression of the 1870s is shown here lining up for a meal at a New York City poorhouse.

ment meant that "many thousand families will be nearer to hunger than for many years" and that "the circle of enforced idleness, disability, and poverty widens daily."[3] Yet, the business press ever more frantically decried not only the attempts of workers to protect their wages through strikes but also the efforts of charity to alleviate the misery of the unemployed. Typical was the response of the *Commercial and Financial Chronicle* in the spring of 1875 to strikes by the building-trade workers in Brooklyn.

> During the winter these very laborers have subsisted, to a great extent, on charity, and they seem to have become so demoralized, so enamored of the charms of living without work, that they now refuse to labor for less than $2.50 a day, or to work more than eight hours a day at any price.

These "mischievous and violent features of modern industrial life," concluded the *Chronicle,* could only be prevented "by stopping the domination of the pestilent ignorance in which these strikes breed and fester and spread."[4] In short, strikes were now widely viewed as a social disease spawned by the unreasoning ignorance of workers deluded enough to engage in them. Labor leaders were denounced as social outlaws and the unemployed as shiftless malcontents too lazy to work.

Although the depression did not hit farmers as suddenly or severely as it did industrial workers, falling farm prices after 1873 did trigger a wave of agrarian protests. The Civil War and the immediate postwar years had been a golden age of prosperity for Northern farmers. Buoyed by the demands of Union armies and of European countries undergoing a series of poor harvests, the prices of corn and wheat, their two main staples, were at historic highs. Prices first cracked in 1869, a year of normal harvests in Europe. Then, and virtually across the board, farm commodities fell in reaction to the panic of 1873. The price for wheat, the major cash crop west of the Mississippi, skidded by forty percent between 1873 and 1880. Economic discontent now fused with the traditional antimonopoly and antibanking sentiments of many western farmers to ignite a political revolt that threatened Republican hegemony in the Midwest.

The farmers focused their anger on railroads, middlemen, bankers, and the politicians who allegedly gave these economic agents monopolistic powers over rural producers. Courted with financial subsidies and hailed in the rhetoric of local boosterism in the years just after the war, the railroads were now attacked as heartless corporations that robbed rural producers of their livelihoods. Much of this anger sprang from the realization of farmers that they no longer controlled their economic destinies. The freight rates charged by the nearest available railroad often meant the difference between a profit or loss for a farmer in the prairie country of the Midwest. Grain dealers, who marketed the farmer's crop, elevator operators, who stored it, and bankers, who supplied the credit to grow it, all wielded tremendous economic power in agricultural communities.

Local producers and shippers in midwestern towns whose economies were disrupted by the coming of the railroads joined farmers in the antimonopoly crusade of the early 1870s. The intensified competition produced by cheap rail transportation broke down the local monopolies of small-town merchants, manufacturers, and craftsmen. They now had to compete with goods and services from outside their previously sheltered local markets, and the lowest-cost producer or shipper set the prices that all competitors had to match in the regional and national markets tied together by the rails. Merchants in river towns had to scramble to make up for trade lost to rivals in interior towns opened up by the railroads. These merchants were the allies of the farmers in fighting against the price differentials charged by the railroads for long and short hauls. Rates for long, continuous hauls, where competition was keen among railroads trying to attract high-volume shippers, were much cheaper than for the short hauls serviced by just one railroad, and they worked to the advantage of merchants in terminal-market cities and of farmers nearest to eastern markets.

The wealthier farmers with larger operations reacted to the falling agricultural prices of the 1870s by preaching the virtues of crop and livestock diversification and extolling the cost efficiencies of a more rationalized, businesslike approach to farming. Smaller, more hard-pressed farmers rushed into the Grange. Founded in 1867 by two government clerks, Oliver H. Kelley and William Saunders, and known officially as the Patrons of Husbandry, the Grange was originally a fraternal organization dedicated to overcoming the social isolation of farmers, especially in the South. Initially indifferent to the Grange, western farmers first joined in significant numbers in 1872 and then in a stampede in 1873. In combination with such militant pressure groups as the Illinois Farmers' Association, formed in 1873, the Grange became a significant new political force in midwestern politics.

In the early 1870s the Granger movement was a vehicle for agrarian protest in the Midwest.

The agrarian protesters attacked the railroads as chartered monopolies that corrupted the legislative process and threatened the republican liberties of the people. The radical wing of the protesters resurrected the imagery of the Money Power, located its conspiratorial source in Wall Street, and called for the abolishment of the National Banking system and its replacement with government-issued greenbacks convertible into low-interest government bonds. Such a program would presumably lighten the debt burden of farmers and raise farm prices through a flexible supply of cheap and plentiful money that would place the needs of the people above the monopolistic profits of the private bankers. The radicals also demanded that state legislatures revoke the railroad charters and set up state commissions to run the railroads on an equitable basis for all the producers and consumers.

Branded as communistic, this program of antimonopoly greenbackism was far too radical for most of the farmers and the town merchants who allied themselves to the agrarian protest. The state leaders of the Grange were much more comfortable with focusing on building cooperative purchasing and marketing organizations for farmers. Aside from some expansion of the greenbacks, the major demand of the agrarian insurgency focused on Granger-supported legislation for the creation of state boards with regulatory power over the rates charged by railroads and operators of grain elevators.

The fall elections in 1873 cut into the Republican majorities in the Midwest. Angry Republican farmers voted for fusion tickets put together by the Democrats, and these Antimonopoly parties, as they usually called themselves, picked up a sizeable protest vote in Minnesota, Wisconsin, Illinois, and Iowa. These reform coalitions successfully pressured legislatures into passing bills for rate regulation, but they did not initiate a permanent political realignment. Most of the bolting Republican farmers soon returned to their party when freight rates, their major complaint, steadily declined after 1873. Meanwhile, the Democrats claimed agrarian protest as their own party issue and absorbed the remaining Republican defectors.

In the Midwest and elsewhere, the responses to the financial panic quickly polarized into battles between inflationists wanting more greenbacks and deflationists demanding a return to a specie currency. These struggles over currency also drew the line between advocates of government activism on one side and of government retrenchment on the other side. Thus, the interminable financial debates that dominated the session of the 43rd Congress in the winter of 1873–1874 were also part of a larger political debate over the role that the federal government should play in coping with the depression and with social questions in general.

Farmers, workers, small entrepreneurs, and credit-hungry manufacturers, who needed to expand production in order to survive, generally favored an inflationary policy based on soft money, that is, the issuing of more greenbacks. What they wanted, as summarized by Senator Wright of Iowa, was "a homogeneous currency, and enough for their wants in view of the increase of our wealth, population, and trade."[5] In their most telling argument, the inflationists stressed that the nation's per-capita money supply had fallen from $30 in 1865 to just over half that a decade later. Arrayed against them were bondholders, creditors, merchants, and well-established manufacturers concerned about the high domestic costs of production—groups who would economically benefit from deflation or not be hurt by it—and all those for whom "sound" money had assumed immense symbolic importance.

The advocates of hard money were dead certain that paper money not redeemable in specie was a fraud and a stain on the nation's honor. "How," rhetorically asked Justin Morrill, a Republican from Vermont, "can we expect to train up a conscientious people where the Government itself gives an example of a daily affront to the true standard of the commercial world by the issue and reissue of paper 'legal tenders,' notoriously above their value in any market, at home or abroad?" Since he believed such money inherently corrupted a nation's morals, Morrill regarded greenbacks as the reason why "work seems to be going out of fashion, and jockeyism is becoming the sole autocrat of the times."[6] For the deflationists, the greenbacks symbolized all the disturbing, speculative excesses of the postwar period, and because they allegedly distorted any true system of values, the greenbacks were also made the scapegoat for labor agitation. Workers going out on strike for the eight-hour day or higher wages had been duped into believing that the false, greenback-inflated prosperity after the war would last forever.

The soft and hard money factions had dramatically different explanations for the panic of 1873 and the persistence of the depression. For the inflationists, the panic was caused by a credit squeeze ultimately traceable to the lack of enough circulating currency. Bankers and railroad promoters had recklessly speculated with the reserves of the National Banking system concentrated in New York, and when their schemes collapsed in the fall of 1873, the economy was paralyzed. For the deflationists, the culprit was the federal government, not private businessmen, and the cause of the panic was too much, not too little, paper money. It was self-evident to Reuben Fenton, a Republican from New York, that "inflated and inconvertible paper money leads to an expansion of debt, visionary schemes, wild speculation, and extravagance, and at last to frightful disasters and wide-spread distress."[7]

Starting from the premise that money is whatever medium of exchange a government declares to be a standard of payment, that is, a dollar is what the government says is a dollar, the inflationists wanted the federal government to lead the economy out of the depression by issuing more greenbacks in order to lower interest rates and raise commodity prices. The contractionists began from the opposite premise. Money to them had to be a currency convertible into a precious metal with an intrinsic and fixed value. The section of the country from which they were disproportionately drawn, the Northeast, had plenty of money. Ironically, much of that money consisted of checks, bank deposits, and clearing-house certificates between financial institutions, forms of money that were just as nonconvertible and nonmetallic as the greenbacks that the inflationists wanted.

Nonetheless, the contractionists insisted that the business confidence necessary to bring back prosperity could be gained only if the federal government put all the nation's currency back on a specie basis. Despite the fact that the supply of greenbacks had not expanded since the end of the war, they believed that the excessive issuing of greenbacks had created the speculative conditions that touched off the panic. Thus, it followed that a return to the gold standard would restore financial stability and pave the way for a recovery based on sound monetary values.

The first session of the 43rd Congress responded to the depression by doing nothing. This in itself was a victory for the fiscal conservatives, most businessmen, and their intellectual supporters among eastern academicians and middle-class reformers. These groups preached an economic philosophy which warned against any popular input into the running of the economy. By defining their economic beliefs as no less than iron laws of nature, they appealed to Americans of all sorts who were searching for doctrines which promised to restore stability in the midst of the social conflicts of the 1870s. According to the economic conservatives, immutable, "natural" laws of supply and demand automatically regulated the economy with a rational impartiality which ultimately rewarded all individuals for pursuing their own economic self-interests. Thus, any government interference with these eternal laws of supply and demand, especially in deviating from gold as the intrinsic standard of exchange and value, was bound to upset the normal, self-regulating workings of the economy and prolong the depression. Indeed, such conservative rhetoric explicitly argued that the popular (and therefore ignorant) basis of American government made politicians inherently unfit to regulate trade or manage the money markets. By the same token, it was argued, any attempt to provide government assistance to those temporarily injured by the depression would only rob individuals of the self-reliance they needed to become productive workers.

Incessant, bipartisan pressure from congressmen from the South and West and a strong lobbying effort by Pennsylvania iron interests did produce a mildly inflationary bill in the spring of 1874. Under its provisions the circulation of national banknotes and greenbacks would have increased by $64 million, about a three percent addition to the nation's currency. Horrified eastern reformers and merchant, banking, and clerical groups launched a counterattack that convinced President Grant to veto the bill. The monetary expansionists were defeated, and all they wound up with was a banking act in June that made minor adjustments in the authorized amount of greenbacks and the reserve requirements for national banknotes.

Grant's veto of the so-called Inflation Bill shattered the patchwork unity the Republicans had been able to achieve on the currency question. The veto was a slap in the face to the Pennsylvania industrialists and the midwestern agrarians in the party. The hopelessly divided Republicans were easy pickings for the Democrats in the congressional elections of 1874. Already the object of the public's wrath over a forty percent retroactive salary increase that Congress had voted itself in 1873, the "salary grab" as it was called, the Republicans now had to pay the full political price for being in power when the depression struck.

The result was a party debacle. A Republican majority of 110 seats in the House was converted into a deficit of sixty seats. The Democrats had made the largest single gain by any party in any nineteenth-century congressional election. The Republicans barely held onto the Senate, and they suffered heavy losses in state and local elections. Although the depressed economy, not Reconstruction, was easily the dominant issue in the elections, Southern whites interpreted the Republican setbacks as a Northern repudiation of what was left of congressional Reconstruction in the South. The final stage in the overthrow of the Southern Republican parties now got under way.

THE END OF RECONSTRUCTION

The depression of the 1870s was the final blow to the slim chances of survival for the southern Republican parties. Cotton prices fell by half between 1872 and the end of the decade, railroad construction grounded to a halt, and most of the railroads that had been so heavily subsidized by the Republicans went bankrupt and were snatched up by Northern receivers. Business failures steadily mounted. In 1875 more than 1,300 firms in the South went under, and their capital losses totaled $36 million. Both figures were three times above the levels of the early 1870s. Set against this deteriorating economic situation, Democratic calls for government reform and fiscal retrenchment found a receptive audience among white farmers already struggling under a heavy tax burden imposed by the Republicans. The Democrats took full advantage of a taxpayers' revolt against government aid to railroads and other state expenditures and rode the issue of tax relief back to power in Texas in 1873 and in Arkansas a year later. Elsewhere, however, the Democrats faced the problems of overcoming the solidly Republican black vote in the states of the Lower South where blacks were in a majority. The winning strategy for doing so was foreshadowed in the Democratic victory of 1874 in the racially balanced state of Alabama.

Alabama Democrats took their cue from the explicitly racist campaign waged by the Democrat James L. Kemper when he won the governorship of Virginia in 1873. As an aide to Kemper explained the strategy, "...we must make the issue *White and Black,* race against race and the canvass red hot—the position must be made so odious that no decent white man can support the radical ticket and look a gentleman in the face."[8] Although Alabama Republicans were quite vulnerable on the fiscal issue as a result of the tripling of state taxes and indebtedness during Reconstruction, impatient Democrats felt that the politics of race offered them the quickest means of recapturing control of the state. By exploiting the emotional explosiveness of the race issue and drawing a sharp color line between the parties, they hoped to win back all the white Alabamians who had flirted with the Republicans, especially the former Unionists in the mountains of north Alabama. This strategy also promised to galvanize formerly apathetic whites into active support for the Democratic party. The main drawback to focusing on race as the campaign issue was that it threatened to bring out an even larger black vote on behalf of the Republicans and thus reduce Democratic whites in black belt countries to a permanent political minority in local affairs. This possibility was countered by resorting to violent intimidation and political terrorism in order to keep down the black vote.

In 1870 the Democrats had temporarily regained power in Alabama by running a conciliatory campaign designed to attract voters of both races. Then, after the Democratic administration of Governor Robert B. Lindsay was scandalized by railroad frauds and bankruptcies, the Republicans elected their last Reconstruction governor in 1872. The Democratic victory in 1874 was a permanent one, and it was based on the white-liners' strategy of making race the issue. They luridly depicted civil rights legislation under discussion in Congress as an example of the loathesome racial amalgamation that all Alabama Republicans would force on whites. They appealed to the wounded racial pride of the whites by declaring that the time had come for them to unite against blacks who had already drawn the color line in politics through their unthinking devotion to the Republicans. Despite running a white slate of their own for state offices, the Republicans were unable to stem the defection of north Alabama whites to the Democrats. Another factor in the Democratic victory was the Republican loss of seven black-belt counties. Here, the Democrats relied on economic threats against potentially Republican voters and a politics of deadly intimidation. Two Republican leaders were assassinated in Sumter county, and, on election day in Barbour county, seven unarmed blacks were shot to death by a white mob outside the polling place in Eufaula.

Shortly after the Democrats had swept to power, a black convention in Montgomery, Alabama, declared, "It is absolutely essential to our protection in our civil and political rights that the laws of the United States shall be enforced so as to compel respect and obedience for them. Before the state laws and state courts, we are utterly helpless."[9] Nonetheless, at the very moment when the Democratic resurgence in the South was emboldening Southern courts to deny blacks the rights and freedoms supposedly guaranteed to them in the Civil War amendments, the Supreme Court was drastically limiting any meaningful role for the federal courts on behalf of black rights.

The *Slaughterhouse Cases* of 1873 registered the first major setback for judicial activism by the federal government. Ostensibly, these cases had nothing to do with black rights. The plaintiffs were white butchers and their Democratic allies who had been shut out of a lucrative monopoly that the Republican legislature in Louisiana had granted to a slaughtering company in New Orleans. However, the 14th Amendment was a focal point of the cases, for the butchers contended that the state-chartered monopoly violated their right as citizens under the 14th Amendment not to be deprived of the opportunity to work without due process of law. The Court rejected this contention by asserting (with little in the way of hard evidence) that the 14th Amendment had distinguished between state and national citizenship. The privileges and immunities traditionally part of state citizenship had not been enlarged or affected by the 14th Amendment, and any alleged violation of these rights was still a matter for the state courts, not the federal judiciary. Furthermore, because the Court defined very narrowly the rights of national citizenship for blacks, its 1873 decision effectively closed off the federal courts as an avenue of redress for blacks whose most meaningful constitutional liberties were being curtailed by discriminatory state laws and hostile state courts.

Three years later, in *U.S. v. Cruikshank* and *U.S. v. Reese*, the Court virtually ruled out any positive role for the federal government in protecting black rights under the Civil War amendments or the enforcement legislation of 1870 and 1871. The *Reese* case originated in Lexington, Kentucky, and concerned black voting rights. Local election officials had rejected black ballots on the alleged grounds of nonpayment of the poll tax. The Court ruled that the election officials could not be indicted for violating the Enforcement Act of 1871 because the voting rights in question were exclusively a matter for the individual states to police and regulate. Unless evidence of voting discrimination solely on grounds of race was overwhelmingly clear, the federal government had no jurisdiction, and any laws that said it did were unconstitutional.

Much the same logic was used in the *Cruikshank* decision. The issue here was whether it was a federal crime to murder blacks attempting to practice their constitutional rights of peaceful assembly and political free speech. Both Republicans and Democrats had claimed victory in the Louisiana election of 1872, and in the ensuing tension, Republican freedmen occupied the courthouse in Colfax, Louisiana, the county seat of Grant Parish, to keep it out of the hands of local Democrats. Whites loyal to the Democratic claimant for the governorship surrounded the town and forced the blacks to relinquish the courthouse. On Easter Sunday, April 13, 1873, surrendering blacks who thought the whites had agreed to a truce were murdered in cold blood and their bodies mutilated. The white savagery was so terrifying that the families of the slain were too frightened even to claim their bodies. About seventy blacks and two whites were killed.

Under the authority of the Enforcement Act of 1870, the Justice Department indicted about 100 whites for their alleged part in the massacre, arrested nine, and, rather remarkably, was able to secure three convictions from a local Louisiana jury. These efforts were in vain. In the *Cruikshank* decision the Supreme Court threw out the indictments and reversed the convictions on the grounds that race had not been stipulated as the reason for the killings. The Court further ruled that the 13th and 14th Amendments, as well as the Enforcement Act of 1870, did not give the federal government the constitutional sanction to protect blacks against the infringement of their rights by individuals. Such protection could be extended only by the state governments. All the federal government was empowered to do was to prevent states from denying blacks their rights as blacks. Southern blacks were understandably dismayed, for the Supreme Court was telling them to look for protection to the very agencies of state government that were in fact depriving them of their rights.

The Colfax massacre was only the most horrifying example of the white terror that played a major role in the overthrow of the last Republican parties in the South. After the elections of 1874, the Republicans controlled only Florida, South Carolina, Mississippi, and Louisiana, the last three of which had black majorities loyal to the Republican regimes. Florida was an exception in that the black presence in its Republican party had been minimized from the very beginning. The radical program for the social restructuring of Florida keyed to the black vote and the disfranchisement of ex-Confederates was rejected at the party's founding in 1868 by a moderate faction anxious to work with conservative Democrats for the development of the state's frontier economy. Supported by General George Meade, the federal commander who oversaw Reconstruction in Florida, the moderates decisively won this intra-party struggle. Their constitution of 1868 was the officially recognized one, and it neutralized black political power by giving the governor vast appointive powers over state offices and by apportioning legislative seats through a formula that underweighted black representation. Here was the least threatening to white interests of any Republican government in the Reconstructed South. Thus, Florida stands out among the last remaining Republican states in the South for the relative lack of violence that the Democrats had to use in finally ousting the Republicans. Elsewhere, the Democrats resorted to a politics of counterrevolutionary terrorism.

Much of the violence unleashed in South Carolina, Mississippi, and Louisiana was an outlet for the economic frustrations of rural white Southerners. The combination of high taxes and a drop form one-third to one-half in the prices of all the major cash staples in the South's agrarian economy after the panic of 1873 was a devastating blow to the fiercely independent white yeomanry. Close to forty percent of all Southern farmers were tenants or croppers by the end of the decade. To be sure, most of these landless farmers were blacks who had never owned land, but white farmers were also joining them in the landless category at an alarming rate in the 1870s. This was especially the case in the upcountry where the arrival of railroads after the war had encouraged formerly subsistence farmers to turn to cotton production as a means of paying off their debts. Having incurred more debt to meet the costs of engaging in commercial agriculture, these farmers lost their land when cotton prices sank.

Planters had more of an economic cushion with which to survive the depression, but falling prices and land values convinced them more than ever of the folly of Republican rule and the need to tighten control over their black labor supply. Much as Northern industrialists now moved to squeeze labor costs, so also did Southern planters. They dominated the Southern Grange, and they used it to push for legislation curbing any economic assertiveness by rural black laborers. As they sought to discipline blacks into greater submission, the planters had every reason to cooperate with Democratic politicians in mobilizing groups of white farmers into armed, anti-black vigilantes. The planters were concerned primarily with regaining the political power they needed to enact their full legislative program of labor controls, while the farmers were seeking to protect their threatened rural worlds of local independence. For both groups, the depression had dramatically heightened the need to purge state governments of the Republicans and overawe their black supporters.

Democratic state leaders coordinated and channeled the political violence as an integral part of a carefully devised party strategy. Rather than relying on such past electoral practices as staging mass meetings in which the voters presumably were ready to turn out, the Democrats now zealously sought out white voters. Democratic clubs, known as the White League in Louisiana, the Rifle Clubs in Mississippi, and the Red Shirts in South Carolina, were carefully organized at the grassroots level. In turn, these clubs acted as the paramilitary arm of the local Democratic party.

Flamboyantly staged parades of club members, often at night in the glare of torches and always with firearms in full display, played up the theme of renewed racial pride and gave blacks a graphic warning that whites were prepared to overpower them by force if necessary. In targeted districts of the black belts the white clubs applied the brutal intimidation that gutted the infrastructure of the Republican organizations and demoralized their followers. At the start of election campaigns, the clubs were used to break up Republican meetings and instigate riots, which served as a pretext to beat and kill blacks, burn their cabins, and destroy their crops. The worst of these contrived riots at Coushatta, Louisiana, in September 1874, Clinton, Mississippi, in September 1875, and Hamburg, South Carolina, in July 1876, added a string of place names to the outrage at Colfax that well might have been applied to Civil War battles. Well-armed and desperate Confederate veterans rallied around the one Southern cause that had not been lost in the official war, mainly the cause of white supremacy.

The calculated rise of violence in campaigns that highlighted the race issue signified a decisive and final shift of strategy for the postwar Democratic parties in the Reconstructed South. After rejecting Reconstruction in the election of 1868 and

Clashes between the White League and the Republican-controlled police force in New Orleans punctuated the violent end of Reconstruction in Louisiana.

waiting in vain for northern Democrats to come to their rescue, southern Democrats then reversed themselves with their New Departure in the election of 1872. They accepted Reconstruction to the extent that they recognized it as a political fact of life, and they attempted to undermine it from within by regaining power through a wooing of black voters and dissident white Republicans. Although they recouped most of their earlier losses among native white Southerners, they made few inroads on the black vote, and the accommodationist strategy of fusing with Liberal Republicans was an overall failure. Greeley had not delivered a single Northern state in 1872, and the net effect of the New Departure in the Lower South was zero. Except for the Border states, Greeley carried only one Southern state, Texas, and the Democratic victory there was counterbalanced by the loss of Louisiana, a Seymour state in 1868. When added to the lackluster Democratic record in state elections and the widely noted apathy of white voters, this dismal performance in 1872 left the New Departure Democrats thoroughly discredited. Power within the southern Democratic parties now swung back to more radical elements who successfully urged that race be made the centerpiece of a new strategy of confrontation.

The issue of white supremacy both unified and energized the disspirited Democrats. By the early 1870s Southern whites were reconciled to the indispensability of free black labor, but they did not, and perhaps could not, accept the political revolution that had given the former slaves a power base independent of local white control. When a Scottish journalist traveled throughout the South in 1870 and 1871, he repeatedly heard that "the main cause of dissatisfaction with the coloured population is the too ready ear they lend to political agitators, and the blind persistency with which they are said to enable such persons to acquire predominance in the State Governments against the will of the white citizens."[10] In order to reassert that will and wash away the shame to racial pride of ever having consented to Republican rule based on the black vote, whites flocked into the paramilitary clubs of the Democrats. Just as the hard-liners had predicted, the Democratic party revived once it jettisoned the confusing image of cooperation with the Republicans and reverted to its straight-out principles of Southernism and exclusive rule by whites.

Once the New Departure had served as a bridge for white Southerners returning to the Democratic party, the rallying cry of race made all the more political sense because of the increasing blackness of the remaining Republican parties. At the same time, black Republicans were becoming more politically assertive. Black office holding, especially on the part of those who had been born into slavery, rose sharply in the early 1870s, and black votes in Republican-controlled legislatures passed civil rights legislation in Mississippi, Louisiana, and Florida. The introduction of a civil rights bill in Congress in 1874 added further ammunition to Democratic charges that blacks were plotting with Republicans in an unholy conspiracy to rob Southern whites of their birth right to local home rule.

The survival strategy of the last Republican governments in the South played into the hands of the Democratic white supremacists. Recoiling from the financial and political disasters of their earlier promotional policies, the Republicans tried to fashion a new party image around the themes of honest government and fiscal accountability. The attempt was bound to fail. Cutting expenses reduced the spending for the social services so desperately needed by blacks. Thus, just as the Democrats were mobilizing their mass constituency of whites, the Republicans were demoralizing their most loyal followers, the blacks. Moreover, the need for reform and retrenchment had first been politicized by the Democrats, and its acceptance by the Northerners who now monopolized the top leadership posts in the Republican parties amounted to an admission that their Democratic opponents had been right all along. It was too late for the Republicans to win back white farmers by reducing taxes, and the effort to do so inevitably strengthened the Democratic claim that race was the most significant issue that divided the parties.

The newly discovered fiscal conservatism of the Republicans placed the party in a no-win situation. In Florida the Republicans cut governmental expenses to the bone and banned the extension of state credit to any corporation, but this only brought them closer to the position of economically conservative Democrats who remained as committed as ever to ridding their state of the party of black suffrage. The Republican administration of William P. Kellogg in Louisiana put through a retrenchment program between 1872 and 1876 that saved taxpayers millions of dollars by scaling back and refunding the state debt. Taxes and state expenditures were slashed by one-third.

Still, the guerrilla war against the Louisiana Republicans raged on. The conservative Democrats and New Orleans businessmen whom Kellogg was trying to placate lost control of the state Democratic party to the White Leaguers. The credibility of the New Departure Democrats had been destroyed when the federal government ruled against their fusion candidate for governor, John McEnery, in the disputed state election of 1872. That decision triggered the explosive growth of the White League, and its terroristic tactics drove Republican officeholders from the outlying rural districts. In September 1874, the murderous attacks on Republicans instigated by the White League at Coushatta in Red River Parish and Liberty Place in New Orleans finally provoked the Grant administration into sending in federal troops to restore order. A truce was worked out in which the White Leagues agreed to back off and permit Kellogg to finish his term in return for a recognition of Democratic control of the lower House of the legislature.

The retrenchment programs of Republican governors Daniel H. Chamberlain in South Carolina and Adelbert Ames in Mississippi alienated most of their black followers and all but destroyed their parties' alliance between Northern whites and blacks, the last bond of biracial cooperation in Southern politics. Former New England abolitionists and Union army officers, Chamberlain and Ames both had impeccable Republican credentials. The party revolts they touched off with their strictly orthodox financial views graphically revealed how Reconstruction had reached an ideological dead end by the mid-1870s.

During his term of office from 1874 to 1876, Chamberlain more than lived up to his promises of giving South Carolina an honest, efficient government. He cut $2 million from the annual expenses of the state, rooted out the corruption of past Republican administrations, and reduced the number of state employees. All this was done to the applause of the merchant community in Charleston and the planters in the low country, the conservative Democrats most willing to cooperate with a reform-minded Republican governor. Meanwhile, black legislators were growing more restive. Chamberlain favored the Democratic fusionists in his political appointments, and his fiscal retrenchment was threatening major cutbacks in the state funding for the public schools. Despite black demands, Chamberlain showed no interest in developing any state programs to provide financial relief to tenants and sharecroppers burdened with growing debt as a result of the agricultural depression.

The simmering feud between Chamberlain and the black politicians climaxed in the party revolt of December 1875. Black legislators in the South Carolina House rejected Chamberlain's nominees for two judgeships in Charleston and substituted two appointees whom Chamberlain in turn rejected as specimens of the disreputable leadership that had to be purged from the Republican party. Citing the actions of the black legislators as proof that the Republicans remained unworthy of the support of decent white citizens, the white-line strategists in the upcountry now captured control of the Democratic party. They swept to victory in the gubernatorial election of 1876 behind a straight Democratic ticket composed entirely of Confederate veterans. The demoralized and divided Republicans watched helplessly as the Democrats clinched their victory through the use of political violence.

Adelbert Ames, Mississippi's last Republican governor, was less successful in his cost-cutting drive than was Chamberlain. In part this was because the Mississippi budget had less fat to cut. Republican rule in Mississippi had been largely free of the fiscal extravagance that plagued the party elsewhere in the South, and, because Mississippi's Reconstruction constitution had prohibited the state from endorsing corporate bonds, the state debt was relatively low. Ames did pare down the debt and introduce some reforms in taxation, but the legislature balked at his request for a drastic reduction in taxes, a cutback that would have impoverished state support for education and welfare. Instead, and against white opposition, the black legislators enacted a program of economic relief for the rural poor. They passed a bill staying the collection of debts and repealed the legislation authorizing the crop–lien system of agricultural credit. In both instances their goal was to restore agricultural opportunities by lifting the crushing load of debt which was driving more and more Mississippians, and especially the blacks, into poverty and abject economic dependency. Although Ames had been a sharp critic of plantation agriculture and the credit system that sustained it, he rejected the new policy direction outlined by the black Republicans. He vetoed both bills on the grounds that they would scare off any capital investment in agriculture and make a bad situation worse.

Ames' vetoes had recommitted the Mississippi Republicans to fiscal respectability, but the refusal of the black legislators to sustain his call for lower taxes gave straight-out Democrats all the pretext they needed to convince taxpaying whites that the misrule of blacks had to be overturned. As in South Carolina, black defiance of the Republicans' white leadership precipitated the final breakup of the fusion movement between the Republicans and conservative Democrats.

The white-liners who took over the Mississippi Democratic party in 1875 rapidly mobilized white farmers into the armed camps of the rifle clubs. Under the leadership of state party chairman, James Z. George, they blended violence, fraud, and martial unity into what became known as the "Mississippi Plan." Its underlying premise, as stated by the Meridian *Mercury* was that, "The negroes are our enemies...we must accept them as our enemies, and beat them as enemies."[11] And the blacks were beaten.

After Democratic rampages of deadly violence in the delta country and the outskirts of Jackson, the state capital, in the late summer of 1875, Ames sent an urgent plea to Washington for federal troops to stop the killing. He received the insulting reply that the North had grown "tired" of these Southern disturbances and that it was high time that the Southern Republicans learned how to defend themselves. The Grant Republicans would do no more than arrange an armistice in which Ames agreed to disband the state militia (only two units were at his disposal) in return for a Democratic promise to call off the violence. The promise was broken. Democratic intimidation of black voters continued up to election day, and in several plantation counties only a handful of blacks dared to vote.

The Mississippi Democrats flouted the Constitution and showed scant regard for either black rights or black lives in their landslide victory in the gubernatorial election of 1875. They could dare to be so contemptuous of the standards of equality that the Republicans had tried to achieve in Reconstruction not only because they were far more unified and better armed than their Republican opponents but also because they correctly reckoned that the Grant Republicans would not intervene. Any chance that they might have had been eliminated back in January 1875 by the uproar in the North over the use of federal troops to oust five Democrats who had forcibly claimed seats in the Louisiana legislature in the aftermath of yet another hotly disputed election in that bitterly divided state. The typical reaction in the North was voiced by the Philadelphia *Inquirer,* a Republican paper.

> Unless the Republican party is content to be swept out of existence by the storm of indignant protest arising against the wrongs of Louisiana from all portions of the country, it will see that this most shameful outrage is redressed wholly and at once....[12]

The tyrannical Republicans, it was charged, had endangered the constitutional liberties of every legislature in the nation. Now that it was unmistakably clear to Republican leaders that Northern voters were dead set against any further federal intervention in Southern affairs, their refusal to heed the plea of Governor Ames for assistance was a foregone conclusion.

The dominant electoral base of the Republicans was always in the North, and, once that base had been badly eroded by the congressional returns in 1874, the Republicans had to protect it at all costs. One of these costs involved cutting loose from their unpopular party brethren in the South. The national party could well afford such a loss if it enhanced the party's chances for victory in the Northern state elections of 1875 and the national election in 1876. As a result of this political arithmetic, southern Republicanism was a lost cause regardless of which party won the presidential race in 1876.

THE CENTENNIAL ELECTION

The Republicans set their basic agenda for the centennial election during the lame-duck session of the 43rd Congress, which convened in December 1874. The 44th Congress would be controlled by the Democrats, and the Republicans were facing their last opportunity to salvage their crumbling Reconstruction policy. Equally important, the party had to heal its divisions over the currency question. Both of these issues had paralyzed and split the party during Grant's second term, and compromises for the sake of party unity had to be worked out if the Democrats were to be kept out of the White House in 1876.

The Republicans nailed sound money to their campaign banner in 1876 with the Specie Resumption Act of January 1875. The act was an artfully contrived compromise put together by Senator John Sherman of Ohio, the older brother of the more famous Union general. Sherman's measure ended the renewed party feuding that had erupted in December when Republican inflationists reacted angrily to the sharply deflationary policy recommended by Grant and Secretary of the Treasury Benjamin Bristow. Intended, as Sherman frankly argued, to save the party's chances in 1876, the Specie Resumption Act offered something to each of the warring sectional and economic interests in the party.

The silver interests in the Rocky Mountain states and inflationists who wanted the nation's currency expanded through the minting of silver coins were temporarily placated with a provision for the limited remonetization of silver. In 1873, silver had been dropped from the nation's coinage at a time when new technological breakthroughs in mining and discoveries of the ore in Nevada and Colorado were rapidly increasing the supply of the metal. Sherman, the head of the Senate Finance Committee, and astute Treasury officials realized that the public credit would be threatened as abundant supplies of the ore caused the price of silver to fall relative to gold. Once that happened, they reasoned, the owners of silver would flood the Treasury with the metal for redemption into coins, and gold dollars would be driven out of circulation. As the Treasury's gold reserves fell, the nation's credit would fall as well because the federal bonds and other government debts would have to be paid off in cheap silver dollars. This was a frightening scenario for the top Treasury officials, who viewed the public credit as a solemn, moral obligation, and they reacted by demonetizing silver. By 1876, Sherman had the foresight to head off the mounting protests from the silver interests by providing that, henceforth, silver coins could be minted to replace the fractional paper currency. This was a minor concession on Sherman's part, but it prevented the silver issue from badly splitting his party before the election of 1876.

Advocates of an expansion of national banknotes were accommodated with the free-banking provision in Sherman's bill, that is, the freeing of the banks from the previous restriction on the total amount of banknotes they could issue. For every $100 of new banknotes that could now be issued, $80 of greenbacks were to be retired, but the greenbackers were mollified by the stipulation that the amount of the greenbacks could dip no lower than $300 million. The heart of the measure, and what Sherman shrewdly chose for its title, was the provision for the redemption of the greenbacks in specie (assumed by everyone to mean gold) as of January 1, 1879. This was the saving grace of the bill for both the party moderates and the conservative deflationists in the Northeast. "The bill is a weak and insufficient measure," explained James Garfield, the Republicans' financial leader in the House, "but I voted for it on the ground that it pledges the Government to resumption and ends, I hope, the attempts at inflating the currency."[13]

Just as Sherman was steering the Specie Resumption Act through Congress, the Republicans were suddenly caught up again in what they were now wearily labeling the "Louisiana question." More so than the divisions over currency, the reactions to the party's recent military intervention under General Phil Sheridan in expelling Democratic claimants from the Louisiana House threatened to split the Republicans and hand the Democrats the 1876 election by default. "It seems as though all the gods had conspired to destroy the Republican Party,"[14] lamented Garfield.

The Republicans restored their unity over Reconstruction through a strategy that they followed for the rest of the century. They reiterated their commitment to Reconstruction through the passage of the Civil Rights Act of 1875 while simultaneously refusing to put any teeth into that commitment. The Republicans had been debating the political wisdom of enacting a major new civil rights bill ever since Charles Sumner had forced the issue on them with a bill that he introduced back in 1870. As envisioned by Sumner, the bill would have extended the 14th Amendment's principle of political equality into social relations by providing for broad federal guarantees of desegregation in schools, juries, churches, cemeteries, and all public accommodations. This was far too sweeping for most Republicans, and the bill languished until Sumner's death in early 1874. Then, in a tribute to Sumner that his Senate colleagues expected House Republicans to spurn, the Senate passed the bill stripped of its church provisions in the spring of 1874, and the House indeed rejected it. Ironically, it was the sheer ferocity of the Democrats' partisan attacks on Sheridan's actions in Louisiana that finally gave the Republicans the courage to pass the civil rights bill in February 1875. Even though Republicans by now were all but apologizing for ever having extended the vote to blacks in the first place, their anger and resentment over the Democratic attacks reunified them against a common enemy. The civil rights bill quickly became a symbol of the idealistic resolve of the Republicans and their refusal to be bullied by the Democrats.

With a rhetoric that reminded Northern voters that the rights of citizenship of the former slaves were forever linked to the great cause of the Union for which the Civil War was fought, the Republicans passed a watered-down version of Sumner's original bill. Deleted of its very controversial provisions relating to churches and schools, the Civil Rights Act of 1875 applied primarily to public accommodations, that is, the right of equal access by race to hotels, restaurants, theaters, and railroads. As the Republicans claimed, the constitutional basis for the bill had come straight out of the war. "Whether right or wrong, whether for good or ill," intoned Republican Representative Benjamin Butler from Massachusetts, "the result of the late war has been that every person born on the soil, or duly naturalized, is a citizen of the United States, entitled to all the rights, privileges, and immunities of a citizen."[15] Its proponents insisted that the act encroached on no state rights but applied only, in Butler's phrase, to state wrongs. Black congressmen spoke eloquently of the need for such legislation. Recalling his own personal experiences, Joseph H. Rainey of South Carolina noted, "So long as [the black man] makes himself content with ordinary gifts, why it is all well; but when he aspires to be a man, when he seeks to have the rights accorded him that other citizens of the country enjoy, then he is asking too much...."[16]

The Civil Rights Act of 1875 did ask too much of white America and especially its spokesmen on the Supreme Court. In the *Civil Rights Cases* of 1883 the Court overturned the 1875 legislation. Citing its *Slaughterhouse* and *Cruikshank* decisions, the Court ruled that the federal protection of civil rights extended only to the violation of those rights by the actions of states, not private individuals.

Republican moderates switched course in 1875 and supported the civil rights legislation on the assumption that the party would go no further in strengthening the lagging federal involvement in Reconstruction. Indeed, the rules change in the House that enabled the bill to come up for a vote was engineered by two of the party's most influential moderates, Garfield and James Blaine, the Speaker of the House. At the insistence of southern Republicans, however, and with the support of radical Northerners led by Benjamin Butler, the party next took up a Federal Elections Bill, which vastly expanded federal powers to police elections. Among its sweeping powers was a fresh authorization for the presidential suspension of the writ of *habeas corpus* in areas where political terrorism prevented peaceful elections. In the light of the escalating violence against blacks in recent Southern elections, this bill was a vital matter of equity and justice for the southern Republicans. For most of their Northern colleagues, the bill was a political disaster. Speaker James G. Blaine later explained why to John Roy Lynch, a black Republican congressman from Mississippi: "If that bill had become a law, the defeat of the Republican party throughout the country would have been a foregone conclusion. We could not have saved the South even if the bill had passed, but its passage would have lost us the North."[17]

Aided immeasurably by the rekindling of intense partisanship over the Louisiana affair, the radical element in the House pushed through the Elections Bill just before adjournment. Many Republicans voted for the bill only because they were certain it would never become a law. As was fully expected, Republicans in the Senate bottled up the bill. The Republican moderates had now cast the party in the centrist direction it would follow into the election of 1876. The party had reconfirmed its commitment to black equality in the Civil Rights Act while reassuring Northern voters that it posed no constitutional threat to the right of Southern whites to local self-government. In reclaiming the high moral ground, the party had also covered its political flank.

Sound money for all Americans and a conciliatory policy for Southern whites emerged as the political planks for 1876 that the Republicans took out of the final session of the 43rd Congress. When another round of scandals hit the Grant administration, the Republicans of necessity added a reformist theme to their party image for the campaign. In Rutherford B. Hayes, the recent victor in the 1875 gubernatorial race in Ohio, they found a candidate whose straitlaced midwestern respectability enabled them to counter Democratic charges of political corruption.

Republican strategists considered the Ohio race in the fall of that year to be far more critical to the party's chances in 1876 than the fate of Republicanism in the South. The party desperately needed a victory in a key Northern state to reverse the tide of Democratic successes in 1874. Somewhat to the surprise of the Republicans, the Ohio campaign centered on the currency question. Secretary of the Treasury Benjamin Bristow had interpreted the Specie Resumption Act in a very deflationary manner by refusing to return to circulation the greenbacks that were being retired even though the net amount of banknotes in circulation was dropping. The provision in the Resumption Act permitting more banknotes to be issued did not produce the expected increase in banknote circulation. National banknotes still had to be secured by holdings of federal bonds, and these bonds could now be sold at a premium to their face value because their rapid retirement by the Treasury was reducing their supply and raising their value. Banks in the Northeast with large deposits available to use as loans found it more profitable to sell their federal bonds than to hold them as a basis for loans in the form of banknotes. Meanwhile, banks in the South and West were not issuing many new banknotes because the demand for them dropped with the depressed business conditions in the wake of the panic of 1873. Thus, the national banknotes in circulation actually fell by fifteen percent between 1874 and 1877. This contraction in the currency added to the deflationary pressure on the economy, and hard times became even harder in the mining and industrial districts of Ohio. Greenbackism revived as a political issue, and the Democratic campaign in Ohio used it to flay the Republicans as the captives of the eastern monied power.

Once they found that they could not duck the money issue in Ohio, the Republicans converted it into a strength. The key to their strategy was the notion of respectability, and it was pitched to a Protestant middle class alarmed by the signs of growing class conflict in the 1870s. Greenbackism was denounced in apocalyptic terms as a revolutionary, communistic scheme to destroy capital, property, and all the civilized values of a God-fearing social order. The clerical and business press rallied behind the Republicans and depicted their stand on sound money and specie resumption as the last defense of social stability, moral honesty, and indeed of Protestant Christianity itself against the unreasoning fanatics in the Democratic camp.

This introduction of Protestantism into the campaign was the other main element in the Republicans' carefully cultivated image of respectability. The women's temperance crusade, a mass movement drawn primarily from middle-class, Protestant households, burst into prominence in Ohio in 1873 and 1874, and it played upon Protestant fears that Catholic immigrants menaced social harmony and public morality through their enslavement to Demon Rum. Hayes, a teetotaler himself, took advantage of this upsurge in Protestant nativism by politically bashing the Catholics in his campaign. Specifically, he charged that a bill recently intro-duced by an Irish Democrat in the Ohio legislature authorizing Catholic chaplains in state prisons and hospitals was the opening wedge in a papal plot to divert tax monies for the support of sectarian Catholic schools. The Democrats were now disreputable on two counts. Their greenbackism would ruin the nation's credit and, in Hayes's phrase, their "subserviency to Roman Catholic demands"[18] would undermine the values of the Protestant majority in Ohio.

The Republicans, by mobilizing Yankee, Protestant, and middle-class voters around the themes of sound money and anti-Catholicism, pulled out a narrow victory in Ohio. The Northern press closely followed the election, and Hayes was immediately added to the list of Republican hopefuls for the party's presidential nomination. The front-runner until early 1876 was James G. Blaine, the popular Speaker of the House who had spent fourteen years in Congress ingratiating himself with party moderates. However, the February trial of Orville Babcock, Grant's personal secretary, for his involvement in the Whiskey Ring scandals, and the impeachment by the House in March of William W. Belknap, the Secretary of War, for taking bribes from Indian traders in return for government contracts at western posts, forced the Republicans to find a candidate with a record of scrupulous honesty. Blaine did not measure up. In the spring he was implicated in some shady financial dealings through which he apparently exerted his considerable political influence on behalf of land-grant railroads in which he had a personal financial stake. Blaine lost his lead, and a deadlocked Republican convention in June settled on Hayes, a rather drab politician who nonetheless fit the need of the party for a reform candidate on good terms with the Liberal Republican bolters of 1872.

The Democrats tried to regain the initiative on the reform issue by nominating Governor Samuel J. Tilden of New York, a millionaire corporate lawyer. Identified with the cause of reform ever since he headed up investigations that helped break up the notorious Tweed Ring in New York City and an equally corrupt ring of state officials who operated out of Albany, Tilden was the hand-picked candidate of the hard-money commercial interests in the eastern wing of the Democratic party. Throughout the 1870s Tilden had attacked the Republicans with the argument that "*Centralism* in the *government*, and *corruption* in *administration* are the twin evils of our times. They threaten with swift destruction civil liberty and the whole fabric of our free institutions."[19] As tailored to fit the needs of the Democratic platform in 1876, this indictment charged the Republicans with financial immorality in issuing the greenbacks and with unconstitutional centralization in forcing corrupt governments on the Reconstructed South. Tilden's candidacy was designed to appeal to conservatives across sectional lines with its call for a specie dollar and an end to "bayonet rule" in the South.

Hayes and Tilden were two right-of-center candidates who tended to cancel each other out. Both preached the need for sound money, governmental reform, and a Southern policy that fully recognized the civil and political liberties of the whites. If Hayes was still officially committed to Reconstruction, that commitment was couched in such conciliatory language that black leaders were rightfully concerned that the Republicans were about to abandon the black cause in the South. This blurring of party differences worked to the advantage of the Democrats, especially in the North. The Democrats expected to carry a nearly solid South, and, with Tilden heading the ticket, they also anticipated victory in New York, New Jersey, and Connecticut. Just a few more swing states in the North would be needed to claim the presidency, and the Democrats hoped to gain them by downplaying the highly emotional and partisan issues relating to the Civil War and Reconstruction, issues guaranteed to bring out the heaviest Republican vote. This strategy well might have worked had it not been for the Hamburg massacre in South Carolina on July 8, 1876.

Four days after a flare-up of racial tensions touched off by a parade of black militia celebrating the Fourth of July, a couple of hundred armed whites descended on the small village of Hamburg, South Carolina, and demanded that its black militia give up their weapons. The blacks refused, and after an exchange of gunfire, which killed one black and one white, five captured members of the black militia were murdered as they tried to escape. This atrocity was a political windfall for the northern Republicans. It enabled them to reactivate all the latent distrust in the North over the Democrats as the party of unrepentant rebels who were still unworthy of controlling the federal government. By September, Hayes was able to report to Garfield that "the prospect of the return of the rebels to power has absorbed all the other issues in the public mind."[20]

Once Civil War loyalties were mobilized in the North, the Republicans had their winning edge. By hammering away at the theme of rebel rule under untrustworthy Democrats returned to power by a united South, they largely neutralized the Northern anger against Grantism and the Republican hard times. Although Hayes ran much weaker throughout the North than had Grant in 1872, he held on to just enough of the party supporters in the marginal states to claim all but four of the Northern states. The outcome of the election, however, turned on who could successfully claim the disputed electoral votes of three Southern states. In South Carolina, Florida, and Louisiana, rival election boards of Republicans and Democrats had sent in two sets of election returns, one for Hayes and the other for Tilden.

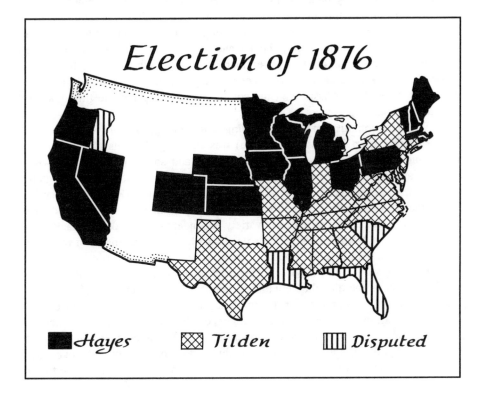

Election of 1876

■ *Hayes*   ▨ *Tilden*   ▥ *Disputed*

If all these returns were counted in favor of Hayes, as well as one electoral ballot from Oregon, which the Democrats challenged on a technicality, the Republicans would win the presidency with a majority of one electoral vote.

Voting fraud and intimidation was so rife in the three disputed Southern states that it is difficult to say who would have won in a fair election. In all likelihood, South Carolina had rightfully gone for Hayes, Florida for Tilden, and Louisiana was anybody's guess. As it turned out, the question of who "actually" won in these states was but a minor consideration in the eventual settlement of the 1876 election. Far more significant than the irreconcilable partisan differences over the presidential vote in these Southern states was the fundamental agreement between the parties at the national level that Reconstruction was over regardless of who gained the presidency.

The Constitution was no more helpful in resolving the electoral crisis than it had been in settling the secession crisis. Congress, where the dispute wound up, was at loggerheads over what to do since the Democrats controlled the House and the Republicans the Senate. Finally, after six weeks of political posturing and much bellicose talk by the Democrats that they were prepared to seize by force what rightfully was theirs, Congress created a special Electoral Commission to arbitrate the dispute.

Congress appointed ten congressmen and four Supreme Court Justices to the commission and evenly balanced them between Republicans and Democrats. The fifteenth, and presumably decisive, member was to be a Supreme Court Justice chosen by his four colleagues already on the commission. This final member turned out to be Joseph P. Bradley, a Republican, and he cast the swing vote by which the commission ruled by an eight to seven margin that all of the disputed returns in favor of Hayes should be accepted. Whether Hayes in fact had carried the three contested states was an issue that the commission had neither the time nor the inclination to take up.

While the commission was deliberating, and a lethargic Tilden (who may have been suffering from Parkinson's disease) was showing all signs of a politician facing inevitable defeat, the Hayes Republicans and southern Democrats were reaching an informal agreement in a series of backroom negotiations in Washington. Through his intermediaries, Hayes conveyed to the southern Democrats what he had privately been telling Republicans during the campaign. He believed that southern Republicanism, at least the variety dependent on the vote of blacks and the leadership of Northern whites, was dead, and he had no intention of trying to prop it up again with federal troops.

Nothing was written down, but Hayes let it be known that he would remove the federal troops guarding the Republican claimants in the statehouses of Louisiana and South Carolina. In return for this implicit promise to end federal interference in Southern affairs, Hayes received assurances that the incoming Democratic administrations in these states would honor the Civil War amendments and respect the civil and political rights of blacks. Rounding out the bargain, though not central to the negotiations, were pledges from Hayes to appoint a Southern white to his cabinet and support federal subsidies for the South, including aid for the long-deferred Southern transcontinental railroad. The Democrats hinted that they would show their gratitude by helping the Republicans organize the next House of Representatives.

The Compromise of 1877, as these set of agreements came to be known, was but the final step in the abandonment of Reconstruction by the Republicans. Throughout the 1870s the Republicans had gradually pulled back from enforcing Reconstruction, and President Grant's refusal in the winter of 1876–1877 to recognize the Republican gubernatorial claimants in Louisiana and South Carolina had the effect of making the bargain struck by Hayes with the southern Democrats into just so much window dressing for a decision that had already been made for Hayes. By simultaneously stationing federal troops to protect these two claimants, Stephen Packard in Louisiana and Daniel Chamberlain in South Carolina, Grant shrewdly kept up the pressure on the southern Democrats to reach a peaceful accommodation and accept Hayes as the presidential winner. The regaining of complete control over their local governments was always the major goal of the southern Democrats, and both Grant and Hayes were ready to concede it as long as federal authority was not directly challenged. As for the northern Democrats in Congress who still had the power to disrupt the inauguration of Hayes by refusing to participate in the official counting of the electoral votes that the Electoral Commission had awarded to Hayes, they swung into line when the commercial interests of the party in the Northeast made it clear that a business recovery demanded an immediate end to the political crisis.

Hayes was duly inaugurated on March 4, 1877, and he soon lived up to his side of the agreement with the southern Democrats. In April he ordered the removal of the federal troops from the statehouses in Louisiana and South Carolina, and the last two Republican governments in the South collapsed. Black aspirations to be treated as legal and political equals in the postwar South also collapsed. Despite white assurances that they would respect black rights, Southern blacks continued to be hounded and persecuted if they dared to act on behalf of the rights supposedly guaranteed to them in the 14th and 15th Amendments. Their role in the civic and political life of the South was now circumscribed more than ever. Hayes had hoped that his policy of conciliation would usher in an age of racial peace and justice in the South. Instead, as the great black leader Frederick Douglass concluded, "The whole four years of this administration were, to the loyal colored citizens, full of darkness and dismal terror."[21] As Southern blacks knew all too well, the Republican retreat from Reconstruction was completed under Hayes.

THE RECONSTRUCTED NATION

Most remnants of the political reconstruction of the South dictated by the settlement of the Civil War were eliminated in 1877 through an agreement between northern Republicans and southern Democrats. Southern whites received home rule in racial matters, and the Republicans got the presidency in return. This agreement was part of a wider consensus that had emerged among propertied interests and their political representatives in both sections. The basis for this consensus was the common response of economic elites and the middle classes of property holders in both sections to the social crisis generated by the depression of the 1870s. The economic reconstruction of the nation, what James Garfield referred to as the financial and industrial revolution that had accompanied the political and military revolutions of the Civil War, turned sour in 1873. In the labor and agrarian protests triggered by the depression, the business and middle classes of the North, as well as the planters of the South, saw nothing less than an impending revolution. They were convinced it was now time to bury sectional differences and reunite the conservatives of the nation by restoring men of property and "intelligence" to power in both the North and the South.

By the time the depression of the 1870s struck, much of the social and economic map of the America of 1850 had been radically redrawn. Most obviously, the South had entered the bourgeois world of a capitalist wage–labor system. Planters were now landlords, and their former slaves were their hired hands. The white yeomanry, a class that had avoided market involvement before the war, were now committed to cotton production in the midst of a commercial revolution made possible by the postwar railroads that broke down the previous isolation of their agricultural communities. The railroads were also the key to the economic transformation of the trans-Mississippi West. Over one-third of America's increase in population between 1860 and 1880 occurred in this region, and it was the railroads that made the West accessible to a mass migration.

The arrival of white Americans triggered a struggle with Native Americans over the land, water, and mineral resources of the Great Plains. For whites, this struggle took on the overtones of a race war in which anti-Indian feelings matched the hatreds expressed by many Southern whites toward blacks. The U.S. Army, staffed with troops hardened in the Civil War and led by an ambitious officer corps trained in that war, defeated the Indians in a decade of fierce fighting. Now, the rail network in the West was able to ship bulky agricultural commodities out of the Great Plains for consumption in eastern cities and, via steamship, for sale in Europe. The low cost of these food exports from the West undercut the small, independent farmer in the Northeast and the peasant proprietor in Europe. Displaced agrarian producers on both sides of the Atlantic moved by increasing numbers into the industrial cities east of the Mississippi.

Immigration in the generation after the Civil War averaged more than 300,000 annually, and most of the foreign born wound up as factory hands whose cheap labor swelled America's growing industrial output. In a process that would continue well into the twentieth century, the mid-century America of the village and farm was giving way to the city and factory. More than seventy percent of Americans still lived in rural areas by 1880, but the urban population had been growing five times as fast in the 1860s and 1870s. And, by the early 1870s, a majority of the labor force was working at nonfarm jobs for the first time in American history.

As compared with 1850, many more Americans in the 1870s were dependent, willingly or not, on a market economy. Farming in the trans-Mississippi West was economically viable only through the production of a cash crop, such as wheat; the crop–lien system that provided the credit for commercial agriculture in the postwar South burdened both white and black Southern farmers with such a load of debt that they had to produce cotton as a cash crop in an effort to pay it off; and industrial workers in the Northeast and Midwest had to accept the discipline of the factory system or face starvation. Many of these farmers and workers experienced their growing market involvement as a loss of personal independence. Commodity prices set in international markets and decisions made by business leaders at the national level were now the crucial factors in determining the economic livelihood of individuals and their local communities. When unemployment soared and agricultural prices fell in the depression of the 1870s, protesting groups of farmers and workers tried to regain some control over their lives and some relief from the miseries of the depression by turning to the government for assistance. Farmers wanted public authorities to regulate and equalize rates charged by the railroads for the shipment of their crops. Workers demanded public-works programs and a return to community standards of fairness in arbitrating labor disputes with management.

This farmer-labor insurgency provoked a sharp reaction from the business and propertied classes. The conservative drift of the 1870s away from the government activism and notions of social equity that had been central to the reform impulse behind Reconstruction now crystallized into a nearly hysterical cry for law and order. In their political discourse, Americans split into two warring camps, with one side seeking an end to economic injustices and the other demanding a suppression of social disorder. About all they had in common was the belief that class lines had hardened into a fundamental division between capital and labor.

The call for government retrenchment was at the heart of the conservative reaction in the mid-1870s. The business press insisted that "there will be no permanent stability for business, and no permanent prosperity or sound growth for the country, until we have good government, and *that* will never be until we have much *less* government."[22] The Northern middle class, chafing under local and state taxes that had risen four times over since the outbreak of the Civil War, provided the broad political base for cutbacks in the scope and financing of government activities. In a marked reversal from the pattern of the 1860s, the new or revised state constitutions of the 1870s sharply limited the power of legislatures and curtailed the borrowing capacities of state governments. Municipal coalitions of taxpayers in Northern cities sought the same objectives. The depression intensified these efforts at reducing the debt load in the North and deepened the emotional commitment of the Northern middle class to the fiscal conservatism that the Republicans embraced as party orthodoxy in the Specie Resumption Act.

Respectable opinion in the North now decried the greenbacks as much as the protests of farm and labor organizations. Both were seen as a grave threat to the stability and rights of private property. Any government attempt to regulate the currency or base it on anything but the enduring value of gold was denounced as unholy meddling with the eternal law of supply and demand. Labeled as a desperate expedient justified only by the fiscal emergency of the Civil War, the greenbacks became for Northern conservatives the arch symbol of entrusting too much power to the government. For Edward Atkinson, a New England textile manufacturer and Liberal Republican in 1872, the greenbacks morally debased workers and business-men alike and corrupted everything that they touched. In an astonishing conclusion that reveals the depths of conservative fears in the 1870s, he argued that this "false" and "vicious" form of money "has done more injustice than the arms and artifices of the enemies of the Union for whose subjugation it was issued."[23]

Northern conservatives viewed themselves as reformers embarked on a cru-sade to return government at all levels to its pristine simplicity of the pre-Civil War years. They were convinced that American government had become bloated and corrupt as the inevitable result of extending the ballot to Southern blacks and Northern immigrants. Universal (male) suffrage produced bad government because the mass electorate of the unpropertied and uneducated was presumably incapable of distinguishing between the true statesman and the venal politician. Corrupt politicians, according to the conservatives, manipulated this electorate and perpet-uated themselves in power by doling out hundreds of thousands of government jobs to the political lackeys who worked for their re-election. They catered to the lazy poor in the electorate by promising them expensive and unnecessary government programs that drained wealth from hard-working taxpayers and taught the poor that they did not have to work at a honest job for a living. An expansive government was therefore inherently evil, they felt, because it put power in the hands of the wrong kinds of Americans, the ignorant and lazy rabble.

Given this prescription of Northern conservatives for what ailed centennial America, Reconstruction was more than expendable. Not only did it seemingly stand as the worst example of the corrupt government that followed in the wake of divorcing political power from intellect and property, it was also condemned for so unsettling political conditions in the South as to prevent indefinitely a national recovery from the depression of the 1870s. Moreover, and most frightening of all, Republican efforts to prop it up raised the specter, in the words of Carl Schurz, of a "National Government so strong that, right or wrong, nobody could resist it."[24]

Just as Reconstruction did not survive the conservatism of the 1870s, neither did a host of beliefs that had been central to the reform impulse of the 1860s. The West as a safety valve for economic discontent and class tensions in the East was the vision of the reformers who pushed for the Homestead Act of 1862. In practice, however, two-thirds of the farms taken up under the act failed, victims of the need for credit in a commercialized agricultural system. By the mid-1870s it was the West that seemed to be closing in on the East. The menacing image of tramps, farm laborers who took to the road in search of work after they had been displaced by agricultural mechanization, now loomed larger in the minds of eastern conserva-tives than Jefferson's idyllic image of the yeomanry as the dominant social product of the West. The hopes of George Julian in 1865 for a model republic of equity and justice had given way a decade later to what the economist David A. Wells called the great "social paradox" of the day, the persistence of poverty amidst the plenty of technologically driven abundance. Along with other commentators, Wells noted that the distribution of wealth had not kept pace with the growing abundance. As a result, the poorest forty percent of American families in the 1870s owned barely one percent of all the property.

The belief in the natural harmony of capital and labor, the core assumption in the free-labor ideology of Lincoln's Republican party, was contradicted by the bitter industrial unrest of the 1870s and the evidence of irreconcilable differences between workers and businessmen. Indeed, the belief that wage labor was but a temporary status as workers moved toward the economic independence of the entrepreneur was already a myth in the 1860s. About two-thirds of the labor force in 1870 were wage or salaried employees, and most of them would continue as the economic dependents of someone else.

Emancipation had not ushered in the expected era of free-labor prosperity in the South, and even most, though by no means all, abolitionists concluded that blacks were not yet ready to stand the test of true moral autonomy. The very notion of reform that the abolitionists had once backed with millennial hopes was radically transformed within a decade of the end of the war. In the 1860s reform meant positive governmental programs to promote meaningful social change in the direction of greater individual opportunity and equality. As foreshadowed in the Liberal Republican movement of 1872, reform to the Hayes Republicans of 1876 meant negative actions of governmental retrenchment based on the distrust of the popular will as a source of corruption and fiscal irresponsibility.

Despite all the hoopla and patriotic oratory proclaiming America's unity and progress, the nation's mood in 1876 as it celebrated the centennial was subdued, even somber. Businessmen worried that what foreign visitors to the Centennial exposition at Philadelphia would most remember about America was the depressed economy and the corrupt politicians. Republicans grumbled that the constitutional objections of congressional Democrats to federal appropriations for the centennial celebration smacked of the same old states rights' heresy that had culminated in the Civil War. Almost everyone was complaining about hard times.

While visitors to the Philadelphia Exposition were marveling at the gigantic Corliss steam engine (it was as tall as a three-story building), the preeminent symbol of America's technological prowess, black field hands in the South and industrial workers in the North were engaging in bloody strikes, a vivid symbol of how American labor was denied its share of the abundance generated by technological innovation. While orators were singing the praises of American democracy, the conservative spokesmen who now dominated both of the major political parties were warning that the excesses of democracy were demoralizing and corrupting the nation. "Is there such a poison in the political system that there is no cure for it?"[26] asked the Reverend Theodore D. Woolsey of Yale University. Conservatives such as Woolsey were calling for an elitest brand of nationalism that, like the victorious Union war effort, stressed loyalty to establish order and the discipline of authoritarian institutions. Blacks and labor leaders simultaneously were calling in vain for

The giant Corliss engine at the Centennial Exposition in Philadelphia dwarfed onlookers and symbolized the machine power of the industrialization which was transforming America in the generation after the Civil War.

a return to the reformist, equalitarian nationalism that had also contributed to Union victory in the Civil War.

Beneath all the celebratory rhetoric of the centennial ran a strong undercurrent of disillusionment. The antebellum republic that had died in 1860 had not been replaced with a compelling sense of national identity and purpose shared by all Americans, regardless of race or class. The reconstructed America of 1876 remained a divided nation. The Civil War had determined that America would indeed be a nation, but what kind of nation, and on whose behalf, was still very much an open question in 1876. For those committed to the equalitarian promise of American democracy, that question remains open today.

NOTES

1. *Congressional Record,* Vol. 2, Pt. 1, 1st Session, 43rd Congress, p. 82.
2. Burke A. Hinsdale (ed.), *The Works of James Abram Garfield,* vol. 2 (Boston: James R. Osgood, 1882–83), p. 101.
3. *Commercial and Financial Chronicle,* vol. 21, August 7, 1875.
4. Ibid., vol. 20, April 24, 1875.
5. *Congressional Record,* Vol. 2, Pt. 1, 1st Session, 43rd Congress, p. 82.
6. Ibid., p. 33.
7. Ibid., p. 252.
8. Quoted in Michael Perman, *The Road to Redemption: Southern Politics, 1869–1879* (Chapel Hill: University of North Carolina, 1984), p. 155.
9. Quoted in W. E. B. Du Bois, *Black Reconstruction in America, 1860–1880* (Cleveland: Meridian, 1962), p. 495.
10. Robert Somers, *The Southern States Since the War, 1870–71* (University, Ala.: University of Alabama Press, 1965 [1872]), pp. 76–77.
11. Quoted in William Gillette, *Retreat from Reconstruction, 1869–1879* (Baton Rouge: Louisiana State University Press, 1982), p. 153.
12. Philadelphia *Inquirer,* Jan. 6, 1875, cited in a speech by Carl Schurz in Frederic Bancroft (ed.), *Speeches, Correspondence and Political Papers of Carl Schurz,* vol. 3 (New York: G. P. Putnam's Sons, 1913), p. 143.
13. Henry James Brown and Frederick D. Williams (eds.), *The Diary of James A. Garfield,* vol. 3 (Lansing: Michigan State University Press, 1973), p. 7.
14. Ibid., p. 7.
15. *Congressional Record,* Vol. 2, Pt. 1, 1st Session, 43rd Congress, p. 340.
16. Ibid., p. 344.
17. John R. Lynch, *Reminiscences of an Active Life: The Autobiography of John Roy Lynch,* (Chicago: University of Chicago Press, 1970), p. 161.
18. Charles Richard Williams (ed.), *Diary and Letters of Rutherford Birchard Hayes,* vol. 3 (Columbus, Ohio: Ohio State Archaeological and Historical Society, 1922–26), p. 274.
19. John Bigelow (ed.), *Letters and Literary Memorials of Samuel J. Tilden,* vol. 1 (New York: Harper & Brothers, 1908), p. 271.
20. *Diary of James A. Garfield,* vol. 3, Sept. 17, 1876, p. 352.

21. [Frederick Douglass], *Life and Times of Frederick Douglass* (New York: Collier Books, 1962 [1892]), p. 536.
22. *Commercial and Financial Chronicle,* vol. 23, July 8, 1876.
23. Edward Atkinson, "Commercial Development," in *The First Century of the Republic: A Review of American Progress* (New York: Harper & Brothers, 1876), p. 210.
24. Bancroft, vol. 3, p. 131.
25. Wells made this observation at the annual convention of the Social Science Association in Detroit in 1875. See the *Commercial and Financial Chronicle,* vol. 20, May 15, 1875.
26. T. D. Woolsey, "The Experiment of the Union, With its Preparations," in *The First Century of the Republic,* p. 277.

SUGGESTED READINGS

BAUM, DALE, *The Civil War Party System: The Case of Massachusetts, 1848-1876.* Chapel Hill, N.C.: University of North Carolina Press, 1984.

CHANDLER, ALFRED D., *The Visible Hand: The Managerial Revolution in American Business.* Cambridge, Mass.: Harvard University Press, 1977.

HOBABAWM, ERIC, *The Age of Capital, 1848-1875.* New York: Scribner, 1975.

KELLER, MORTON, *Affairs of State: Public Life in Late Nineteenth Century America.* Cambridge, Mass.: Harvard University Press, 1977.

KIRKLAND, EDWARD C., *Industry Comes of Age: Business, Labor and Public Policy, 1860-1897.* New York: Quadrangle, 1961.

NEVINS, ALLAN, *The Emergence of Modern America, 1865-1878.* New York: Macmillan, 1927.

NUGENT, WALTER T.K., *Money and American Society, 1865-1880.* New York: Free Press, 1968.

POLAKOFF, KEITH I., *The Politics of Inertia: The Election of 1876 and the End of Reconstruction.* Baton Rouge, La.: Louisiana State University Press, 1973.

RABLE, GEORGE C., *But There Was No Peace: The Role of Violence in the Politics of Reconstruction.* Athens, Ga.: University of Georgia Press, 1984.

RANSOM, ROGER L., and SUTCH, RICHARD, *One Kind of Freedom: The Economic Consequences of Emancipation.* New York: Cambridge University Press, 1977.

SPROAT, JOHN C., *"The Best Men": Liberal Reformers in the Gilded Age.* New York: Oxford University Press, 1968.

TRELEASE, ALLEN W., *White Terror: The Ku Klux Klan Conspiracy and Southern Reconstruction.* New York: Harper and Row, 1971.

TUNNELL, TED, *Crucible of Reconstruction: War, Radicalism, and Race in Louisiana, 1862-1877.* Baton Rouge, La.: Louisiana State University Press, 1984.

UNGER, IRWIN, *The Greenback Era: A Social and Political History of American Finance, 1865-1879.* Princeton, N.J.: Princeton University Press, 1964.

WHARTON, VERNON LANE, *The Negro in Mississippi, 1865-1890.* Chapel Hill, N.C.: University of North Carolina Press, 1947.

WILLIAMSON, JOEL, *After Slavery: The Negro in South Carolina During Reconstruction.* Berkeley, Calif.: University of California Press, 1968.

WOODWARD, C. VANN, *Reunion and Reaction: The Compromise of 1877 and the End of Reconstruction.* Boston, Mass.: Little, Brown, 1951.

Index

---

* Denotes entry from end of chapter notes.

Photo Credits